HANDBOOKS

ZION & BRYCE

W. C. McRAE & JUDY JEWELL

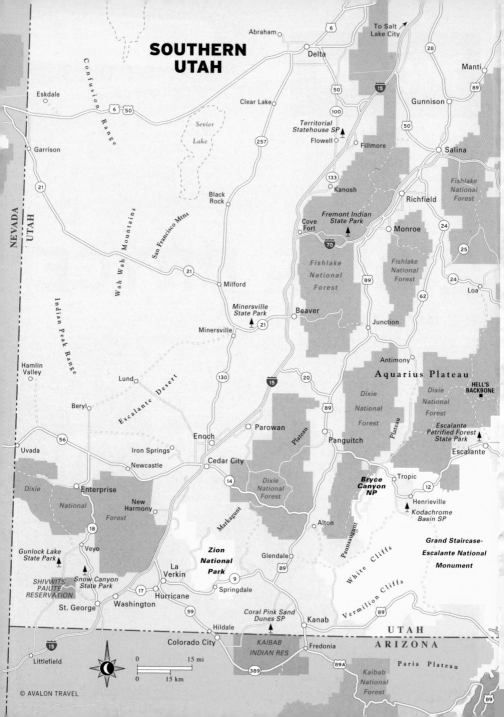

SOUTHERN UTAH

To Salt Lake City

Abraham

Delta

Eskdale

Confusion Range

Garrison

Clear Lake

Sevier Lake

Manti

Gunnison

Territorial Statehouse SP

Flowell

Fillmore

Salina

Black Rock

Kanosh

Richfield

Fishlake National Forest

NEVADA

UTAH

San Francisco Mtns

Wah Wah Mountains

Cove Fort

Fremont Indian State Park

Monroe

Fishlake National Forest

Loa

Milford

Fishlake National Forest

Indian Peak Range

Minersville State Park

Beaver

Junction

Antimony

Aquarius Plateau

Minersville

HELL'S BACKBONE

Hamlin Valley

Lund

Escalante Desert

Dixie National Forest

Dixie National Forest

Escalante Petrified Forest State Park

Beryl

Enoch

Parowan

Panguitch

Escalante

Uvada

Iron Springs

Plateau

Plateau

Tropic

Newcastle

Cedar City

Dixie National Forest

Bryce Canyon NP

Dixie National Forest

Henrieville

Kodachrome Basin SP

Enterprise

New Harmony

Markagunt

Alton

Pausaugunt

Grand Staircase-Escalante National Monument

Gunlock Lake State Park

Veyo

Zion National Park

Glendale

White Cliffs

SHIVWITS PAIUTE RESERVATION

Snow Canyon State Park

La Verkin

Springdale

Vermilion Cliffs

St. George

Washington

Hurricane

Kanab

UTAH

ARIZONA

Littlefield

Hildale

Coral Pink Sand Dunes SP

Paria Plateau

Colorado City

KAIBAB INDIAN RES

Fredonia

© AVALON TRAVEL

0   15 mi
0   15 km

Kaibab National Forest

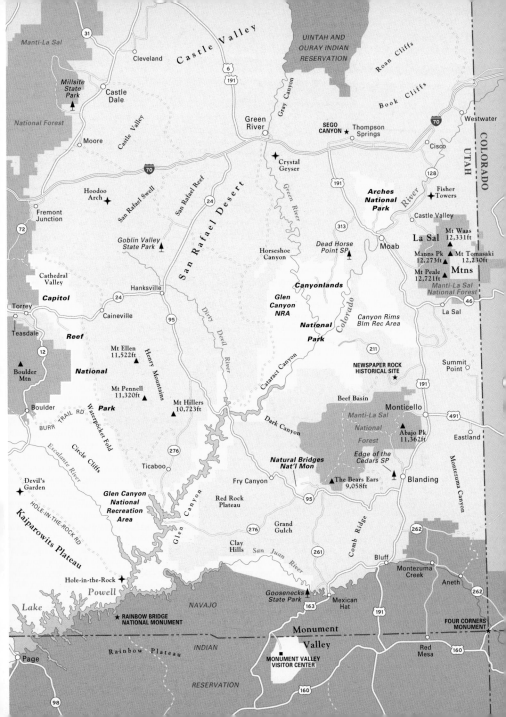

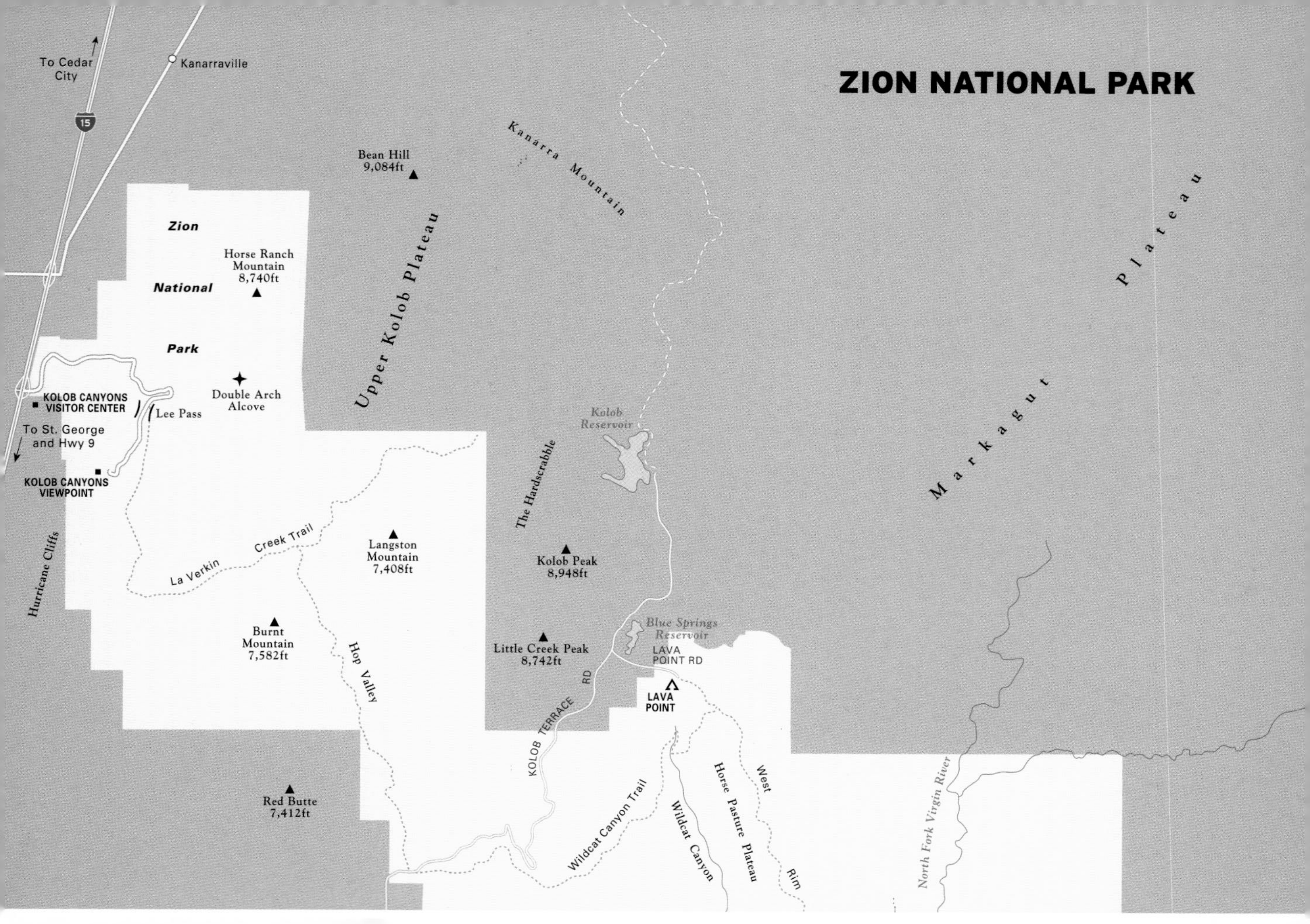

ZION NATIONAL PARK

Kaibab Plateau

Markagunt Plateau

North Fork Virgin River

West Rim

Horse Pasture Plateau

Wildcat Canyon

Blue Springs Reservoir

Kolob Reservoir

LAVA POINT RD

LAVA POINT

Kanarra Mountain

The Hardscrabble

Kolob Peak
8,948ft

Little Creek Peak
8,742ft

KOLOB TERRACE RD

Wildcat Canyon Trail

Bean Hill
9,084ft

Upper Kolob Plateau

Langston Mountain
7,408ft

Hop Valley

Horse Ranch Mountain
8,740ft

Double Arch Alcove

Creek Trail

Burnt Mountain
7,582ft

Red Butte
7,412ft

Zion

National

Park

Lee Pass

La Verkin

KOLOB CANYONS
VISITOR CENTER

To St. George
and Hwy 9

KOLOB CANYONS
VIEWPOINT

Hurricane Cliffs

Kanarraville

To Cedar
City

15

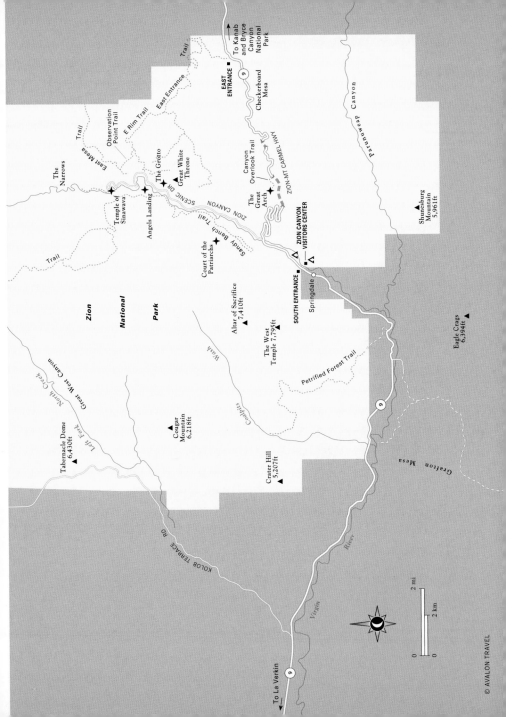

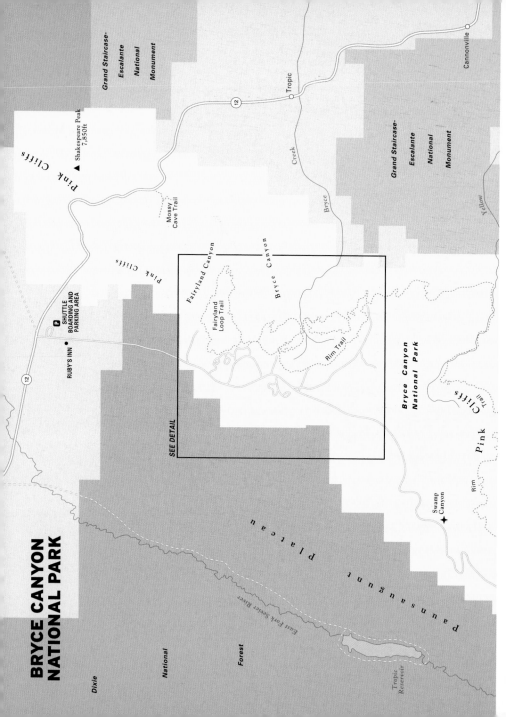

BRYCE CANYON NATIONAL PARK

Dixie

National

Forest

East Fork Sevier River

Tropic Reservoir

Paunsaugunt Plateau

Swamp Canyon

Rim Trail

Pink Cliffs

Cliffs Trail

Bryce Canyon National Park

SEE DETAIL

Fairyland Canyon

Fairyland Loop Trail

Bryce Canyon

Rim Trail

12

RUBY'S INN

P SHUTTLE BOARDING AND PARKING AREA

Pink Cliffs

Pink Cliffs

Mossy Cave Trail

▲ Shakespeare Peak 7,850 ft

Grand Staircase- Escalante National Monument

12

Tropic

Bryce Creek

Yellow

Grand Staircase- Escalante National Monument

Grand Staircase- Escalante National Monument

Cannonville

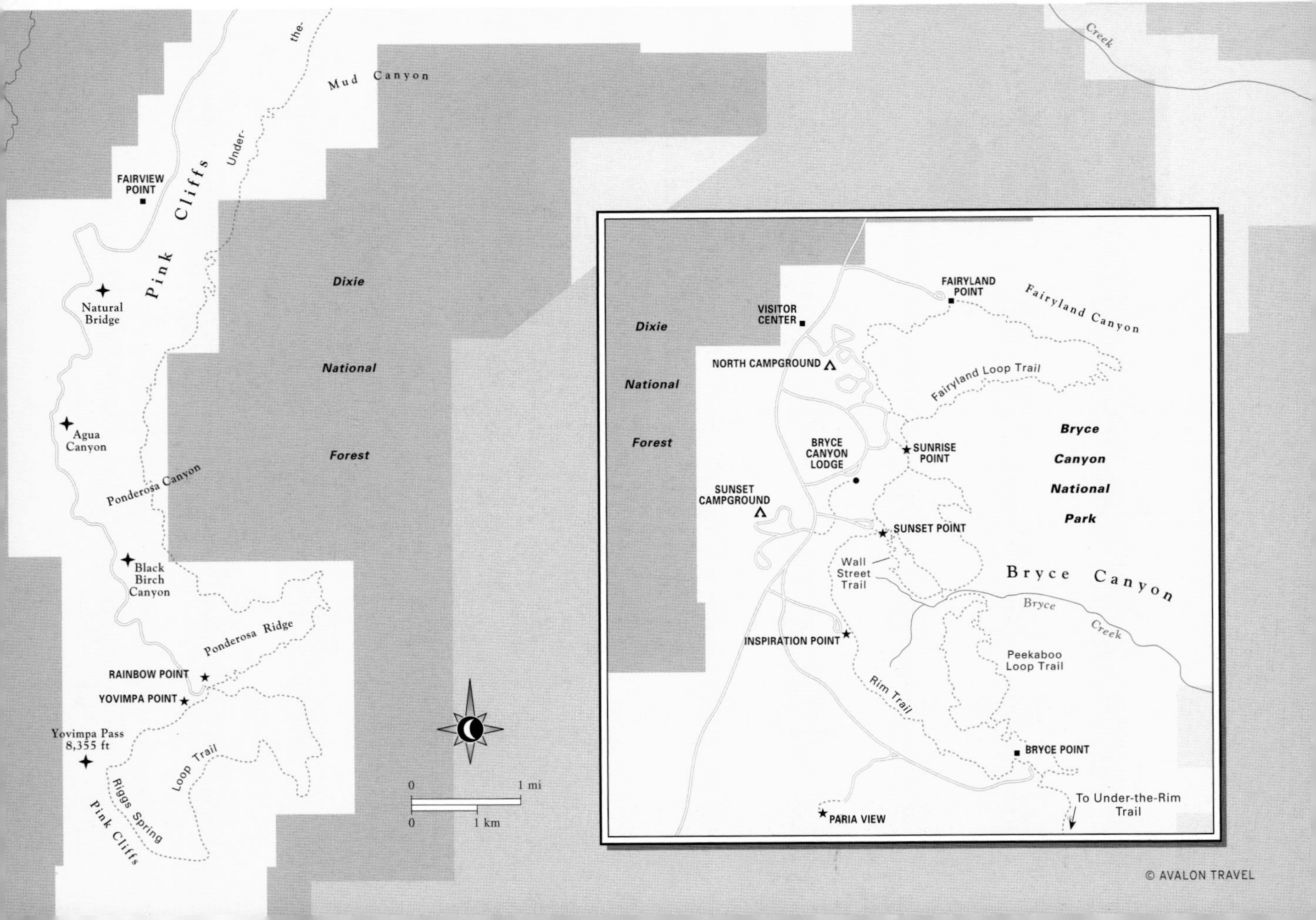

Bryce Canyon National Park

Bryce Canyon

Fairyland Canyon

Fairyland Point

Fairyland Loop Trail

SUNRISE POINT

SUNSET POINT

Bryce Creek

Peekaboo Loop Trail

BRYCE POINT

Wall Street Trail

Rim Trail

INSPIRATION POINT

PARIA VIEW

To Under-the-Rim Trail

BRYCE CANYON LODGE

VISITOR CENTER

NORTH CAMPGROUND

SUNSET CAMPGROUND

Dixie National Forest

Dixie National Forest

Mud Canyon

Under-the-

Pink Cliffs

FAIRVIEW POINT

Natural Bridge

Agua Canyon

Ponderosa Canyon

Black Birch Canyon

Ponderosa Ridge

RAINBOW POINT

YOVIMPA POINT

Yovimpa Pass 8,355 ft

Riggs Spring Loop Trail

Pink Cliffs

Creek

1 mi

1 km

0

0

© AVALON TRAVEL

Contents

Discover Zion & Bryce

Southern Utah is so filled with staggering beauty, drama, and power that it seems like a place of myth. Five spectacular national parks and several national monuments are all within a day's drive of one another. The colorful canyons, arches, and mesas found within this high dry area are surprisingly diverse, and each park has its own characteristic landscape.

Zion National Park contains stunning contrasts, with towering rock walls deeply incised by steep canyons containing a verdant oasis of cottonwood trees and wildflowers. Bryce National Park is famed for its red and pink hoodoos, delicate fingers of stone rising from a steep mountainside. At sunrise the lighting is especially magical, the air crisp, and the trails empty.

A large section of the Grand Staircase-Escalante National Monument preserves the dry washes and slot canyons trenched by the Escalante River and its tributaries. Long-distance hikers descend into the deep, narrow river channels here to experience the near-mystical harmony of flowing water and stone.

The highlight of Capitol Reef National Park is the Waterpocket Fold, an enormous wrinkle of rock rising from the desert. The Fremont River carves a magnificent canyon through the formation, offering a leafy, well-watered sanctuary from the otherwise arid landscapes of southern Utah.

In Canyonlands National Park, the Colorado River carves through deep red sandstone. From the Island in the Sky unit, expansive vistas take in hundreds of miles of canyon country, while rafting the Colorado's Cataract Canyon is the wet and thrilling climax of many a vacation. The beauty is more serene and mystical at Arches National Park, where delicate rock arches provide vast windows into the solid rock. Short trails draw hikers into an eerily beautiful land of slickrock promontories and stone arches. High-spirited Moab is the recreational mecca of southeastern Utah, known for its mountain biking and comfortable—even sophisticated—dining and lodging.

Southern Utah is more than a showcase of erosion. Its cliffs and canyons have been home to Native Americans for thousands of years, and the haunting beauty of Native American rock art is on display at hundreds of locations.

Although many people first visit as part of a grand tour of the Southwest, they often return to further explore a smaller and distinctive corner of this vast landscape. After a small glimpse of the magnificence and variety, some latch on to one special place and return year after year, growing to know it intimately.

Planning Your Trip

▶ WHERE TO GO

Zion National Park

In Zion National Park, hiking trails lead up narrow canyons cut into massive stone cliffs, passing quiet pools of water and hanging gardens. The park's main canyon, carved by the Virgin River, is an easy place to find a day hike; however, the rest of the park's canyons are the province of canyoneers and long-distance hikers.

Bryce Canyon National Park

Bryce Canyon has famous vistas across an eroded amphitheater of pink sandstone hoodoos. Short trails lead down from the canyon edge into a wonderland of fanciful formations and outcrops, and you'll have quite a different experience from the amateur photographers perched along the rim if you venture into the park's backcountry.

Grand Staircase-Escalante National Monument

Grand Staircase preserves some of the Southwest's best canyon hiking. Numerous day hikes and long-distance hiking trails follow the slot canyons of the Escalante River. Mountain bikers can head down the Hole-in-the-Rock Road or the Burr Trail to visit some of the same landscape via jeep road; even cruising scenic Highway 12 in a car is an eye-popping experience.

Capitol Reef National Park

Capitol Reef preserves a vast wrinkle of rock called the Waterpocket Fold, which buckles up into a vertical barricade across more than 100 miles of southeast Utah. Of the few canyons that penetrate Waterpocket Fold, the Fremont River Canyon is most accessible along Highway 24. Ancient petroglyphs, pioneer farms and orchards, and soaring rock

IF YOU HAVE . . .

- **A WEEKEND:** Visit Zion National Park.
- **FIVE DAYS:** Add Bryce Canyon National Park and Kodachrome Basin State Park.
- **ONE WEEK:** Add Grand Staircase and Capitol Reef.
- **TEN DAYS:** Add Canyonlands, Arches, and Moab.

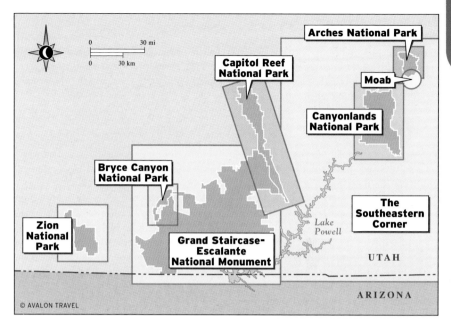

formations extend the length of the canyon. A paved scenic highway explores more canyons along the fold's western face. The rest of the park is remote backcountry—just the way hikers and backpackers like it.

Canyonlands National Park

Canyonlands National Park is made up of four sections: the River District, containing the canyons of the Colorado and Green Rivers; the Needles District, with hiking trails and backcountry roads through a standing-rock desert; the Maze District, a remote area filled with geologic curiosities and labyrinthine canyons; and the Island in the Sky District, a flat-topped mesa that overlooks the rest. A separate area, the Horseshoe Canyon Unit, lies to the west and contains a significant cache of prehistoric rock art.

Arches National Park

Just up the road from Moab is Arches National Park, with its famous rock bridges. Arches is a great family park: It's not too large and there are lots of accessible hikes to explore. Unlike other Utah national parks, there's plenty to see even if you can't get out of the car and hike. Be sure to hike the Windows Section, a series of arches and rock fins at the center of the park, and to Delicate Arch, overlooking the Colorado River.

Moab

At the heart of Utah's slickrock country, Moab is the recreation capital of southeastern Utah. Although mountain biking put Moab on the map, old mining roads make four-wheel-driving an increasingly popular alternative. Arches National Park is just minutes from downtown, and Canyonlands' districts are an easy drive from Moab. But Moab is a destination in itself: a youthful, high-energy town that offers good restaurants, brewpubs, and coffee shops.

The Southeastern Corner

Although Arches and Canyonlands parks get most of the attention from first-time visitors, veterans of the area know that southeastern Utah has abundant other wonders in national recreation areas, national monuments, and state parks. After you have explored the national parks, be sure to save time to visit such fascinating destinations as Natural Bridges and Hovenweep National Monuments, Dead Horse Point State Park, and the lovely alpine glades of La Sal National Forest.

▶ WHEN TO GO

The parks are all open year-round, although spring (Apr.-early June) and early fall (Sept.-Oct.) are the most pleasant times to visit. They are also the busiest seasons, and travelers may find that popular campgrounds and hotels are booked well in advance.

Spring rain can also dampen trails, and late winter-early spring storms can play havoc with backcountry roads. Bryce Canyon, at 6,600-9,100 feet, can be snowy well into the spring, but it is pleasant during the summer when other areas of southern Utah bake.

Thunderstorms are fairly common in summer (late July-early Sept.) and bring the threat of flash flooding, especially in slot canyons. In Canyonlands, Arches, and Moab, summer temperatures can reach the 100s.

A few highways close for the winter, most notably the roads around Cedar Breaks National Monument. However, winter can be a great time to visit the high country around Bryce, where cross-country skiers take to the park roads. Around Escalante, the canyons can be quite nice in the winter during the day, but nights are freezing. In Canyonlands and Arches, winter days tend to be bright and sunny, but nighttime temperatures can dip into the teens or lower.

near Goblin Valley State Park

cactus flowers   trail to Tapestry Arch, Arches National Park

► BEFORE YOU GO

Although the national parks of Utah are located in a geographically compact area, connecting the dots to visit each of them isn't always straightforward. The rugged topography of the area has made road building difficult, so visiting all of the parks requires a lot of driving. Unpaved back roads can serve as shortcuts if you have a high-clearance vehicle, but check locally before setting out to determine current conditions: Rainstorms and snowmelt can render these roads impassable.

If you're planning on making the rounds of the national parks, buy an America the Beautiful–National Parks and Federal Recreational Lands Pass (valid for one year, $80) at your first stop to cover entrance to all national parks. Senior passes (lifetime pass $10) and free passes for residents with permanent disabilities are also available.

Many national parks now offer reserved campsites. If you want to camp in a park, reserve ahead—this is especially important at Arches—or plan to arrive early in the day to get an unreserved site.

What to Take

Prepare for wide variations in temperature; nights in the desert can be very chilly even when summer highs soar above 100°F. Remember to use lots of sunscreen.

There's no need to pack dressy clothes. Casual clothes are acceptable nearly everywhere, even in what passes for a classy restaurant.

Alcohol presents another issue. If you want to drink, especially away from Moab or Springdale, pack your own, especially if you have discerning tastes. While many restaurants in the towns around these parks now offer a selection of alcoholic beverages, southern Utah does not have a drinking culture.

Bring your cell phone, but don't count on reception in the canyons of southern Utah.

Explore Zion & Bryce

▶ THE BEST OF UTAH'S NATIONAL PARKS

Despite their proximity, visiting all of Utah's national parks is a bit complicated because of the rugged terrain. You must plan on a lot of driving. So get in a road-trip frame of mind, cue up some good music, and head out. The following itinerary only scratches the surface of what there is to see, but after this sampler, you'll know where to focus your next Utah adventure.

Days 1-2

If you fly into Salt Lake City or Las Vegas, you'll probably get to Zion National Park sometime in the afternoon. Settle into your motel in Springville and head into the park to check out the visitors center and take a ride up Zion Canyon on the park shuttle bus. Hop off for views of the Court of the Patriarchs and to take an easy hike up the Riverside Walk. Start the next day with a hike up the West Rim Trail to Angels Landing or, if you want something a bit easier going, hike the Emerald Pools trails.

Spend the afternoon visiting Springville's galleries, and if your legs are up for it, go for an early evening hike up the Watchman Trail.

Day 3

Head east out of the park via the Zion-Mt. Carmel Highway (Hwy. 9); turn north onto U.S. 89 and east onto Highway 12 to reach Bryce Canyon National Park (84 miles from Zion). Park the car and spend the day riding the park shuttle to vista points and exploring hoodoos from trailheads along the road. Camp in the park, or stay at the historic park lodge or one of the motels just outside the park entrance.

Day 4

Get up in time to see the rising sun light up the hoodoos, then drive 42 miles east on Highway 12 through the town of Escalante to the dramatic Lower Calf Creek Falls Trail. Cool your toes in the pool under the falls, then continue east to Boulder, where you'll

AVOIDING THE CROWDS

Many areas outside Utah's national parks are often less crowded but are equally compelling.

- **Cedar Breaks National Monument** preserves an area with formations similar to Bryce Canyon, but without the crowds.

- **Red Canyon** is immediately west of Bryce Canyon and shares its geology, but because it's not a national park, you can mountain bike amid the red-rock formations.

- **Kodachrome Basin State Park,** between Bryce Canyon and Grand Staircase-Escalante, is ringed by

remarkable pink cliffs plus odd rock pillars called sand pipes.

- **Hovenweep National Monument** contains the ruins of ancient Anasazi stone villages.

- **Natural Bridges National Monument** contains rock formations that rival Arches National Park.

- **Dead Horse State Park,** on the road into Canyonlands, provides an eagle's-eye view over the Colorado River Canyon.

- **Goblin Valley State Park** has trails among goblin-shaped hoodoos.

Capitol Reef National Park

spend the night at the Boulder Mountain Lodge (be sure to make reservations for dinner at Hells Backbone Grill when you book your hotel room).

Day 5

Explore more of the Escalante River canyons. Drive 12.5 miles south from Highway 12 and turn onto Hole-in-the-Rock Road to traipse around Devils Garden. You can also visit the canyons of Dry Fork of Coyote Gulch, 26 miles south of Highway 12. Return to Boulder for the night.

Day 6

From Boulder, follow Highway 12 north 39 miles over Boulder Mountain to Highway 24 and Torrey, your base for exploring Capitol Reef National Park. In the park, explore the old pioneer town of Fruita, hike to see petroglyphs, and drive the scenic park road. Add a hike up the Chimney Rock Trail or along Capitol Wash, then return to Torrey for dinner and a bed.

Day 7

Head to the east side of Capitol Reef and turn south from Highway 24 onto the Notom-Bullfrog Road and follow this well-maintained (but mostly dirt) road 68 miles south to Bullfrog Bay, where a ferry (May-Oct.) crosses Lake Powell. Ride the ferry, and once on the other side, head away from the lake for 40 miles on Highway 276 to Highway 95 and Natural Bridges National Monument. (If you'd rather stick to pavement, or if the ferry isn't in season, continue east on Highway 24 to Hanksville, then turn south on Highway 95 to reach Natural Bridges.) Often overlooked, this small park is a gem, with three massive rock bridges and an Anasazi cliff dwelling along a nine-mile loop highway. Unfortunately, there's no lodging at Natural Bridges, except for a small campground, so you'll have to head back to Highway 95 and continue east to U.S. 191 to find a room for the night.

Balanced Rock, Arches National Park

cactus flower

The first town you'll come to on U.S. 191 is Blanding, which has plenty of options; however, tiny Bluff, 26 miles south, is more charming.

Day 8

Get an early start if you want to explore the Needles District of Canyonlands National Park. Head north 46 miles from Bluff and turn west off U.S. 191 at Monticello. Follow well-marked paved roads west and north to BLM Newspaper Rock Historical Monument, one of the finest and most accessible petroglyph sites in Utah. From Newspaper Rock, continue west on Highway 211 to the Needles District, where a good short hike is along the Cave Spring Trail. Unless you're camping in Canyonlands, head back to Highway 191 and north 40 miles to spend the night in Moab.

Days 9-10

Moab is just a few miles south of Arches National Park. You can tour Arches in half a day if you take only short hikes to viewpoints; if you want to visit all of the sites along the park road and hike to famed Delicate Arch, you'll spend all day in the park. If you have one more day left in your trip, uses it to explore Canyonlands' Island in the Sky District, taking in the astonishing vista points (particularly Grand View Point) and saving time for a hike to the cliff edge. In the evening, enjoy the lively scene in Moab, with its good restaurants and brewpubs.

BEST VISTAS

one of many stunning views in Dead Horse Point State Park

With a landscape characterized by mountain peaks and deep canyons, southern Utah is filled with big views. With a few exceptions, you won't need to hike uphill for miles to get a bird's-eye view—most of the vista points below are easily reached by a short hike or detour by car.

ZION
OK, forget what we just said about not needing to hike uphill. If you really want the views, hike up to **Angels Landing.** But if you're not up for this steep hike and just want an eyeful, jump off the shuttle bus at the **Court of the Patriarchs.**

BRYCE
Don't dismiss **Sunrise Point** just because the name is a cliché. The angle of the rising sun does make this viewpoint special. If you can't quite make it by sunrise, try a sunset view at **Sunset Point.**

GRAND STAIRCASE-ESCALANTE
Between Escalante and Boulder, Highway 12 climbs up a steep fin of rock called the **Hog's Back,** from which the slot canyons of the Escalante River and the cliffs of the Aquarius Plateau form a jaw-dropping 360-degree vista.

The end of the 57-mile **Hole-in-the-Rock Road** dead-ends at a cliff over the Colorado River. Mormon pioneers blasted a trail down the 600-foot-high precipice, but views from the top, with the Colorado in a maze of red-rock canyons below, are enough for most modern explorers.

CAPITOL REEF
It's hard to get a handle on the fact that Waterpocket Fold is a vast wrinkle of rock more than 100 miles long. Unless, of course, you climb up and look down on it. From **Navajo Knobs,** 1,500 feet above the Fremont River Canyon, reached after a six-mile climb from Hickman Natural Bridge Trailhead, you'll take in most of southern Utah and the snakelike ridge of the Waterpocket Fold winding to the south.

CANYONLANDS
From the main access road into the Island in the Sky section of Canyonlands, two road-end vista points provide swallow-your-gum views over the incredible Colorado River Canyon. From **Dead Horse Point State Park,** a 30-foot-wide neck of land extends into the void over the twisting channels of the river 2,000 feet below. Continue to **Grand View Point,** above the confluence of the Colorado and the Green Rivers, for vistas of canyons, sheer rock walls, and pinnacles and distant mountains. This incredible vantage point displays hundreds of miles of the Southwest.

ARCHES
In its sheer concentration of incredible scenery, it's hard to beat Arches for dramatic vistas. Drive 16 miles from the park gates to Wolfe Ranch, and then take the three-mile round-trip hike up a slickrock trail for the park's most incredible view. Looking across the Colorado River Canyon to the distant La Sal Mountains through **Delicate Arch** is a memory-of-a-lifetime experience.

▶ BEST DAY HIKES

It's difficult to imagine more dramatic landscapes than those found in Utah's national parks. These day hikes through epic canyons, arches, and needles of sandstone invite you to get out of your vehicle and explore.

Zion

The Emerald Pools trails start from Zion Lodge and make good variable-length hikes. Depending on your stamina and time available, hike to Lower, Middle, or Upper Emerald Pool, or take more time and visit all three.

Bryce

Given the high elevation and the fact that all of Bryce's best hikes descend from the rim (meaning a climb back up to the rim at the hike's end), it's good to start with the relatively easy 1.5-mile trek to Queen's Garden. This will get you off the rim and down into the hoodoos and, unless you're acclimated to the 8,000-foot elevation, give you a bit of a workout. If you need a longer hike, connect with the Navajo Loop Trail to bring the total distance to about three miles.

Grand Staircase-Escalante

The hike up Calf Creek to Lower Calf Creek Falls is a delectable sampler of the kinds of sights that make the slickrock canyon country of Escalante such a compelling destination. From a trailhead right off Highway 12 (15 miles northeast of Escalante), a trail follows a desert canyon past rock art, ruins of an ancient Native American village, and beaver ponds, and terminates at a delicate 126-foot waterfall. The 5.5-mile round-trip trail is easy enough for families.

Capitol Reef

Many of the hikes in Capitol Reef involve quite a bit of climbing to reach high viewpoints over

Mesa Arch, atop Canyonlands' Island in the Sky

hiking the Navajo Loop Trail, Bryce Canyon

Pine Tree Arch on Devils Garden Trail, Arches

the Fremont River and the Waterpocket Fold. However, hiking Grand Wash is easy and scenic. Grand Wash is one of only five canyons that cut through the rock reef, with walls up to 800 feet high and narrows of just 20 feet. Pick up the trail from Highway 24, five miles south of the visitors center, where Grand Wash enters Fremont Canyon. For a view over the wash, continue on the trail and climb up to Cassidy Arch (3.5 miles round-trip), named after outlaw Butch Cassidy.

Canyonlands

The hike into Horseshoe Canyon to view the phenomenal rock art at the Great Gallery is a near-mystical experience for many. The 6.5-mile trail requires negotiating a steep canyon wall, but experiencing the stunning petroglyphs in a verdant canyon is well worth the effort. The trailhead is 30 miles east of Highway 24 on gravel roads.

In Canyonlands' Island in the Sky District, the landscape is nearly all vertical, and many hiking trails explore the rock faces and canyon walls. The Grand View Trail traverses more level ground, ending at the southernmost tip of the Island in the Sky peninsula, where you'll have views over much of the park, including the gorges of the Green and Colorado Rivers.

Stretch your legs on the hike to Chesler Park, in the Needles District. Although the hike begins at the busy four-wheeling Elephant Hill parking area, it quickly leads away from the noisy crowds to a lovely meadow, complete with old cowboy line camp.

Arches

The three-mile round-trip hike to Delicate Arch is a fantastic experience, a moderately demanding trail up a slickrock formation to the arch and transcendent views over the Colorado River Canyon. If you'd prefer a trail without the crowds, go to Devils Garden, at the end of the paved parkway, and hike the 7.2-mile loop trail past eight arches and the weird formations in Fin Canyon.

ANCIENT ROCK ART LEGACY

Sego Canyon pictographs

The Colorado Plateau contains a rich tapestry of pictographs (drawings painted on rock using natural dyes) and petroglyphs (images carved into stone). Searching out rock-art panels can easily become an obsession, and it's a good one, since it will lead you far off the beaten path and deep into canyons that were once central for the area's ancient inhabitants.

- **Boynton Overlook:** Stop between the towns of Escalante and Boulder and scan the cliff face across the river to see a pictograph of many handprints.

- **Delicate Arch:** On this popular hiking trail in Arches is an often-overlooked panel of Ute-style rock art images.

- **Fremont River Canyon:** Petroglyphs of horned mountain sheep and humans in headdresses are easily viewed from a parking area along Highway 24.

- **Great Gallery:** One of the most important rock art sites in the United States is in Canyonlands' Horseshoe Canyon Unit.

- **Holly Ruins:** You'll find many petroglyphs at Hovenweep National Monument, one of Utah's best-preserved Anasazi villages.

- **Newspaper Rock:** Near Canyonlands' Needles District, this is another easily reached showcase of rock art.

- **Parowan Gap:** East of Cedar City is this narrow rock pass where ancient artists chiseled images over 1,000 years ago.

- **Sego Canyon:** An hour north of Moab you'll find hundreds of etched images, starting with ghostly, shamanic-looking creatures right out of sci-fi movies.

► FUN FOR ALL AND ALL FOR FUN

Utah is famously family friendly, and national parks are traditional places for summertime family vacations, so it's not hard to find activities in southern Utah that are fun for both kids and adults. The national parks all have programs for children; generally they run Memorial Day-Labor Day. Junior Ranger programs are essentially workbooks that will keep kids occupied for a while.

Zion

Zion National Park has a wide array of summertime programs for school-age children (who must be accompanied by an adult for all activities). Daily programs at the Zion Nature Center focus on geology, animals, and ecosystems; short hikes on weekdays may even include a lesson on using a global positioning system (GPS) unit. Reservations are required for some programs; ask at the visitors center.

Horseback rides, which start at the corrals near the Emerald Pools trailhead, are a hit with kids age seven and up.

After a few hours of hiking and riding, spend an afternoon or evening at the Zion Canyon Giant Screen Theatre.

Bryce

Bryce Canyon National Park's fantastically sculpted rocks give even the stodgiest hikers a child's sense of imagination. Wander down the Queen's Garden Trail and make up your own names for the rock formations. Bryce has the usual Junior Ranger and ranger-talk programs for kids, but a special treat might be staying up late for a look at the night sky—the stars are fantastic here. Night sky programs run over 100 times per year, and include a multimedia show followed by a chance to look at the sky through telescopes.

Capitol Reef

Capitol Reef's Ripple Rock Nature Center offers a number of special programs, including some geared toward pioneer life. Kids can spin wool, pretend to milk a cow, make cornmeal on a prehistoric grinding stone, identify fossils, or play with animal puppets.

Canyonlands

Although much of Canyonlands National Park is too rugged and remote for most family outings, the Needles and Island in the Sky Districts have a number of shorter trails. In the Needles District, the short Cave Spring Trail gives hikers a chance to scamper across slickrock, scale ladders up steep (but not too high) cliffs, examine pictographs, and visit an old cowboy line camp. Stop by the visitors center at either district to borrow an Explorer Pack (deposit required) loaded with binoculars, a hand lens, a notebook, and other naturalist tools.

Arches

Arches National Park's many short trails and dramatic rock sculptures make it one of the most appealing national parks for visitors of all ages. Although there are few kid-specific activities beyond the Junior Ranger booklet, regular ranger-led activities are suitable for older children. A ranger-led hike in the Fiery Furnace requires a bit of hiking experience and agility; children under age five are not permitted, but older kids, including teens, will probably enjoy the scenery and the scrambling.

Cap off a visit to canyon country with a raft trip down the Colorado River. The trip from Fisher Towers toward town has quiet stretches punctuated by white water; it's offered in half-day and full-day versions and is a good bet for families.

CAMP IT UP

camping in Arches National Park

Southern Utah is flush with campgrounds, including many great spots just outside national parks.

- **Snow Canyon State Park** is a beautiful spot just outside busy St. George. Even though it's at a higher elevation than the town, this area gets very hot in the summer, and the campground is fairly lightly used then. But during spring, it's quite popular; reserve a site well in advance.

- **Zion National Park** has two park-maintained campgrounds in popular Zion Canyon, both with good sites. If you're planning in advance, some sites in **Watchman Campground** can be reserved. Spend a couple of nights here to really see the park.

- The campgrounds at **Bryce Canyon National Park** are perfectly nice, but the high elevation of this park means cold nights in the spring and fall (there are significant patches of snow on the ground in early May). Find a warmer spot at **Kodachrome Basin State Park,** about 20 miles south of Bryce. Kodachrome itself is quite scenic, with great campsites and several hiking trails.

- Two campgrounds near Escalante make a good base for exploring the northern edge of the Grand Staircase-Escalante National Monument. Of the two, the **Calf Creek Campground,** east of town, is more scenic, but **Escalante Petrified Forest State Park,** just west of town, has showers.

- Don't skip a visit to Capitol Reef. The most noteworthy thing about the park's **Fruita Campground** is its easy access to the local fruit trees (free for the picking in the right season) and hiking trails. Because no reservations are accepted, it's best to arrive here early in the day to claim a spot.

- In the Needles District of Canyonlands National Park, both loops of the **Squaw Flat Campground** have excellent sites. This place is popular, though, and it's easy to be unable to find a site. If necessary, head east and camp either at the private **Needles Outpost** or at Bureau of Land Management sites along Lockhart Basin Road, east of the park entrance.

- Reserve a site at Arches National Park's sublimely beautiful **Devils Garden Campground** well in advance. If that isn't possible, rest assured that there are many campsites in the Moab area, from primitive sites along the Colorado River to shady comfort in town at the private tents-only **Up the Creek Campground.**

ZION NATIONAL PARK

Zion is a magnificent park with stunning, soaring scenery. The canyon's name is credited to Isaac Behunin, who believed this spot to be a refuge from religious persecution. When Brigham Young later visited the canyon, however, he found tobacco and wine in use and declared the place "not Zion"—which some dutiful followers then began calling it.

The geology here is all about rocks and water. Little trickles of water, percolating through massive chunks of sandstone, have created both dramatic canyons and markedly undesertlike habitats, enabling an incredible variety of plants to find niches.

The first thing that catches the attention of visitors are the sheer cliffs and great monoliths of Zion Canyon, reaching high into the heavens. Energetic streams and other forces of erosion created this land of finely sculptured rock. The park spreads across 147,000 acres and contains eight geologic formations and four major vegetation zones. Elevations range from 3,666 feet, in lower Coalpits Wash, to 8,726 feet, atop Horse Ranch Mountain.

The highlight for most visitors is Zion Canyon, which is approximately 2,400 feet deep. Zion Canyon Scenic Drive winds through the canyon along the North Fork of the Virgin River, past some of the most spectacular scenery in the park. A shuttle bus ferries visitors along this route spring-early fall. Hiking trails branch off to lofty viewpoints and narrow side canyons.

© BILL MCRAE

HIGHLIGHTS

◖ Zion Canyon Visitor Center: It's always a good idea to drop by a park's visitors center, and this one is an especially interesting place to explore. The highlights are the outdoor exhibits, the excellent bookstore, and a shuttle bus stop that will ferry you up the canyon (page 29).

◖ Court of the Patriarchs Viewpoint: Hop off the shuttle bus to spend a few moments trying to fit all three mountains into your camera's viewfinder. The Patriarchs, along with the Great White Throne, are emblematic of Zion's massive sandstone rocks (page 31).

◖ Emerald Pools Trails: A little bit like in the story of the three bears, there's an Emerald Pool Trail that's right for just about everyone. The trail to the lower pool is paved (though non-electric wheelchair users may need a push), the trail to the middle pool offers a good short hike, and the trail to the upper pool will make most hikers break a sweat. All three pools are indeed emerald green, and the trails are lined with wildflowers (page 38).

◖ West Rim Trail to Angels Landing: If you want to do one vigorous day hike, this is a classic. Be prepared for spectacular views and some tenuous footing along the way—not for acrophobes or children (page 39).

◖ Hidden Canyon Trail: Hike up the East Rim Trail to the turnoff for Hidden Canyon. After a chain-assisted traverse of a cliff face, you'll pop into a shady, steep-walled narrow canyon with caves, pools, a small arch, and moisture-loving plants (page 41).

◖ Riverside Walk: If you're a die-hard hiker, don't count this level paved path as a hiking trail—save it for an after-dinner stroll. But for those who aren't up to steep trails, this walk along the Virgin River is a good way to see the water, the plantlife, and the soaring canyon walls. At the end of the trail you can watch hikers set off up the Narrows (page 41).

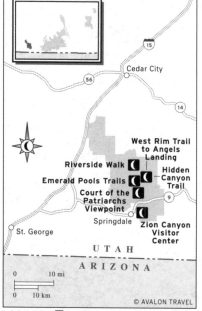

LOOK FOR **◖** TO FIND RECOMMENDED SIGHTS, ACTIVITIES, DINING, AND LODGING.

Water-loving adventurers can continue past the pavement's end and hike at the Virgin River at the Narrows in upper Zion Canyon.

The spectacular Zion-Mt. Carmel Highway, with its switchbacks and tunnels, provides access to the canyons and high plateaus east of Zion Canyon. Two other roads enter the rugged Kolob section northwest of Zion Canyon. Kolob is a Mormon name meaning "the brightest star, next to the seat of God." The Kolob section includes wilderness areas rarely visited by humans.

Zion's grandeur is evident all through the year. Even rainy days can be memorable as waterfalls plunge from nearly every crevice in the cliffs above. Spring and fall are the choice seasons for pleasant temperatures and the

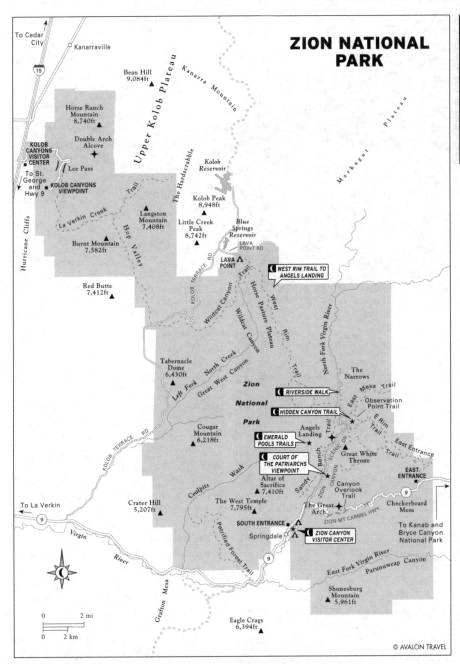

ZION NATIONAL PARK

To Cedar City

Kanarraville

Bean Hill
9,084ft

Upper Kolob Plateau

Kanarra Mountain

Horse Ranch
Mountain
8,740ft

Double Arch
Alcove

KOLOB
CANYONS
VISITOR
CENTER

To St.
George
and
Hwy 9

Lee Pass

KOLOB CANYONS
VIEWPOINT

Kolob
Reservoir

The Hardscrabble

Markagut Plateau

La Verkin Creek

Trail

Hop Valley

Langston
Mountain
7,408ft

Kolob Peak
8,948ft

Little Creek
Peak
8,742ft

Blue
Springs
Reservoir

KOLOB TERRACE RD

LAVA
POINT RD

LAVA
POINT

◖ **WEST RIM TRAIL TO
ANGELS LANDING**

Burnt Mountain
7,582ft

Hurricane Cliffs

Red Butte
7,412ft

Wildcat Canyon

Wildcat Canyon

Horse Pasture Plateau

West Rim Trail

North Fork Virgin River

Tabernacle
Dome
6,430ft

North Creek

Great West Canyon

Left Fork

Zion

National

Park

The
Narrows

East Mesa Trail

◖ **RIVERSIDE WALK**

◖ **HIDDEN CANYON TRAIL**

Observation
Point Trail

Cougar
Mountain
6,218ft

◖ **EMERALD
POOLS TRAILS**

Angels
Landing

Bench Trail

E Rim
Trail

East Entrance

◖ **COURT OF
THE PATRIARCHS
VIEWPOINT**

Great White
Throne

ZION CANYON SCENIC DR

Trail

**EAST
ENTRANCE**

KOLOB TERRACE RD

Wash

Altar of
Sacrifice
7,410ft

Sandy

Canyon
Overlook
Trail

9

To La Verkin

9

Coalpits

Crater Hill
5,207ft

The West Temple
7,795ft

The Great
Arch

Checkerboard
Mesa

To Kanab and
Bryce Canyon
National Park

Virgin

Petrified Forest Trail

River

SOUTH ENTRANCE
Springdale

ZION-MT CARMEL HWY

9

◖ **ZION CANYON
VISITOR CENTER**

9

East Fork Virgin River

Parunuweap Canyon

Grafton Mesa

Shunesburg
Mountain
5,961ft

Eagle Crags
6,394ft

0	2 mi
0	2 km

© AVALON TRAVEL

ZION NATIONAL PARK

© PAUL LEVY

The Virgin River lies at the bottom of Zion Canyon.

best chances of seeing wildlife and wildflowers. From about mid-October through early November, cottonwoods and other trees and plants blaze with color. Summer temperatures in the canyons can be uncomfortably hot, with highs hovering above 100°F. Summer is also the busiest season. In winter, nighttime temperatures drop to near freezing, and the weather tends to be unpredictable, with bright sunshine one day and freezing rain the next. Snow-covered slopes contrast with colorful rocks. Snow may block some of the high-country trails and the road to Lava Point, but the rest of the park is open and accessible year-round.

PLANNING YOUR TIME

Visitors short on time should drop in at the Zion Canyon Visitor Center and ride the shuttle along Zion Canyon Scenic Drive, stopping for short walks on the Weeping Rock and Riverside Walk trails. If you have a full day, you can also include an easy hike to the Emerald Pools or an ambitious trek up to Angels Landing.

It's always worth spending part of a day hiking with a park ranger. If you can join a ranger hike, spend the morning of your second day going wherever the ranger leads you. In the afternoon, depending on your energy, hike to Weeping Rock (short) or Hidden Canyon (longer).

After this, it's time for longer hikes: Angels Landing is a classic for those who are in good shape and not afraid of heights. Alternatively, if weather conditions and your own abilities are suitable, the hike up the Virgin River (largely in the river) is a spectacular way to spend another full day.

For visitors with more time and a desire to leave busy Zion Canyon, the Kolob is great for longer hikes. It's also worth taking just a couple of hours to drive Kolob Canyons Road, which begins at I-15. Motorists with more time may also want to drive Kolob Terrace Road to Lava Point for another perspective of the park; this drive is about 44 miles round-trip from the town of Virgin and has some unpaved sections.

Exploring the Park

Zion National Park (435/772-3256, www.nps. gov/zion, $25 per vehicle, $12 pedestrians, bicyclists, and motorcyclists) is 43 miles northeast of St. George, 60 miles south of Cedar City, 41 miles northwest of Kanab, and 86 miles southwest of Bryce Canyon National Park. There are two entrances to the main section of the park: From Springdale, you enter the south end of Zion Canyon, near the visitors center and the Zion Canyon shuttle buses; from the east, you come in on the Zion-Mt. Carmel Highway, pass through a long tunnel, then pop into Zion Canyon a few miles north of the visitors center.

There's also a separate entrance for the Kolob Canyons area, in the park's northwest corner. A third entrance leads to the less-traveled part of the park and is accessed by the Kolob Terrace Road, which heads north from Highway 9 at the tiny town of Virgin and goes to backcountry sites. (There's no entrance station on Kolob Terrace Road.) Kolob Canyons Road, in the extreme northwestern section of the park, begins just off I-15's exit 40 at the Kolob Canyons Visitor Center and climbs to an overlook for great views of the Finger Canyons of the Kolob; the drive is 10 miles round-trip.

Large RVs and bicycles must heed special regulations for the long tunnel on the Zion-Mt. Carmel Highway.

VISITORS CENTERS
◖ Zion Canyon Visitor Center
The park's sprawling visitors center (8am-6pm daily winter-spring, 8am-7:30pm daily summer, 8am-5pm daily fall), between Watchman and South Campgrounds, is a hub of activity. The plaza outside the building features several interpretive plaques, including some pointing out environmentally sensitive design features of the visitors center. Inside, a large area is devoted

to backcountry information; staff members can answer your questions about various trails, give you updates on the weather forecast, and help you arrange a shuttle to remote trailheads. The backcountry desk opens at 7am daily late April-late October, an hour earlier than the rest of the visitors center. A Backcountry Shuttle Board allows hikers to coordinate transportation between trailheads.

The busiest part of the visitors center is the bookstore, stocked with an excellent selection of books covering natural history, human history, and regional travel. Topographic and geologic maps, posters, and postcards are also sold here.

Kolob Canyons Visitor Center
Although it is small and has just a handful of exhibits, this visitors center (435/772-3256, 8am-6pm daily summer, 8am-5pm daily spring and fall, 9am-5pm winter) is a good place to stop for information on exploring the Kolob region. Hikers can learn about current trail conditions and obtain the permits required for overnight trips and Zion Narrows day trips. Books, topographic and geologic maps, posters, postcards, slides, and film are sold. The visitors center and the start of Kolob Canyons Road are just off I-15's exit 40.

TOURS
With the exception of ranger-led hikes, Zion Canyon Field Institute classes, horseback rides from Zion Lodge, and the running commentary from the more loquacious shuttle-bus drivers, Zion is a do-it-yourself park. Outfitters are not permitted to lead trips within the park. If you'd like a guided tour outside park boundaries, there are several outfitters in Springdale that lead biking, canyoneering, and climbing trips.

The best way to get a feel for Zion's impressive geology and variety of habitats is to take a

ZION NATIONAL PARK

THE GEOLOGY OF ZION

Faulting has broken the Colorado Plateau into a series of smaller plateaus. At Zion you are on the Kolob Terrace of the Markagunt Plateau, whose rock layers are younger than those of the Kaibab Plateau at Grand Canyon National Park and older than those exposed on the Paunsaugunt Plateau at Bryce Canyon National Park.

The rock layers at Zion began as sediments of oceans, rivers, lakes, or sand dunes deposited 65-240 million years ago. The soaring Navajo sandstone cliffs that form such distinctive features as the **Great White Throne** and the **Three Patriarchs** were originally immense sand dunes. Look for the slanting lines in these rock walls, which result from shifting winds as the sand dunes formed. Calcium carbonate in the sand piles acted as a glue to turn the dunes into rock, and it's also responsible for the white color of many of the rocks. The reddish rocks are also Navajo sandstone, but they've been stained by iron oxides—essentially rust.

Kayenta shale is the other main rock you'll see in Zion. For an up-close look, check out the streambed at **Middle Emerald Pool.** The rippled gray rock is Kayenta shale. This shale, found beneath the Navajo sandstone, is much less permeable than the sandstone. Water can easily trickle through the relatively porous sandstone, but when it hits the impermeable Kayenta shale, it runs along the top surface of the rock and seeps out on the side of the near-est rock face. **Weeping Rock,** with its lush cliff-side springs, is a good place to see the boundary between Navajo sandstone and Kayenta shale.

A gradual uplift of the Colorado Plateau, which continues today, has caused the formerly lazy rivers on its surface to pick up speed and knife through the rock layers. You can really appreciate these erosive powers during flash floods, when the North Fork of the Virgin River and other streams roar through their canyons. Erosion of some of the Virgin River's tributaries couldn't keep up with the main channel, and they were left as "hanging valleys" on the canyon walls. A good example is **Hidden Canyon,** which is reached by a steep trail up from Zion Canyon.

Although some erosive forces, like flash floods, are dramatic, the subtle freezing and thawing of water and the slow action of tree roots are responsible for most of the changes in the landscape. Water seeps into the Navajo sandstone, accumulating especially in the long vertical cracks in the cliffs. The dramatic temperature changes, especially in spring and fall, cause regular freezing and thawing, slowly enlarging the cracks and setting the stage for more dramatic rock falls. Erosion and rock falls continue to shape Zion Canyon. In 1995 a huge rock slide blocked the Zion Canyon Scenic Drive and left hundreds of people trapped at the lodge for several days until crews were able to clear a path.

hike with a park ranger. Many nature programs and hikes are offered late March-November; check the posted schedule at the Zion Canyon Visitor Center. Children's programs, including the popular Junior Ranger program, are held Memorial Day-Labor Day at Zion Nature Center near South Campground; ask at the visitors center for details.

The **Zion Canyon Field Institute** (435/772-3265, www.zionpark.org) is authorized to run educational programs in the park, which include animal tracking, photography, and archaeology; fees vary.

ZION NATURE CENTER

At the northern end of South Campground, the Zion Nature Center (noon-5pm daily summer) houses programs for kids, including Junior Ranger activities for ages 6-12. Although there's no shuttle stop for the Nature Center, it's an easy walk along the Pa'rus Trail from the Zion Canyon Visitor Center or the Human History Museum. Check the park newsletter for kids' programs and family hikes. Programs focus on natural history topics such as insects and bats in the park. Many Junior Ranger activities can be done on your own—pick up a booklet ($1) at the visitors center bookstore.

ZION'S FLORA AND FAUNA

Many different plant and animal communities live in the rugged terrain of deep canyons and high plateaus. Because the park is near the meeting place of the Colorado Plateau, the Great Basin, and the Mojave Desert, species representative of all three regions can be found here.

Only desert plants can endure the long dry spells and high temperatures found at Zion's lower elevations; they include cacti (prickly pear, cholla, and hedgehog), blackbrush, creosote bush, honey mesquite, and purple sage. Cacti and yucca are common throughout the park. Pygmy forests of piñon pine, Utah juniper, live oak, mountain mahogany, and the fragrant cliffrose grow at elevations of about 3,900-5,600 feet.

Once you get above the canyon floor, Zion's plants are not so different from what you'd find across the West. Trees such as ponderosa pine and Douglas fir can thrive here thanks to the moisture they draw from the Navajo sandstone. White fir and aspen are also common on high cool plateaus. Permanent springs and streams support a profusion of greenery such as cottonwood, box elder, willow, red birch, horsetail, and ferns. Watch out for poison ivy in moist shady areas.

Colorful wildflowers pop out of the ground— indeed, even out of the rocks—at all elevations, spring-fall. In early spring, look for the Zion shooting star, a plant in the primrose family found only in Zion. Its nodding pink flowers are easily spotted along the **Emerald Pools trails**

and at **Weeping Rock.** You're also likely to see desert phlox, a low plant covered with pink flowers, and, by mid-May, golden columbine.

Mule deer are common throughout the park. Also common are bank beavers, which live along the banks of the Virgin River rather than in log lodges, which would be too frequently swept away by flash floods. Even though they don't build log lodges, they still gnaw like crazy on trees—look around the base of riverside trees near **Zion Lodge** for their work. Other wildlife includes elk, mountain lions, bobcats, black bears, reintroduced bighorn sheep, coyotes, gray foxes, porcupines, ringtail cats, black-tailed jackrabbits, rock squirrels, cliff chipmunks, and many species of mice and bats.

Birders have spotted more than 270 species in and near the park, but most common are red-tailed hawks, turkey vultures, quail, mallard, great horned owls, hairy woodpeckers, ravens, scrub jays, black-headed grosbeaks, blue-gray gnatcatchers, canyon wrens, Virginia's warblers, white-throated swifts, and broad-tailed hummingbirds. Zion's high cliffs are good places to look for peregrine falcons and the park's reintroduced California condors; try spotting them from the cliff at **Angels Landing** trail.

Hikers and campers will undoubtedly see northern sagebrush lizards, and they should watch for Western rattlesnakes, although these relatively rare reptiles are unlikely to attack unless provoked.

ZION HUMAN HISTORY MUSEUM

The old park visitors center has been retooled as the Zion Human History Museum (9am-7pm daily summer, 10am-6pm daily spring, 9am-6pm daily fall, closed Dec.-early Mar.), covering southern Utah's cultural history with a schmaltzy film introducing the park and fairly bare-bones exhibits focusing on Native American and Mormon history. It's at the first shuttle stop after the visitors center. This is a good place to visit when you're too tired to hike any farther or if the weather forces you to seek shelter.

ZION CANYON

During the busy seasons, April-October, the road is closed to private cars, and you must travel up and down Zion Canyon in a shuttle bus (90 minutes round-trip, free). Most visitors find the shuttle an easy and enjoyable way to visit the following sites.

◖ Court of the Patriarchs Viewpoint

A short trail from the parking area leads to the viewpoint. The Patriarchs, a trio of peaks to the west, overlook Birch Creek; they are, from left to right, Abraham, Isaac, and Jacob. Mount

NAVAJO SANDSTONE

Take a look anywhere along Zion Canyon and you'll see 1,600-2,200-foot cliffs of Navajo sandstone. The big walls of Zion were formed from sand dunes deposited during a hot dry period about 200 million years ago. Shifting winds blew the sand from one direction, then another—a careful inspection of the sandstone layer reveals the diagonal lines resulting from this "cross-bedding." Studies by researchers at the University of Nebraska-Lincoln conclude that the vast dunes of southern Utah were formed when the landmass on which they sit was about 15 degrees north of the equator, at about the same location as Honduras is today. The shift patterns apparent in the sandstone—the slanting striations easily seen in cliff faces—were caused in part by intense monsoon rains, which served to compact and move the dunes each rainy season.

Eventually, a shallow sea washed over the dunes. Lapping waves left shells behind, and as the shells dissolved, their lime seeped down into the sand and cemented it into sandstone. After the Colorado Plateau lifted, rivers cut deeply through the sandstone layer. The formation's lower layers are stained red from iron oxides.

Moroni, the reddish peak on the far right, partially blocks the view of Jacob. Although the official viewpoint is a beautiful place to relax and enjoy the view, you'll get an even better view if you cross the road and head about 0.5 miles up Sand Bench Trail.

Zion Lodge

Rustic Zion Lodge (435/772-7700 or 888/297-2757, www.zionlodge.com), with its big front lawn, spacious lobby, snack bar, restaurant, and restrooms, is a natural stop for most park visitors. You don't need to be a guest at the lodge to enjoy the ambiance of its public areas, and the snack bar is not a bad place to grab lunch.

Cross the road from the lodge to catch the Emerald Pools trails, or walk a 0.5 miles north from the Zion Lodge shuttle stop to reach the Grotto.

The Grotto

The Grotto is a popular place for a picnic. From here, a trail leads back to the lodge, and across the road, the Kayenta Trail links up with the Emerald Pools trails or goes farther on to Angels Landing.

Visible from several points along Zion Canyon Drive is the **Great White Throne.** Topping out at 6,744 feet, this bulky chunk of Navajo sandstone has become, along with the Three Patriarchs, emblematic of the park. Ride the shuttle in the evening to watch the rock change color in the light of the setting sun.

Weeping Rock

Several trails, including the short and easy Weeping Rock Trail, start here. Weeping Rock is home to hanging gardens and many moisture-loving plants, including the striking Zion shooting star. The rock "weeps" because this is a boundary between porous Navajo sandstone and denser Kayenta shale. Water trickles down through the sandstone, and when it can't penetrate the shale, it moves laterally to the face of the cliff.

While you're at Weeping Rock, scan the cliffs for the remains of cables and rigging that were used to lower timber from the top of the rim down to the canyon floor. During the early 1900s, this wood was used to build pioneer settlements in the area.

Big Bend

Look up: This is where you're likely to see rock climbers on the towering walls or hikers on Angels Landing. Because outfitters aren't allowed to bring groups into the park, these climbers presumably are quite experienced and know what they're doing.

Temple of Sinawava

The last shuttle stop is at this canyon, where 2,000-foot-tall rock walls reach up from the sides of the Virgin River. There's not really enough room for the road to continue farther up the canyon, but it's spacious enough for a fine paved wheelchair-accessible walking path. The Riverside Walk heads one mile upstream to the Virgin Narrows, a place where the canyon becomes too narrow even for a sidewalk to squeeze through. You may see people hiking up the Narrows (in the river) from the end of the Riverside Walk. Don't join them unless you're properly outfitted.

EAST OF ZION CANYON

The east section of the park is a land of sandstone slickrock, hoodoos, and narrow canyons. You can see much of the dramatic scenery along the Zion-Mt. Carmel Highway (Hwy. 9) between the east entrance station and Zion Canyon. Most of this region invites exploration on your own. Try hiking a canyon or heading up a slickrock slope (the pass between Crazy Quilt and Checkerboard Mesas is one possibility). Highlights on the plateau include views of the White Cliffs and Checkerboard Mesa, both near the east entrance station, and a hike on the Canyon Overlook Trail, which begins just east of the long tunnel. Checkerboard Mesa's distinctive pattern is caused by a combination of vertical fractures and horizontal bedding planes, both accentuated by weathering. The highway's spectacular descent into Zion Canyon goes first through a 530-foot tunnel, then a 5,600-foot tunnel, followed by a series of six switchbacks to the canyon floor. Because the tunnel, completed in 1930, is narrow, any vehicle more than 7 feet, 10 inches wide, 11 feet, 4 inches high, or 40 feet long (50 feet with trailer) must be escorted through in one-way traffic; a $15 fee, good for two passages, is charged at the tunnel to do this. Bicycles must be carried through the long tunnel on a car or truck; it's too dangerous to ride.

hanging garden at Weeping Rock

© BILL MCRAE

KOLOB CANYONS

North and west of Zion Canyon is the remote backcountry of the Kolob. This area became a second Zion National Monument in 1937, and then was added to Zion National Park in 1956. From here you'll see all but one of the rock formations in the park and evidence of past volcanic eruptions. Two roads lead into the Kolob. The paved five-mile Kolob Canyons Road begins at the Kolob Canyons Visitor Center just off I-15 and ends at the Timber Creek Overlook and picnic area; it's open year-round. Kolob Terrace Road is paved from the town of Virgin (Hwy. 9, 15 miles west of the south entrance station) and runs 20 steep miles to the turnoff for Lava Point; snow usually blocks the way in winter.

Kolob Canyons Road

This five-mile scenic drive winds past the dramatic Finger Canyons of the Kolob to Timber Creek Overlook and a picnic area at the end

ZION CANYON SHUTTLE

In the late 1990s, visitors to Zion remembered the traffic nearly as vividly as they remembered the Great White Throne: Throughout much of the summer, the canyon road was simply a parking lot for enormous RVs. To relieve the congestion, the National Park Service has instituted an April-October **shuttle bus service** through the canyon.

There are actually two separate bus lines: One line travels between Springdale and the park entrance, stopping within a short walk of every Springdale motel and near several large visitor parking lots; the other bus line starts just inside the park entrance, at the visitors center, and runs the length of Zion Canyon Road, stopping at scenic overlooks, trailheads, and Zion Lodge. Lodge guests may obtain a pass authorizing them to drive to the lodge, but in general, private vehicles are not allowed to drive up Zion Canyon.

This is less of a pain than it might seem. It's still fine to drive to the campgrounds; in fact, the road between the park entrance and the Zion-Mt. Carmel Highway junction is open to all vehicles. Buses run frequently, so there's rarely much of a wait, and most of the bus drivers are friendly and well-informed, offering an engaging commentary on the sights that they pass (even pointing out rock climbers on the canyon walls).

If you get to Zion before 10am or after 3pm, there may be parking spaces available in the visitors center lot. Midday visitors should just park in Springdale (at your motel or in a public lot) and catch a shuttle bus to the park entrance.

Riding the bus is free; its operating costs are included in the park admission fee. Buses run as often as every six minutes 5:30am-11pm daily, less frequently early in the morning and in the evening. No pets are allowed on the buses.

November-March, private vehicles are allowed on all roads, and the buses are out of service.

Zion Canyon Scenic Drive is a six-mile road that follows the North Fork of the Virgin River upstream. Impressive natural formations along the way include the Three Patriarchs, Mountain of the Sun, Lady Mountain, Great White Throne, Angels Landing, and Weeping Rock. The bus stops at eight points of interest along the way; you can get on and off the bus as often as you want at these stops. The road ends at Temple of Sinawava and the beginning of the Riverside Walk Trail.

© BILL MCRAE

Zion Canyon shuttle

of the road. The road is paved and has many pullouts where you can stop to admire the scenery. The first part of the drive follows the 200-mile-long Hurricane Fault, which forms the west edge of the Markagunt Plateau. Look for the tilted rock layers deformed by friction as the plateau rose nearly one mile. **Taylor Creek Trail,** which begins two miles past the visitors center, provides a close look at the canyons.

Lee Pass, four miles beyond the visitors center, was named after John D. Lee, who was the only person ever convicted of a crime in the infamous Mountain Meadows Massacre; he's believed to have lived nearby for a short time

© PAUL LEVY

East of Zion Canyon, Checkerboard Mesa's unusual facade is due to oppositional fracturing.

KOLOB TERRACE

The Kolob Terrace section of the park is a high plateau roughly parallel to and west of Zion Canyon. From the town of Virgin, the road runs north through ranch land and up a narrow tongue of land, with drop-offs on either side, and then the land widens into a high plateau. The Hurricane Cliffs rise from the gorge to the west, and the back side of Zion Canyon's big walls are to the east. The road passes in and out of the park and terminates at Kolob Reservoir, a popular boating and fishing destination outside the park. This section of the park is much higher than Zion Canyon, so it is a good place to explore when the canyon swelters in the summertime. It's also much less crowded than the busy canyon.

Lava Point

The panorama from Lava Point (elevation 7,890 feet) takes in the Cedar Breaks area to the north, the Pink Cliffs to the northeast, Zion Canyon Narrows and tributaries to the east, the Sentinel and other monoliths of Zion Canyon to the southeast, and Mount Trumbull on the Arizona Strip to the south. Signs help identify features. Lava Point, which sits atop a lava flow, is a good place to cool off in summer—temperatures are about 20 degrees cooler than in Zion Canyon. Aspen, ponderosa pine, Gambel oak, and white fir grow here. A small primitive campground near the point offers sites during warmer months (free) but there is no water. From Virgin, take the Kolob Terrace Road about 21 miles north to the Lava Point turnoff; the viewpoint is 1.8 miles farther on a well-marked spur road.

Kolob Reservoir

This high-country lake north of Lava Point has good fishing for rainbow trout. An unpaved boat ramp is at the south end near the dam. People sometimes camp along the shore, although there are no facilities. Most of the

after the 1857 incident, in which a California-bound wagon train was attacked by an alliance of Mormons and local Native Americans. About 120 people in the wagon train were killed. Only small children too young to tell the story were spared. The close-knit Mormon community tried to cover up the incident and hindered federal attempts to apprehend the killers. Only Lee, who was in charge of Indian affairs in southern Utah at the time, was ever brought to justice; he was later executed.

La Verkin Creek Trail begins at Lee Pass Trailhead and offers trips to Kolob Arch and beyond. Signs at the end of the road identify the points, buttes, mesas, and mountains. The salmon-colored Navajo sandstone cliffs glow a deep red at sunset. **Timber Creek Overlook Trail** begins from the picnic area at road's end and climbs 0.5 miles to the overlook (elevation 6,369 feet); views encompass the Pine Valley Mountains, Zion Canyon, and distant Mount Trumbull.

© PAUL LEVY

The Kolob Terrace overlooks Zion National Park's canyons.

surrounding land is private. To reach the reservoir, continue north 3.5 miles on Kolob Terrace Road from the Lava Point turnoff. The fair-weather road can also be followed past the reservoir to the Cedar City area. Blue Springs Reservoir, near the turnoff for Lava Point, is closed to the public.

Recreation

Zion's hiking trails are tailored to all abilities, making it easy to explore. Both the Pa'rus Trail and Riverside Walk are wheelchair accessible. Casual hikers can spend several days riding the shuttle bus up Zion Canyon and hopping off for short hikes. These hikes, past lush hanging gardens or up to vertiginous viewpoints, may whet your appetite for extended backpacking trips or an in-water hike up the Virgin River Narrows.

Experienced hikers can do countless off-trail routes in the canyons and plateaus surrounding Zion Canyon; rangers can suggest areas. Rappelling and other climbing skills may be needed to negotiate drops in some of the more remote canyons. Groups cannot exceed 12 hikers per trail or drainage. Overnight hikers must obtain backcountry permits from the Zion Canyon or Kolob Canyons visitors centers or from https://zionpermits.nps.gov. The permit fees are based on group size: $10 for 1-2 people, $15 for 3-7, and $20 for 8-12. Some areas of the park—mainly those near roads and major trails—are closed to overnight use. Ask about shuttles to backcountry trailheads outside Zion Canyon at the visitors center's backcountry desk (435/772-0170). Shuttles are also available from Zion Rock and Mountain Guides

(435/772-3303) and the Zion Adventure Company (435/772-1001) in Springdale.

HIKING IN ZION CANYON

The trails in Zion Canyon provide perspectives of the park that are not available from the roads. Many of the hiking trails require long ascents but aren't too difficult at a leisurely pace. Carry water on all but the shortest walks. Descriptions of the following trails are given in order from the mouth of Zion Canyon to the Virgin River Narrows.

Pa'rus Trail

- Distance: 3.5 miles round-trip
- Duration: 2 hours
- Elevation change: 50 feet
- Effort: easy
- Trailheads: South Campground and Canyon Junction
- Shuttle stops: Zion Canyon Visitor Center and Canyon Junction

This paved, wheelchair-accessible trail runs from South Campground to the Canyon Junction shuttle-bus stop. For most of its distance, it skirts the Virgin River, and it makes for a nice early-morning or evening stroll. Listen for the trilling song of the canyon wren, then try to spot the small bird in the bushes. The Pa'rus Trail is the only trail in the park open to bicycles and pets.

Watchman Trail

- Distance: 2.7 miles round-trip
- Duration: 2 hours
- Elevation change: 370 feet
- Effort: easy-moderate
- Trailhead: just north of Watchman Campground
- Shuttle stop: Zion Canyon Visitor Center

No, this hike doesn't go to the top of 6,555-foot Watchman Peak, but it does lead to a mesa southeast of the visitors center with a good view of this

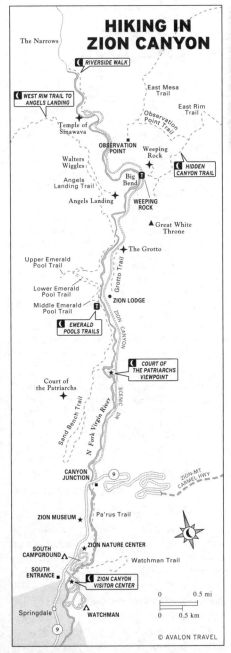

ZION NATIONAL PARK

THE ZION-MT. CARMEL TUNNEL

If your vehicle is 7 feet, 10 inches wide, 11 feet, 4 inches tall, or larger, you will need a traffic-control escort through the narrow mile-long Zion-Mt. Carmel Tunnel. Vehicles of this size are too large to stay in one lane while traveling through the tunnel, which was built in the 1920s, when autos were not only small but few and far between. Most RVs, buses, trailers, and fifth-wheels, and some camper shells, will require an escort.

If your vehicle requires an escort, expect to pay a $15 fee per vehicle in addition to the park entrance fee (payable at the park entrance station before entering the tunnel). The fee is good for two trips through the tunnel for the same vehicle over a seven-day period.

Although the park service persists in using the term *escort*, you're really on your own through the tunnel. Park staff will stop oncoming traffic, allowing you enough time to drive down the middle of the tunnel, but you do not follow an escort vehicle. Traffic-control staff are present at the tunnel 8am-8pm daily April 1-mid-September. During the winter season, oversized vehicle passage must be arranged at the entrance stations (8am-7pm daily late Sept., 8am-6pm daily Oct., 8am-4:30pm daily Nov.-Mar.) at Zion Canyon Visitor Center, at Zion Lodge, or by phoning 435/772-3256. Bicycles and pedestrians are not allowed in the tunnel.

early or late in the day. In fact, it's a good shake-down hike to do on the evening you arrive at Zion. As soon as the sun drops behind the canyon walls, set out—on long summer evenings, you'll have plenty of time to complete it before dark.

Sand Bench Trail

- Distance: 1.7 miles round-trip
- Duration: 3 hours
- Elevation change: 500 feet
- Effort: easy
- Trailhead: Zion Lodge
- Shuttle stops: Court of the Patriarchs or Zion Lodge

This loop trail has good views of the three Patriarchs, the Streaked Wall, and other monuments of lower Zion Canyon. During the main season, Zion Lodge organizes three-hour horseback rides on the trail. The horses churn up dust and leave an uneven surface, though, so hikers usually prefer to go elsewhere during those times. The trail soon leaves the riparian forest along Birch Creek and climbs onto the dry benchland. Piñon pine, juniper, sand sage, yucca, prickly pear cactus, and other high-desert plants and animals live here. Hikers can get off the shuttle at the Court of the Patriarchs Viewpoint, walk across the scenic drive, and then follow a service road to the footbridge and trailhead. A 1.2-mile trail along the river connects the trailhead with Zion Lodge. In warmer months, try to hike in the early morning or late afternoon.

prominent mountain. The hike starts off fairly unspectacularly, but it gets more interesting as it gains elevation. Be sure to look back over your shoulder for views of Zion Canyon's high walls.

At the top of the mesa, the Watchman pops into view. The short mesa-top loop trail is worth taking for its views of Springdale and its nice assortment of wildflowers, including barrel cacti. During the middle of the day, this trail can bake in the sun. Try to hike it on a cool day or

◖ Emerald Pools Trails

- Distance: 0.6 miles one-way to Lower Emerald Pool; 1 mile to Middle Emerald Pool; 1.4 miles to Upper Emerald Pool
- Duration: 1-3 hours
- Elevation change: 70 feet to Lower Emerald Pool; 150 feet to Middle Emerald Pool; 350 feet to Upper Emerald Pool
- Effort: easy-moderate

- Trailhead: across the footbridge from Zion Lodge
- Shuttle stop: Zion Lodge

Three spring-fed pools, small waterfalls, and views of Zion Canyon make this hike a favorite. You have a choice of three trails. The easiest is the paved trail to the Lower Pool; cross the footbridge near Zion Lodge and turn right. The Middle Pool can be reached by continuing 350 yards on this trail or by taking a totally different trail from the footbridge at Zion Lodge (after crossing the bridge, turn left, then right up the trail). Together these trails make a 1.8-mile round-trip loop. A third trail begins at the Grotto Picnic Area, crosses a footbridge, and turns left before continuing for 0.7 miles; the trail forks left to the Lower Pool and right to the Middle Pool. A steep 0.4-mile trail leads from the Middle Pool to Upper Emerald Pool. This magical spot has a white sand beach and towering cliffs rising above. Don't expect to find solitude; these relatively easy trails are quite popular.

West Rim Trail to Angels Landing

- Distance: 5.4 miles round-trip
- Duration: 4 hours
- Elevation change: 1,488 feet
- Effort: strenuous
- Trailhead: Grotto Picnic Area
- Shuttle stop: The Grotto

This strenuous trail leads to some of the best views of Zion Canyon. Start from Grotto Picnic Area (elevation 4,300 feet) and cross the footbridge, then turn right along the river. The trail climbs the slopes and enters the cool and shady depths of Refrigerator Canyon. Walter's Wiggles, a series of 21 closely spaced switchbacks, wind up to Scout Lookout and a trail junction—it's four miles round-trip and a 1,050-foot elevation gain if you decide to turn around here. Scout Lookout has fine views of Zion Canyon. The trail is paved and well graded to this point. Turn

right at the junction and continue 0.5 miles to the summit of Angels Landing.

Angels Landing rises as a sheer-walled monolith 1,500 feet above the North Fork of the Virgin River. Although the trail to the summit is rough, chains provide security in the more exposed places. The climb is safe with care and good weather, but don't go if the trail is covered with snow or ice or if thunderstorms threaten. Children must be closely supervised, and people who are afraid of heights should skip this trail. Once on top, you'll see why Angels Landing got its name—the panorama makes all the effort worthwhile. It's most pleasant to do this hike during the cooler morning hours.

Energetic hikers can continue 4.8 miles on the main trail from Scout Lookout to **West Rim Viewpoint,** which overlooks the Right Fork of North Creek. This strenuous 12.8-mile round-trip hike from Grotto Picnic Area includes 3,070 feet of elevation gain. West Rim Trail continues through Zion's backcountry to Lava Point (elevation 7,890 feet), where there's a primitive campground. A car shuttle and one or more days are needed to hike the 13.3 miles (one-way) from Grotto Picnic Area. You'll have an easier hike if you start at Lava Point and hike down to the picnic area; even so, be prepared for a long day hike. The trail has little or no water in some seasons.

Weeping Rock Trail

- Distance: 0.5 miles round-trip
- Duration: 30 minutes
- Elevation change: 100 feet
- Effort: easy
- Trailhead: Weeping Rock parking area
- Shuttle stop: Weeping Rock

A favorite with visitors, this easy trail winds past lush vegetation and wildflowers to a series of cliff-side springs above an overhang. Thousands of water droplets glisten in the afternoon sun. The springs emerge where water seeping through more than 2,000 feet of

ZION NATIONAL PARK

© SABRINA YOUNG

ANGELS LANDING

STRENUOUS CLIMB

NARROW ROUTE WITH
CLIFF EXPOSURES

HAZARDOUS DURING
THUNDERSTORMS, DARKNESS,
AND ICE / SNOW CONDITIONS

Everything this sign says about the trail to Angels Landing is true!

Navajo sandstone meets a layer of impervious shale. Signs along the way identify some of the trees and plants.

Observation Point Trail

- Distance: 8 miles round-trip
- Duration: 5 hours
- Elevation change: 2,148 feet
- Effort: strenuous
- Trailhead: Weeping Rock parking area
- Shuttle stop: Weeping Rock

This strenuous trail climbs to Observation Point (elevation 6,507 feet) on the edge of Zion Canyon. Trails branch off along the way to Hidden Canyon, upper Echo Canyon, the east entrance, East Mesa, and other destinations. The first of many switchbacks begins a short way up from the trailhead at Weeping Rock parking area. You'll reach the junction for Hidden Canyon Trail after 0.8 miles. Several switchbacks later, the trail enters sinuous Echo

Canyon. This incredibly narrow chasm can be explored for short distances upstream and downstream to deep pools and pour-offs. **Echo Canyon Trail** branches to the right at about the halfway point; this rough trail continues farther up the canyon and connects with trails to Cable Mountain, Deertrap Mountain, and the east entrance station (on Zion-Mt. Carmel Highway). The East Rim Trail then climbs slickrock slopes above Echo Canyon with many fine views. Parts of the trail are cut right into the cliffs; this work was done in the 1930s by the Civilian Conservation Corps. You'll reach the rim at last after three miles of steady climbing, and then it's an easy 0.6 miles hike through a forest of piñon pine, juniper, Gambel oak, manzanita, sage, and some ponderosa pine to Observation Point. Impressive views take in Zion Canyon below and mountains and mesas all around. The **East Mesa Trail** turns right about 0.3 miles before Observation Point and follows the plateau northeast to a dirt road outside the park.

© PAUL LEVY

hiking Zion's trails

Hidden Canyon Trail

- Distance: 3 miles round-trip
- Duration: 2.5-3 hours
- Elevation change: 850 feet
- Effort: strenuous
- Trailhead: Weeping Rock parking area
- Shuttle stop: Weeping Rock

See if you can spot the entrance to Hidden Canyon from below. Inside the narrow canyon are small sandstone caves, a little natural arch, and diverse plantlife. The high walls, rarely more than 65 feet apart, block sunlight except for a short time at midday. From the trailhead at the Weeping Rock parking area, follow the East Rim Trail 0.8 miles up the cliff face, then turn right and go 0.7 miles on Hidden Canyon Trail to the canyon entrance. Footing can be a bit difficult in places, but chains provide handholds on the exposed sections. Steps chopped into the rock just inside Hidden Canyon help bypass some deep pools. After heavy rains and

spring runoff, the creek forms a small waterfall at the canyon entrance. The canyon itself is about one mile long and mostly easy walking, although the trail fades away. Look for the arch on the right about 0.5 miles up the canyon.

Riverside Walk

- Distance: 2.2 miles round-trip
- Duration: 1.5-2 hours
- Elevation change: 57 feet
- Effort: easy
- Trailhead: Temple of Sinawava parking area
- Shuttle stop: Temple of Sinawava

This is one of the most popular hikes in the park, and except for the Pa'rus, it's the easiest. The nearly level paved trail begins at the end of Zion Canyon Scenic Drive and heads upstream along the Virgin River to the Narrows. Allow about two hours to fully take in the scenery—it's a good place to get a close-up view of Zion's lovely hanging gardens. Countless springs and seeps on the canyon walls support luxuriant plant growth and swamps. Most of the springs occur at the boundary between the porous Navajo sandstone and the less permeable Kayenta Formation below. The water and vegetation attract abundant wildlife; keep an eye out for birds and animals and their tracks. Late morning is the best time for photography. In autumn, cottonwoods and maples display bright splashes of color. At trail's end, the canyon is wide enough only for the river. Hikers continuing upstream on the Narrows hike must wade and sometimes even swim.

The Narrows

- Distance: 16 miles one-way
- Duration: 12 hours
- Elevation change: 200 feet
- Effort: strenuous
- Trailheads: end of Riverside Walk or Chamberlain's Ranch

© BILL MCRAE

entering the Narrows

• Shuttle stop: Temple of Sinawava

Upper Zion Canyon is probably the most famous backcountry area in the park, yet it's also one of the most strenuous. There's no trail and you'll be wading in the river much of the time, which can be knee- to chest-deep. In places, the high fluted walls of the upper North Fork of the Virgin River are only 20 feet apart, and very little sunlight penetrates the depths. Mysterious side canyons beckon.

Hikers should be well prepared and in good condition—river hiking is more tiring than hiking over dry land. The major hazards are flash floods and hypothermia. Finding the right time to go through can be tricky: Spring runoff is too high, summer thunderstorms bring hazardous flash floods, and winter is too cold. That leaves just early summer (mid-June–mid-July) and early autumn (mid-Sept.–mid-Oct.) as the best bets. You can get through the entire 16-mile (one-way) Narrows in about 12 hours, although two days is best to enjoy

the beauty of the place. Children under 12 shouldn't attempt to hike the entire canyon.

Don't be tempted to wear river sandals or sneakers up the Narrows; it's easy to twist an ankle on the slippery rocks. If you have a pair of hiking boots that you don't mind drenching, they'll work, but an even better solution is available from the **Zion Adventure Company** (36 Lion Blvd., Springdale, 435/772-1001, www.zionadventures.com) and other Springdale outfitters. They rent specially designed river-hiking boots, along with neoprene socks, walking sticks, and in cool weather, dry suits. Boots, socks, and sticks rent for $21 for the first day, $10.50 for each additional day; with a dry suit the package costs $49 for the first day, $24.50 for each additional day. They also provide a valuable orientation to hiking the Narrows and lead tours of the section below Orderville Canyon (about $150 pp, depending on group size and the season).

Talk with rangers at the Zion Canyon Visitor Center before starting a trip; they also have a handout with useful information on planning a Narrows hike. No permit is needed if you're just going partway in and back in one day, although you must first check conditions and the weather forecast with rangers. Permits are required for overnight hikes, which must be "top down," starting at Chamberlain's Ranch and hiking downstream to the Riverside Walk; get permits from the backcountry desk at the visitors center the day before you plan to hike or the morning of your hike (7am–noon) or by applying at https://zionpermits.nps.gov. You will also be issued a plastic bag specially designed to collect human waste. Only one-night stays are allowed. No camping is permitted below Big Springs. Group size for hiking and camping is limited to 12 along the entire route.

A downstream hike saves not only climbing but also the work of fighting the river currents. If you're planning to hike the full length of the Narrows, it is strongly recommended that you take the downstream route. The main hitch is that this requires a shuttle to the upper trailhead near Chamberlain's Ranch, reached via an 18-mile dirt road that turns north from Highway 9 east of the park. The lower trailhead is at the end of the Zion Canyon Scenic Drive. The elevation change is 1,280 feet. During the summer, **Zion Rock and Mountain Guides** (1458 Zion Park Blvd., 435/772-3303, www.zionrockguides.com, 6:30am and 9:30am, $35 pp) offers a daily shuttle to Chamberlain's Ranch. Make shuttle reservations 9am-6pm the day before you want to ride. There is a small discount in the fare if you also rent gear from them. **Zion Adventure Company** (435/772-1001, www.zionadventures.com) has a similar service.

A good half-day trip begins at the end of the Riverside Walk and follows the Narrows 1.5 miles (about 2 hours) upstream to Orderville Canyon, then back the same way. Orderville Canyon makes a good destination itself; you can hike quite a ways up from Zion Canyon.

HIKING EAST OF ZION CANYON

You can't take the park shuttle bus to trailheads east of Zion Canyon, although the long-distance East Rim Trail, which starts just inside the park's eastern boundary, joins trails that lead down into Zion Canyon's Weeping Rock trailhead.

Canyon Overlook Trail

- Distance: 1 mile round-trip
- Duration: 1 hour
- Elevation change: 163 feet
- Effort: easy
- Trailhead: parking area just east of the long (westernmost) tunnel on the Zion-Mt. Carmel Highway

This fun hike starts on the road east of Zion Canyon and features great views from the heights without the stiff climbs found on most other Zion trails. A booklet available at the start or at the Zion Canyon Visitor Center describes the geology, plantlife, and clues to the presence of wildlife. The trail winds in and out along the ledges of Pine Creek Canyon, which opens into a great valley. Panoramas at trail's end take in lower Zion Canyon in the distance. A sign at the viewpoint identifies Bridge Mountain, Streaked Wall, East Temple, and other features. The Great Arch of Zion—termed a "blind arch" because it's open only on one side—is below; the arch is 580 feet high, 720 feet long, and 90 feet deep.

East Rim Trail

- Distance: 10.6 miles one-way
- Duration: 6-8 hours
- Elevation change: 1,340 feet
- Effort: strenuous
- Trailheads: east entrance of Zion National Park; Weeping Rock trailhead

This trail is best done as a one-way trek. It's possible to do it as a long day hike but beautiful enough to encourage a slower-paced overnight trip. The great views start with a look at Checkerboard Mesa and continue as the big features of Zion Canyon come into view. The first half of the hike involves a steady climb, but then the trail tops out on a mesa and finishes by dropping into Zion Canyon. This downhill stretch is amazingly beautiful—even the slickrock that you walk on in places seems like a work of art. In the slickrock section, keep an eye out for the rock cairns that mark the way.

The Observation Point trail joins this trail at nine miles; it's a steep two miles on this spur trail to Observation Point. The main trail continues down a paved path to Weeping Rock and the Zion Canyon shuttle bus.

The East Rim Trail tops out at 6,725 feet, high enough that snow may linger into the spring. Check with the staff at the visitors center backcountry desk if you're hiking early in the season.

HIKING OFF HIGHWAY 9

During the summer, this area of the park can be extremely hot, and in the early spring, it's often too muddy to hike. These trails, which head north from Highway 9 west of the town of Springdale, are accessible without paying the park entrance fee.

Huber Wash

- Distance: 5 miles round-trip
- Duration: 2.5 hours
- Elevation change: 163 feet
- Effort: easy
- Trailhead: Highway 9, about 6 miles west of park entrance, near a power substation

From the parking area, this trail heads up Huber Wash through painted desert and canyons. One of the highlights of hiking in this area, besides the desert scenery, is the abundance of petrified wood. There's even a log-jam of petrified wood at the 2.5-mile mark, where the trail ends in a box canyon decked with a hanging garden. If you're up for a tricky climb over the petrified logjam, you can clamber up and catch the Chinle Trail, then hike five miles back to the road. The Chinle Trail emerges onto Highway 9 about 2.5 miles east of the Huber Wash trailhead.

This is an ideal autumn hike. Even then, it'll be quite warm. Remember to bring plenty of water.

Coalpits Wash

- Distance: 3.5 miles round-trip
- Duration: 2 hours
- Elevation change: 100 feet
- Effort: easy
- Trailhead: Highway 9, about 7.3 miles west of park entrance. The trailhead parking area may not be marked; it's between Rockville and Virgin, almost directly across Highway 9 from the turnoff to Grafton.

At 3,666 feet, the Coalpits Wash trailhead is the lowest spot in Zion. This low elevation makes it an ideal winter hike, and it's also the best place to look for early spring wildflowers, including mariposa lilies, purple sagebrush, and pale evening primrose. Birders also like this shrubby area. If you have the opportunity to take a ranger-led tour up this wash, take it—you'll likely be introduced to many new plants.

The stream in this wash carries water for much of the year. After about 1.5 miles, Coalpits joins Scroggins Wash. Though most hikers turn around at this point, it's possible to keep going up the ever-narrowing wash (the Chinle Trail joins in at 3.75 miles) and turn this into a good cool-season backpacking trip.

HIKING IN KOLOB CANYONS

Access these hikes from Kolob Canyons Road, which begins at I-15 south of Cedar City. You're likely to have the trails to yourself in this section of the park.

Taylor Creek Trail

- Distance: 5 miles round-trip
- Duration: 4 hours
- Elevation change: 450 feet
- Effort: easy-moderate
- Trailhead: 2 miles east of Kolob Canyons Visitor Center, left side of the road

This excellent day hike from Kolob Canyons Road heads upstream into the canyon of the Middle Fork of Taylor Creek. Double Arch Alcove is 2.7 miles from the trailhead; a dry fall 350 yards farther blocks the way (water flows over it during spring runoff and after rains). A giant rockfall occurred here in June 1990. From this trail you can also explore the North Fork of Taylor Creek. A separate trail along the South Fork of Taylor Creek leaves the drive at a bend 3.1 miles from the visitors center, then goes 1.2 miles upstream beneath steep canyon walls.

La Verkin Creek Trail to Kolob Arch

• Distance: 14 miles round-trip

• Duration: 8 hours

• Elevation change: 700 feet

• Effort: strenuous

• Trailhead: Lee Pass

Kolob Arch vies with Landscape Arch in Arches National Park as the world's longest natural rock span. Differences in measurement techniques have resulted in controversy: Kolob Arch's span has been measured variously at 292-310 feet, while Landscape Arch measures at 291-306 feet. Kolob probably takes the prize because its 310-foot measurement was done using an accurate electronic method. Kolob's height is 330 feet, and its vertical thickness is 80 feet. The arch makes a fine destination for a backpacking trip. Spring and autumn are the best seasons to go; summer temperatures rise above 90°F, and winter snows make the trails hard to follow.

You have a choice of two moderately difficult trails. La Verkin Creek Trail begins at Lee Pass (elevation 6,080 feet) on Kolob Canyons Scenic Drive, four miles beyond the visitors center. The trail drops into Timber Creek (intermittent flow), crosses over hills to La Verkin Creek (flows year-round), then turns up side canyons to the arch. The 14-mile round-trip hike can be done as a long day trip, but you'll enjoy the best lighting for photos at the arch if you camp in the area and see it the following morning. Carry plenty of water for the return trip; the climb to the trailhead can be hot and tiring.

HIKING FROM KOLOB TERRACE ROAD

From the town of Virgin, Kolob Terrace Road runs north and passes several trailheads, including the Subway, a popular canyoneering spot, and a couple of great trails at Lava Point. These trails are far less traveled than those in Zion Canyon, and at about 7,000 feet, they stay fairly cool in summer.

Snow blocks the access road to Lava Point for much of the year; the usual season is May or June-early November. Check road conditions with the Zion Canyon or Kolob Canyons Visitor Center. From the south entrance station in Zion Canyon, drive west 15 miles on Highway 9 to Virgin, travel north 21 miles on Kolob Terrace Road (signed for "Kolob Reservoir"), then turn right and continue 1.8 miles to Lava Point.

The Subway

• Distance: 9 miles round-trip

• Duration: 7 hours

• Elevation change: 2,000 feet

• Effort: strenuous

• Trailheads: Left Fork or Wildcat Canyon

The Left Fork of North Creek, a.k.a. "The Subway," is a special semitechnical canyoneering hike for strong swimmers. This challenging day hike involves, at the very least, lots of route-finding, many stream crossings, and some rope work. Obviously, the Left Fork is not for everyone.

Like the Narrows, the Left Fork can be hiked either partway up and then back down, starting and ending at the Left Fork Trailhead; or, with a shuttle, from an upper trailhead at Wildcat Canyon downstream to the Left Fork Trailhead. The "top-to-bottom" route requires rappelling skills and at least 60 feet of climbing rope or webbing. It also involves swimming through several deep sections of very cold water.

Even though the hike is in a day-use-only zone, the Park Service requires a special permit, which, unlike other Zion backcountry permits, is available ahead of time through a somewhat convoluted lottery process. Prospective hikers should visit the park's website (www.nps.gov/zion), click on "Wilderness Information," then click on "The Subway," and follow links to the permit. From there, you will be introduced to the complicated lottery system of applying for a permit to hike the Subway. Lotteries are run monthly for hiking dates several months in the future. Each lottery entry costs $10 for two hikers, and each individual hiker can apply only once per month.

If you're planning this hike at the last minute, try calling 435/772-0170 or checking www.nps.gov/zion to see if there are any openings. The Left Fork trailhead is on Kolob Terrace Road, 8.1 miles north of Virgin.

Hop Valley Trail to Kolob Arch

- Distance: 14 miles round-trip
- Duration: 8 hours
- Elevation change: 1,050 feet
- Effort: strenuous
- Trailhead: Hop Valley trailhead, 13 miles north of Virgin off the Kolob Terrace Road

Although most hikers reach Kolob Arch via the La Verkin Creek Trail, you can also hike to the scenic arch on the Hop Valley Trail from Kolob Terrace Road. The Hop Valley Trail is seven miles one-way to Kolob Arch with an elevation drop of 1,050 feet; water is available in Hop Valley and La Verkin Creek. You may have to do some wading in the creek, and the trail crosses private land (no camping).

Northgate Peaks Trail

- Distance: 4 miles round-trip
- Duration: 2 hours
- Elevation change: 50 feet
- Effort: easy
- Trailhead: Wildcat Canyon trailhead (southern end), 16 miles north of Virgin off Kolob Terrace Road

Most of the trails in this remote area of the park are long and challenging. Northgate Peaks is the exception: an easy family hike along a sandy trail. Hike out from the southern Wildcat Canyon Trailhead and pass the turnoff to the Hop Valley Trail; about 200 yards

farther, turn right (south) onto the Northgate Peaks Trail. The trail passes through a pine-strewn meadow to a trail's end overlook of the Great West Canyon, surrounded by highly textured sandstone domes. Wildflowers, including the strikingly pretty shooting stars, are abundant near the end of the trail. This is also a good place to look for raptors.

West Rim Trail

- Distance: 13.3 miles one-way
- Duration: 8 hours or overnight
- Elevation change: 3,600 feet
- Effort: strenuous
- Trailhead: Lava Point trailhead

The West Rim Trail goes southeast to Zion Canyon, with an elevation drop of 3,600 feet (3,000 of them in the last six miles). This is the western end of the same trail that takes hikers from Zion Canyon to Angels Landing. Water can normally be found along the way at Sawmill, Potato Hollow, and Cabin Springs.

From its start on the edge of the Kolob Plateau to its end in Zion Canyon, the West Rim Trail passes through a wide range of ecosystems, including sandstone domes and an unexpected pond at Potato Hollow, and many great views. The trail is most often done as a two-day backpacking trip, which gives hikers time to explore and enjoy the area.

You can also reach the Lava Point trailhead by hiking the one-mile Barney's Trail from Site 2 in Lava Point Campground.

Wildcat Canyon Trail

- Distance: 10 miles round-trip
- Duration: 5 hours
- Elevation change: 450 feet
- Effort: moderate
- Trailhead: Lava Point trailhead

The Wildcat Canyon Trail heads southwest from Lava Point to a trailhead on Kolob Terrace

Road (16 miles north of Virgin), so if it's possible to arrange a shuttle, you can do this as a one-way hike in about three hours. The trail, which travels across slickrock, through forest, and past cliffs, has views of the Left Fork North Creek drainage, but it lacks a reliable water source. You can continue north and west toward Kolob Arch by taking the four-mile Connector Trail to Hop Valley Trail.

You can also reach the Lava Point trailhead by hiking the one-mile **Barney's Trail** from Site 2 in Lava Point campground.

BIKING

One of the fringe benefits of the Zion Canyon shuttle bus is the great bicycling that's resulted from the lack of automobile traffic. It used to be way too scary to bike along the narrow, traffic-choked Zion Canyon Scenic Drive, but now it's a joy.

On the stretch of road where cars are permitted—between the Zion Canyon Visitor Center and Canyon Junction (where the Zion-Mt. Carmel Highway meets Zion Canyon Scenic Drive)—the two-mile paved **Pa'rus Trail** is open to cyclists as well as pedestrians and makes for easy stress-free pedaling. Bicycles are allowed on the park road, but they must pull over to allow shuttle buses to pass.

If you decide you've had enough cycling, every shuttle bus has a rack that can hold two bicycles. Bike parking is plentiful at the visitors center, Zion Lodge, and most trailheads.

Outside the Zion Canyon area, **Kolob Terrace Road** is a good place to stretch your legs; it's 22 miles to Kolob Reservoir.

There's no place to mountain bike off-road within the park, but there are good mountain-biking spots, including places to practice slickrock riding, just outside the park boundaries. It's best to stop by one of the local bike shops for advice and a map of your chosen destination.

Bike rentals and maps are available in Springdale at **Bike Zion** (1458 Zion Park Blvd.,

435/772-0320, www.bikingzion.com) and at **Zion Cycles** (868 Zion Park Blvd., 435/772-0400, www.zioncycles.com).

HORSEBACK RIDING

Trail rides on horses and mules leave from the corral near Zion Lodge (435/679-8665, www.canyonrides.com) and head down the Virgin River. A one-hour trip ($40) goes to the Court of the Patriarchs, and a half-day ride ($80) follows the Sand Bench Trail. Riders must be at least age 7 for the short ride and age 10 for the half-day ride, and riders can weigh no more than 220 pounds.

CLIMBING

Rock climbers come to scale the high Navajo sandstone cliffs; after Yosemite, Zion is the nation's most popular big-wall climbing area. However, Zion's sandstone is far more fragile than Yosemite's granite, and it has a tendency to crumble and flake, especially when wet. Beginners should avoid these walls—experience with crack climbing is a must.

For route descriptions, pick up a copy of *Desert Rock* by Eric Bjørnstad or *Rock Climbing Utah* by Stewart M. Green. Both books are sold at the Zion Canyon Visitor Center bookstore. The backcountry desk in the visitors center also has a notebook full of route descriptions supplied by past climbers. Check here to make sure your climbing area is open—some are closed to protect nesting peregrine falcons—and remember to bring a pair of binoculars to scout climbing routes from the canyon floor.

If you aren't prepared to tackle the 2,000-foot-high canyon walls, you may want to check out a couple of bouldering sites, both quite close to the south entrance of the park. One huge boulder is 40 yards west of the park entrance; the other is a large slab with a crack, located 0.5 miles north of the entrance.

During the summer, it can be intensely hot on

unshaded walls. The best months for climbing are March-May and September-early November.

If watching the climbers at Zion gives you a hankering to scale a wall, the **Zion Adventure Company** (36 Lion Blvd., Springdale, 435/772-1001, www.zionadventures.com) runs half-day and day-long climbing clinics for beginning and experienced climbers. Similar offerings are provided by **Zion Rock and Mountain Guides** (1458 Zion Park Blvd., Springdale, 435/772-3303, www.zionrockguides.com). Because no outfitters are permitted to operate inside the park, these classes are held near St. George.

OUTFITTERS

Several good outfitters have shops in Springdale, just outside the park. Here you can buy all manner of gear and outdoor clothing. You can also pick up canyoneering skills, take a guided mountain-bike ride (outside the park), or learn to climb big sandstone walls.

Campers who left that crucial piece of equipment at home should visit **Zion Outdoor** (868 Zion Park Blvd., Springdale, 435/772-0630, www.zionoutdoor.com), as should anybody who needs to spruce up their wardrobe with some stylish outdoor clothing.

Zion Cycles (868 Zion Park Blvd., Springdale, 435/772-0400, www.zioncycles.com) and **Bike Zion** (1458 Zion Park Blvd., Springdale, 435/772-0320, www.bikingzion.com) both offer rentals of all sorts of bikes, from kids bikes ($12 half-day) to road bikes ($28 half-day) to full-suspension mountain bikes ($40 half-day).

Canyoneering supplies, including gear to hike the Narrows or the Subway, are available from **Zion Adventure Company** (36 Lion Blvd., Springdale, 435/772-1001, www.zionadventures.com) and **Zion Rock and Mountain Guides** (1458 Zion Park Blvd., Springdale, 435/772-3303, www.zionrockguides.com).

Accommodations and Food

Within the park, lodging is limited to Zion Lodge and three park campgrounds. Look to Springdale or the east entrance of the park for more options.

ZION LODGE

This rustic lodge (435/772-7700 or 888/297-2757, www.zionlodge.com) is in the heart of Zion Canyon, three miles up Zion Canyon Scenic Drive. Zion Lodge provides the only accommodations and food options within the park. It's open year-round; reservations for guest rooms can be made up to 13 months in advance. During high season, all rooms are fully booked months in advance. Doubles begin at $175; cute cabins are $183.

The **Red Rock Grill** (435/772-7760, dinner reservations required, 6:30am-10am, 11:30am-3pm, 5:30pm-9pm daily, dinner entrées $15-20), the lodge restaurant, offers a Southwestern

and Mexican-influenced menu for breakfast, lunch, and dinner daily. A snack bar, the **Castle Dome Café** (breakfast, lunch, and dinner daily spring-fall) serves decent fast food, including salads and coffee.

The lodge also has evening programs, a post office (Mon.-Sat.), and a gift shop.

CAMPGROUNDS
Zion Canyon Campgrounds

Campgrounds in the park often fill up on Easter and other major holidays. During summer, they're often full by early afternoon, so it's best to arrive early in the day. The **South Campground** and **Watchman Campground** (information 435/772-3256, $16), both just inside the south entrance, have sites with water but no showers. Watchman (164 sites) has some sites with electrical hookups ($18) along with prime riverside spots ($20). Reservations can be made in advance for some sites at Watchman Campground (877/444-6777, www.recreation.gov, $10 reservation fee) but not at South Campground. One of the campgrounds stays open year-round.

South Campground (126 sites) is a bit smaller than Watchman, with a few choice walk-in sites and easy access to the Pa'rus Trail, but tenters shouldn't eschew Watchman; loops C and D are for tents, and these sites are more spacious than those at South. Some of the fruit trees planted in the campgrounds by early pioneers are still producing; you can pick your own.

It should be noted that camping in Zion's two big campgrounds can be pretty laid-back; indeed, it can be luxurious. Campers have easy access, via the park's free shuttles, to good restaurants in Springdale. It's also simple enough to find showers in Springdale; just outside the park, the privately owned Zion Canyon Campground charges $4.

Private campgrounds are just outside the park in Springdale and just east of the park's east entrance. Camping supplies and groceries are available just outside the park entrance at **Sol Foods** (Springdale shuttle stop, 95 Zion Park Blvd., 435/772-0277, www.solfoods.com, 8am-4pm daily).

Kolob Campgrounds

Up the Kolob Terrace Road are six first-come, first-served sites at **Lava Point Campground** (no water, free), a small primitive campground open during warmer months. The **Red Ledge Campground** in Kanarraville (435/586-9150, $25) is the closest commercial campground to the Kolob Canyons area, and there's no campground in this part of the park; go two miles north on I-15, take exit 42, and continue 4.5 miles into downtown Kanarraville. The campground is open year-round with tent and RV sites, cabins, a store, showers, and a laundry room. The tiny agricultural community of Kanarraville was named after a local Paiute chief. A low ridge south of town marks the southern limit of prehistoric Lake Bonneville. Hikers can explore trails in Spring and Kanarra Canyons within the Spring Canyon Wilderness Study Area just east of town.

Springdale and Vicinity

Mormons settled tiny Springdale (population 457) in 1862, but with its location just outside the park's south entrance, the town is not a typical Mormon settlement but rather is geared toward serving park visitors. Its many high-quality motels and B&Bs, as well as frequent shuttle bus service to the park's entrance, make Springdale an appealing base for a visit to Zion. Farther down the road toward Hurricane are the little towns of Rockville and Virgin, both quickly becoming B&B suburbs of Springdale.

SIGHTS
Zion Canyon Giant Screen Theatre

You know you should be in the park, not looking at movies of it on a six-story-tall screen at Zion Canyon Giant Screen Theatre (145 Zion Park Blvd., 435/772-2400 or 888/256-3456, www.zioncanyontheatre.com, films start on the hour 11am-8pm daily summer, winter hours vary, $8 adults, $6 under age 12). But assuming you've been out hiking all day and need a little rest, come here to meet the Anasazi, watch Spanish explorers seek golden treasure, witness the hardships of pioneer settlers, enter remote slot canyons, and join rock climbers hundreds of feet up vertical cliff faces. The feature program is *Treasure of the Gods*, but there's nearly always a big-screen version of a Hollywood movie showing as well. Don't

© PAUL LEVY

Just outside the park, the Watchman stands guard above Springdale.

expect to see current hits; all the movies are a few years old.

O. C. Tanner Amphitheater

The highlight at the open-air O. C. Tanner Amphitheater (435/652-7994, www.dixie.edu/tanner) is a series of musical concerts held on Saturday evenings throughout the summer. The amphitheater is just outside the park entrance.

ACCOMMODATIONS

The quality of lodgings in the area just outside Zion National Park is quite high. Springdale offers a wide range of lodging. Rockville has several B&Bs, and Hurricane, the next town west of the park, has all the standard chain motels and the least expensive rooms in the area. Just down the road toward Hurricane are the little towns of Rockville and Virgin, both of which are quickly becoming suburbs of Springdale.

$50-100

The hosts at the **Bunkhouse at Zion B&B** (149 E. Main St., Rockville, 435/772-3393, www.bunkhouseatzion.com, $61-89) are dedicated to living sustainably, and they bring this ethic into their two-room B&B. The views are remarkable from this quiet spot in Rockville.

The least expensive lodgings in Springdale are the motel rooms at **Zion Park Motel** (865 Zion Park Blvd., Springdale, 435/772-3251, www.zionparkmotel.com, $84-149), an older well-kept motel with a small pool, located about one mile from the park entrance. The **Canyon Ranch Motel** (668 Zion Park Blvd., Springdale, 435/772-3357 or 866/946-6276, www.canyonranchmotel.com, $99-109) is another good value, with small units—some with kitchenettes—scattered around a grassy shaded lawn.

$100-150

In Springdale, **Under the Eaves B&B** (980 Zion Park Blvd., Springdale, 435/772-3457, www.undertheeaves.com, $95-185) features six homey guest rooms, two with a shared bath, the rest with private baths, plus a spacious suite, all in a vintage home and a garden cottage. Children over age eight are welcome, and all guests get free breakfast at nearby Oscar's Café.

Also in Springdale, **Rockville Rose Inn** (125 E. Main St., Rockville, 435/772-0800, www.rockvillerose.com, $95-115) has guest rooms in a large Victorian set back from the road.

An attractive motel and a good value is **Best Western Zion Park Inn** (1215 Zion Park Blvd., Springdale, 435/772-3200 or 800/934-7275, www.zionparkinn.com, $135-155), part of a complex with a restaurant, a swimming pool, a gift shop, and some of the nicest guest rooms in Springdale. In addition to regular guest rooms, there are also various suites and kitchen units available.

For a place with a bit of personality, or perhaps more accurately, with multiple personalities, try the **Novel House Inn at Zion** (73 Paradise Rd., Springdale, 435/772-3650 or 800/711-8400, www.novelhouse.com, $139-159), a B&B with 10 guest rooms, each

The Cliffrose is a longtime favorite motel in Springdale.

decorated with a literary theme and named after an author, including Mark Twain, Rudyard Kipling, and Louis L'Amour. All guest rooms have private baths and great views, and the B&B is tucked off the main drag.

The renovated **Driftwood Lodge** (1515 Zion Park Blvd., Springdale, 435/772-3262 or 800/801-8811, www.driftwoodlodge.net, $129-199) has a pool and spa on its spacious grounds, pet-friendly guest rooms, and a seriously good restaurant on-site. It's a big step up from the area's budget motels.

Over $150

Flanigan's Inn (428 Zion Park Blvd., Springdale, 435/772-3244 or 800/765-7787, www.flanigans.com, $169-219) is a quiet and convenient place to stay. Guest rooms are set back off the main drag and face onto a pretty courtyard. Up on the hill behind the inn, a labyrinth provides an opportunity to take a meditative walk in a stunning setting. An excellent restaurant (The Spotted Dog Café), a pool, and spa services make this an inviting place to spend several days. Two villas, essentially full-size houses, are also available.

Red Rock Inn (998 Zion Park Blvd., Springdale, 435/772-3139, www.redrockinn.com, $139-192) offers accommodations in individual cabins and a cottage suite, all with canyon views. Full-breakfast baskets are delivered to your door.

Probably the most elegant place to stay is the **Desert Pearl Inn** (707 Zion Park Blvd., Springdale, 435/772-8888 or 888/828-0898, www.desertpearl.com, $178-198), a very handsome lodge-like hotel perched above the Virgin River. Some guest rooms have views of the river; others face the pool. Much of the wood used for the beams and the finish moldings was salvaged from a railroad trestle made of century-old Oregon fir and redwood that once spanned the north end of the Great Salt Lake. The guest rooms are all large and beautifully furnished, with a modern look.

The closest lodging to the park is at **Cable Mountain Lodge** (147 Zion Park Blvd., Springdale, 435/772-3366 or 877/712-3366, www.cablemountainlodge.com, $169-279), in the same complex as the big-screen theater. Along with being extremely convenient, it's very nicely fitted out, with a pool, guest rooms with microwaves and fridges or small kitchens, and appealing architecture and decor to go along with the spectacular views.

Just outside the south gates to Zion, the **C Cliffrose Lodge** (281 Zion Park Blvd., Springdale, 435/772-3234 or 800/243-8824, www.cliffroselodge.com, $159-269) sits on five acres of lovely well-landscaped gardens with riverfront access. The guest rooms are equally nice, especially the riverside rooms, and there's a pool and a laundry room. The Cliffrose is favored by many longtime Zion fans.

Campgrounds

If you aren't able to camp in the park, the **Zion Canyon Campground** (479 Zion Park Blvd., 435/772-3237, www.zioncamp.com) is a short walk from the park entrance. Along with tent sites (no dogs allowed, $30) and RV sites ($39), there are motel rooms ($65). The sites are crammed pretty close together, but a few are situated right on the bank of the Virgin River. Facilities include a store, a pizza parlor, a game room, a laundry room, and showers.

FOOD

Just outside the park entrance, near the Springdale shuttle stop, **Sol Foods** (95 Zion Park Blvd., 435/772-0277, www.solfoods.com, 8am-4pm daily) is a short walk from either park campground and a good place for a salad or sandwich ($8-10). Sol Foods also runs the town's only supermarket (995 Zion Park Blvd., 435/772-3100, 7am-11pm daily spring) and stocks groceries and camping supplies in the store near the park entrance.

C Mean Bean Coffee (932 Zion Park Blvd.,

435/772-0654, 6:30am-afternoon daily) is the hip place to hang out in the morning. Besides excellent coffee drinks, they serve breakfast burritos and a few pastries and sandwiches. For a more substantial meal, head across the way to **Oscar's Café** (948 Zion Park Blvd., 435/772-3232, www.cafeoscars.com, 8am-2 hours after sunset daily, $8-19), where you can get a good burger or a Mexican-influenced breakfast or lunch. The patio is set back off the main road and is especially pleasant.

An old gas station has become the **C Whiptail Grill** (445 Zion Park Blvd., 435/772-0283, noon-10pm daily, $8-15), a casual spot serving innovative homemade food, such as incredibly good spaghetti squash enchiladas. There's very little seating inside, so plan to eat at the outdoor tables or take your meal to go.

Also good, and reasonably priced, is **Zion Pizza and Noodle** (868 Zion Park Blvd., 435/772-3815, www.zionpizzanoodle.com, 4pm-close daily, $11-16), housed in an old church and serving a good selection of microbrews.

Springdale's other good place for pizza is **Flying Monkey** (975 Zion Park Blvd., 435/772-3333, www.flyingmonkeyzion.com, 11am-9:30 or 10pm daily, $8-10), tucked into the back of a newer development near the local supermarket. A wood-fired oven turns out very good pizza and sandwiches.

The following restaurants all offer full liquor service: The **C Spotted Dog Café** (Flanigan's Inn, 428 Zion Park Blvd., 435/772-3244, www.flanigans.com, dinner 5pm-9:30pm daily spring-fall, 5pm-9:30pm Tues.-Sun. winter, breakfast buffet 7am-11am daily spring-fall, dinner $13-25) is one of Springdale's top restaurants; it uses high-quality ingredients for its American bistro cuisine. Be sure to order a salad with (or for) your dinner—the house salad is superb. If you want to eat outside, try to get a table on the back patio, which is quieter and more intimate than the dining area out front.

Another good, and very popular, place

for dinner in Springdale is the **Bit & Spur Restaurant** (1212 Zion Park Blvd., 435/772-3498, reservations recommended during busy season, www.bitandspur.com, 5pm-close daily, $15-23), a lively Mexican-influenced place with a menu that goes far beyond the usual south-of-the-border concoctions. The sweet-potato tamales keep us coming back year after year.

Another strong player in Springdale's fine-dining scene is the refined but still casual **Parallel 88** (1515 Zion Park Blvd., 435/772-3588, www.paralleleighty-eightrestaurant.com, 7am-10:30am and 5pm-close daily, dinner entrées $15-25), at the Driftwood Lodge. Dinners include a delicious braised lamb shank and an equally tasty vegetable *parmentier* (layered spinach, yams, and other veggies topped with red pepper coulis). The wine selection is relatively extensive for Utah but pretty pedestrian.

INFORMATION AND SERVICES

People traveling with their dogs have a bit of a dilemma when it comes to visiting Zion. No pets are allowed on the trails (except the Pa'rus Trail) or in the shuttle buses, and it's absolutely unconscionable to leave a dog inside a car here in the warmer months. Fortunately, the **Doggy Dude Ranch** (Hwy. 9, Rockville, 435/772-3105, www.doggyduderanch.com) provides conscientious daytime and overnight pet care.

The **Zion Canyon Medical Clinic** (120 Lion Blvd., 435/772-3226) provides urgent-care services.

You may want to check out the art galleries along Zion Park Boulevard; some of them have high-quality merchandise.

GETTING THERE

Springdale is located at the mouth of Zion Canyon, just outside the park's main (south) entrance. From I-15 just north of St. George, take exit 16 and head east on Highway 9; it's about 40 miles to Springdale. If you're coming from the north, take I-15's exit 22, head southeast through Toquerville, and meet Highway 9 at the town of La Verkin.

St. George

Southern Utah's largest city, St. George (population about 73,000) is between lazy bends of the Virgin River on one side and rocky hills of red sandstone on the other. Although it has gained a reputation as a retirement haven, thanks in part to its warm winter climate and its plethora of golf courses, the city won't have much appeal to most travelers. In order to appreciate St. George, it may be necessary to visit its outskirts, where Snow Canyon State Park and a couple of spas can be found.

In 1861, more than 300 Mormon families in the Salt Lake City area answered the call to go south to start the Cotton Mission, of which St. George became the center (hence the frequent use of the term "Dixie" to describe the area). The settlers overcame great difficulties to start farms and to build an attractive city in this remote desert. Brigham Young chose the city's name to honor George A. Smith, who had served as head of the Southern (Iron) Mission during the 1850s. The title *Saint* means simply that he was a Mormon—a Latter-day Saint.

SIGHTS

Visits to some of the historic sites will add to your appreciation of the city's past; ask for the "St. George Historic Walking Tour" brochure at the **Chamber of Commerce** (97 E. St. George Blvd., 435/628-1658, www.stgeorge-chamber.com, 9am-5pm Mon.-Fri.). The warm climate, dramatic setting, and many year-round recreation opportunities have helped make St. George the fastest-growing city in the state.

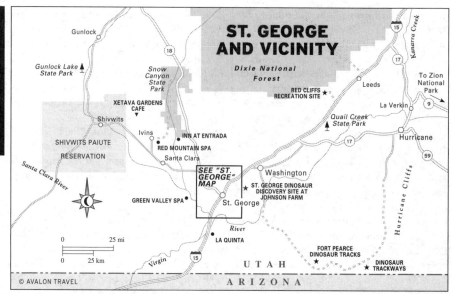

St. George and Vicinity

© AVALON TRAVEL

Visitors can see the **St. George Temple** (250 E. 400 S., 435/673-5181) from the outside and stop in its visitors center, and you can tour **Brigham Young's Winter Home** (67 W. 200 N., 435/673-2517), but if your focus is Zion, you'll most likely just use St. George as a jumping-off point.

Dinosaur Trackways

Back in the early Jurassic, when the supercontinent of Pangaea was just beginning to break up, lakes covered this part of present-day Utah, and dinosaurs were becoming the earth's dominant vertebrates. Two sites southeast of St. George preserve dinosaur tracks from this era. Of the two, the more recently discovered site at Johnson Farm is more impressive and much easier to get to; indeed, it has been called one of the world's 10 best dinosaur-track sites. The Fort Pearce site is good if you're hankering for some back-road travel and like scouting dino tracks and petroglyphs in remote washes.

ST. GEORGE DINOSAUR DISCOVERY SITE AT JOHNSON FARM

Tracks at the St. George Dinosaur Discovery Site at Johnson Farm (2180 E. Riverside Dr., 435/574-3466, www.dinotrax.com, 10am-6pm Mon.-Sat., 11am-5pm Sun. Mar.-Sept., 10am-5pm Mon.-Sat. Oct.-Feb., $6 adults, $3 ages 3-11) were discovered in 2000 by a retired optometrist. Since then, a vast number of tracks, including those of three species of theropods (meat-eating dinosaurs), and important "trace fossils" of pond scum, plants, invertebrates, and fish have also been uncovered.

Excavation work is ongoing, and a visitors center provides a good look at some of the most exciting finds, including a wall-size slab of rock with footprints going to and fro. Also quite remarkable are the "swim tracks," which settled a long-standing argument over whether dinosaurs actually swam.

The track site is on the outskirts of St. George, about two miles south of I-15's exit 10.

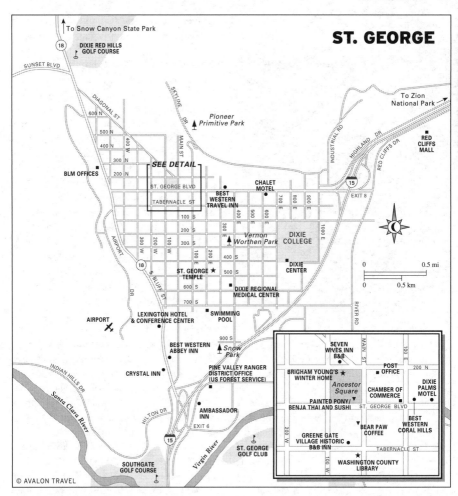

ST. GEORGE

To Snow Canyon State Park

18 DIXIE RED HILLS GOLF COURSE

SUNSET BLVD

DIAGONAL ST

600 N
500 N
400 N
300 N
200 N

SKYLINE DR

MAIN ST

Pioneer Primitive Park

To Zion National Park

HIGHLAND DR

RED CLIFFS DR

INDUSTRIAL RD

RED CLIFFS MALL

BLM OFFICES

SEE DETAIL

ST. GEORGE BLVD

TABERNACLE ST

100 S
200 S
300 S
400 S
500 S
600 S
700 S

BEST WESTERN TRAVEL INN

CHALET MOTEL

15 EXIT 8

700 E
800 E
900 E
1000 E

Vernon Worthen Park

DIXIE COLLEGE

DIXIE CENTER

0   0.5 mi
0   0.5 km

ST. GEORGE TEMPLE ★

DIXIE REGIONAL MEDICAL CENTER

AIRPORT DR

S. BLUFF ST

18

AIRPORT ✈

LEXINGTON HOTEL & CONFERENCE CENTER

SWIMMING POOL

900 S

Snow Park

BEST WESTERN ABBEY INN

CRYSTAL INN

PINE VALLEY RANGER DISTRICT OFFICE (US FOREST SERVICE)

INDIAN HILLS DR

Santa Clara River

HILTON DR

AMBASSADOR INN

EXIT 6

15

ST. GEORGE GOLF CLUB

SOUTHGATE GOLF COURSE

Virgin River

© AVALON TRAVEL

RIVER RD

SEVEN WIVES INN B&B

MAIN S

POST OFFICE

100 E

200 N

BRIGHAM YOUNG'S WINTER HOME ★

Ancestor Square

CHAMBER OF COMMERCE

DIXIE PALMS MOTEL

PAINTED PONY ▼

BENJA THAI AND SUSHI

ST. GEORGE BLVD

BEST WESTERN CORAL HILLS

250 W

BEAR PAW COFFEE

GREENE GATE VILLAGE HISTORIC B&B INN

TABERNACLE ST

100 W

WASHINGTON COUNTY LIBRARY ★

FORT PEARCE DINOSAUR TRACKS

A scenic back-road drive through the desert between St. George and Hurricane passes the ruins of Fort Pearce and more dinosaur tracks. Much of the road is unpaved, and it has rough and sandy spots, but it's usually suitable for cautious drivers in dry weather.

This group of tracks documents the passage of at least two different dinosaur species more than 200 million years ago. The well-preserved tracks, in the Moenave Formation, were made by a 20-foot-long herbivore weighing an estimated 8-10 tons and by a carnivore half as long. No remains of the dinosaurs themselves have been found here.

In 1861 ranchers arrived in Warner Valley to run cattle on the desert grasslands. Four years later, however, troubles with the Native Americans threatened to drive the settlers out. The Black Hawk War and periodic raids by

ZION NATIONAL PARK

© PAUL LEVY

St. George spa-goers often hike in Snow Canyon State Park, but it's there for anyone to use.

Navajo made life precarious. Springs in Fort Pearce Wash—the only reliable water for many miles—proved the key to domination of the region. In December 1866 work began on a fort overlooking the springs. The stone walls stood about 8 feet high and were more than 30 feet long. No roof was ever added. Much of the fort and the adjacent corral (built in 1869) have survived to the present. Local cattle ranchers still use the springs for their herds. Petroglyphs can be seen in various places along the wash, including 0.25 miles downstream from the fort along ledges on the north side of the wash.

To reach this somewhat remote site from St. George, head south on River Road, cross the Virgin River Bridge, and turn left on 1450 South. Continue on this main road and keep bearing east through several 90-degree left and right turns. Turn left (east) onto a dirt road at the Fort Pearce sign and continue 5.6 miles to a road that branches right along a small wash to the Fort Pearce parking lot. The dinosaur tracks are

in a wash about two miles farther down the road from Fort Pearce; the parking area is signed.

Snow Canyon State Park

If St. George's outlet stores and chain restaurants threaten to close in on you, head a few miles north of town to the red-rock canyons, sand dunes, volcanoes, and lava flows of Snow Canyon (435/628-2255, http://stateparks.utah.gov, 6am-10pm daily year-round, $6 per vehicle). Walls of sandstone 50-750 feet high enclose the five-mile-long canyon. Hiking trails trace the canyon bottom and lead into the backcountry for a closer look at the geology, flora, and fauna. Common plants are barrel, cholla, and prickly pear cacti; yucca; Mormon tea; shrub live oak; cliffrose; and cottonwood. Delicate wildflowers bloom mostly in the spring and autumn, following the wet seasons, but cacti and the sacred datura can flower in the heat of summer.

Wildlife includes sidewinder and Great Basin rattlesnakes, Gila monsters, desert tortoises, kangaroo rats, squirrels, cottontails, kit foxes, coyotes, and mule deer. You may find some Native American rock art, arrowheads, bits of pottery, and ruins. Many of the place-names in the park honor Mormon pioneers. Snow Canyon was named for Lorenzo and Erastus Snow, not for the rare snowfalls.

Summer is too hot for comfortable hiking, except in the early morning. Highway 18 leads past an overlook on the rim of Snow Canyon and to the paved park road (Hwy. 300) that drops into the canyon and follows it to its mouth and the small town of Ivins. Snow Canyon is about 12 miles northwest of St. George. It is reached either by Highway 18—the faster way—or through the towns of Santa Clara and Ivins. The campground here has a few lovely sites.

RECREATION
Golf

With 10 golf courses in the area, St. George enjoys a reputation as Utah's winter golf capital.

Greens fees are highest in the winter (listed here) and drop by nearly 50 percent during the hot summer months. Red sandstone cliffs serve as the backdrop for **Dixie Red Hills** (1250 N. 645 W., 435/634-5852, $20.50), the city's first golf course, built in the 1960s on the northwest edge of town; it's a nine-hole par-34 municipal course. The 18-hole par-71 **Green Spring Golf Course** (588 N. Green Spring Dr., 435/673-7888, $64), just west of I-15's exit 10, has a reputation as one of the finest courses in Utah.

Professionals favor the cleverly designed 27-hole par-72 **Sunbrook Golf Course** (2366 Sunbrook Dr., 435/634-5866, $56) off Dixie Downs Road, between Green Valley and Santa Clara. The **St. George Golf Club** (2190 S. 1400 E., 435/634-5854, $33) has a popular 18-hole par-73 course south of town in Bloomington Hills. The **Southgate Golf Course** (1975 S. Tonaquint Dr., 435/628-0000, $33), on the southwest edge of town, has 18 holes. The adjacent Southgate Game Improvement Center (435/674-7728) can provide golfers with computerized golf-swing analyses plus plenty of indoor practice space and lots of balls.

Entrada (2511 W. Entrada Tr., 435/674-7500) is a newer 18-hole private course that's fast on its way to becoming St. George's most respected. The Johnny Miller-designed course is northwest of St. George at beautiful Snow Canyon and incorporates natural lava flows, rolling dunes, and arroyos (dry riverbeds) into its design. Guests at the Inn at Entrada can get a package deal to golf; in peak winter season rates are $175, including lodging for two and golf for one. The 18-hole par-72 **Sky Mountain** (1030 N. 2600 W., 435/635-7888, $45), northeast of St. George in nearby Hurricane, has a spectacular setting.

Mountain Biking

Mountain bikers in the know come to St. George fall-early spring to ride single-track trails and slickrock that is just as good as what you'll find in Moab. One of Utah's most spectacular trails is **Gooseberry Mesa,** southeast of Hurricane, a challenging but fun ride with both slickrock and single track. The **Green Valley Loop** starts at the Green Valley Spa and is mostly advanced single track.

Less intense cycling can be found at **Snow Canyon State Park,** where the paved six-mile Whiptail Trail and the eight-mile gravel and sand West Canyon Road are open to bicycles.

Rock Climbing

Snow Canyon State Park (435/628-2255, http://stateparks.utah.gov, 6am-10pm daily year-round, $6 per vehicle) offers many technical rock-climbing routes in the park.

ACCOMMODATIONS

St. George offers many places to stay and eat. Motel prices stay about the same year-round, although they may drop if business is slow in summer. Considering the popularity of this destination, prices are reasonable. Golfers should ask about golf-and-lodging packages. You'll find most lodgings along the busy I-15 business route of St. George Boulevard (exit 8) and Bluff Street (exit 6). As for food, you'll find almost every fast-food place known to humanity just off the interstate on St. George Boulevard.

Under $50

Many of St. George's less expensive lodging choices are chains operating at exit 8 off I-15. Near downtown, there are some decent locally owned choices. The **Chalet Motel** (664 E. St. George Blvd., 435/628-6272, from $40) offers fridges and microwaves, some efficiency kitchens in larger guest rooms, and a pool. **◖Dixie Palms Motel** (185 E. St. George Blvd., 435/673-3531, $40) is a classic old-fashioned courtyard motel on the main strip right downtown, with an outdoor pool and fridges and microwaves in the guest rooms. It's a top pick for budget travelers.

$50-100

In the downtown area, the Spanish-style **Best Western Travel Inn** (316 E. St. George Blvd., 435/673-3541 or 800/528-1234, www.stgeorgebestwestern.com, $63-70) is a relatively small motel with an outdoor pool and an indoor spa. It's a good mid-range choice.

Close to downtown is one of St. George's best: the **Best Western Coral Hills** (125 E. St. George Blvd., 435/673-4844 or 800/542-7733, www.coralhills.com, $77-132), a very attractive property with indoor and outdoor pools and two spas, an exercise room, and a complimentary continental breakfast.

Look for more motels at I-15's exit 6. The **Lexington Hotel & Conference Center** (850 S. Bluff St., 435/628-4235 or 877/539-7070, www.lexingtonhotels.com, $89) is a large complex complete with indoor and outdoor pools, a whirlpool, recreation and fitness facilities, a tennis court, a putting green, and a good on-site restaurant. At the **Best Western Abbey Inn** (1129 S. Bluff St., 435/652-1234 or 888/222-3946, www.bwabbeyinn.com, $80-110), all guest rooms have microwaves and fridges. There's a small outdoor pool, an indoor spa, recreation and fitness facilities, and a hot breakfast included.

Quite comfortable is the **Ambassador Inn** (1481 S. Sunland Dr., 435/673-7900 or 877/373-7900, http://ambassadorinn.net, $70), located at the south end of town near the convention center, east of I-15's exit 6. Near the interstate, **LaQuinta** (91 E. 2680 S., 435/674-2664 or 888/788-2457, www.laqstgeorge.com, $69-129) is a comfortable place to crash on the edge of town.

$100-150

A couple of B&Bs are good alternatives to the more generic lodgings that dominate St. George. Just across from Brigham Young's Winter Home, the **🅲 Seven Wives Inn Bed & Breakfast** (217 N. 100 W., 435/628-3737 or 800/600-3737, www.sevenwivesinn.com, $100-189) offers guest rooms in two historic homes,

including one that served as a safe house for polygamists after the practice was banned in the 1880s, and a cute cottage. All guest rooms have private baths and are decorated with antiques. Children are welcome, and pets are permitted in the cottage. There's an outdoor pool, in-room massage service, and good weekday "business rates" ($70) are offered.

You'll find an entire compound of pioneer-era homes at the **Greene Gate Village Historic Bed & Breakfast Inn** (76 W. Tabernacle St., 435/628-6999 or 800/350-6999, www.greengatevillage.com, $99-199). Nine beautifully restored homes offer a variety of lodging options—groups or families can rent an entire home. Many guest rooms come with kitchens and private baths, some with private whirlpools. There's also a pool shared by all guests. Children are welcome.

A particularly nice standard motel is the **Crystal Inn** (1450 S. Hilton Inn Dr., 435/688-7477 or 800/662-2525, www.crystalinns.com, $119-200, online specials as low as $75) is located on a golf course and has beautiful public areas and nicely appointed guest rooms. Facilities include a pool, a sauna, and private tennis courts.

Over $150

Golfers and those who want a bit of plushness should seriously consider the **Inn at Entrada** (2588 W. Sinagua Tr., 435/634-7100, www.innatentrada.com, from $179), located near Snow Canyon State Park. A stay at the inn is the easiest way to gain access to the resort community's top-notch golf course. It's a lovely setting, lodging is in "casitas," and there's a spa and restaurant on-site.

Spa Resorts

St. George is home to two large spa resorts and recreation centers in gorgeous natural settings. The **Green Valley Spa** (1871 W. Canyon View Dr., 435/628-8060 or 800/237-1068, www.greenvalleyspa.com, from $189 B&B package, spa packages with lodging and all meals from $400, depending on treatments and activities, many specials offered) is a fitness, sports, health, and beauty spa with all-inclusive rates. Facilities include three pools, racquetball courts, a fully equipped gym with an array of fitness, yoga, and meditation classes as well as tennis instruction, golf privileges, and hiking and climbing in neighboring canyons. There's also a whole catalog of beauty and rejuvenation treatments, which may be included in a package deal or tacked on at extra cost, including massage, wraps, and aromatherapy as well as more spiritual renewals such as personal meditation guidance. Guest rooms flank a park-like pool and garden area. Three spa meals are served daily; they're included in the cost of most packages. Rates vary widely, with summer the least expensive time to visit.

Slightly less swanky, the **Red Mountain Spa** (202 N. Snow Canyon Rd., 877/246-4453, www.redmountainspa.com) focuses even more intently on outdoor adventure and fitness. It's located near Snow Canyon, and morning hikes in the beautiful state park are a great part of the routine. Facilities include numerous swimming and soaking pools, a fitness center and gym, tennis courts, a salon, a spa, and conference rooms, plus access to lots of hiking and biking trails. Prices, which include all meals, lodging, and use of most spa facilities and recreation, start at about $230 pp double, with special deals often available online. Spa services, including massage, facials, body polishing, and aromatherapy, cost extra.

Campgrounds

The best camping in the area is at **Snow Canyon State Park** (435/628-2255, reservations 800/322-3770, www.reserveamerica.com, $8 reservation fee, reservations required in spring, $16 without hookups, $20 with hookups). Sites are in a pretty canyon and include showers. From downtown St. George, go 12 miles north on Highway 18, then turn left and continue two miles.

The other public campgrounds in the area are **Quail Creek State Park** (435/879-2378, www.stateparks.utah.gov, $13) and the Bureau of Land Management (BLM) **Red Cliffs Recreation Site** (435/688-3200, $8), both north of town off I-15 (take exit 16 when coming from the south; take exit 23 when approaching from the north). Quail Creek is on a reservoir and is a good option if you have a boat. Red Cliffs is a little more scenic and has hiking trails.

If you need a place to park an RV for the night right in town, **McArthur's Temple View RV Resort** (975 S. Main St., 435/673-6400 or 800/776-6410, $31 tents, $42 RVs) is near the temple district but has little shade.

FOOD

For a major recreation and retirement center, St. George is curiously lacking in unique places to eat. Almost every chain restaurant can be found, but don't expect a bevy of local fine-dining houses.

The best place to head for lunch or dinner is Ancestor's Square, a trendy shopping development downtown at the intersection of St. George Boulevard and Main Street. ◖**Painted Pony** (435/634-1700, www.painted-pony.com, 11:30am-10pm Mon.-Sat., 4pm-9pm Sun., lunch $8-10, dinner $24-34) is a stylish restaurant where the kitchen puts Southwestern and, in some cases, Asian touches on American standards; try salmon rolls with a carrot orange sauce. Downstairs from the Painted Pony is another pretty good restaurant, **Benja Thai and Sushi** (435/628-9538, www.benjathai. com, 11:30am-10pm Mon.-Sat., 5pm-9pm Sun., $11-20), one of the very few Thai restaurants in southern Utah. Just across St. George Boulevard, **Bear Paw Coffee** (75 N. Main St., 435/634-0126, 7am-3pm daily, $7-9) is a bright spot for coffee drinkers and anyone who wants a good breakfast.

There's a sweetly elegant spot up by Snow Canyon: **Xetava Gardens Cafe** (815 Coyote Gulch, 435/656-0165, www.coyotegulchart-village.com, 8am-9:30pm Thurs.-Sat., 8am-5pm Sun.-Wed., dinner $10-30). Dinners range from excellent burgers and pizza to rack of lamb; this is also a great place to come for breakfast ($7-9) after a morning hike.

INFORMATION AND SERVICES

The **St. George Chamber of Commerce** (97 E. St. George Blvd., 435/628-1658, www.stgeorgechamber.com, 9am-5pm Mon.-Fri.), in the old county courthouse, can tell you about the sights, events, and services of southwestern Utah. Better online sources of information are www.utahsdixie.com and www.utahstgeorge.com.

For recreation, visit the **Interagency Visitor Office** (196 E. Tabernacle St., 435/688-3246, www.fs.fed.us/r4/dixie, 8am-5pm Mon.-Fri.) for information on fishing, hiking, and camping in the national forest and BLM lands around town.

There is a **post office** (180 N. Main St., 435/673-3312). The **Dixie Regional Medical Center** (544 S. 400 E., 435/688-4000) provides hospital care.

GETTING THERE

St. George's new airport (SGU), located five miles southeast of downtown off I-15's exit 2, opened in early 2011 and, depending on the economy, should lead to an increase in air service. **Delta** (800/323-2323, www.delta.com), in partnership with **Skywest Airlines** (www.skywest.com), offers several daily direct flights to and from Salt Lake City, while **United** (800/864-8331, www.ual.com) offers flights to and from Los Angeles.

Several of the usual rental-car companies operate at the St. George airport: **Budget** (435/673-6825 or 800/527-0700), **Avis** (435/627-2002 or 800/230-4898), and **Hertz** (435/652-9941 or 800/654-3131).

It's an easy two-hour drive from Las Vegas to St. George, so travelers may want to consider flying into Vegas and renting a car there.

Greyhound (435/673-2933) buses depart from McDonald's (1235 S. Bluff St.) for Salt Lake City, Denver, Las Vegas, and other destinations. The **St. George Shuttle** (790 S. Bluff St., 435/628-8320 or 800/933-8320, www.stgshuttle.com) will take you to Las Vegas ($25) or Midvale ($55), a Salt Lake City suburb, in a 15-passenger van. Trips depart from the Shuttle Lodge Inn (915 S. Bluff St.).

Cedar City

Cedar City (population about 28,000), known for its scenic setting and its summertime Utah Shakespearean Festival, is a handy base for exploring a good chunk of southern Utah. Just east of town are the high cliffs of the Markagunt Plateau—a land of panoramic views, colorful rock formations, desolate lava flows, extensive forests, and flower-filled meadows. Also on the Markagunt Plateau is the Cedar Breaks National Monument, an immense amphitheater eroded into the vividly hued underlying rock.

Within an easy day's drive are Zion National Park to the south and Bryce Canyon National Park and Grand Staircase-Escalante National Monument to the east.

SIGHTS
Utah Shakespearean Festival

Cedar City's lively festival (general info 435/586-7880, box office 435/586-7878 or 800/752-9849, www.bard.org) presents three Shakespearean plays or other classics each

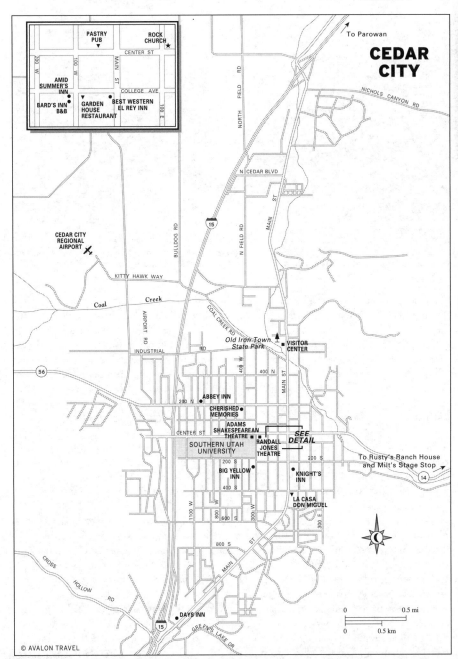

To Parowan

CEDAR CITY

NICHOLS CANYON RD

DETAIL INSET:

PASTRY PUB ▼

ROCK CHURCH ★

CENTER ST

200 W

100 W

MAIN ST

100 E

COLLEGE AVE

AMID SUMMER'S INN ●

BARD'S INN B&B ▼

GARDEN HOUSE RESTAURANT ●

BEST WESTERN EL REY INN ●

N FIELD RD

NORTH

N CEDAR BLVD

MAIN ST

BULLDOG RD

15

CEDAR CITY REGIONAL AIRPORT ✈

KITTY HAWK WAY

N FIELD RD

AIRPORT RD

Coal Creek

COAL CREEK RD

Old Iron Town State Park

VISITOR CENTER

INDUSTRIAL

400 W

400 N

MAIN ST

56

200 N

ABBEY INN ●

CHERISHED MEMORIES ●

ADAMS SHAKESPEAREAN THEATRE ■

SEE DETAIL

CENTER ST

RANDALL JONES THEATRE

SOUTHERN UTAH UNIVERSITY

200 S

To Rusty's Ranch House and Milt's Stage Stop

BIG YELLOW INN ●

400 S

KNIGHT'S INN ●

14

1100 W

800 W

600 S

300 W

LA CASA DON MIGUEL ▼

300 E

800 N

MAIN ST

CROSS HOLLOW RD

DAYS INN ●

15

GREEN'S LAKE DR

0   0.5 mi
0   0.5 km

© AVALON TRAVEL

© BILL MCRAE

Narrow Parowan Gap, etched with ancient petroglyphs, has long been a thoroughfare.

summer season in the Adams Shakespearean Theatre (351 W. Center St.), an open-air theater in the round, closely modeled on the original Globe Theatre of Elizabethan London. The indoor Randall Jones Theatre presents the "Best of the Rest"—often recent Broadway hits. A total of eight or nine plays are staged each season (late June-mid-Oct.).

Costumed actors stage the popular free Greenshow (7pm Mon.-Sat.) before the performances, with a variety of Elizabethan comedy skits, *Punch and Judy* shows, period dances, music, juggling, and other good-natured 16th-century fun. Backstage tours of the costume shop, makeup room, and stage show you how the festival works. At literary seminars each morning, actors and Shakespearean scholars discuss the previous night's play. Production seminars, held daily except Sunday, take a close look at acting, costumes, stage props, special effects, and other details of play production.

The Greenshow and seminars are free, but most other events are $22-71, and it's wise to purchase tickets well in advance; last-minute theatergoers, however, can usually find tickets to something.

The theaters are on the Southern Utah University campus near the corner of Center Street and 300 West. Rain occasionally dampens the performances (the Elizabethan theater is open to the sky), and plays may move to a conventional theater next door, where the box office is located.

Old Iron Town State Park

This in-town state park (635 N. Main St., 435/586-9290, $3) focuses on history rather than recreation. The ironworks had their start in 1850, when Brigham Young, hoping to increase Utah's self-sufficiency, sent workers to develop an "Iron Mission." The ironworks eventually became a private company, and although it never really prospered financially, the area has become Iron County. Here, indoor and outdoor exhibits focus on the iron foundry and other aspects of local history.

SCENIC DRIVES
Parowan Gap

Ten miles west of the small I-15 town of Parowan is a pass where Native Americans created many petroglyphs, designs pecked into the rocks. People hunting in the Red Hills and wildlife commonly passed through this gap, and it may have served as an important site for hunting rituals. The meaning of the rock art hasn't been deciphered, but it probably represents the thoughts of many different Native American groups over the past 1,000 or more years. Geometric designs, snakes, lizards, mountain sheep, bear claws, and human figures are all still recognizable. You can get here on a good gravel road from Parowan by going north on Main Street and turning left and continuing 10.5 miles on the last street (400 North). Or, from Cedar City, go north on Main Street, which becomes Highway 130 at I-15's exit 62, and follow signs for north for 13.5 miles, then turn right and go 2.5 miles on a good gravel road (near milepost 19). In Cedar City, you can get an interpretive brochure and map at the Bureau of Land Management (BLM) office (176 E. D. L. Sargent Dr., Cedar City, 435/586-2401).

Markagunt Scenic Byway

Starting at Cedar City's eastern boundary, Highway 14 plunges into a narrow canyon flanked by steep rock walls before climbing up to the top of the Markagunt Plateau. This is a very scenic route, passing dramatic rock cliffs and pink-rock hoodoos that echo the formations at Zion and Bryce Canyon National Parks. Although it's not a quick drive—especially if you get caught behind a lumbering RV—the scenic qualities of the canyon and the incredible vistas, which extend across Zion and down into Arizona, will amply repay your patience. The route also passes several wooded campgrounds and small mountain resorts. Because of their elevations—mostly 8,000-9,000 feet—these high-mountain getaways are popular when the temperatures in the desert basin towns begin to soar. The route ends at Long Valley Junction, at U.S. 89, which is 41 miles east of Cedar City.

ACCOMMODATIONS

During the Shakespearean Festival, Cedar City is a popular destination, so it's best to reserve a room at least a day or two in advance during the summer. There are two major concentrations of motels. A half dozen large chain hotels cluster around the I-15 exits together with lots of fast-food restaurants and strip malls. Downtown along Main Street are even more motels. You can easily walk from most of the downtown motels to the Shakespeare Festival. Many of Cedar City's B&Bs are also within a stroll of the festival grounds.

Note that the following prices are for the summer festival high season. Outside high season, expect rates to drop by about one-third.

$50-100

Right downtown, the **Best Western El Rey Inn** (80 S. Main St., 435/586-6518 or 800/528-1234, www.bwelrey.com, $85-130) offers a breakfast bar.

Also downtown, the **Knight's Inn** (281 S. Main St., 435/586-9916, www.knightsinncedarcity.com, $52-62) has a bit of a budget ambience, but it's pleasant and a good deal, with a pool and complimentary continental breakfast.

At I-15's exit 57, the **Days Inn** (1204 S. Main St., 435/867-8877 or 888/556-5637, $70-103) is a well-kept place with an indoor pool and complimentary continental breakfast.

One of the best places to stay in Cedar City is the **Abbey Inn** (940 W. 200 N., 435/586-9966 or 800/325-5411, www.abbeyinncedar.com, $89-99), which has remodeled guest rooms, an indoor pool, and a good breakfast included.

$100-150

Bed-and-breakfast inns and Shakespeare seem to go hand-in-hand. The **Bard's Inn Bed & Breakfast** (150 S. 100 W., 435/586-6612, www.bardsbandb.com, $109-129), two blocks from the Shakespearean Festival, has seven guest rooms, all with private baths, as well as a two-bedroom cottage. It's open during festival season only. Right next door, the antiques-filled **Amid Summer's Inn** (140 S. 100 W., 435/867-4691, www.amidsummersinn.com, $115-185) has eight sumptuously decorated guest rooms in a restored 1930s cottage. Also near the Shakespearean Festival, at the edge of the Southern Utah University campus, the **C Big Yellow Inn** (234 S. 300 W., 435/586-0960, www.bigyellowinn.com, $100-199) is easy to spot; it's yellow, full of antiques, and several of the guest rooms are in a house directly across the street from the main inn.

Campgrounds

East of Cedar City on Highway 14 are a handful of campgrounds in the Dixie National Forest. The closest, **Cedar Canyon** (635/865-3200, www.fs.fed.us/r4/Dixie, early June-mid-Sept., $12), is 12 miles from town in a pretty canyon along Cow Creek. It's at 8,100 feet elevation and has water.

Cedar City KOA (1121 N. Main St., 435/586-9872 or 800/562-9873, year-round, $27 tents, $45 RVs) has cabins, showers, a playground, and a pool. **Country Aire RV Park** (1700 N. Main St., 435/586-2550, year-round, $32) has showers and a pool.

FOOD

Cedar City has some good casual restaurants. At the **C Pastry Pub** (86 W. Center St., 435/867-1400, www.cedarcitypastrypub.com, 10am-10pm Mon.-Sat., $6-9) you'll find pastries, good sandwiches, and coffee; it's a good place for lunch or a quick bite to eat before a play. Stop by **La Casa Don Miguel** (453 S. Main St., 435/586-6855, lunch and dinner daily, $6-12) for the best Mexican food you'll find for miles around.

The **Garden House Restaurant** (164 S. 100 W., 435/586-6110, dinner from 5pm Mon.-Sat.,

$12-19) is housed in a charming cottage off the main drag. It offers what passes for fine dining in Cedar City; the food (pasta, salmon, grilled trout) is OK but not great. Alcohol is not served.

East of Cedar City on Highway 14 is a dramatic desert canyon with two steak houses that share an owner and Western ambience. **Rusty's Ranch House** (2275 E. Hwy. 14, 435/586-3839, www.rustysranchhouse.com, dinner from 5:30pm Mon.-Sat., $15-28) is two miles east of town on Highway 14 and serves good steak and seafood dinners in a dramatic canyon setting. Two miles farther up the same road is **Milt's Stage Stop** (3560 E. Hwy. 14, 435/586-9344, www.miltsstagestop.com, 5pm-9pm daily, $15-25), serving steak, prime rib, and seafood.

INFORMATION AND SERVICES

The **Cedar City Brian Head Tourism Bureau** (581 N. Main St., 435/586-5124 or 800/354-4849, www.scenicsouthernutah.com) is just south of Iron Mission State Park. The Dixie National Forest's **Cedar City Ranger District Office** (1789 Wedgewood Lane, 435/865-3200) has information on recreation and travel on the Markagunt Plateau. The **BLM's Cedar City District Office** (176 E. D. L. Sargent Dr., 435/586-2401) is just off Main Street on the north edge of town.

GETTING THERE

Cedar City is just east of I-15, 52 miles northeast of St. George and 253 miles southwest of Salt Lake City; take I-15's exit 57, 59, or 62. **Delta** (800/323-2323, www.delta.com) has flights operated by SkyWest between the small **Cedar City Regional Airport** (CDC, 2560 Aviation Way, 435/586-2950) and Salt Lake City. Rent a car from **Enterprise** (435/865-7636) or **Hertz** (435/586-9806) at the airport.

BRYCE CANYON NATIONAL PARK

In Bryce Canyon, a geologic fairyland of rock spires rises beneath the high cliffs of the Paunsaugunt Plateau. This intricate maze, eroded from soft limestone, now glows with warm shades of red, orange, pink, yellow, and cream. The rocks provide a continuous show of changing color through the day as the sun's rays and cloud shadows move across the landscape.

Looking at these rock formations is like looking at puffy clouds in the sky; it's easy to find images in the shapes of the rocks. Some see the natural rock sculptures as Gothic castles, others as Egyptian temples, subterranean worlds inhabited by dragons, or vast armies of a lost empire. The Paiute tale of the Legend People relates how various animals and birds once lived in a beautiful city built for them by Coyote; when the Legend People began behaving badly toward Coyote, he transformed them all into stone.

Bryce Canyon isn't a canyon at all, but rather the largest of a series of massive amphitheaters cut into the Pink Cliffs. In Bryce Canyon National Park, you can gaze into the depths from viewpoints and trails on the plateau rim or hike down moderately steep trails and wind your way among the spires. A 17-mile scenic drive traces the length of the park and passes many overlooks and trailheads. Away from the road, the nearly 36,000 acres of Bryce Canyon National Park offer many

HIGHLIGHTS

◖ Sunrise and Sunset Points: At the namesake hours, these overlooks are irresistible, especially if you have a camera in hand. Unless you are utterly jaded, don't pass these off as mere clichés (page 70).

◖ Inspiration Point: From Sunset Point, walk south along the Rim Trail to see a fantastic maze of hoodoos in the "Silent City." Vertical joints in the rocks have weathered to form many rows of narrow gullies, some more than 200 feet deep (page 70).

◖ Yovimpa and Rainbow Points: Really, all of Bryce's viewpoints are pretty spectacular, but this 9,115-foot-high spot at the end of the scenic road is particularly dramatic. From this spot you can start a day hike, a backpacking trip, or a stroll along a nature trail (page 73).

◖ Queen's Garden Trail: The easiest hike below the rim, it can still leave flatlanders huffing and puffing. The trail drops from Sunrise Point through impressive features in the middle of Bryce Amphitheater to a hoodoo resembling a portly Queen Victoria (page 75).

◖ Navajo Loop Trail: From Sunset Point, hike down through a narrow canyon. At the bottom, the loop leads into deep, dark Wall Street—an even narrower canyon—then returns to the rim. From the bottom you can hook up with other trails, including one leading to the town of Tropic (page 75).

◖ Red Canyon Bike Trails: As lovely as Bryce Canyon is, sometimes the crowds, the tour buses, and all the synchronized oohing

and aahing can begin to close in on you. In that case, put rubber to the road on the wonderful paved bike trail that parallels Highway 12 through Red Canyon. If the paved path is too tame, take a mountain bike up Red Canyon's trails (page 83).

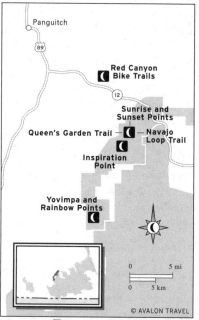

LOOK FOR ◖ TO FIND RECOMMENDED SIGHTS, ACTIVITIES, DINING, AND LODGING.

opportunities to explore spectacular rock features, dense forests, and expansive meadows.

The park's elevation ranges 6,600-9,100 feet, so it's usually much cooler here than at Utah's other national parks. Expect pleasantly warm days in summer, frosty nights in spring and fall, and snow at almost any time of year. The visitors center, the scenic drive, and a campground stay open throughout the year.

PLANNING YOUR TIME

Allow a full day to see the visitors center exhibits, enjoy the viewpoints along the scenic drive, and take a few short walks. Because of the layout of the park, with viewpoints all on the east side of the scenic drive, rangers recommend driving all the way south to Rainbow Point, and then stopping at viewpoints on your way back toward the park entrance; this means

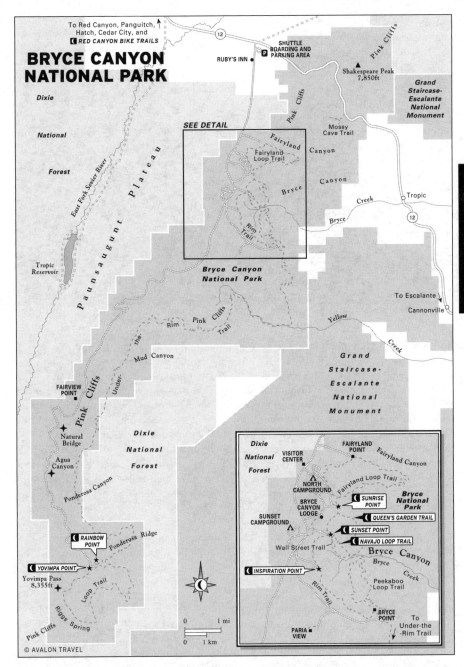

BRYCE CANYON

BRYCE CANYON

© PAUL LEVY

Bryce isn't a canyon at all, but a highly eroded amphitheater.

you won't constantly need to turn left across oncoming traffic.

The hike into Queen's Garden is a good, relatively short hike, and it's easy to fit into a one-day tour of the park. If you have more time to hike, the Navajo Loop Trail is also good; it can be combined with the Queen's Garden for a pretty substantial trek. Another good bet for strong hikers is the outstanding Peekaboo Loop. These trails are often crowded near the rim, but less so the farther out you get. But if the crowds begin to get to you, it's time to visit the Fairyland Loop Trail, which is off the main drag and less trafficked.

If you're interested in photographing the hoodoos—and it's hard to resist the urge—it makes sense to spend the night in or near the park. Photographers usually obtain the best results early and late in the day, when shadows set off the brightly colored rocks. Memorable sunsets and sunrises reward visitors who stay overnight. Moonlit nights reveal yet another spectacle.

If you want to travel into the backcountry, be sure to consult with a ranger about your plans. Remember that winter can last a long time at this elevation, and many trails can be blocked by snow and ice into the spring. The weather can also take a toll on the trails, and it's not uncommon to learn that your selected trail has been closed by rockfall.

Exploring the Park

Bryce Canyon National Park (435/834-5322, www.nps.gov/brca, $25 per vehicle, $12 cyclists, pedestrians, and motorcycles, admission good for 7 days and unlimited shuttle use) is just south of the incredibly scenic Highway 12, between Bryce Junction and Tropic. To reach the park from Bryce Junction (at the intersection of U.S. 89 and Hwy. 12, 7 miles south of Panguitch), head 14 miles east on Highway 12, then south three miles on Highway 63. From Escalante, it's about 50 miles west on Highway 12 to the turnoff for Bryce; turn south onto Highway 63 for the final three miles into the park (winter snows occasionally close this section). Both approaches have spectacular scenery.

Special hazards you should be aware of include crumbly ledges and lightning strikes. People who have wandered off trails or got too close to the drop-offs have had to be pulled out by rope. Avoid cliffs and other exposed areas during electrical storms, which are most common in late summer.

VISITORS CENTER

From the turnoff on Highway 12, follow signs past Ruby's Inn for 4.5 miles south to the park entrance; the visitors center (435/834-5322, 8am-8pm daily May-Sept., 8am-6pm daily Apr. and Oct., 8am-4:30pm daily Nov.-Mar.) is a short distance farther on the right. A brief slide show, shown every 30 minutes, introduces the park. Geologic exhibits illustrate how the land was formed and how it has changed. Historic displays cover the Paiute people, early nonnative explorers, and the first settlers; trees, flowers, and wildlife are identified. Rangers present a variety of naturalist programs, including short hikes, mid-May-early September; see the posted schedule.

TOURS

The most basic tour of the park, which comes with the price of admission, is a ride on the park shuttle bus. Shuttle buses run every 12 minutes or so during the peak part of the day, and the trip through the park takes 50 minutes. Of course, the beauty of the shuttle is that you can get off at any stop, hike for a while, and then catch another bus. Shuttle season is early May-mid-October.

Beyond a shuttle ride, **Ruby's Inn** (26 S. Main St., 866/866-6616, www.rubysinn.com), a hotel, restaurant, and recreation complex at the park entrance, is a good place to take measure of the opportunities for organized recreation and sightseeing excursions around Bryce Canyon. The lobby is filled with outfitters who are anxious to take you out on the trail; you'll find lots of recreational outfitters, along with vendors who organize hayrides, barn dances, and chuckwagon dinners. **Ruby's Horseback Adventures** (435/834-5341 or 866/782-0002, www.horserides.net, Apr.-Oct.) offers horseback riding in and near Bryce Canyon. There's a choice of half-day ($85) and full-day ($135, including lunch) trips, as well as a 1.5-hour trip ($65). During the summer, Ruby's also sponsors a rodeo (7pm Wed.-Sat., $10 adults, $7 ages 3-12) across from the inn.

You can also explore the area around Bryce Canyon on a noisier steed. Guided all-terrain vehicle (ATV) tours of Red Canyon are offered by **Ruby's ATV Tours** (435/834-5232, 1-hour trip $45).

Horseback rides are also offered by a concessionaire inside the park at the Lodge at Bryce Canyon. **Canyon Trail Rides** (435/679-8665, www.canyonrides.com) offers a two-hour ride ($60) that goes to the canyon floor. Half-day rides are also available.

If you'd like to get a look at Bryce and the surrounding area from the air, take a scenic flightseeing tour with **Bryce Canyon Airlines** (Ruby's Inn, 435/834-8060), which offers both plane and helicopter tours. There's quite

BRYCE CANYON

BRYCE CANYON SHUTTLE

When rangers and visitors alike began to complain seriously about the "Bryce Canyon national parking lot," park administrators took note. But bigger parking lots, obviously, weren't the environmentally friendly solution.

In 2000 the National Park Service instituted a shuttle service through Bryce Canyon National Park. Buses run during the peak summer season from the shuttle parking and boarding area at the intersection of Highways 12 and 63 to the visitors center, with stops at Ruby's Inn and Ruby's Campground. From the visitors center, the bus travels to the park's developed areas, including all the main amphitheater viewpoints, Sunset Campground, and the Bryce Canyon Lodge. Passengers can take as long as they like at any viewpoint, then catch a later bus. The shuttle bus service also makes it easier for hikers, who don't need to worry about car shuttles between trailheads.

Use of the shuttle bus system is not mandatory; you can still bring in your own vehicle. However, even if you do drive into the park, don't plan to pull a trailer all the way to Rainbow Point. Trailers aren't allowed past Sunset Campground. Trailer parking is available at the visitors center.

a range of options, but a 35-minute airplane tour ($159 pp, 2-person minimum) provides a good look at the surroundings.

SCENIC DRIVE

From elevations of about 8,000 feet near the visitors center, the park's scenic drive gradually winds 1,100 feet higher to Rainbow Point. About midway you'll notice a change in the trees from largely ponderosa pine to spruce, fir, and aspen. On a clear day, you can enjoy vistas of more than 100 miles from many of the viewpoints. Because of parking shortages

on the drive, trailers must be left at the visitors center or your campsite. Visitors wishing to see all of the viewpoints should take a walk on the Rim Trail.

Note that even though the viewpoints are described here in north-to-south order, when the park is bustling, it's better to drive all the way to the southern end of the road and visit the viewpoints from south to north, thus avoiding left turns across traffic. Of course, if you're just heading to one viewpoint or trailhead, it's fine to drive directly to it.

Fairyland Point

The turnoff for Fairyland Point is just inside the park boundary; go north 0.8 miles from the visitors center, then east one mile. Whimsical forms line Fairyland Canyon a short distance below. You can descend into the fairyland on the **Fairyland Loop Trail** or follow the **Rim Trail** for other panoramas.

◖ Sunrise and Sunset Points

These overlooks are off to the left about one mile south of the visitors center; they're connected by a 0.5-mile paved section of the **Rim Trail.** Panoramas from each point take in large areas of Bryce Amphitheater and beyond. The lofty Aquarius and Table Cliff Plateaus rise along the skyline to the northeast; you can see the same colorful Claron Formation in cliffs that faulting has raised about 2,000 feet higher. A short walk down either the **Queen's Garden Trail** or the **Navajo Loop Trail** from Sunset Point will bring you close to Bryce's hoodoos and provide a totally different experience from what you get atop the rim.

◖ Inspiration Point

It's well worth the 0.75-mile walk south along the **Rim Trail** from Sunset Point to see a fantastic maze of hoodoos in the "Silent City." It's also accessible by car, from a spur road near the Bryce Point turnoff. Weathering

THE GEOLOGY OF BRYCE CANYON

As the top step of the Grand Staircase, Bryce's rocks are young by geologic standards. The park's Pink Cliffs lie on top of older rock layers, which are exposed in stair-step form as you head south toward the Grand Canyon.

This fantastic landscape got its start about 60 million years ago as sediment dropped to the bottom of a large body of water, named Lake Flagstaff by geologists. Silt, calcium carbonate, and other minerals settled on the lake bottom, then consolidated and became the Claron Formation—a soft, silty limestone with some shale and sandstone.

Lake Flagstaff had long since disappeared when the land began to rise as part of the Colorado Plateau uplift about 16 million years ago. Uneven pressures beneath the plateau caused it to break along fault lines into a series of smaller plateaus at different levels known as the "Grand Staircase." Bryce Canyon National Park occupies part of one of these plateaus, the Paunsaugunt.

The spectacular **Pink Cliffs** on the east edge of the Paunsaugunt Plateau contain the famous erosional features known as hoodoos, carved in the Claron Formation. Variations in hardness of the rock layers result in these strange features, which seem almost alive. Water flows through cracks, wearing away softer rock around hard erosion-resistant caps. Finally, a cap becomes so undercut that the overhang allows water to drip down, leaving a "neck" of rock below the harder cap. Traces of iron and manganese provide the distinctive coloring. The hoodoos continue to change; new ones form and old ones fade away. The plateau cliffs, meanwhile, recede at a rate of about one foot every 50-65 years; look for trees on the rim that now overhang the abyss. Listen and you might hear the sounds of pebbles falling away and rolling down the steep slopes.

© PAUL LEVY

Bryce's spectacular hoodoos were carved by ice and wind.

along vertical joints has cut many rows of narrow gullies, some more than 200 feet deep. It's a short but steep 0.2-mile walk up to Upper Inspiration Point.

Bryce Point

This overlook at the south end of Bryce Amphitheater has expansive views to the north and east. It's also the start for the **Rim, Peekaboo Loop,** and **Under-the-Rim Trails.** From the turnoff two miles south of the visitors center, follow signs 2.1 miles in.

Paria View

Cliffs drop precipitously into the headwaters of Yellow Creek, a tributary of the Paria River. You can see a section of Under-the-Rim Trail winding up a hillside near the mouth of the amphitheater below. Distant views take in the Paria River Canyon, White Cliffs (of Navajo sandstone), and Navajo Mountain. The plateau rim in the park forms a drainage divide. Precipitation falling west of the rim flows gently into the East Fork of the Sevier River and the Great Basin; precipitation landing east of the

BRYCE CANYON'S FLORA AND FAUNA

Bryce's plantlife changes considerably with elevation; higher elevations are moister than the lowlands and can support relatively lush vegetation. The warm dry slopes beneath the canyon's rim, below about 7,000 feet, are dominated by piñon pine, Utah juniper, and Gambel oak.

Ponderosa pines rise majestically over greenleaf manzanita and other shrubs at 7,000-8,500 feet. You'll find these species in the area around the **visitors center, campground,** and **lodge.**

Blue spruce, white fir, Douglas fir, limber pine, bristlecone pine, and aspen thrive in the cool moist conditions above 8,500 feet. It's easy to see these trees at **Rainbow** and **Yovimpa Points,** which are just above 9,100 feet.

Wildflowers put on a showy display spring-early fall. Springs and seeps below the rim support pockets of water birch, bigtooth maple, willows, and narrow-leaf cottonwood.

Larger wildlife visit the higher elevations in summer, then move down out of the park as winter snows arrive. It's no shock that mule deer frequent **Bryce's meadows,** especially in morning and evening, but it's a little more surprising to see wild turkeys grazing there. Other residents include mountain lions, black bears, coyotes, bobcats, gray foxes, striped skunks, badgers, porcupines, Utah prairie dogs, yellow-bellied marmots, Uinta chipmunks, and golden-mantled ground squirrels. Beavers live near the park on the **East Fork of the Sevier River** (*Paunsaugunt* is Paiute for "home of the beaver"). Despite the cool climate, you can find a few reptiles; look for the short-horned lizard, skink, and Great Basin rattlesnake.

Birds appear in greatest numbers May-October. Violet-green swallows and white-throated swifts dive and careen among the hoodoos in hot pursuit of flying insects. Other summer visitors are the golden eagle, red-tailed hawk, Western tanager, and mountain bluebird. Year-round residents include woodpeckers, owls, ravens, Steller's jays, Clark's nutcrackers, and blue grouse.

Bryce's cliffs have become home to a thriving population of California condors. Six condors were released in the Vermilion Cliffs south of Bryce in 1996, and the population has grown to about 100. Peregrine falcons are another avian success story here; several pairs of these raptors nest in the park. Look for them from **Paria View.**

Although some wild creatures may seem quite tame, they must not be fed or handled–rodents may have diseases such as hantavirus, and young deer contaminated with human scent might be abandoned by their mothers. Also, animals that become dependent on humans may die in winter when left to forage for themselves after the summer crowds have left.

rim rushes through deep canyons in the Pink Cliffs to the Paria River and on to the Colorado River and the Grand Canyon. Take the turnoff for Bryce Point, and then keep right at the fork.

Farview Point

This sweeping panorama takes in a lot of geology. You'll see levels of the Grand Staircase that include the Aquarius and Table Cliff Plateaus to the northeast, Kaiparowits Plateau to the east, and White Cliffs to the southeast. Look beyond the White Cliffs to see a section of the Kaibab Plateau that forms the north rim of the Grand Canyon in Arizona. The overlook is on the left, nine miles south of the visitors center.

Natural Bridge

This large feature lies just off the road to the east, 1.7 miles past Farview Point. The span is 54 feet wide and 95 feet high. Despite its name, this is an arch formed by weathering from rain and freezing, not by stream erosion, as with a true natural bridge. Once the opening reached ground level, runoff began to enlarge the hole and to dig a gully through it.

HOODOOS

Although many visitors assume that wind shaped Bryce Canyon's hoodoos, they were, in fact, formed by water, ice, and gravity, and the way those elements and forces have interacted over the years on rocks of varying hardness.

When the Colorado Plateau uplifted, vertical breaks—called joints—formed in the plateau. Joints allowed water to flow into the rock. As water flowed through these joints, erosion widened them into rivulets, gullies, and eventually deep slot canyons. Even more powerful than water, the action of ice freezing, melting, then freezing again, as it does about 200 days a year at Bryce, causes ice wedges to form within the rock joints, eventually breaking the rock.

Bryce Canyon is composed of layers of limestone, siltstone, dolomite, and mudstone. Each rock type erodes at a different rate, carving the strange shapes of the hoodoos. The word *hoodoo* derives from the same sources as *voodoo;* both words are sometimes used to describe folk beliefs and practices. Early Spanish explorers transferred the mystical sense of the word to the towering, vaguely humanoid rock formations that rise above Southwestern landscapes. The Spaniards believed that Native Americans worshipped these statue-like "enchanted rocks." In fact, while early indigenous people considered many hoodoo areas sacred, there is no evidence that they worshipped the stones themselves.

© PAUL LEVY

It's easy to imagine Sunrise Point's hoodoos as statues or fanciful creatures.

Agua and Ponderosa Canyons

You can admire sheer cliffs and hoodoos from the Agua Canyon overlook to the east, 1.4 miles past Natural Bridge. With a little imagination, you may be able to pick out the Hunter and the Rabbit below. Ponderosa Canyon overlook, to the east 1.8 miles farther, offers a panorama similar to that at Farview Point.

◖ Yovimpa and Rainbow Points

The land drops away in rugged canyons and fine views at the end of the scenic drive, 17 miles south of the visitors center. At an elevation of 9,115 feet, this is the highest area of the park. Yovimpa and Rainbow Points are only a short walk apart yet offer different vistas. The **Bristlecone Loop Trail** is an easy one-mile loop from Rainbow Point to ancient bristlecone pines along the rim. The **Riggs Spring Loop Trail** makes a good day hike; you can begin from either Yovimpa Point or Rainbow Point and descend into canyons in the southern area of the park. The **Under-the-Rim Trail** starts from Rainbow Point and winds 22.5 miles to Bryce Point; day hikers can make a 7.5-mile trip by using the Agua Canyon Connecting Trail and a car shuttle.

Recreation

Although it's possible to have an entirely pleasant visit to Bryce by just riding the shuttle and hopping off to snap pictures at various viewpoints, a short hike or horseback ride down off the rim will give you an entirely different perspective on the hoodoos, native plants, and, perhaps, wildlife of the park.

HIKING

Hikers enjoy close-up views of the wonderfully eroded features and gain a direct appreciation of Bryce's geology. Because almost all of the trails head down off the canyon's rim, they're moderately difficult, with many ups and downs, but the paths are well graded and signed. Hikers not accustomed to the 7,000-9,000-foot elevation will find the going relatively strenuous and should allow extra time. Be sure to carry water and drink frequently—staying well hydrated will give you more energy.

Wear a hat and sunscreen to protect against sunburn, which can be a problem at these elevations. Don't forget rain gear, because storms can come up suddenly. Always carry water for day trips; only a few natural sources exist. Ask at the visitors center for current trail conditions and water sources; you can also pick up a free hiking map at the visitors center. Snow may block some trail sections in winter and early spring. Horses are permitted only on Peekaboo Loop. Pets must stay above the rim; they're allowed on the Rim Trail only between Sunset and Sunrise Points.

Overnight hikers can obtain the required backcountry permit ($5-15) at the visitors center. Camping is allowed only on the Under-the-Rim and Riggs Spring Loop trails. Backpack stoves must be used for cooking; wood fires are prohibited. Although there are several isolated springs in Bryce's backcountry, it's prudent to carry at least one gallon of water per person per day. Ask about the location and flow of springs when you register for the backcountry permit.

Don't expect much solitude during the summer on the popular Rim, Queen's Garden, Navajo, and Peekaboo Loop Trails. Fairyland Loop Trail is less used, and the backcountry trails are almost never crowded. September-October are the choice hiking months—the weather is best and the crowds smallest, although nighttime temperatures in late October can dip well below freezing.

Rim Trail

- Distance: 11 miles round-trip
- Duration: 5-6 hours
- Elevation change: 540 feet
- Effort: easy
- Trailheads: Fairyland Point, Bryce Point

© BILL MCRAE

Short hiking trails lead to scenic overlooks.

GREENLEAF MANZANITA

One of the easiest plants to identify at Bryce is greenleaf manzanita. The leaves on this low-lying shrub are dark green and leathery; the bark is cinnamon-colored. Look closely and you may see fine hairs on the stems. Pink urn-shaped flowers dangle from the stems in May, followed in late summer by fruit that resembles tiny cream-colored apples (*manzanita* is a Spanish word for "little apple"). Manzanita, which is common in California and the inland Pacific Northwest, easily survives snowy winters, though parts of the plant that aren't covered by an insulating blanket of snow may die from the cold. To conserve water during the hot summers, manzanita leaves stand straight up in a vertical position, reducing the surface area exposed to the sun and slowing transpiration.

Native Americans brewed a diuretic tea from manzanita leaves and made cider from its ripe fruit. They also used the crushed leaves and fruit as a poultice for poison ivy. Patient (or lucky) visitors may spot wildlife browsing on the manzanita—both mule deer and wild turkeys are fond of it.

• Shuttle stops: Fairyland Point, Bryce Point

This easy trail follows the edge of Bryce Amphitheater. Most people walk short sections of the rim in leisurely strolls or use the trail to connect with five other trails that head down beneath the rim. The 0.5-mile stretch of trail near the lodge between Sunrise and Sunset Points is paved and nearly level; other parts are gently rolling.

Fairyland Loop Trail

• Distance: 8 miles round-trip
• Duration: 4-5 hours
• Elevation change: 900 feet
• Effort: strenuous
• Trailheads: Fairyland Point or Sunrise Point

• Shuttle stops: Fairyland Point or Sunrise Point

This trail winds in and out of colorful rock spires in the northern part of Bryce Amphitheater, a somewhat less-visited area one mile off the main park road. Although the trail is well graded, remember the climb of 900 vertical feet you'll make when you exit. You can take a loop hike of eight miles from either Fairyland Point or Sunrise Point by using a section of the **Rim Trail**; a car shuttle saves three hiking miles. The whole loop is too long for many visitors, who enjoy short trips down and back to see this "fairyland."

◖ Queen's Garden Trail

• Distance: 1.5 miles round-trip
• Duration: 1.5 hours
• Elevation change: 320 feet
• Effort: moderate
• Trailhead: Sunrise Point
• Shuttle stop: Sunrise Point

A favorite of many people, this trail drops from Sunrise Point through impressive features in the middle of Bryce Amphitheater to a hoodoo resembling a portly Queen Victoria. This is the easiest excursion below the rim. Queen's Garden Trail also makes a good loop hike with the **Navajo Loop** and **Rim Trails**; most people who do the loop prefer to descend the steeper Navajo and climb out on Queen's Garden Trail for a 3.5-mile hike. Trails also connect with the **Peekaboo Loop Trail** and go to the town of Tropic.

◖ Navajo Loop Trail

• Distance: 1.3 miles round-trip
• Duration: 1.5 hours
• Elevation change: 520 feet
• Effort: moderate
• Trailhead: Sunset Point
• Shuttle stop: Sunset Point

From Sunset Point, the trail drops 520 vertical feet in 0.75 miles through a narrow

© PAUL LEVY

Hike down the Navajo Loop Trail to get up close and personal with the hoodoos.

canyon. At the bottom, the loop leads into deep, dark **Wall Street**—an even narrower canyon 0.5 miles long—then returns to the rim. Other destinations from the bottom of Navajo Trail are **Twin Bridges, Queen's Garden Trail, Peekaboo Loop Trail,** and the town of Tropic. The 1.5-mile trail to Tropic isn't as scenic as the other trails, but it does provide another way to enter or leave the park; ask at the visitors center or in Tropic for directions to the trailhead.

Peekaboo Loop Trail

- Distance: 5.5-7 miles round-trip
- Duration: 4 hours
- Elevation change: 500-800 feet
- Effort: moderate-strenuous
- Trailhead: Bryce Point
- Shuttle stop: Bryce Point

This enchanting walk is full of surprises at every turn—and there are lots of turns. The trail is in the southern part of Bryce Amphitheater, which has some of the most striking rock features. You can start from Bryce Point (6.5 miles round-trip), from Sunset Point (5.5 miles round-trip via Navajo Trail), or from Sunrise Point (7 miles round-trip via Queen's Garden Trail). The loop segment itself is 3.5 miles long, with many ups and downs and a few tunnels. The elevation change is 500-800 feet, depending on the trailhead you choose. This is the only trail in the park where horses are permitted; remember to give horseback travelers the right of way and, if possible, to step to higher ground when you allow them to pass.

Under-the-Rim Trail

- Distance: 23 miles one-way
- Duration: 2 days or longer
- Elevation change: 1,500 feet
- Effort: strenuous
- Trailheads: Bryce Point, Rainbow Point
- Shuttle stops: Bryce Point, Rainbow Point

The longest trail in the park winds 23 miles below the Pink Cliffs, between Bryce Point to the north and Rainbow Point to the south. Allow at least two days to hike the entire trail; the elevation change is about 1,500 feet, with many ups and downs. Four connecting trails from the scenic drive also make it possible to travel the Under-the-Rim Trail as a series of day hikes. Another option is to combine the Under-the-Rim and **Riggs Spring Loop** Trails for a total of 31.5 miles.

The **Hat Shop,** an area of delicate spires capped by erosion-resistant rock, makes a good day hiking destination; begin at Bryce Point and follow the Under-the-Rim Trail for about two miles. Most of this section is downhill (elevation change of 900 feet); you'll have to climb it on the way out.

BRYCE CANYON

BRISTLECONE PINE

Somewhere on earth, a bristlecone pine tree may be among the planet's oldest living organisms. The trees here, while not the world's oldest, are up to 1,700 years old (there's a bristlecone in California that's nearly 4,800 years old). These twisted, gnarly trees are easy to spot in the area around Rainbow Point because they look their age.

What makes a bristlecone live so long? For one, its dense, resinous wood protects it from insects, bacteria, and fungi that kill many other trees. It grows in a harsh dry climate where there's not a lot of competition from other plants. During droughts that would kill most other plants, the bristlecone can slow down its metabolism until it's practically dormant, then spring back to life when conditions are less severe. Although the dry desert air poses its own set of challenges, it also keeps the tree from rotting.

Besides its ancient look, a bristlecone pine can be recognized by its distinctive needles—they're packed tightly, five to a bunch, with the bunches running along the length of a branch, making it to look like a bottle brush.

Swamp Canyon Loop

- Distance: 4.3 miles round-trip
- Duration: 2 hours
- Elevation change: 628 feet
- Effort: moderate
- Trailhead: Swamp Canyon
- Shuttle stop: Swamp Canyon

This loop comprises three trails: the Swamp Canyon Connecting Trail, a short stretch of the Under-the-Rim Trail, and the Sheep Creek Connecting Trail. Drop below the rim on the Swamp Canyon trail to a smaller sheltered canyon that is, by local standards, a wetland. Swamp Canyon's two tiny creeks and a spring provide enough moisture for a lush growth of grass and willows. Salamanders live here, as do

a variety of birds; this is usually a good trail for bird-watching.

Bristlecone Loop Trail

- Distance: 1 mile round-trip
- Duration: 30 minutes
- Elevation change: 150 feet
- Effort: easy
- Trailheads: Rainbow Point, Yovimpa Point
- Shuttle stop: Rainbow Point

This easy one-mile loop begins from either Rainbow or Yovimpa Point and goes to viewpoints and ancient bristlecone pines along the rim. These hardy trees survive fierce storms and extremes of hot and cold that no other tree can. Some of the bristlecone pines here are 1,700 years old.

Riggs Spring Loop

- Distance: 8.5 miles round-trip
- Duration: 5 hours
- Elevation change: 1,625 feet
- Effort: strenuous
- Trailhead: Rainbow Point
- Shuttle stop: Rainbow Point

One of the park's more challenging day hikes or a leisurely overnighter, this trail begins from Rainbow Point and descends into canyons in the southern area of the park. Of the three backcountry campgrounds along the trail, the Riggs Spring site is most conveniently located; it's about halfway around the loop. Great views of the hoodoos, lots of aspen trees, a couple of pretty meadows, and good views off to the east are some of the highlights of this hike. Day hikers often take a shortcut that bypasses Riggs Spring and saves 0.75 miles.

Mossy Cave Trail

- Distance: 1 mile round-trip
- Duration: 30 minutes
- Elevation change: 209 feet
- Effort: easy

BRYCE CANYON

VISITING BRYCE CANYON IN WINTER

Although Bryce is most popular during the summer months, it is especially beautiful and otherworldly during the winter, when the rock formations are topped with snow. Because Bryce is so high (elevation ranges 8,000-9,000 feet), winter lasts a long time, often into April.

The main park roads and most viewpoints are plowed, and the Rim Trail is an excellent, easy snowshoe or cross-country ski route. **Paria Ski Trail** (a 5-mile loop) and **Fairyland Ski Trail** (a 2.5-mile loop) are marked for snowshoers and cross-country skiers. Whenever snow depth measures 18 inches or more, snowshoes are loaned free of charge at the visitors center (credit-card deposit required). Rent cross-country ski equipment just outside the park at Ruby's Inn (435/834-5341 or 866/866-6616, www.rubysinn.com). Miles of snowmobile trails are groomed outside the park.

During the winter, most of the businesses around the park entrance shut down. The notable exception is Ruby's Inn, which is a wintertime hub of activity. During the winter months, rates drop precipitously—January-March, most guest rooms go for less than $60.

Ruby's Inn hosts the **Bryce Canyon Winter Festival** during Presidents Day weekend in February. The three-day festival includes free cross-country skiing and snowshoeing clinics, demos, and tours. This is also the time and place to pick up tips on ski archery and winter photography.

- Trailhead: Highway 12, between mileposts 17 and 18

This easy trail is just off Highway 12, northwest of Tropic, near the east edge of the park (which means that park entrance fees aren't required). Hike up Water Canyon to a cool alcove of dripping water and moss. Sheets of ice and icicles add beauty to the scene in winter. The hike is only one mile round-trip with a small elevation change. A side trail just before the cave branches right a short distance to a little waterfall; look for several small arches in the colorful canyon walls above. Although the park lacks perennial natural streams, the stream in Water Canyon flows even during dry spells. Mormon pioneers labored three years to channel water from the East Fork of the Sevier River through a canal and down this wash to the town of Tropic. Without this irrigation, the town might not even exist. From the visitors center, return to Highway 12 and turn east, then travel 3.7 miles toward Escalante; the parking area is on the right just after a bridge, between mileposts 17 and 18. Rangers schedule guided walks to the cave and the waterfall during the spring-fall season.

HORSEBACK RIDING

If you'd like to get down among the hoodoos but aren't sure you'll have the energy to hike back up to the rim, consider letting a horse help you along. **Canyon Trail Rides** (Lodge at Bryce Canyon, 435/679-8665, www.canyonrides. com), a park concessionaire, offers guided rides near Sunrise Point, and both two-hour ($60) and half-day ($80) trips are offered. Both rides descend to the floor of the canyon; the longer ride follows the Peekaboo Loop Trail. Riders must be at least seven years old and weigh no more than 220 pounds; the horses and wranglers are accustomed to novices.

OUTFITTERS

You guessed it: If there's a piece of gear or clothing that you need, the **General Store** at Ruby's Inn (26 S. Main St., 435/834-5484, www.rubysinn.com, 7am-10:30pm daily) is the best place to look for it. Here you'll find a large stock of groceries, camping and fishing supplies, film and processing, Native American crafts, books, souvenirs, and a post office. Horseback rides, helicopter tours, and airplane rides are arranged in the lobby just outside the store. In winter, cross-country skiers can rent gear and use trails located near the inn as well as in the park. Snowmobile trails are also available, but snowmobiles may not be used within the park. Western-fronted shops across from Ruby's Inn offer trail rides, chuckwagon dinners, mountain bike rentals, souvenirs, and a petting farm.

Inside the park, there's another general store (mid-Apr.-late Sept.), with groceries, camping supplies, coin-operated showers, and a laundry room. It is located between North Campground and Sunrise Point.

If you need specialized outdoor gear, you're more likely to find it 50 miles east in the town of Escalante than in the Bryce Canyon neighborhood.

Accommodations and Food

Travelers may have a hard time finding accommodations and campsites April-October in both the park and nearby areas. Advance reservations at lodges, motels, and the park campground are a good idea; otherwise, plan to arrive by late morning if you expect to find a room without reservations. You'll also find that there's a huge variation in room prices from day to day and from season to season. Use the prices cited below, for summer high season, only as a general guide; what you may find on the Internet or by phone on a particular evening may differ markedly.

The Lodge at Bryce Canyon is the only lodge inside the park, and you'll generally need to make reservations months in advance to get a room in this historic landmark (although it doesn't hurt to ask about vacancies). Other motels are clustered near the park entrance road, but many do not offer much for the money. The quality of lodgings is somewhat better in Tropic, 11 miles east on Highway 12, and in Panguitch, 25 miles to the northwest.

$50-100

During the winter, it's easy to find inexpensive accommodations in this area; even guest rooms at Ruby's Inn start at about $60. Several motels are clustered on Highway 12, right outside the park boundary. Many of these have seen a lot of use over the years, usually without a lot of attendant upkeep. **Foster's Motel** (1150 Hwy. 12, 435/834-5227 or 800/372-4750, www.fostersmotel.com, $79) has pine-paneled motel rooms best suited for budget travelers who don't want to camp and don't plan to spend a lot of time in their rooms. It's four miles west of the park entrance in a small complex with a restaurant and a supermarket.

$100-150

A full-service hotel complex with pleasant guest rooms is the **Bryce Canyon Resort** (13500 E. Hwy. 12, 435/834-5351 or 866/834-0043, www.brycecanyonresort.com, from $89-194), with an indoor pool, a restaurant, a store, and lodging options that include standard motel rooms, suites, and cottages that sleep up to six.

The sprawling **Best Western Ruby's Inn** (26 S. Main St., 435/834-5341 or 800/468-8660, www.rubysinn.com, $125-140) offers many year-round services on Highway 63 just north of the park boundary; winter rates are about half high-season rates. The hotel features an indoor pool and a hot tub and all the bustling activity you could ever want. Kitchenettes and family rooms are also available; pets are allowed. Ruby's Inn is more than just a place to stay, however: This is one of the area's major centers for all manner of recreational outfitters, dining, entertainment, and shopping. Many tour bus groups bed down here. Although it is kind of a zoo, the quality of the guest rooms at Ruby's is generally higher than at other lodgings in the immediate area. If you want something more sumptuous and relaxing, consider staying at a B&B in nearby Tropic.

One of the newer hotels, and a good value for the area, is the **Bryce View Lodge** (991 S. Hwy. 63, 435/834-5180 or 888/279-2304, www.bryceviewlodge.com, $103-120), which has guest rooms in handsome buildings near the park entrance, across the road from Ruby's Inn (it's owned by Ruby's).

Six miles west of the park turnoff, **Bryce Canyon Pines Motel** (Hwy. 12, Milepost 10, 435/834-5441 or 800/892-7923, www.brycecanyonmotel.com, $110-135) is an older motel with both motel rooms and cottages, a seasonal covered pool, horseback rides, an RV park, and a restaurant (breakfast, lunch, and dinner daily early Apr.-late Oct.).

OVER $150

Set among ponderosa pines a short walk from the rim, the ◖ **Lodge at Bryce Canyon** (435/834-8700 or 877/386-4383, http://brycecanyonforever.com, Apr.-Oct., rooms $139-243, cabins $198) was built in 1923 by a division of the Union Pacific Railroad; a spur line once terminated at the front entrance. The lodge has lots of charm and is listed on the National Register of Historic Places. It also has by far the best location of any Bryce-area accommodations; it's the only lodging in the park itself. Accommodations options include suites in the lodge, motel-style guest rooms, and lodgepole pine cabins; all are clean and pleasant but fairly basic in terms of amenities. The location, however, could not be better.

Activities at the lodge include horseback rides, park tours, evening entertainment, and ranger talks; a gift shop sells souvenirs, while food can be found at both a restaurant and a snack bar. Try to make reservations as far in advance as possible.

CAMPGROUNDS
Bryce Canyon Campgrounds

The park's two campgrounds ($15) both have water and some pull-through spaces. Reservations are accepted seasonally for 13 RV sites at North Campground and 20 tent and RV sites at Sunset Campground. Make reservations at least two days in advance (877/444-6777, www.recreation.gov, May-Sept., $10 reservation fee). Otherwise, try to arrive early for a space during the busy summer season, because both campgrounds usually fill by 1 or 2pm. **North Campground** is on the left just past the visitors center. The best sites here are just a few yards downhill from the Rim Trail, with easy hiking access to other park trails. At least one loop is open year-round. **Sunset Campground** (late spring-early fall) is about 2.5 miles farther on the right, across the road from Sunset Point. Sunset has campsites accessible to people with disabilities (Loop A).

Basic groceries, camping supplies, coin-operated showers, and a laundry room are available at the General Store (mid-Apr.-late Sept.), between North Campground and Sunrise Point. During the rest of the year, you can go outside the park to Ruby's Inn for these services.

Public Campgrounds

The Dixie National Forest has three Forest Service campgrounds ($10-12) located in scenic settings among ponderosa pines. They often have room when campgrounds in the park are full. Sites can be reserved at Pine Lake, King Creek, and Red Canyon Campgrounds (877/444-6777, www.recreation.gov, $10 reservation fee). **Pine Lake Campground** (mid-May-mid-Sept.) is at 7,700 feet elevation, just east of its namesake lake, in a forest of ponderosa pine, spruce, and juniper. From the highway junction north of the park, head northeast 11 miles on Highway 63 (gravel), then turn southeast and go six miles. Contact the Escalante Ranger District office in Escalante (435/826-5400) for information on Pine Lake.

King Creek Campground (usually May-late Sept.) is on the west shore of Tropic Reservoir, which has a boat ramp and fair trout fishing. Sites are at 8,000 feet elevation. Go 2.8 miles west of the park turnoff on Highway 12, and then head seven miles south on the gravel East Fork Sevier River Road. **Red Canyon Campground** (late May-late Sept.) is just off Highway 12, four miles east of U.S. 89. It's at 7,400 feet elevation, below brilliantly colored cliffs. Contact the Powell Ranger District office (435/676-9300) in Panguitch for more information on King Creek and Red Canyon Campgrounds.

Camping is available a little farther away at beautiful **Kodachrome Basin State Park** (801/322-3770 or 800/322-3770, www.reserveamerica.com, $16). From Bryce, take Highway 12 east to Cannonville, then head nine miles south to the park.

Private Campgrounds

Private campgrounds in the area tend to cost $25 or more. The **Ruby's Inn Campground** (26 S. Main St., 435/834-5301, www.rubysinn.com, early Apr.-late Oct.) is at the park junction and has spaces for tents ($25) and RVs ($35-46); showers and a laundry room are open year-round. They've also got a few tepees (from $38) and bunkhouse-style cabins (bedding not provided, $62). All of the considerable facilities at Ruby's are available to campers. **Bryce Canyon Pines Campground** (milepost 10, Hwy. 12, 435/834-5441 or 800/892-7923, www.brycecanyonmotel.com, Apr.-Oct., $20 tents, $30 RVs), four miles west of the park

entrance, has an indoor pool, a game room, groceries, and shaded sites.

FOOD

The dining room at the ◖ **Lodge at Bryce Canyon** (435/834-8700, http://brycecanyonforever.com, 6:30am-10am, reservations not accepted, 11am-3pm, and 5pm-10pm daily Apr.-Oct., $12-22) is atmospheric and offers food that's as good as you're going to find in the area. For lunch, the snack bar is a good bet in nice weather; the only seating is outside on the patio or in the hotel lobby.

If you really want a high-volume dining experience, Ruby's Inn **Cowboy Buffet and Steak Room** (26 S. Main St., 435/834-5341, www.rubysinn.com, 6:30am-10pm daily, $10-25) is an incredibly busy place. It's also one of Bryce Canyon's better restaurants, with sandwiches, steaks, and a buffet with a salad bar. Casual lunch and dinner fare, including pizza, is served in the inn's snack bar, the **Canyon Diner** (11:30am-10pm daily Apr.-Oct.).

Bryce Canyon Resort (13500 E. Hwy. 12, 435/834-5351 or 800/834-0043, www.brycecanyonresort.com, 7am-10pm daily, $8-22), near the turnoff for the park, has an on-site restaurant that features burgers and Mexican food.

Two long-established restaurants west of the park entrance have a low-key, noncorporate atmosphere and pretty good food. The small family-run restaurant attached to **Bryce Canyon Pines** (milepost 10, Hwy. 12, 435/834-5441 or 800/892-7923, 7am-10pm daily, $8-17) is a homey place to stop for burgers, soup, or sandwiches. The restaurant is famous for its fruit pies. Two miles west of the park turnoff is **Foster's** (Hwy. 12, 435/834-5227, 7am-10pm daily, $11-26), a well-regarded steak house with an Old West atmosphere.

BRYCE CANYON

Vicinity of Bryce Canyon

Sometimes the bustle at Bryce's rim and at the large commercial developments right at the entrance to the park can be a little off-putting. It's easy to escape the crowds by heading just a few miles west on scenic Highway 12.

RED CANYON

The drive on Highway 12 between U.S. 89 and the turnoff for Bryce Canyon National Park passes through this well-named canyon. Because Red Canyon is not part of Bryce—it's part of Dixie National Forest—many of the trails are open to mountain biking and ATV riding. In fact, this canyon has become very popular as other Utah mountain biking destinations have become crowded. Red Canyon's bike trails are spectacularly scenic and exhilarating to ride. Ruby's Inn provides a shuttle service for Red Canyon mountain bikers.

Staff members at the **Red Canyon Visitor Center** (Hwy. 12, between mileposts 3 and 4, 435/676-2676, www.fs.fed.us, 9am-6pm Fri.-Mon. Apr.-May, 9am-6pm daily Memorial Day-Labor Day, 9am-6pm Thurs.-Mon. Sept.-Oct.) can tell you about the trails and scenic backcountry roads that wind through the area. Books and maps are available.

The U.S. Forest Service maintains many scenic hiking trails that wind back from the highway for a closer look at the geology. The following trails are open to hikers only. Because this is not part of the national park, dogs are permitted on these trails.

Pink Ledges Trail

- Distance: 1 mile round-trip
- Duration: 30 minutes
- Elevation change: 100 feet
- Effort: easy
- Trailhead: Red Canyon Visitor Center

The Pink Ledges Trail, the easiest and most popular trail in the area, loops past intriguing geological features. Signs identify some of the trees and plants.

Birds Eye Trail

- Distance: 1.4 miles round-trip
- Duration: 1 hour
- Elevation change: 150 feet
- Effort: easy-moderate
- Trailhead: Red Canyon Visitor Center

The Birds Eye Trail winds by red-rock formations, including a supposedly bird-shaped rock, and connects the visitors center with the Photo Trail and its parking area on Highway 12, just inside the forest boundary.

Buckhorn Trail

- Distance: 1.8 miles round-trip
- Duration: 1.5 hours
- Elevation change: 250 feet
- Effort: moderate-strenuous
- Trailhead: Red Canyon Campground, site 23

This trail climbs to views of the interesting geology of Red Canyon. It's a good choice if you'd like to burn off a little energy and get a sense of the surrounding country. The campground is on the south side of Highway 12 between mileposts 3 and 4.

For a longer hike (4 miles one-way), turn left off the Buckhorn Trail after about 0.6 miles onto the Golden Wall Trail. Follow the Golden Wall Trail south past yellow limestone walls, and then north again back to Highway 12, where it comes out across from the visitors center. A short spur, the Castle Bridge Trail, climbs to a ridge overlooking the Golden Wall before rejoining the Golden Wall Trail.

VICINITY OF BRYCE CANYON

two miles east of U.S. 89. Turn north from Highway 12 onto Forest Road 118, and continue about three miles to the Casto Canyon parking lot. For part of the way, the trail is shared with ATVs, but then the bike trail splits off to the right. The usual turnaround point is at Sanford Road.

This ride can be linked with other trails to form a 17-mile one-way test of biking skills and endurance, with the route starting and ending along Highway 12. If you don't have a shuttle vehicle at each of the trailheads, you'll need to pedal back another eight miles along the paved roadside trail to retrieve your vehicle. Start at Tom Best Road, just east of Red Canyon. You'll climb through forest, turning onto Berry Spring Creek Road and then Cabin Hollow Road. Once the trail heads into Casto Canyon, you'll have five downhill miles of wonderful red-rock scenery. When you reach the Casto Canyon trailhead, you can choose to return to Highway 12 or pedal out to U.S. 89 and Panguitch. Much of the trail is strenuous, and you must take water along because there's no source along the way. There are several side trails you could use to make this into a shorter ride; stop by the Red Canyon Visitor Center for more information.

Tunnel Trail

- Distance: 0.8 miles round-trip
- Duration: 1 hour
- Elevation change: 300 feet
- Effort: moderate
- Trailhead: Highway 12 pullout, just west of the tunnels

The Tunnel Trail ascends to fine views of the canyon and the two highway tunnels. The trail crosses a streambed and then climbs a ridge to access excellent views.

🄲 Red Canyon Bike Trails

A rather wonderful paved bike trail parallels Highway 12 for five miles through Red Canyon. Parking lots are located at either end of the trail, at the Thunder Mountain Trailhead and Coyote Hollow Road.

True mountain bikers will eschew the pavement and head to **Casto Canyon Trail,** a 5.5-mile one-way trail that winds through a variety of red-rock formations and forest. This ride starts west of the visitors center, about

Campground

Red Canyon Campground (Hwy. 12, 435/676-9300, www.fs.fed.us/r4/dixie, late May-late Sept., $12) is located at 7,400 feet and has 37 first-come, first-served sites. Drinking water and showers ($2) are available.

BRYCE MUSEUM AND WILDLIFE ADVENTURE

A museum and natural history complex, Bryce Museum and Wildlife Adventure (1945 W. Hwy. 12, 435/834-5555, www.brycewildlifeadventure.com, 9am-7pm daily Apr. 1-Nov. 15, $8) is a wildlife showcase housed in a large building just west of the turnoff to Bryce

Canyon. This taxidermy collection depicts more than 800 animals from around the world displayed in dioramas resembling their natural habitats. It's actually quite well done, and kids seem to love it. There's also a good collection of Native American artifacts and a beautiful butterfly display. You can also rent ATVs and mountain bikes here.

CEDAR BREAKS NATIONAL MONUMENT

If you're driving between Zion and Bryce National Parks, consider stopping at Cedar Breaks. But take note: This is high country, and the road is closed mid-October–late May.

Cedar Breaks National Monument (www. nps.gov/cebr, $4) is much like Bryce Canyon, but it's on a different high plateau and lacks the crowds that flock to Bryce. Here on the west edge of the Markagunt Plateau, a giant amphitheater 2,500 feet deep and more than three miles across has been eroded into the stone. A fairyland of forms and colors appears below the rim. Ridges and pinnacles extend like buttresses from the steep cliffs. Traces of iron, manganese, and other minerals have tinted the normally white limestone a rainbow of warm hues. The intense colors blaze during sunsets and glow even on cloudy days. Rock layers look much like those at Bryce Canyon National Park, but here they're 2,000 feet higher. Elevations range from 10,662 feet at the rim's highest point to 8,100 feet at Ashdown Creek. Cottony patches of clouds often drift above the craggy landscape. In the distance, beyond the amphitheater, are Cedar City and the desert's valleys and ranges. Dense forests broken by large alpine meadows cover the rolling plateau country away from the rim. More than 150 species of wildflowers brighten the meadows during summer; the colorful display peaks during the last two weeks of July, when the Annual Wildflower Festival (435/586-9451, www.nps.gov/cebr) takes place.

Two easy trails near the rim provide an added appreciation of the geology and forests. Allow extra time on foot—walking can be tiring at high elevations. Regulations prohibit pets on the trails.

A five-mile scenic drive leads past four spectacular overlooks, each with a different perspective. Avoid overlooks and other exposed areas during thunderstorms, which are common on summer afternoons. Heavy snows close the road for much of the year. You can drive in only from about late May, sometimes later, until the first big snowstorm of autumn, usually in October. Winter visitors can ski, snowshoe, or travel by snowmobile (only on unplowed roads) from Brian Head (2 miles north of the monument) or Highway 14 (2.5 miles south).

Cedar Breaks National Monument is 24 miles east of Cedar City, 17 miles south of Parowan, 30 miles southwest of Panguitch, and 27 miles northwest of Long Valley Junction (Hwy. 14 and U.S. 89).

Visitors Center

A log cabin visitors center (435/586-0787 summer, 435/586-0787 winter, www.nps.gov/cebr, 9am–6pm daily June 5–mid-Oct.) includes exhibits, an information desk, and a bookstore. The exhibits provide a good introduction to the Markagunt Plateau and identify local rocks, wildflowers, trees, animals, and birds. Staff members offer nature walks, geology talks, and campfire programs; see the schedules posted in the visitors center and at the campground. The Point Supreme Overlook is located west of the visitors center. The entrance fee ($4 per vehicle) is collected near the visitors center; there's no charge if you're just driving through the monument without stopping.

Spectra Point/Ramparts Trail

- Distance: 4 miles round-trip
- Duration: 2 hours
- Elevation change: 400 feet

BRYCE CANYON

© BILL MCRAE

Lose the crowds at Cedar Breaks National Monument.

- Effort: moderate-strenuous
- Trailhead: visitors center

The Spectra Point/Ramparts Trail begins at the visitors center, then follows the rim along the south edge of the amphitheater to an overlook. Hikers who are short on time or feeling the effects of the 10,000-foot elevation can cut the distance in half by stopping after one mile at Spectra Point, where weather-beaten bristlecone pines grow. The trail's end is marked by an overlook.

Alpine Pond Trail

- Distance: 2 miles round-trip
- Duration: 1 hour
- Elevation change: 20 feet
- Effort: easy
- Trailhead: visitors center

The Alpine Pond Trail drops below the rim into one of the few densely wooded areas of the amphitheater. The trail winds through enchanting forests of aspen, subalpine fir, and Engelmann spruce. You can cut the hiking distance in half

with a car shuttle between the two trailheads or by taking a connector trail that joins the upper and lower parts of the loop near Alpine Pond. Begin from either Chessmen Ridge Overlook or the trailhead pullout 1.1 miles farther north. A trail guide ($1) is available at the start or at the visitors center.

Accommodations and Food

Point Supreme Campground (mid-June-late Sept., $14), east of the visitors center, offers 28 first-come, first-served sites with water. If you plan to visit in June or September, it's best to call ahead to check that it's open; in some years the season is short. There's a picnic area near the campground.

The nearest accommodations and restaurants are two miles north in Brian Head, where **Cedar Breaks Lodge** (223 Hunter Ridge Rd., Brian Head, 435/677-3000 or 888/282-3327, www.cedarbreakslodge.com, $94-109 summer; $120-139 winter) has fairly plush guest rooms, a day spa, and good deals during the summer (Brian Head is busiest during the ski season).

Tropic

Mormon pioneer Ebenezer Bryce homesteaded near the town site of Tropic in 1875, but the work of scratching a living from the rugged land became too difficult. He is remembered as saying of the area, "Well, it's a hell of a place to lose a cow." He left five years later for more promising land in Arizona. The name of the park commemorates his efforts. Other pioneers settled six villages near the upper Paria River between 1876 and 1891. The towns of Tropic, Cannonville, and Henrieville still survive.

SIGHTS

A **log cabin** built by Ebenezer Bryce has been moved to a site beside the Bryce Pioneer Village Motel (80 S. Main St.); ask to see the cabin's small collection of pioneer and Native American artifacts. There is a **visitor** **information booth** (11am-7pm daily early May-late Oct.) in the center of town.

ACCOMMODATIONS

Travelers think of Tropic primarily for its cache of motels lining Main Street (Hwy. 12), but several pleasant B&Bs also grace the town.

$50-100

At the **Bryce Canyon Inn** (21 N. Main St., 435/679-8502 or 800/592-1468, www.bryce-canyoninn.com, Mar.-Oct., $70 motel rooms, $99 cabins), the tidy cabins are nicely furnished and are one of the more appealing options in the Bryce neighborhood. The economy motel rooms are small but clean and a good deal.

Up on a bluff on the outskirts of town, the **Buffalo Sage B&B** (980 N. Hwy. 12,

Bryce Valley, east of the park, is visible from the town of Tropic.

© PAUL LEVY

435/679-8443 or 866/232-5711, www.buffalo-sage.com, $80) has great views and guest rooms decorated in an upscale Southwestern style.

America's Best Value Bryce Valley Inn (199 N. Hwy. 12, 435/679-8811 or 800/442-1890, www.brycevalleyinn.com, $68-105) has conventional motel rooms in an attractive wood-fronted Western-style motel with an adjoining restaurant. Pets are permitted, but an extra fee is charged.

$100-150

One of the most pleasant places to stay in Tropic is in the **Bryce Country Cabins** (320 N. Hwy. 12, 435/679-8643 or 888/679-8643, www.brycecountrycabins.com, $99-139). The cabins overlook a meadow, and each has a private bath.

At the other end of town, the **Bullberry Inn B&B** (412 S. Hwy 12, 435/679-8820 or 800/249-8126, www.bullberryinn.com, from $105) has wraparound porches, and the guest rooms have private baths and rustic-style pine furniture.

At **Bryce Canyon Livery B&B** (660 W. 50 S., 435/679-8780 or 888/889-8910, www.brycecanyonbandb.com, $115) every guest room has a private bath; several have balconies with views of Bryce Canyon.

Over $150

The **[** **Stone Canyon Inn** (435/679-8611 or 866/489-4680, www.stonecanyoninn.com, $145-225 rooms, $275-330 cottages), just west of Tropic with views of Bryce, is a strikingly handsome modern structure with comfortable

uncluttered rooms, all with private baths. Stone Canyon also has two-bedroom guest cabins that can be divided into smaller units. The owners are happy to point you toward their favorite trails.

Campgrounds

In town, you can find tent ($12) and RV ($30) camping at **Bryce Pioneer Village Motel** (80 S. Main St., 435/679-8546 or 800/222-0381, www.brycepioneervillage.com) in addition to guest rooms and cabins ($70-95). Head east to Cannonville for **Cannonville/ Bryce Valley KOA** (175 N. Red Rock Dr., Cannonville, 435/679-8988 or 888/562-4710, www.koa.com, $30-35), or continue south from Cannonville to **Kodachrome Basin State Park** (801/322-3770 or 800/322-3770, www.reserveamerica.com, $16).

FOOD

There are a few dining options in town. The best place to start your search for a meal is **Clarke's** (141 N. Main St., 435/679-8633, 7am-10pm daily, $7-22), an all-around institution that, in addition to selling groceries, serves Mexican food, pasta, pizza, ice cream, and steaks from a variety of venues within a complex that's essentially the town center.

GETTING THERE

Tropic is 11 miles east of Bryce Canyon National Park on Highway 12, and it is visible from many of the park's viewpoints.

Panguitch

Pioneers arrived here in 1864, but the Ute people forced them to evacuate just two years later. A second attempt by settlers in 1871 succeeded, and Panguitch (the name is from the Paiute word for "big fish") is now the largest town in the area.

Panguitch is one of the more pleasant towns in this part of Utah, and it has an abundance of reasonably priced motels, plus a couple of good places to eat. It's a good stopover on the road between Zion and Bryce National Parks.

SIGHTS

The early-20th-century commercial buildings downtown have some of their original facades. On side streets you can see sturdy brick houses built by the early settlers. Stop by the **Daughters of Utah Pioneers Museum** (125 E. Center St., 4pm-8pm Mon.-Sat. Memorial Day-Labor Day, free) in the old bishop's storehouse to see historic exhibits about Panguitch. During the off-season, the museum is open by appointment; phone numbers of volunteers are on the door.

The **city park** on the north edge of town has picnic tables, a playground, tennis courts, and a visitor information cabin. A **swimming pool** (250 E. Center St., 435/676-2259) is by the high school.

Travelers in the area during the second weekend in June should try to swing by for the annual **Quilt Walk,** an all-out festival with historic home tours, quilting classes, and lots of food. The Quilt Walk commemorates a group of seven pioneers who trudged through snow to bring food back to starving townspeople—they spread quilts on the deep, soft snow and walked on them in order not to sink.

ACCOMMODATIONS
$50-100

Panguitch is the best place in greater Bryce Canyon to find an affordable motel

room—there are more than a dozen older motor court lodgings, most very nicely maintained. Of these, the **Color Country Motel** (526 N. Main St., 435/676-2386 or 800/225-6518, www.colorcountrymotel.com, $69-89) is one of the most attractive, with an outdoor pool and clean well-furnished guest rooms.

The **Adobe Sands** (390 N. Main St., 435/676-8874 or 800/497-9261, www.adobesandsmotel.com, May-Oct., $55-70) is pet friendly, and it offers clean basic guest rooms at budget prices.

Another good midrange pick is the **Canyon Lodge** (210 N. Main St., 435/676-8292 or 800/440-8292, www.color-country.net/~cache, $69-89) with clean basic guest rooms plus a three-bed suite.

Along U.S. 89, the **New Western Motel** (180 E. Center St., 435/676-8876 or 800/528-1234, http://newbrycewesterninn.com, $74-99) has a swimming pool and a hot tub plus laundry facilities. Some guest rooms are in an older building, but all guest rooms have recently been refurbished.

$100-150

Stay in one of the town's landmark red-brick homes: the tidy ◖ **Red Brick Inn of Panguitch B&B** (161 N. 100 W., 435/676-2141 or 866/733-2745, www.redbrickinnutah.com, $119) has distinctive barnlike architecture and cozy bedrooms, including two adjoining bedrooms that share a bath—perfect for families. If you like B&Bs, this is definitely the best place in town to stay.

Campgrounds

Hitch-N-Post Campground (420 N. Main St., 435/676-2436, www.hitchnpostrv.com, year-round) offers spaces for tents ($15) and RVs ($27) and has showers and a laundry

© BILL MCRAE

Panguitch makes the most of its Old West facades.

room. The **Big Fish KOA Campground** (555 S. Main St., 435/676-2225, mid-Apr.-mid-Oct., from $25 tents, $36 RVs, $49 cabins) on the road to Panguitch Lake includes a pool, a recreation room, laundry, and showers. The closest public campground is in **Red Canyon** (Hwy. 12, 435/676-9300, www.fs.fed.us/r4/dixie, $12).

FOOD

The culinary high point of a visit to Panguitch will likely be the mesquite-grilled meats at **Cowboy's Smokehouse Bar-B-Q** (95 N. Main St., 435/676-8030, 6:30pm-9pm Mon.-Sat. mid-Mar.-mid-Oct., $10-18), where live country music and Western atmosphere are regular features. The **Flying M Restaurant** (580 N. Main St., 435/676-8008, 7am-9pm daily, $8-18) is a favorite for its hearty breakfasts and standard American comfort-food dinners, including homemade turkey potpies.

INFORMATION AND SERVICES

Contact the **Bryce Canyon Country** (55 S. Main St., 435/676-1160 or 800/444-6689, www.brycecanyoncountry.com) for information on Panguitch and the nearby area. The **Powell Ranger District Office** (225 E. Center St., 435/676-9300, 8am-4:30pm Mon.-Fri.) of the Dixie National Forest has information on campgrounds, hiking trails, fishing, and scenic drives in the forest and canyons surrounding Bryce Canyon National Park.

There is a **post office** (65 N. 100 W.), and **Garfield Memorial Hospital** (200 N. 400 E., hospital 435/676-8811, clinic 435/676-8842) is the main hospital in this part of the state.

GETTING THERE

Panguitch is on U.S. 89, seven miles north of Bryce Junction (Hwy. 12 and U.S. 89). From Bryce Junction, it is 11 miles east on Highway 12 to Bryce Canyon National Park.

GRAND STAIRCASE-ESCALANTE NATIONAL MONUMENT

The 1.9-million-acre Grand Staircase-Escalante National Monument (GSENM) contains a vast and wonderfully scenic collection of slickrock canyon lands and desert, prehistoric village sites, Old West ranch land, arid plateaus, and miles of back roads linking stone arches, mesas, and abstract rock formations. The monument even preserves a historic movie set (think vintage Westerns).

The monument contains essentially three separate districts: On the eastern third are the narrow wilderness canyons of the Escalante River and its tributaries. In the center of the monument is a vast swath of arid rangeland and canyons called the Kaiparowits Plateau, with few developed destinations. The western third of the monument edges up against the Gray, White, and Pink Cliffs of the Grand Staircase. These thinly treed uplands are laced with former Forest Service roads. The GSENM is the largest land grouping designated as a national monument in the Lower 48.

There's little dispute that the Escalante canyons are the primary reason people visit the monument. The river and its tributaries cut deep and winding slot canyons through massive slickrock formations, and hiking these canyon bottoms is an extremely popular adventure. A multiday trek is a rite of passage for many devoted hikers, but you don't have to be a hardened backcountry trekker to enjoy this landscape: Two backcountry roads wind through the area, and some day hikes are possible.

© PAUL LEVY

HIGHLIGHTS

◖ Kodachrome Basin State Park: Strange-looking rock pillars or "sand pipes" are the attraction at this state park on the edge of the Grand Staircase-Escalante National Monument. Hiking trails and a campground make this a good base for exploring Cottonwood Canyon Road south into the monument (page 97).

◖ Grosvenor Arch: In a remote yet drivable location off Cottonwood Canyon Road is the magnificent Grosvenor Arch, which is actually two sandstone arches. Photographers, including those from a *National Geographic* expedition in the 1940s, have continually been drawn to it (page 98).

◖ Anasazi State Park: In addition to the good indoor exhibits at this park's museum, there's an excavated Anasazi village out back displaying a wide range of Anasazi building styles. This is an excellent opportunity to learn about the Anasazi (page 103).

◖ Burr Trail Road: From its start in Boulder, through the astounding Long Canyon, to views of the Waterpocket Fold, the Circle Cliffs, and distant mountains, Burr Trail Road is a treat to drive. Don't expect a fast trip; if the weather has been wet, inquire about the condition of the unpaved section (page 104).

◖ Lower Calf Creek Falls: Easy enough for families, accessible with a regular car, and offering a different highlight every 0.5 miles or so, this hike is definitely worth taking. Expect to see desert varnish, beaver ponds, Native American ruins, pictographs, and the misty 126-foot-high Lower Calf Creek Falls (page 115).

◖ Dry Fork of Coyote Gulch: To explore the enchanting slot canyons of this area, it's necessary to drive 26 miles along the bumpy dirt Hole-in-the-Rock Road. If you and your vehicle are up for such a drive, don't miss it. The slot canyons are easy enough for reasonably fit people to explore, and they'll give you a taste of canyoneering (page 117).

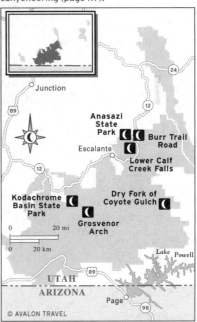

LOOK FOR ◖ TO FIND RECOMMENDED SIGHTS, ACTIVITIES, DINING, AND LODGING.

The other districts offer less-well-defined opportunities for adventure. Backcountry drivers and long-distance mountain bikers will find mile after mile of desert and canyon to explore. Grosvenor Arch, with double windows, is a popular back-road destination. At the southern edge of the park, along the Arizona border, is another rugged canyon system that's popular with long-distance hikers. The Paria River Canyon is even more remote than the Escalante, and hiking these slot canyons requires experience and preparation.

PLANNING YOUR TIME

If you only have one day, plan to drive stunning Highway 12. The Lower Calf Creek Falls hike begins right off the highway between Escalante and Boulder, and hiking it is a great way to spend half a day.

If you have an additional day or two, it makes sense to base yourself either in Escalante (convenient camping and moderately priced accommodations) or in Boulder (where it's possible to sleep and eat in luxury). Spend your second day here exploring Hole-in-the-Rock Road, where you can hike slot canyons in the Dry Fork of Coyote Gulch and explore Devils Garden. It's possible to stay in this area of the monument for several days, either backpacking along the Escalante River or exploring its various canyons as day hikes. If you're at all up to backpacking, it's only a one-nighter to hike from the town of Escalante along the river to the river's highway crossing.

If you have more time, drive between the Kanab area and Cannonville on Cottonwood Canyon Road (be sure to check on road conditions before heading out). Stop and walk up through the Cottonwood Narrows, and at the north end of the road, visit Grosvenor Arch and Kodachrome State Park. If you want to make a loop drive, return on the Johnson Canyon and Skutumpah Roads, with a hike along Lick Wash.

GRAND STAIRCASE

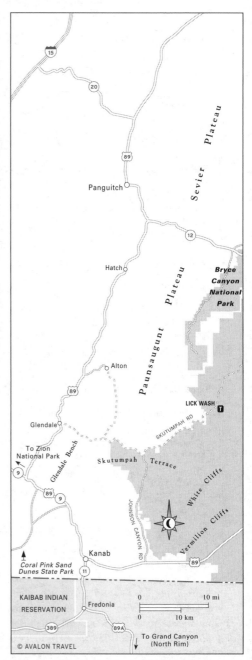

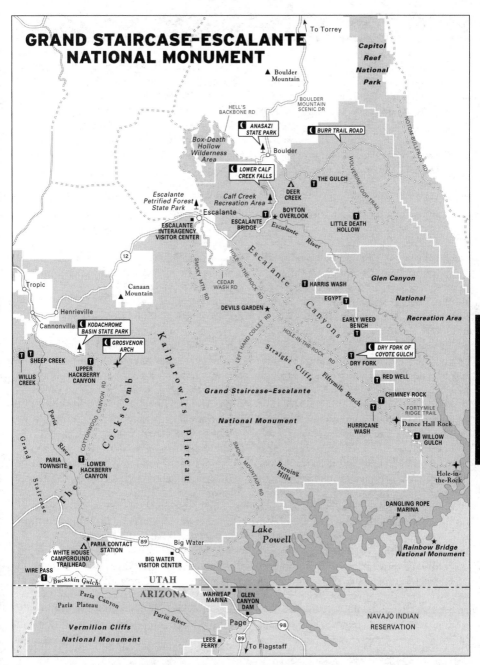

GRAND STAIRCASE-ESCALANTE NATIONAL MONUMENT

To Torrey

Capitol Reef National Park

Boulder Mountain

HELL'S BACKBONE RD

BOULDER MOUNTAIN SCENIC DR

ANASAZI STATE PARK

BURR TRAIL ROAD

Box-Death Hollow Wilderness Area

Boulder

LOWER CALF CREEK FALLS

Calf Creek Recreation Area

DEER CREEK

THE GULCH

WOLVERINE LOOP TRAIL

Escalante Petrified Forest State Park

Escalante

ESCALANTE BRIDGE

BOYTON OVERLOOK

LITTLE DEATH HOLLOW

ESCALANTE INTERAGENCY VISITOR CENTER

Escalante River

12

SMOKY MTN RD

CEDAR WASH RD

HOLE-IN-THE-ROCK RD

Escalante Canyons

HARRIS WASH

Glen Canyon

Tropic

Canaan Mountain

DEVILS GARDEN

EGYPT

National

EARLY WEED BENCH

Recreation Area

Henrieville

Cannonville

KODACHROME BASIN STATE PARK

LEFT HAND COLLET RD

HOLE-IN-THE-ROCK RD

DRY FORK OF COYOTE GULCH

DRY FORK

GROSVENOR ARCH

Straight Cliffs

RED WELL

SHEEP CREEK

UPPER HACKBERRY CANYON

Kaiparowits Plateau

Fiftymile Bench

CHIMNEY ROCK

FORTYMILE RIDGE TRAIL

WILLIS CREEK

The Cockscomb

COTTONWOOD CANYON RD

Grand Staircase-Escalante

HURRICANE WASH

Dance Hall Rock

Paria River

National Monument

WILLOW GULCH

PARIA TOWNSITE

LOWER HACKBERRY CANYON

SMOKY MOUNTAIN RD

Burning Hills

Hole-in-the-Rock

The Grand Staircase

DANGLING ROPE MARINA

Lake Powell

Rainbow Bridge National Monument

PARIA CONTACT STATION

89

Big Water

WHITE HOUSE CAMPGROUND/ TRAILHEAD

BIG WATER VISITOR CENTER

WIRE PASS

Buckskin Gulch

UTAH

ARIZONA

WAHWEAP MARINA

GLEN CANYON DAM

NAVAJO INDIAN RESERVATION

Paria Canyon

Paria Plateau

Paria River

Page

98

Vermilion Cliffs National Monument

LEES FERRY

89

To Flagstaff

GRAND STAIRCASE

Exploring the Park

There is no entrance fee to visit Grand Staircase-Escalante National Monument (435/644-4600, www.ut.blm.gov/monument). Free permits are required for all overnight backcountry camping or backpacking. There is a fee to camp in the monument's three developed campgrounds.

Hikers in the Paria Wilderness area, which includes Paria Canyon and Coyote Buttes, are required to buy a permit, as are hikers at the Calf Creek Recreation Area.

It's best to have a travel strategy when visiting this huge national monument. Just as important, especially for a visit of more than a couple of days, is a vehicle that can take on some rugged roads. (A Subaru wagon proved perfectly adequate in dry weather, but when the clay was wet and muddy, the back roads were virtually impassable in all but 4WD vehicles with significantly higher clearance than a station wagon.)

Only two paved roads pass through the monument, both on a west-east trajectory. Highway 12, on the northern boundary of the park, links Bryce Canyon and Capitol Reef National Parks with access to the Escalante canyons. This is one of the most scenic roads in Utah—in fact, *Car and Driver* magazine rates this route as one of the 10 most scenic in the United States. Its innumerable vistas and geologic curiosities will keep you on the edge of your seat. U.S. 89, which runs along the southern edge of the monument between Kanab and Lake Powell, is no scenery slouch either. It is also the access road for the north rim of the Grand Canyon in Arizona.

Three fair-weather dirt roads, each with a network of side roads and trails, cut through the rugged heart of the monument, linking the two paved roads. Before heading out on these back roads, check with the visitors center for conditions; high-clearance vehicles are recommended.

VISITORS CENTERS

The **administrative headquarters** of the GSENM (669 S. U.S. 89A, Kanab, 435/644-1200, www.ut.blm.gov/monument, 8am-4:30pm Mon.-Fri.) is about 15 miles from the southwestern edge of the monument in Kanab, but the regional visitors centers, listed below, are the best places for practical travel information.

Escalante Interagency Visitor Center (755 W. Main St., Escalante, 435/826-5499, 8am-4:30pm daily mid-Mar.-mid-Nov., 8am-4:30pm Mon.-Fri. mid-Nov.-mid-Mar.) is housed in a sprawling building at the west end of the town of Escalante. Staff are very knowledgeable and helpful, and exhibits focus on the monument's ecology and biological diversity.

Kanab Visitor Center (745 E. U.S. 89, Kanab, 435/644-1300, 8am-4:30pm daily) is the place to stop if you're planning to drive Cottonwood or Johnson Canyon and Skutumpah Roads from the south. Staff can give you updates on the road conditions and suggest driving and hiking strategies. Exhibits at this visitors center concentrate on geology and archaeology.

Cannonville Visitor Center (10 Center St., Cannonville, 435/826-5640, 8am-4:30pm daily mid-Mar.-mid-Nov.) is an attractive building at the north end of Cottonwood and Johnson Canyon-Skutumpah Roads. Even if the office is closed, stop by to look at the outdoor exhibits, which depict the different cultures that have lived in the area.

Big Water Visitor Center (100 Upper Revolution Way, Big Water, 435/675-3200, 9am-5:30pm daily Apr.-Oct., 8am-4:30pm daily Nov.-Mar.), a spiral-shaped building designed to resemble an ammonite, is home to a small but distinctive collection of dinosaur bones and a wild mural depicting

THE LIFE AND LANDSCAPE OF GRAND STAIRCASE-ESCALANTE

GEOLOGY

About 300 million years ago, this land was at times a great Sahara-like desert, with dunes towering hundreds of feet high. At other times the land sank below sea level and was covered by water. Thick layers of sediment built up, one on top of the next. During the last 50 million years, powerful forces within the earth slowly pushed the entire region one mile upward. The ancestral Colorado River began to carve the deep gorges seen today at the Grand Canyon. In turn, the tributaries of the Colorado, such as the Escalante River, were trenched deeper and deeper in order to drain their watershed.

The most characteristic rocks in the monument are the ancient dunes turned to stone, called slickrock. They make up many of the sheer canyon cliffs, arches, and spires of the region. Delicate cross-bedded lines of the former dunes add grace to these features. Forces within the restless plateau have also buckled and folded rock layers into great reefs as long as 100 miles. Weathering then carved them into rainbow-hued rock monuments. The aptly named **Cockscomb,** visible from Cottonwood Canyon Road, which cuts through the center of the monument, is an example of these massive rock wrinkles.

FLORA AND FAUNA

The dry conditions and thin or nonexistent soils limit both plantlife and wildlife in the Escalante region. Annual plants simply wait for a wet year before quickly flowering and spreading their seeds. Piñon pines, junipers, and other plants often adapt by growing in rock cracks that concentrate moisture and nutrients. Small mammals such as mice, wood rats, rock squirrels, and chipmunks find food and shelter in these outposts of vegetation. Even meager soils permit the growth of hardy shrubs like blackbrush, greasewood, sagebrush, rabbitbrush, and Mormon tea. Prickly pear and other types of cacti also do well in the desert.

Perhaps the most unusual plant communities are the cryptobiotic crusts found on sandy soils. Mosses, lichens, fungi, algae, and diatoms live together in a gray-green or black layer up to several inches thick. Microclimates surrounding canyon seeps and springs provide a haven for hanging gardens of grasses, ferns, orchids, columbines, mosses, and other water-loving plants. River and stream banks have their own vegetation, including river willows, cattails, tamarisks, and cottonwoods.

Wildlife that you might see in the semiarid desert are mule deer, desert bighorn sheep, pronghorns, coyotes, bobcats, foxes, skunks, porcupines, and many species of rodents. Ravens, eagles, hawks, owls, falcons, magpies, and smaller birds fly overhead. Watch out for poisonous rattlesnakes and scorpions, although these shy creatures won't attack unless provoked.

GRAND STAIRCASE

late-Cretaceous life in the area. Stop here to learn about local paleontology.

Anasazi State Park (460 N. Hwy. 12, Boulder, 435/335-7382, www.stateparks.utah. gov, 9am-5pm daily mid-Mar.-mid-Nov., $5) has a ranger on duty at an information desk inside the museum. The museum is worth a visit, so don't be stingy with your five bucks!

Paria Contact Station (U.S. 89, 44 miles east of Kanab, no phone, 9am-3pm daily Mar. 15-Nov. 15) is a small visitors center, but it's an important stop for anyone planning to hike Paria Canyon.

TOURS

For guided tours of the Escalante canyons, contact **Utah Canyons Outback Adventures** (325 W. Main St., Escalante, 435/826-4967, www. utahcanyons.com). Trips focus on day hikes (full-day from $110), with popular trips going to slot canyons and scenic Phipps Arch. It also offers hiker shuttles and runs a good gear shop

Escalante Interagency Visitor Center, in the town of Escalante, is a good place to plan trips into the monument.

© BILL MCRAE

GRAND STAIRCASE

in the salmon-colored building in downtown Escalante.

The guides at **Excursions of Escalante** (125 E. Main St., Escalante, 800/839-7567, www.excursionsofescalante.com) lead trips into more remote canyons, including some that require some technical canyoneering to explore, and some multiday backpacking trips. Straightforward hiking trips (from $130) are also offered, either cross-country (easiest) or in slot canyons (more challenging). A day of basic canyoneering ($150) includes instruction.

Many local outfitters use pack animals. With **Escape Goats** (435/826-4652, www.utahpackgoats.com), you can hike with goats (and a friendly, goat-loving human guide) into canyons. This is a good bet for families with kids. A variety of hikes are available; full-day hikes start at $80 pp.

Hike into the canyon backcountry (let horses

carry your gear) and spend a few days exploring with **Escalante Canyon Outfitters** (435/335-7311 or 888/326-4453, www.ecohike.com). Five-day trips run about $1,600.

Red Rock 'n Llamas (435/559-7325 or 877/955-2627, www.redrocknllamas.com) offers a variety of fully outfitted hiking adventures in the Escalante area. Llamas will carry most of the gear, leaving you to explore in comfort. Most trips are for 3-4 nights and cost $900-1,000.

Boulder-based **Earth Tours** (435/691-1241, www.earth-tours.com) offers full-day (from $100 pp) to six-day (price varies with number of guests) tours of the area. Most trips are led by a geologist with a wide-ranging interest in natural history.

ALONG HIGHWAY 12

Highway 12 runs west-east from Bryce Canyon National Park and Tropic along the north edge of the monument to the towns of Escalante and Boulder. Stop at the **Cannonville Visitor Center** (10 Center St., Cannonville, 435/826-5640, 8am-4:30pm daily mid-Mar.-mid-Nov.) for information about back-road conditions and hikes in this part of the monument. Two backcountry roads depart from Cannonville and lead to remote corners of the monument.

Johnson Canyon-Skutumpah Road

The northern end of the Johnson Canyon-Skutumpah Road (46 miles one-way) is in Cannonville, and its southern terminus is at U.S. 89, just east of Kanab. From the northernmost stretch of this road, Bryce Canyon rises to the west; about six miles from the southern end and off to the east on private land (look from the road but don't trespass) is the set from the TV show *Gunsmoke*.

The unpaved portions of the road are usually in good condition, except after rains, when the bentonite soils that make up the roadbed turn to goo. In good weather, cars can usually make the journey. The road follows the Pink and White Cliff terraces of the Grand Staircase, with access to some excellent and

DOWN THE GRAND STAIRCASE

The broad tilted terraces of the Grand Staircase step down through time. Some 200 million years of sedimentation are visible here, starting with pink in the north, then traveling through gray, white, and vermilion cliffs.

A freshwater lake deposited the limey siltstones that became the Pink Cliffs (see these same rocks in Bryce Canyon National Park). This layer formed on top of the shale of the Gray Cliffs, deposited when an ocean covered the area; the Gray Cliffs step is rich with marine fossils and coal, formed from ancient wetland plants. The next older step, the White Cliffs, is composed of Navajo sandstone, one of the main rocks seen in Zion National Park. The bottom step, the bright Vermilion Cliffs, visible around Kanab, is also sandstone, laden with fossils of fish and dinosaurs. At the base of the whole staircase, the striped brick-colored Chinle badlands form the bed for the Paria River.

These sandstone steps are stacked like pancakes. As in much of the Colorado Plateau region, erosion by water and wind produces amazing geological displays, including the intricate network of deep canyons, uplifted plateaus, sheer cliffs, beautiful sandstone arches and natural bridges, water pockets, sandstone monoliths, pedestals and balanced rocks, domes, and buttes.

comparatively undersubscribed hiking trails. Several steep slot canyons make for excellent canyoneering. The lower 16 miles of Johnson Canyon Road are paved.

Scenic Back Way: Cottonwood Canyon Road

The 46-mile Cottonwood Canyon Road also connects Cannonville with U.S. 89, but it passes through quite different terrain and landscapes. One of the most scenic backcountry routes in the monument, Cottonwood Canyon Road not only offers access to dramatic Grosvenor Arch; it also passes along the Cockscomb, a soaring buckle of rock that divides the Grand Staircase and the Kaiparowits Plateau. Cottonwood Creek, which this road parallels, is a normally dry streambed that cuts through the angular rock beds of the Cockscomb. Several excellent hikes lead into the canyons and narrows, where the Paria River, Hackberry Canyon, and Cottonwood Creek all meet, about 20 miles south of Cannonville.

Check at the Cannonville or Big Water Visitor Center for information about road conditions. Although the road is sometimes passable for cars, several road crossings are susceptible to washouts after rainstorms, and the northern portion is impassable even to 4WD vehicles when wet because of the extremely unctuous nature of the roadbed. Check conditions before setting out if you plan to go beyond Grosvenor Arch.

◖ Kodachrome Basin State Park

Visitors come to Kodachrome Basin State Park (435/679-8562, www.stateparks.utah.gov, 6am-10pm daily, $6), located in a basin southeast of Bryce, to see not only colorful cliffs but also strange-looking rock pillars that occur nowhere else in the world. Sixty-seven rock pillars (here called "sand pipes") found in and near the park range in height from 6 feet to nearly 170 feet. One theory of their origin is that earthquakes caused sediments deep underground to be churned up by water under high pressure. The particles of calcite, quartz, feldspar, and clay in the sand pipes came from underlying rock formations, and the pipes appeared when the surrounding rock eroded away. Most of the other rocks visible in the park are Entrada sandstone: The lower orange layer is the Gunsight Butte Member, and the white layer with orange bands is the Cannonville Member.

Signs name some of the rock features. "Big

© BILL MCRAE

sandstone spires, called "pipes," at Kodachrome Basin State Park

Stoney," the phallus-shaped sand pipe overlooking the campground, is so explicit that it doesn't need a sign. The article "Motoring into Escalante Land" by Jack Breed in the September 1949 *National Geographic* magazine brought attention to the scenery and earned the area the name "Kodachrome Flat," for the then-experimental Kodak film used by the expedition. The state park is a worthwhile stop, both as a day trip to see the geology and as a pleasant spot to camp. The park also offers several good half-day hiking trails and a host of shorter hikes.

PRACTICALITIES

Supplies and accommodations are available in the park at the **Kodachrome General Store,** which also operates **Red Stone Cabins** (435/679-8536, www.redstonecabins.com, summer high season $99), six well-maintained log structures in a lovely setting. All have private baths and efficiency kitchens.

The state park's **campground** (435/679-8562, reservations 800/322-3770 or www.reserveamerica.com, year-round, $16) is in a natural amphitheater at an elevation of 5,800 feet. It has restrooms, showers, and a dump station. During the winter, restrooms and showers may close, but pit toilets are available. The campground usually has space except on summer holidays.

GETTING THERE

To reach the park, take Highway 12 south to Cannonville and follow the signs for seven miles along paved Cottonwood Canyon Road. Adventurous drivers can also approach the park from U.S. 89 to the south via Cottonwood Canyon Road (35 miles) or Skutumpah Road through Bull Valley Gorge and Johnson Canyon (48 miles). These routes may be impassable in wet weather but are generally OK in dry weather for cars with good clearance.

Grosvenor Arch

Just one mile off Cottonwood Canyon Road, a side road leads to the magnificent Grosvenor Arch. It takes a bit of effort to get here (the 10-mile dirt road between the turnoff to Kodachrome Basin State Park and the arch can be bumpy and should be avoided in wet weather), so a visit to the arch can take on the qualities of a pilgrimage. There are actually two arches here, which is a rare occurrence for such erosion-formed arches. Their position, jutting like flying buttresses out of a soaring cliff, is also quite stunning. The larger of the two openings is 99 feet across. A 1949 National Geographic Society expedition named the double arch in honor of the society's president. From Highway 12, take the Cottonwood Canyon Road turnoff to Kodachrome Basin State Park. Continue for 10 miles to the Grosvenor Arch parking area. Alternatively, the turnoff is 29 miles north from U.S. 89.

© BILL MCRAE

Kodachrome Basin has one of the nicest campgrounds in the area.

Escalante Petrified Forest State Park

The pleasant Escalante Petrified Forest State Park (435/826-4466, www.stateparks.utah. gov, 7am-10pm daily summer, 8am-10pm daily winter, $6), just northwest of the town of Escalante, offers camping, boating, fishing, picnicking, hiking, a visitors center with displays of petrified wood and dinosaur bones, and a chance to see petrified wood along hiking trails. Rivers of 140 million years ago carried trees to the site of present-day Escalante and buried them in sand and gravel. Burial prevented decay as crystals of silicon dioxide gradually replaced the wood cells. Mineral impurities added a rainbow of colors to the trees as they turned to stone. Weathering has exposed this petrified wood and the water-worn pebbles and sand of the Morrison Formation.

For a look at some colorful petrified wood, follow the **Petrified Forest Trail** from the campground up a hillside wooded with piñon

pine and juniper. At the top of the 240-foot-high ridge, continue on a loop trail to the petrified wood; allow 45-60 minutes for the one-mile round-trip hike. The steep **Rainbow Loop Trail** (0.75 miles) branches off the Petrified Forest Trail to more areas of petrified wood.

The **campground** (reservations 800/322-3770, www.reserveamerica.com, year-round, $16) offers drinking water, flush toilets, showers, and RV hookups ($20). The adjacent 139-acre Wide Hollow Reservoir offers fishing, boating, and bird-watching. The park is 1.5 miles west of Escalante on Highway 12, then 0.7 miles north on a gravel road.

Town of Escalante

The town of Escalante, 38 miles east of Bryce Canyon and 23 miles south of Boulder, has a full range of services and is the headquarters for explorations of the Escalante River canyons. The **Escalante Interagency Visitor Center** (755 W. Main St., Escalante, 435/826-5499) provides information on local hikes and road conditions.

Smokey Mountain Road

From Escalante, it's 78 miles south to U.S. 89 at Big Water, just shy of Lake Powell, along Smokey Mountain Road. This road is rougher than other cross-monument roads. Be sure to check on conditions before setting out; a 4WD vehicle is required. As this route passes across the Kaiparowits Plateau, the landscape is bleak and arid. After that, the road drops precipitously down onto a bench where side roads lead through badlands to Lake Powell beaches. Big Water is 19 miles from Page, Arizona, and 57 miles from Kanab.

Hole-in-the-Rock Road

The building of this road by determined Mormons is an epic story of the colonization of the West. Church leaders organized the Hole-in-the-Rock Expedition to settle the wildlands around the San Juan River of southeastern

© PAUL LEVY

With its flying buttresses, Grosvenor Arch is one of the most distinctive of Utah's many arches.

GRAND STAIRCASE

Utah, believing that a Mormon presence would aid in ministering to the Native Americans there and prevent non-Mormons from moving in. In 1878 the Parowan Stake issued the first call for a colonizing mission to the San Juan, even before a site had been selected.

Preparations and surveys took place the following year as the 236 men, women, and children received their calls. Food, seed, farming and building tools, 200 horses, and more than 1,000 head of cattle were brought along. Planners ruled out lengthy routes through northern Arizona or eastern Utah in favor of a straight shot via Escalante that would cut the distance in half. The expedition set off in the fall of 1879, convinced that they were part of a divine mission.

Hints of the trouble to come filtered back from the group as they discovered the Colorado River crossing to be far more difficult than first believed. Lack of water sources along the

way added to their worries. From their start at Escalante, road building progressed rapidly for the first 50 miles, then slowly over rugged slickrock for the final six miles to Hole-in-the-Rock. A sheer 45-foot drop below this narrow notch was followed by almost one mile of extremely steep slickrock to the Colorado River. The route looked impossible, but three crews of workers armed with picks and blasting powder worked simultaneously to widen the notch and construct a precarious wagon road down to the river and up the cliffs on the other side.

The job took six weeks. Miraculously, all of the people, animals, and wagons made it down and were ferried across the Colorado River without serious incident. Canyons and other obstacles continued to block the way as the weary group pressed on. Only after six months of exhausting travel did they stop at the present-day site of Bluff on the San Juan River.

Today, on a journey from Escalante, you

© BILL MCRAE

Near the town of Escalante, the Escalante River begins to trench through a layer cake of colorful rock.

can experience a bit of the same adventure the pioneers knew. Except for scattered signs of ranching, the land remains unchanged. If the road is dry, vehicles with good clearance can drive to within a short distance of Hole-in-the-Rock. The rough conditions encountered past Dance Hall Rock require more clearance than most cars allow. Bring sufficient gas, food, and water for the entire 126-mile round-trip from Escalante; there are no services along this route.

SIGHTS

Metate Arch and other rock sculptures decorate **Devils Garden,** 12.5 miles down Hole-in-the-Rock Road. Turn west and continue 0.3 miles at the sign to the parking area, because you can't really see the "garden" from the road. Red and cream-colored sandstone formations sit atop pedestals or tilt at crazy angles. Delicate bedding lines run through the rocks. There are no trails or markers—just wander around as

you like. The Bureau of Land Management (BLM) has provided picnic tables, grills, and outhouses for day use. No overnight camping is permitted at Devils Garden.

Dance Hall Rock (38 miles down Hole-in-the-Rock Rd.) jumped to the fiddle music and lively steps of the expedition members in 1879. Its natural amphitheater has a relatively smooth floor and made a perfect gathering spot when the Hole-in-the-Rock group had to wait three weeks at nearby Fortymile Spring for road work to be completed ahead. Dance Hall Rock is an enjoyable place to explore and only a short walk from the parking area. Solution holes, left by water dissolving in the rock, pockmark the sandstone structure.

At road's end, 57 miles from Highway 12, continue on foot across slickrock to the notch and views of the blue waters of **Lake Powell** below. Rock slides have made the descent impossible for vehicles, but hikers can scramble down to the

A PIONEER ACCOUNT OF ESCALANTE TRAVEL

Mormon pioneer Elizabeth Morris Decker described the descent from Hole-in-the-Rock Road in a letter to her parents on February 22, 1880:

If you ever come this way, it will scare you to death to look down it. It is about a mile from the top down to the river and it is almost strait [sic] down, the cliffs on each side are five hundred feet high and there is just room enough for a wagon to go down. It nearly scared me to death. The first wagon I saw go down, they put the brake on and rough locked the hind wheels and had a big rope fastened to the wagon and about ten men holding back on it, and then they went down like they would smash everything. I'll never forget that day. When we was walking down Willie looked back and cried and asked me how we would get back home.

lake and back in about one hour. The elevation change is 600 feet. The 0.5-mile round-trip hike is strenuous. After a steep descent over boulders, look for steps of Uncle Ben's Dugway at the base of the notch. Below this point, the grade is gentler. Drill holes in the rock once held oak stakes against which logs, brush, and earth supported the outer wagon wheels. The inner wheels followed a narrow rut 4-6 inches deep. About two-thirds of the route down is now under water, although the most impressive road work can still be seen.

GETTING THERE

The turnoff from Highway 12 is five miles east of Escalante. In addition to rewarding you with scenic views, Hole-in-the-Rock Road passes many side drainages of the Escalante River to the east and some remote country of the Kaiparowits Plateau high above to the west. Staff at the **Escalante Interagency Visitor Center** (755 W. Main St., Escalante, 435/826-5499, 8am-4:30pm daily mid-Mar.-mid-Nov., 8am-4:30pm Mon.-Fri. mid-Nov.-mid-Mar.), just west of Escalante, can give current road conditions and suggest hikes.

Boynton Overlook and Hundred Hands Pictograph

Be sure to pull off Highway 12 at the Boynton Overlook (Hwy. 12, 14 miles east of Escalante, at the Escalante River Bridge) and scan the walls on the far side of the Escalante River for the Hundred Hands pictograph (binoculars help immensely). For a closer look, take a 30-minute hike up from the parking lot at the bottom of the hill at the Escalante River crossing. Rather than hike along the river, go up above the house (don't stray onto fenced-in private property), scramble up the face of the first cliff, and follow faint trails and rock cairns across the bench. It is easiest if you've located the pictographs first from the overlook. The Hundred Hands are high up on a cliff face that's larger than the one you scrambled up. Follow the cliff to the right, where pictographs of goats are lower on the wall.

Back down at river level, head downstream a few hundred yards and look up to the left to see Anasazi ruins, known as the Moki House.

Calf Creek Recreation Area

This stunning canyon and park at Calf Creek Recreation Area (day-use $2 per vehicle) offers the most accessible glimpse of what Escalante canyon country is all about. The trailhead to 126-foot **Lower Calf Creek Falls** is here, and you should definitely make plans for the half-day hike (6 miles round-trip, 3-4 hours), especially if you have no time for further exploration of

© PAUL LEVY

It takes binoculars and a little looking, but the Hundred Hands pictograph is visible from the Boynton Overlook.

this magical landscape. Otherwise, stop here to picnic in the shade of willows and cottonwoods. This is also the most convenient and attractive **campground** ($7) for dozens of miles. The 13 campsites have water, fire pits, and picnic tables.

The Million-Dollar Road

Highway 12 between Escalante and Boulder was completed in 1935 by workers from the Civilian Conservation Corps. The cost was a budget-busting $1 million. Before then, mules carried supplies and mail across this wilderness of slickrock and narrow canyons. The section of Highway 12 between Calf Creek and Boulder is extraordinarily scenic—even jaded travelers used to the wonders of Utah will have to pull over and ogle the views from the **Hog's Back,** where the road crests a fin of rock above the canyons of the Escalante. Be here for sunset on a clear evening and you'll have a memory to carry for the rest of your life.

Boulder

Boulder is a tiny community in a lovely location at the base of Boulder Mountain, where the alpine air mixes with the desert breezes. The single best lodging choice in the Escalante region—the Boulder Mountain Lodge—is here, so plan accordingly.

◖ Anasazi State Park

At the excellent Anasazi State Park (Hwy. 12, 1 mile north of Boulder, 435/335-7308, www.stateparks.utah.gov, 8am-6pm daily Apr.-Oct., 9am-5pm Mon.-Sat. Nov.-Mar., $5 pp), museum exhibits, an excavated village site, and a pueblo replica provide a look into the life of these ancient people. The Anasazi stayed here for 50-75 years some time between 1050 and 1200. They grew corn, beans, and squash in fields nearby. The village population peaked at about 200, with an estimated 40-50 dwellings. Why the Anasazi left or where they went isn't known for certain, but a fire swept through

© BILL MCRAE

Anasazi State Park features excavated Anasazi structures.

much of the village before they abandoned it. Perhaps they burned the village on purpose, knowing they would move on. University of Utah students and faculty excavated the village, known as the Coombs Site, in 1958 and 1959. You can view pottery, ax heads, arrow points, and other tools found at the site in the museum, along with delicate items like sandals and basketry that came from more protected sites elsewhere. A diorama shows how the village might have appeared in its heyday. You can see video programs on the Anasazi and modern Native Americans on request.

The self-guided tour of the ruins begins behind the museum, one mile north of Boulder. You'll see a whole range of Anasazi building styles—a pit house, masonry walls, jacal walls (mud reinforced by sticks), and combinations of masonry and jacal. Replicas of habitation and storage rooms behind the museum show complete construction details.

◖ Burr Trail Road

Burr Trail Road, originally a cattle trail blazed by stockman John Atlantic Burr, extends from the town of Boulder on Highway 12 to the Notom-Bullfrog Road, which runs between Highway 24 near the eastern entrance to Capitol Reef National Park and Bullfrog Marina on Lake Powell, off Highway 276. Starting at Boulder, the road is paved as far as the boundary between the GSENM and Capitol Reef National Park (31 miles), where the route traverses the Circle Cliffs, as well as spectacular canyon areas such as Long Canyon and the Gulch. As the route meets the Waterpocket Fold in Capitol Reef National Park, breathtaking switchbacks drop some 800 feet in just 0.5 miles. These switchbacks are not considered suitable for RVs or vehicles towing trailers. The unpaved sections of the road may be impassable in poor weather. Visitors should inquire about road and weather conditions

THE POLITICS OF ESTABLISHING THE NATIONAL MONUMENT

In September 1996, President Bill Clinton declared 1.9 million acres of south-central Utah a national monument, ending a decades-old debate about preserving the wilderness canyons in this part of the Southwest. The federal government's move sought to prevent the establishment of coal mines in the area by a Dutch resource-extraction consortium. The monument was formed by combining existing public land into a single administrative unit: The land now preserved as Grand Staircase-Escalante National Monument consists of land formerly supervised by the Bureau of Land Management (BLM), the Forest Service, and the state of Utah. The responsibility for administering the new monument was assigned to the BLM.

Preservation of the canyons as a national monument angered the Utah Republican legislative delegation and many others in this deeply conservative state. They were angry that they had not been consulted about the formation of the monument, and they argued that the federal government should not interfere with local agriculture and the existing community. The move pleased environmentalists and backcountry recreationists, however, who feared that the existence of a mining operation, no matter how environmentally sound, would destroy the area's unique scenic splendor and ancient Anasazi art and ruins.

Feelings pro and con about the monument can still run deep around Escalante and southern Utah, but a whole new breed of business is springing up to address the needs of the sightseers and recreationists who flock here. For people who have adapted to the changing economic and environmental forces, hostility toward the monument and the crowds it attracts is subsiding, although certain issues, especially concerning the size of the monument and activities permitted within its boundaries, are still being litigated, and may continue to be for years.

The irony in all of this is that so far, in terms of land usage, very little has changed for either the farmers and ranchers who have leased these federal lands for generations or for the hikers and bikers who want to explore the wilds of this canyon country. The BLM has moved slowly to reassess access to the land and is trying to preserve the land's tradition as a multiuse area, with ranchers retaining grazing leases on federal land. Certain restrictions are in place, but these mostly affect the use of all-terrain vehicles (ATVs) and other vehicles that are not street-legal (off-road vehicles, dune buggies, and certain kinds of dirt bikes).

GRAND STAIRCASE

before setting out. Also inquire about hiking trails that depart from side roads.

Burr Trail Road joins Notom-Bullfrog Road just before it exits Capitol Reef National Park.

ALONG U.S. 89

In this region, U.S. 89 runs from Kanab to the Utah-Arizona border. From Kanab to Page, Arizona, at the Colorado River's Glen Canyon Dam, is 80 miles.

Johnson Canyon Road

Eight miles east of Kanab, Johnson Canyon Road heads north along the western border of the monument before joining Skutumpah Road and Glendale Bench Road. This road system links up with several more remote backcountry roads in the monument, and it eventually leads to Cannonville along Highway 12. From U.S. 89, Johnson Canyon Road is paved for the first 16 miles. The road passes an abandoned movie set, where the TV series *Gunsmoke* was sometimes filmed. The road then climbs up through the scenic Vermilion and then White Cliffs of the Grand Staircase. The road eventually passes over Skutumpah Terrace, a rather featureless plateau covered with scrub.

Paria Townsite Road

This road has several names, including Paria Valley and Paria Breaks Road. It turns north off U.S. 89 at milepost 31. The five-mile dirt road is passable to cars when dry. It passes some towering and colorful canyons and mesas, among which the remains of a **1930s Western movie set** are slowly decaying. From the parking area, walking trails lead to the abandoned bleached wood buildings, which make for great photo opportunities against the rugged backdrop. Farther along the road, as it approaches the Paria River, are the remains of Pahreah, although there's not much left of this ghost town.

Paria Canyon and Vermilion Cliffs National Monument

Paria Canyon—a set of magnificent slot canyons that drain from Utah down through northern Arizona to the Grand Canyon—is the focus of popular multiday canyoneering expeditions. Paria Canyon and 293,000 acres of surrounding desert grasslands are now protected as Vermilion Cliffs National Monument (www. blm.gov). Although the monument spreads south from the Utah-Arizona border, access to the monument's most famous sites is from back roads in Utah. In addition to the long Paria Canyon backpacking route, some shorter but strenuous day hikes explore this area. For more information, contact the Kanab Visitor Center (745 E. U.S. 89, Kanab, 435/644-4680, 9am-3pm daily Mar. 15-Nov. 15) or stop at the Paria Contact Station (U.S. 89, 44 miles east of Kanab, no phone, 9am-3pm daily Mar. 15-Nov. 15), near milepost 21 on U.S. 89.

Cottonwood Canyon Road

A few miles east of the Paria Contact Station (milepost 21 on U.S. 89), Cottonwood Canyon Road leads north. The unpaved road's lower portions, usually passable with a car in dry weather, pass through scenic landscapes as the road pushes north. The route climbs up across a barren plateau before dropping down to the Paria River. Several good hikes lead from roadside trailheads into steep side canyons. The route continues north along the Cockscomb, a long wrinkle of rock ridges that run north and south across the desert. At the northern end of this 46-mile route are Grosvenor Arch, Kodachrome State Park, and Highway 12.

Big Water and Smokey Mountain Road

At the little crossroads of Big Water, the GSENM has built a **visitors center** (100 Upper Revolution Way, Big Water, 435/675-3200, 9am-5:30pm daily Apr.-Oct. and 8am-4:30pm daily Nov.-Mar.) to serve the needs of travelers to the monument and to Glen Canyon National Recreation Area (NRA), which is immediately adjacent to this area. The visitors center is definitely worth a stop—it houses bones from a 75-million-year-old, 30-foot-long duck-billed dinosaur. The backbone, bearing tooth marks from a tyrannosaur, and the 13-foot-long tail are especially impressive.

Joining U.S. 89 at Big Water is Smokey Mountain Road. This long and rugged road links Big Water to Highway 12 at Escalante, 78 miles north. The southern portions of the route pass through Glen Canyon NRA, and side roads lead to remote beaches and flooded canyons. The original *Planet of the Apes* movie was shot here, before the area was inundated by Lake Powell.

From Big Water it is 19 miles to Page, Arizona, on U.S. 89.

Recreation

The GSENM preserves some of the best long-distance hiking trails in the American Southwest, but it also has shorter trails for travelers who want to sample the wonderful slot canyons and backcountry without venturing too far afield.

Be sure to check at local visitors centers for road and trail conditions, up-to-date maps, and if you're backpacking, a free backcountry permit, which is required for overnight stays. Many of the following hikes require extensive travel on backcountry roads, which can be impassable after rains and rough the rest of the

WALKING SOFTLY

Only great care and awareness can preserve the pristine canyons of the Escalante. You can help if you pack out all trash, avoid trampling the fragile cryptobiotic soils (dark areas of symbiotic algae and fungus on the sand), travel in groups of 12 or fewer, don't disturb Native American artifacts, and protect wildlife by leaving your dogs at home. Most important, bury human waste well away from water sources, trails, and camping areas; unless there's a fire hazard, burn toilet paper to aid its decomposition. Campfires in developed or designated campgrounds are allowed only in fire grates, fire pits, or fire pans. Wood collection in these areas is not permitted. The use of backpacking stoves is recommended by the National Park Service and the Bureau of Land Management. Visitors are encouraged to maximize efforts to leave no trace of their passage in the area.

Leave No Trace is a national organization dedicated to awareness, appreciation, and respect for our wildlands. The organization also promotes education about outdoor recreation that is environmentally responsible. More information about Leave No Trace is available at www.lnt.org.

time. In summer, these trails are hot and exposed; always carry plenty of water and sunscreen, and wear a hat.

Hiking the **Escalante River Canyon** is one of the world's greatest wilderness treks. Most people devote 4-6 days to exploring these slickrock canyons, which involves frequent scrambling (if not rock climbing), stream fording (if not swimming), and exhausting detours around rock falls and logjams. Most of the day hikes are along side canyons of the Escalante River and can be reached by trailheads off Hole-in-the-Rock Road or Burr Trail. A couple of shorter hikes—Lower Calf Creek Falls and Escalante Natural Bridge—start quite conveniently from Highway 12. Another good jumping-off point for day hikers is the Dry Fork Coyote Gulch Trailhead, 26 miles south of Highway 12 on Hole-in-the-Rock Road; trails here lead to two fascinating and beautifully constricted slot canyons.

The **Paria Canyon** is another famed long-distance slickrock canyon hike that covers 37 miles between the border of Utah and the edge of the Colorado River's Marble Canyon. Several long day hikes leave from trailheads on the Paria Plateau, along the border with Arizona.

Other areas with developed hiking trails include the Skutumpah Road area and Cottonwood Canyon, in the center of the park. Otherwise, hiking in the monument is mostly on unmarked routes. Although the park is developing more day hiking options, the rangers encourage hardy adventurers to consider extended hikes across the rugged and primitive outback, beyond the busy canyon corridors. Call one of the visitors centers and ask for help from the rangers to plan a hiking adventure where there are no trails.

GRAND STAIRCASE

HIKING JOHNSON CANYON-SKUTUMPAH ROAD

The northern portions of this road pass through the White Cliffs area of the Grand Staircase, and several steep and narrow canyons are trenched into these terraces. Rough hiking trails explore these slot canyons. As when hiking any slot canyon, be sure to check the weather report before venturing up-canyon, and beware of changes in weather; flash floods can strike fast, and they are especially common in mid-late summer.

Willis Creek Narrows

- Distance: 4.4 miles round-trip
- Duration: 3-4 hours
- Elevation change: 40 feet
- Effort: easy
- Trailhead: 9 miles south of Cannonville along Skutumpah Road

This relatively easy trail follows a small stream as it etches a deep and narrow gorge through the sandstone. From the parking area, where Skutumpah Road crosses Willis Wash, walk downstream along the wash. Follow the streambed, which quickly descends between slickrock walls. The canyon is at times no more than 6-10 feet across, while the walls rise 200-300 feet. The trail follows the streambed through the canyon for nearly 2.5 miles. To return, backtrack up the canyon. Use caution when hiking during flash flood season.

Bull Valley Gorge

- Distance: 2 miles round-trip
- Duration: 1-2 hours
- Elevation change: 850 feet
- Effort: moderate-strenuous
- Trailhead: 10.5 miles south of Cannonville along Skutumpah Road

Approximately 1.5 miles south of Willis Creek on Skutumpah Road, a narrow bridge vaults over the Bull Valley Gorge. Like the Willis Creek Narrows, this is a steep and narrow cleft in the slickrock; however, scrambling along the canyon bottom is a greater challenge. From the bridge, walk upstream along a faint trail on the north side of the crevice until the walls are low enough to scramble down. From here, the canyon deepens quickly, and you'll have to negotiate several dry falls along the way (a rope will come in handy). When you reach the area below the bridge, look up to see a 1950s-era pickup truck trapped between the canyon walls. Three men died in this 1954 mishap; their bodies were recovered, but the pickup was left in place. The canyon continues another mile from this point; after that the valley widens out a bit. There is no loop trail out of the canyon, so turn back when you've seen enough.

Lick Wash

- Distance: 4 miles one-way to Park Wash
- Duration: 4-5 hours
- Elevation change: 200 feet
- Effort: easy
- Trailhead: 20 miles south of Cannonville along Skutumpah Road

From Lick Wash, trails lead downstream into slot canyons to a remote arroyo (dry riverbed) surrounded by rock-topped mesas. One of these lofty perches contains a preserve of now-rare native grasses. Although this area can be reached in a day's hike, this is also a good place to base a multiday camping trip. The trail starts just below the road crossing on Lick Wash and follows the usually dry streambed as it plunges into a narrow slot canyon. The canyon bottom is mostly level and easy to hike. After one mile, the canyon begins to widen; after four miles, Lick Wash joins Park Wash, a larger desert canyon.

Looming above this canyon junction are mesas topped with deep sandstone terraces. Rising to the east is **No Mans Mesa,** skirted on all sides by steep cliffs. The 1,788 acres atop the mesa were grazed by goats for six months in the 1920s, but since then the pristine grassland has been protected by the BLM as an Area of Critical Environmental Concern. Hardy hikers can scramble up a steep trail—used by the goats—to visit this wilderness preserve. The ascent of No Mans Mesa is best considered an overnight trip from Lick Wash Trailhead.

HIKING COTTONWOOD CANYON ROAD

The northern portions of this route pass by Kodachrome Basin State Park, with a fine selection of hiking trails through colorful rock formations. The first five hikes in this section are in Kodachrome Park. For a brief introduction to the park's ecology, follow the short **Nature Trail.**

Panorama Trail

- Distance: 3 miles round-trip
- Duration: 2 hours
- Elevation change: 350 feet
- Effort: easy
- Trailhead: west side of park road, south of Trailhead Station

The Panorama Trail loops through a highly scenic valley with sand pipes and colorful rocks. The trail then leaves the valley and climbs up the rocks, offering good views of the park's formations. The most spectacular views are found at Panorama Point, which requires a short steep climb up a few switchbacks. If the three-mile loop leaves you thirsty for more hiking (and you're carrying an adequate supply of water), several spur trails offer the opportunity for a longer loop. Be sure to pick up a map of the park's hiking trails before you begin; they're available in several locations, including the Kodachrome General Store.

Angel's Palace Trail

- Distance: 1.5 miles round-trip

- Duration: 30-45 minutes
- Elevation change: 300 feet
- Effort: easy-moderate
- Trailhead: Kodachrome Basin State Park, just east of group campground

From the trailhead, hike up the butte to its top, where you're rewarded with fine views of the park and surrounding area, including Bryce Canyon. Once on top of the butte, the trail is level, and the hike becomes an easy amble. It's easy to spend quite a bit of time exploring the plateau. Note that horseback riders share this trail.

Grand Parade Trail

- Distance: 1.5 miles round-trip
- Duration: 1.5 hours
- Elevation change: 100 feet
- Effort: easy
- Trailhead: Kodachrome Basin State Park, Trailhead Station

The Grand Parade Trail makes a loop with good views of rock pinnacles. It stays on the floor of the canyon, so it's much gentler than some of the park's other hikes. But it's not dull—the trail visits a couple of box canyons and rock formations that resemble marchers in a parade. Horses and bicycles are permitted on this trail.

Eagle's View Trail

- Distance: 1 mile round-trip
- Duration: 30 minutes
- Elevation change: 1,000 feet
- Effort: moderate-strenuous
- Trailhead: north of Kodachrome Basin State Park campground

Eagle's View Trail, a segment of a historic cattle trail, climbs steep cliffs above the campground. The highest overlook is a steep 0.25-mile ascent from the campground, but if you just want a good view, hike just to the top of the second set of stairs—after this point, the trail gets very narrow and exposed. Because this trail is so steep and has significant exposure, it's not good for young children. It's also best to avoid it in gusty winds.

Shakespeare Arch Trail

- Distance: 1 mile round-trip
- Duration: 30 minutes
- Elevation change: 50 feet
- Effort: easy
- Trailhead: From the main park road, head east past the Arch group campground, turn right (south), and follow signs to Shakespeare Arch.

Although the arch is the destination of this trail, the trailside plants and excellent views are other highlights of this easy hike. Pick up a brochure at the trailhead to help with plant identification. The arch, which is 20 feet across and 90 feet high, is tucked into a small out-of-the-way cove and was not discovered until 1976, when a ranger searching for a coyote den stumbled across it. Note that just because you've seen this arch doesn't mean you should skip Grosvenor Arch. Think of Shakespeare Arch as an appetizer for the main course down the road at Grosvenor.

Hackberry Canyon

- Distance: 22 miles one-way
- Duration: 3 days
- Elevation change: 1,300 feet
- Effort: strenuous
- Trailhead: southern end of BLM Road 422
- Directions: Head south on Cottonwood Canyon Road for 7.5 miles, from where the pavement ends at Kodachrome Basin State Park to the crossing of Round Valley Draw. From here, turn south on BLM Road 422.

Hikers can travel the 22-mile length of this scenic canyon in three days, or take day hikes from either end of the trail. The lower canyon meets Cottonwood Canyon at an elevation of 4,700 feet, just above the mouth of the Paria River. Cottonwood Canyon Road provides access to both ends. A small spring-fed stream flows down the lower half of Hackberry Canyon; hikers should expect to get their feet wet. Many side canyons invite exploration. One of them, Sam Pollock Canyon, is on the west side, about 4.5 miles upstream from the junction of Hackberry and Cottonwood Canyons; follow it 1.75 miles up to **Sam Pollock Arch** (60 feet high and 70 feet wide). Available topographic maps include the metric 1:100,000 Smoky Mountain or the 7.5-minute Slickrock Bench and Calico Peak. Michael Kelsey's *Hiking and Exploring the Paria River* contains trail and trailhead information and a history of the Watson homestead, located a short way below Sam Pollock Canyon.

Cottonwood Narrows

- Distance: 3 miles round-trip
- Duration: 2 hours

Cottonwood Narrows

© PAUL LEVY

- Elevation change: minimal
- Effort: easy
- Trailhead: From the pavement's end at Kodachrome Basin State Park, head south on Cottonwood Canyon Road. The northern end of the Cottonwood Narrows is 15 miles down the dirt road; the southern end is 1 mile farther south. Access is easier from the southern end.

This hike, through a narrow high-walled Navajo sandstone canyon, is good for casual hikers. The sandy-bottomed wash offers an easy path through the Cockscomb and a good look at the layers of warped rocks. Several side canyons join the wash; if you're up for some scrambling, they can make for good exploring. Even on this short hike, remember to bring water. Use caution during flash flood season.

Box of the Paria River

- Distance: 7 miles round-trip
- Duration: 4-5 hours
- Elevation change: 500 feet
- Effort: strenuous
- Trailhead: at the confluence of Cottonwood Creek and Paria River, 2.5 miles south of lower Hackberry Canyon trailhead (29 miles south of the pavement's end at Kodachrome State Park, or from the south, 11.5 miles north of U.S. 89)

The confluence of Paria, Hackberry, and Cottonwood Canyons provides the backdrop to an excellent if strenuous day hike. The Box of the Paria River involves some steep climbs up rocky slopes as it traverses a tongue of slickrock between the mouth of the Hackberry and Paria Canyons. The route then follows the Paria River through its "box," or cliff-sided canyon, in the Cockscomb Formation. The trail returns to the trailhead by following Cottonwood Canyon upstream to the trailhead. For an easier hike up the box, start at the Old Paria town site, at the northern end of Movie Set Road.

Hike one mile down the Paria River, and then turn east into the box. Inquire at visitors centers for maps and about conditions.

HIKING THE ESCALANTE RIVER

The maze of canyons that drain the Escalante River presents exceptional hiking opportunities. You'll find everything from easy day hikes to challenging backpacking treks. The Escalante's canyon begins just downstream from the town of Escalante and ends at Lake Powell, about 85 miles beyond. In all this distance, only one road, Highway 12, bridges the river. Many side canyons provide additional access to the Escalante, and most are as beautiful as the main gorge. The river system covers such a large area that you can find solitude even in spring, the busiest hiking season. The many eastern canyons remain virtually untouched.

The Escalante canyons preserve some of the quiet beauty once found in Glen Canyon, which is now lost under the waters of Lake Powell. Prehistoric Anasazi and Fremont people have left ruins, petroglyphs, pictographs, and artifacts in many locations. These archaeological resources are protected by federal law: Don't collect or disturb them.

Before setting out, visit the rangers at the **Escalante Interagency Visitor Center** (755 W. Main St., 435/826-5499, 8am-4:30pm daily mid-Mar.-mid-Nov., 8am-4:30pm Mon.-Fri. mid-Nov.-mid-Mar.), on the west edge of Escalante, for the required free permit to backpack overnight in the GSENM, and to check on the latest trail and road conditions. Restrictions on group size may be in force on some of the more popular trails. You can also obtain topographic maps and literature that show trailheads, mileages, and other information that may be useful in planning trips. Some of the more popular trailheads have self-registration stations for permits.

The best times for a visit are early March-early June and mid-September-early November.

GRAND STAIRCASE

© PAUL LEVY

the deeply etched canyon of the Escalante River

Summertime trips are possible, but be prepared for higher temperatures and greater flash-flood danger in narrow canyons. Travel along the Escalante River involves frequent crossings, and there's always water in the main canyon, usually ankle- or knee-deep. Pools in the Narrows between Scorpion Gulch and Stevens Canyon can be up to chest-deep in spots (which you can bypass), but that's the exception. Occasional springs, some tributaries, and the river itself provide drinking water. Always purify the water first; the BLM warns of the unpleasant disease giardiasis, which is caused by the invisible giardia protozoan. Don't forget insect repellent—mosquitoes and deer flies seek out hikers in late spring and summer. Long-sleeved shirts and long pants also discourage biting insects and protect against the brush.

For guided day hikes and hiking shuttles into the Escalante canyons, contact **Utah Canyons** (325 W. Main St., Escalante, 435/826-4967, www.utahcanyons.com).

Escalante Canyon Trailheads

The many approaches to the area allow all sorts of trips. Besides the Highway 12 access at Escalante and the Highway 12 bridge, hikers can reach the Escalante River through western side canyons from Hole-in-the-Rock Road or eastern side canyons from Burr Trail Road. The western-canyon trailheads on Hole-in-the-Rock Road can be more easily reached by car, thus facilitating vehicle shuttles. To reach eastern-canyon trailheads, with the exceptions of Deer Creek and the Gulch on Burr Trail Road, you'll need lots of time and, if the road is wet, a sturdy 4WD vehicle. You must carry water for trips in these more remote canyons. With the exception of Deer Creek, they're usually dry.

Escalante to Highway 12 Bridge

- Distance: 15 miles one-way
- Duration: 1-2 days
- Elevation change: 500 feet

- Effort: moderate-strenuous
- Trailhead: near the town of Escalante
- Directions: Follow signs from Highway 12 on the east side of town, by the high school, to the trailhead.

This section of the Escalante River offers easy walking and stunning canyon scenery. Tributaries and sandstone caves invite exploration. You'll find good camping areas the entire way (be sure to get a permit for overnight camping). Usually the river here is only ankle deep. Almost immediately, the river knifes its way through the massive cliffs of the Escalante Monocline, leaving the broad valley of the upper river behind. Although there is no maintained trail along this stretch of the east-flowing river, it is relatively easy to pick your way along the riverbank.

Death Hollow, which is far prettier than the name suggests, meets the Escalante from the north after 7.5 miles. Several good swimming holes carved in rock are a short hike upstream from the Escalante; watch for poison ivy among the greenery. Continue farther up Death Hollow to see more pools, little waterfalls, and outstanding canyon scenery. You can bypass some pools, but others you'll have to swim—bring a small inflatable boat, air mattress, or waterproof bag to ferry backpacks.

Sand Creek, on the Escalante's north side, 4.5 miles downstream from Death Hollow, is also worth exploring; deep pools begin a short way up from the mouth. Another 0.5 miles down the Escalante, a natural arch appears high on the canyon wall. Then Escalante Natural Bridge comes into view, just two miles from the Highway 12 bridge.

Escalante Natural Arch and Bridge

- Distance: 2 miles one-way
- Duration: 2 hours
- Elevation change: 100 feet

- Effort: easy
- Trailhead: Highway 12 bridge over the Escalante River, between Escalante and Boulder

This hike upstream from the highway gives day hikers a taste of the Escalante River. After about 1.5 miles of hiking, you'll see the arch (look up) and then the 130-foot-high natural bridge. Hike upstream from the bridge for better views of the arch. Continue hiking for another 0.5 miles beyond the arch to the point where Sand Creek enters the Escalante. Hot-weather hikers may want to head a short distance up Sand Creek to find deep pools.

Phipps Wash

- Distance: 2 miles one-way to Maverick Bridge
- Duration: 3 hours
- Elevation change: 300 feet
- Effort: easy
- Trailhead: Highway 12 bridge over the Escalante River, between Escalante and Boulder

Start this hike from the highway crossing and follow the Escalante River downstream to Phipps Wash, a lovely side canyon. A sign directs you to cross the Escalante River; heed it. Highlights of the hike are Maverick Bridge, about 0.5 miles up the wash in a side canyon, and Phipps Arch, visible high on the canyon wall above the wash. If you want to continue up the wash, the streambed trail gives way to a sandy wash, then slickrock. The head of Phipps Wash is about four miles from the Escalante River.

Highway 12 Bridge to Harris Wash

- Distance: 26.5 miles one-way
- Duration: 4-6 days
- Elevation change: 700 feet
- Effort: moderate
- Trailhead: Highway 12 bridge over the Escalante River

This is where many long-distance trekkers begin their exploration of the Escalante canyons. In

GRAND STAIRCASE

this section, the Escalante Canyon offers a varied show: In places the walls close in to make constricted narrows; at others they step back to form great valleys. Side canyons filled with lush greenery and sparkling streams contrast with dry washes of desert, yet all can be fun to explore. A good hike of 4-6 days begins at the Highway 12 bridge, goes down the Escalante to Harris Wash, then up Harris to a trailhead off Hole-in-the-Rock Road (37 miles total).

From the Highway 12 bridge parking area, a trail leads to the river. Canyon access goes through private property; cross the river at the posted signs. **Phipps Wash** comes in from the south (the right side) after 1.5 miles and several more river crossings. Turn up its wide mouth for 0.5 miles to see Maverick Bridge in a drainage to the right. To reach Phipps Arch, continue another 0.75 miles up the main wash, turn left into a box canyon, and scramble up the left side (see the 7.5-minute Calf Creek topographic map).

Bowington (Boynton) Arch is an attraction in a north side canyon known locally as Deer Creek. Look for this small canyon on the left, one mile beyond Phipps Wash; hike up it for about one mile, past three deep pools, and then turn left into a tributary canyon. In 1878 gunfire resolved a quarrel between local ranchers John Boynton and Washington Phipps. Phipps was killed, but both their names live on.

Waters of **Boulder Creek** come rushing into the Escalante from the north in the next major side canyon, 5.75 miles below the Highway 12 bridge. The creek, along with its Dry Hollow and Deer Creek tributaries, provides good canyon walking; deep areas may require swimming or climbing up on the plateau. (You could also start down Deer Creek from Burr Trail Road, where they meet, 6.5 miles southeast of Boulder at a primitive BLM campground. Starting at the campground, follow Deer Creek 7.5 miles to Boulder Creek, then 3.5 miles down Boulder Creek to the Escalante.) Deer and Boulder Creeks have water year-round.

High sheer sandstone walls constrict the Escalante River in a narrow channel below Boulder Creek, but the canyon widens again above the **Gulch** tributary, 14 miles below the highway bridge. Hikers can head up the Gulch on a day hike.

Alternatively, hikers can descend the Gulch from Burr Trail Road to join the Escalante Canyon at this point (the Gulch trailhead is 10.8 miles southeast of Boulder). The hike from the road down to the Escalante is 12.5 miles, but there's only one difficult spot: a 12-foot waterfall in a section of narrows about halfway down. When Rudi Lambrechtse, author of *Hiking the Escalante,* tried friction climbing around the falls and the pool at their base, he fell and broke his foot. That meant a painful three-day hobble out. Instead of taking the risk, Rudi recommends backtracking about 300 feet from the falls and climbing out from a small alcove in the west wall (look for a cairn on the ledge above). Climb up Brigham Tea Bench, walk south, then look for cairns leading back east to the narrows, and finally descend to the streambed (a rope helps to lower packs in a small chimney section).

Most springs along the Escalante are difficult to spot. One that's easy to find is in the first south bend after the Gulch; water comes straight out of the rock a few feet above the river. Escalante Canyon becomes wider as the river lazily meanders along. Hikers can cut off some of the bends by walking in the open desert between canyon walls and riverside willow thickets. A bend cut off by the river itself loops to the north just before Horse Canyon, three miles below the Gulch. Along with its tributaries **Death Hollow** and **Wolverine Creek, Horse Canyon** drains the Circle Cliffs to the northeast. Floods in these mostly dry streambeds wash down pieces of black petrified wood. Vehicles with good clearance can reach the upper sections of all three canyons from a loop road off Burr Trail Road. Horse and Wolverine Creek Canyons offer good easy-moderate hiking, but if you really want a challenge, try Death Hollow, sometimes called Little Death Hollow to distinguish it from the larger one near Hell's Backbone Road. Starting from the Escalante River, go about two miles up Horse Canyon and turn right into Death Hollow; rugged scrambling over boulders takes you back into a long section of twisting narrows. Carry water for Upper Horse Canyon and its tributaries. Lower Horse Canyon usually has water.

About 3.5 miles down the Escalante from Horse Canyon, you'll enter Glen Canyon NRA and come to Sheffield Bend, a large grassy field on the right. Only a chimney remains from Sam Sheffield's old homestead. Two grand amphitheaters are beyond the clearing and up a stiff climb in loose sand. Over the next 5.5 river miles to Silver Falls Creek, you'll pass long bends, dry side canyons, and a huge slope of sand on the right canyon wall. Don't look for any silver waterfalls in **Silver Falls Creek**—the name comes from streaks of shiny desert varnish on the cliffs. You can approach Upper Silver Falls Creek by a rough road from Burr Trail Road, but a car shuttle between here and any of the trailheads on the west side of the Escalante River would take all day. Most hikers visit this drainage on a day hike from the river. Carry water with you.

Harris Wash is to the right (west) side of the Escalante River almost opposite Silver Falls Creek. When the Hole-in-the-Rock route proved so difficult, pioneers figured there had to be a better way to the San Juan Mission. Their new wagon road descended Harris Wash to the Escalante River, climbed part of Silver Falls Creek, crossed the Circle Cliffs, descended Muley Twist Canyon in the Waterpocket Fold, and then followed Hall's Creek to Hall's Crossing on the Colorado River. Charles Hall operated a ferry there 1881-1884. Old maps show a jeep road through Harris Wash and Silver Falls Creek Canyons, used before the National Park Service closed off the Glen Canyon NRA section. Harris Wash is just 0.5 miles downstream and across the Escalante from Silver Falls Creek.

◖ Lower Calf Creek Falls

- Distance: 2.75 miles one-way
- Duration: 4 hours
- Elevation change: 250 feet
- Effort: easy-moderate
- Trailhead: Calf Creek Campground ($2 day-use), 16 miles east of Escalante on Highway 12

Calf Creek is a tributary of the Escalante River, entering it near Highway 12. The hike to Lower Calf Creek Falls is quite accessible for ordinary folks and is, for many people, the highlight of their first trip to the Escalante area. It's the dazzling enticement that brings people back for longer and more remote hiking trips. From the trailhead and park just off Highway 12, the trail winds between high cliffs of Navajo sandstone streaked with desert varnish, where you'll see beaver ponds, Native American ruins and pictographs, and the misty 126-foot-high Lower Calf Creek Falls. A brochure available at the trailhead next to the campground identifies many of the desert and riparian plant species along the way. Bring water and perhaps lunch. Summer temperatures can soar, but the falls and the crystal-clear pool beneath stay cool. Sheer cliffs block travel farther upstream.

Calf Creek Campground (early Apr.-late Oct., $7), near the road, has 13 sites with drinking water. Reserve group sites through the **Escalante Interagency Visitor Center** (755 W. Main St., Escalante, 435/826-5499, 8am-4:30pm daily mid-Mar.-mid-Nov., 8am-4:30pm Mon.-Fri. mid-Nov.-mid-Mar.).

Upper Calf Creek Falls

- Distance: 1 mile one-way
- Duration: 1.5 hours
- Elevation change: 500 feet
- Effort: moderate

- Trailhead: just east of milepost 81 on Highway 12
- Directions: From Escalante, drive about 20.5 miles east on Highway 12. Turn left onto a dirt road between mileposts 80 and 81; the road may be marked by a black boulder with a white stripe. Drive 0.25 miles up the bumpy dirt road to the trailhead (park low-clearance vehicles at the turnoff and walk to the trailhead).

The hike to Upper Calf Creek Falls is more strenuous and less used than the trail to the lower falls. It's also entirely different in nature, so don't feel that, if you've hiked to the lower falls, the upper falls trip will be a mere repeat. This hike starts with a fairly steep descent across slickrock and then continues along a sandy trail. At a fork, you can choose to hike down to the base of the 87-foot-high falls or stay high and continue across more slickrock to the top of the falls and some deep pools in the stream. Near the bottom of the falls are hanging gardens and thick vegetation. At the top, paintbrush grows out of cracks in the slickrock.

Harris Wash

- Distance: 10.25 miles one-way from trailhead to Escalante River
- Duration: 2 days round-trip
- Elevation change: 700 feet
- Effort: moderate
- Trailhead: Harris Wash Trailhead off Hole-in-the-Rock Road
- Directions: From Highway 12, turn south and travel on Hole-in-the-Rock Road for 10.8 miles, then turn left and go 6.3 miles on a dirt road (keep left at the fork near the end).

Clear shallow water glides down this gem of a canyon. High cliffs streaked with desert varnish are deeply undercut and support lush hanging gardens. Harris Wash provides a beautiful route to the Escalante River, but it can also be a destination in itself; tributaries and caves invite exploration along the way. The sand and gravel streambed makes for easy walking. Don't be dismayed by the drab appearance of upper Harris Wash. The canyon and creek appear a few miles downstream. The Harris Wash Trailhead is restricted to a maximum of 12 people per group.

Harris Wash to Lake Powell

- Distance: 42.75 miles one-way
- Duration: 8-9 days
- Elevation change: 1,000 feet
- Effort: moderate
- Trailhead: Harris Wash Trailhead off Hole-in-the-Rock Road
- Directions: From Highway 12, turn south on Hole-in-the-Rock Road and take it 10.8 miles, then turn left and go 6.3 miles on a dirt road (keep left at the fork near the end).

The Escalante continues its spectacular show of wide and narrow reaches, side canyons, and intriguing rock formations. A trip all the way from Harris Wash Trailhead to the Escalante, down the Escalante River to near Lake Powell, then out to the Hurricane Wash trailhead is 66.25 miles and requires 8-10 days. Many shorter hikes using other side canyons are also possible.

Still in a broad canyon, the Escalante flows past **Fence Canyon** (to the west), 5.5 miles from Harris Wash. Fence Canyon has water and is a strenuous 3.5-mile cross-country route out to the end of Egypt Road. Get trail directions from a ranger, and bring a topographic map. (Adventurous hikers could do a three-day, 20-mile loop via Fence Canyon, the Escalante River, and the northern arm of Twentyfive Mile Wash. To reach the trailheads, take Hole-in-the-Rock Road 17.2 miles south of Highway 12, then turn left—east—and go 3.7 miles on Egypt Road to Twentyfive Mile Wash trailhead, or 9.1 miles to Egypt trailhead.)

Twentyfive Mile Wash, on the west side, 11.5 miles below Harris Wash, is a good route for entering or leaving the Escalante River. The moderately difficult hike is 13 miles one-way from trailhead to river. Scenery changes from an uninteresting dry wash in the upper part to a beautiful canyon with water and greenery in the lower reaches. To get to the trailhead, take Hole-in-the-Rock Road 17.2 miles south of Highway 12, then turn left and drive 3.7 miles on Egypt Road.

Moody Creek enters the Escalante six meandering river miles below Twentyfive Mile Wash (or just 2.25 miles as the crow flies). A rough road off Burr Trail Road gives access to Moody Creek, Purple Hills, and other eroded features. The distance from trailhead to river is seven miles one-way (moderately strenuous), although most hikers find it more convenient to hike up from the Escalante. **Middle Moody Creek** enters Moody Creek three miles above the Escalante. Moody and Middle Moody Canyons feature colorful rock layers, petrified wood, a narrows, and solitude. Carry water because springs and water pockets cannot be counted on. Canyons on the east side of the Escalante tend to be much drier than those on the west side.

East Moody Canyon enters the Escalante 1.5 miles downstream from Moody Canyon, and it also makes a good side trip. There's often water about 0.5 miles upstream. Continuing down the Escalante, look on the left for a *rincón,* a meander cut off by the river. **Scorpion Gulch** enters through a narrow opening on the right, 6.5 miles below Moody Canyon. A strenuous eight-mile climb up Scorpion Gulch over rockfalls and around deep pools brings you to a trailhead on Early Weed Bench Road. Experience, directions from a ranger, and a topographic map are needed. A challenging four-day, 30-mile loop hike uses Fox Canyon, Twentyfive Mile Wash, the Escalante River, and Scorpion Gulch. Water is found only in lower Twentyfive Mile Wash, the river, and lower Scorpion Gulch. The Early Weed Bench turnoff is 24.2 miles south on Hole-in-the-Rock Road from Highway 12; head in 5.8 miles to Scorpion Gulch Trailhead.

In the next 12 miles below Scorpion Gulch,

Escalante Canyon is alternately wide and narrow. Then the river plunges into **The Narrows,** a five-mile-long section choked with boulders; plan on spending a day picking a route through this stretch. Watch out for chest-deep water here. Remote and little-visited **Stevens Canyon** enters from the east near the end of the Narrows; Stevens Arch stands guard 580 feet above the confluence. The upper and lower parts of Stevens Canyon usually have water.

Coyote Gulch, on the right 1.5 miles below Stevens Canyon, marks the end of the Escalante for most hikers. In some seasons, Lake Powell comes within one mile of Coyote Gulch and occasionally floods the canyon mouth. Coyote Gulch can stay flooded for several weeks, depending on the release flow of Glen Canyon Dam. The river and lake don't have a pretty meeting place—quicksand and dead trees are found here. Logjams make it difficult to travel in from the lake by boat.

Coyote Gulch has received more publicity than other areas of the Escalante, and you're more likely to meet other hikers here. Two arches, a natural bridge, graceful sculpturing of the streambed and canyon walls, deep undercuts, and a cascading creek make a visit well worthwhile. The best route in starts where Hole-in-the-Rock Road crosses Hurricane Wash, 34.7 miles south of Highway 12. It's 12.5 miles one-way from the trailhead to the river, and the hike is moderately strenuous. Coyote Gulch, which has water, is 5.25 miles from the trailhead. Another way into Coyote Gulch begins at the Red Well Trailhead; it's 31.5 miles south on Hole-in-the-Rock Road, then 1.5 miles east (keep left at the fork). Starting from Red Well adds almost one mile to the hike, but this route is also less crowded.

◖ Dry Fork of Coyote Gulch

- Distance: 3.5 miles round-trip
- Duration: 5 hours

GRAND STAIRCASE

© PAUL LEVY

GRAND STAIRCASE

A little scrambling is necessary to enter Peek-a-boo Canyon, a tributary canyon of the Dry Fork of Coyote Gulch.

• Elevation change: 300 feet
• Effort: moderate
• Trailhead: Dry Fork of Coyote Gulch
• Directions: From Highway 12, turn south on Hole-in-the-Rock Road and follow it for 26 miles. Turn left at the sign for Dry Fork and continue 1.7 miles along a rutted dirt road to the trailhead.

Twenty-six miles south of Highway 12 is a series of narrow, scenic, and exciting slot canyons reached by a moderate day hike. The canyons feed into the Dry Fork of Coyote Gulch, reached from the Dry Fork Trailhead. These three enchanting canyons are named **Peek-a-boo,** **Spooky,** and **Dry Creek.** Exploring these slots requires basic canyoneering skills and the ability to pass through some fairly narrow (12-inch) spaces. From the trailhead parking lot, follow cairns down into the sandy bottom of the Dry Fork of Coyote Gulch. The slot canyons all enter the gulch from the north; watch for cairns and trails because the openings can be easy to miss. You'll have to scramble up some rocks to get into Peek-a-boo. The slots sometimes contain deep pools of water; choke stones and pour-offs can make access difficult. No loop trail links the three slot canyons; follow each until the canyon becomes too narrow to continue, then come back out. Making a full circuit of these canyons requires about 3.5 miles of hiking.

HIKING IN PARIA CANYON AND VERMILION CLIFFS

The wild and twisting canyons of the Paria River and its tributaries offer a memorable experience for experienced hikers. Silt-laden waters have sculpted the colorful canyon walls, revealing 200 million years of geologic history. *Paria* means "muddy water" in the Paiute language. You enter the 2,000-foot-deep gorge of the Paria in southern Utah, then hike 37 miles downstream to Lee's Ferry in Arizona, where the Paria empties into the Colorado River. A handful of shorter but rugged day hikes lead to superb scenery and geologic curiosities.

Ancient petroglyphs and campsites show that Pueblo people traveled the Paria more than 700 years ago. They hunted mule deer and bighorn sheep while using the broad lower end of the canyon to grow corn, beans, and squash. The Dominguez-Escalante Expedition stopped at the mouth of the Paria in 1776, and these were the first nonnatives to see the river. John D. Lee and three companions traveled through the canyon in 1871 to bring a herd of cattle from the Pahreah settlement to Lee's Ferry. After Lee began a Colorado River ferry service in 1872, he and others farmed the lower Paria Canyon. Prospectors came here to search for gold, uranium, and other minerals, but much of the canyon remained unexplored. In the late 1960s, the BLM organized a small expedition whose research led to protection of the canyon as a primitive area. The Arizona Wilderness

slot canyons at the Dry Fork of Coyote Gulch

Act of 1984 designated Paria Canyon a wilderness, along with parts of the Paria Plateau and Vermilion Cliffs. Vermilion Cliffs National Monument was created in 2000.

The **BLM Paria Canyon Ranger Station** is in Utah, 43 miles east of Kanab on U.S. 89 near milepost 21. It's on the south side of the highway, just east of the Paria River. Self-serve day-use permits ($6) are required for hiking in Paria Canyon and to visit other sites in Vermilion Cliffs National Monument.

Paria Canyon

- Distance: 38.5 miles one-way
- Duration: 4-6 days
- Elevation change: 1,300 feet
- Effort: moderate
- Trailhead: Whitehouse Campground
- Directions: The trailhead is two miles south of the Paria Contact Station, on a dirt road near a campground and old homestead site

called White House Ruins. The exit trailhead is in Arizona at Lonely Dell Ranch of Lee's Ferry, 44 miles southwest of Page via U.S. 89 and U.S. 89A (or 98 miles southeast of Kanab on U.S. 89A).

Allow plenty of time to hike Paria Canyon—there are many river crossings, and you'll want to make side trips up at least some of the tributary canyons. Hikers should have enough backpacking experience to be self-sufficient, as help may be days away. Flash floods can race through the canyon, especially during summer. Rangers close the Paria if they think a danger exists. Because the upper end is narrowest (between miles 4.2 and 9.0), rangers require that all hikers start here so they have up-to-date weather information for their passage.

You must register at a trailhead or the **Kanab BLM office** (318 N. 100 E., Kanab, 435/644-2672, 8am-4:30pm Mon.-Fri. year-round). Permits to hike the canyon are $6 pp per day; overnight permits are $5. Backpackers should get a permit at the ranger station or online (www.blm.gov/az/paria), but day hikers can just register and pay the fee at the trailhead. The visitors center and the office both provide weather forecasts and brochures with map and hiking information. The visitors center always has the weather forecast posted at an outdoor information kiosk.

The hike requires a 150-mile round-trip car shuttle. For a list of shuttle services, check the BLM website (www.blm.gov) or ask at the Paria Contact Station (U.S. 89, 44 miles east of Kanab, no phone, 9am-3pm daily Mar. 15-Nov. 15) or Kanab BLM Office. Expect to pay about $100 for this service.

All visitors should take special care to minimize their impact on this beautiful canyon. Check the BLM's "Visitor Use Regulations" for the Paria before you go. Regulations include no campfires in the Paria and its tributaries, a pack-in/pack-out policy, and require that latrines be made at least 100 feet away from

© PAUL LEVY

GRAND STAIRCASE

river and campsite locations. Human waste and toilet paper must be transported out in plastic bags (available at the ranger station).

The Paria rangers recommend a maximum group size of six, though regulations specify a 10-person limit. No more than 20 people per day can enter the canyon for overnight trips. The best times to travel along the Paria are usually mid-March-June and October-November. May, especially Memorial Day weekend, tends to be crowded. Winter hikers often complain of painfully cold feet. Wear shoes suitable for frequent wading; canvas shoes are better than heavy leather hiking boots. You can get good drinking water from springs along the way (see the BLM hiking brochure for locations); it's best not to use the river water because of possible chemical pollution from farms and ranches upstream. Normally the river is only ankle-deep, but in spring or after rainy spells, it can become much deeper. During thunderstorms, levels can rise to more than 20 feet in the Paria Narrows, so heed weather warnings. Quicksand, which is most prevalent after flooding, is more a nuisance than a danger—usually it's just knee-deep. Many hikers carry a walking stick to probe the opaque waters for good crossing places.

Wrather Canyon Arch, one of Arizona's largest natural arches, is about one mile up a side canyon of the Paria. The massive structure has a 200-foot span. Turn right (southwest) at mile 20.6 on the Paria hike. (The mouth of Wrather Canyon and other points along the Paria are unsigned; you have to follow your map.)

Buckskin Gulch and Wire Pass

- Distance: 1.7 miles one-way
- Duration: 3 hours
- Elevation change: 300 feet
- Effort: moderate
- Trailhead: Wire Pass Trailhead

- Directions: From Kanab, head 37 miles east on U.S. 89 to BLM Road 700 (also called House Rock Valley Road), between mileposts 25 and 26. Turn south for 8.5 bumpy miles to the trailhead.

Buckskin Gulch is an amazing slot-canyon tributary of the Paria, with convoluted walls reaching hundreds of feet high and narrowing to as little as four feet in width. In places the walls block out so much light that it's like walking in a cave. Be very careful to avoid flash floods.

Day hikers can get a taste of this incredible canyon country by driving to the Wire Pass trailhead. From the trailhead, a relatively easy trail leads into Wire Pass, a narrow side canyon that joins Buckskin Gulch. The trail runs the length of Wire Pass to its confluence with Buckskin Gulch. From here, you can explore this exceptionally narrow canyon or follow Buckskin Gulch to its appointment with Paria Canyon (12.5 miles).

For the full experience of Buckskin Gulch, long-distance hikers can begin at Buckskin Gulch Trailhead, 4.5 miles south of U.S. 89 on BLM Road 700. From here, it's 16.3 miles (one-way) to Paria Canyon. Hikers can continue down the Paria or turn upstream and hike six miles to exit at the White House trailhead near the ranger station. Hiking this gulch can be strenuous, with rough terrain, deep pools of water, and log and rock jams that may require the use of ropes. Conditions vary considerably from one year to the next. Regulations mandate packing your waste out of this area.

Hiking permits ($6 pp per day) are required; backpackers should get an overnight permit ($5) at the ranger station, but day hikers can simply register and pay the fee at the trailhead.

Coyote Buttes

You've probably seen photos of these dramatic rock formations: towering sand dunes frozen into rock. These much-photographed buttes are located on the Paria Plateau, just south of Wire

Pass. Access is strictly controlled, and you can only enter the area with advance reservations and by permit. The number of people allowed into the area is also strictly limited; however, the permit process, fees, and restrictions are exactly the same as for Paria Canyon.

Advance permits are required for day use and are available online and at the Paria Contact Station (U.S. 89, 44 miles east of Kanab, no phone, 9am-3pm daily Mar. 15-Nov. 15); no overnight camping is allowed. Group size is limited to no more than six people. Dogs are allowed. All trash must be packed out and campfires are not allowed. See the Vermilion Cliffs Monument website (www.az.blm.gov/vermilion/vermilion.htm) for complete information and to obtain permits.

The BLM has divided the area into Coyote North and Coyote South. The Wave—the most photographed of the buttes—is in Coyote North, so this region is the most popular (and easiest to reach from Wire Pass trailhead); BLM staff will give you a map and directions when you get your permit. After the trailhead, you're on your own, because the wilderness lacks signs. Permits are more difficult to obtain in spring and fall—the best times to visit—and on weekends. The fragile sandstone can break if climbed on, so it's important to stay on existing hiking routes and wear soft-soled footwear.

MOUNTAIN BIKING

Mountain bikes are allowed on all roads in the monument but not on hiking trails. Mountain bikers are not allowed to travel cross-country off roads or to make their own routes across slickrock; however, there are hundreds of miles of primitive roads in the monument, with dozens of loop routes available for cyclists on multiday trips. In addition to following the scenic **Burr Trail** from Boulder to the Waterpocket Fold in Capitol Reef National Park, cyclists can loop off this route and follow the Circle Cliffs-Wolverine trail. This 45-mile loop traverses the

headwaters of several massive canyons as they plunge to meet the Escalante River.

Hole-in-the-Rock Road is mostly a one-way-in, one-way-out affair, but cyclists can follow side roads to hiking trailheads and big vistas over the Escalante canyons. Popular side roads include a 10-mile round-trip road to the area known as Egypt and the Fifty Mile Bench Road, a 27-mile loop from Hole-in-the-Rock Road that explores the terrain above Glen Canyon. Left Hand Collet Road, a rough jeep trail that a mountain bike can bounce along easily enough, links Hole-in-the-Rock Road with the Smoky Mountain Road system, with links to both Escalante in the north and Big Water in the south.

Other popular routes in the **Big Water area** include the Nipple Butte loop and the steep loop around Smoky Butte and Smoky Hollow, with views over Lake Powell. **Cottonwood Canyon Road,** which runs between U.S. 89 and Cannonville, is another long back road with access to a network of less-traveled trails.

Request more information on mountain biking from the visitors centers. They have handouts and maps and can help cyclists plan backcountry bike adventures. This country is remote and primitive, so cyclists must carry everything they are likely to need. Also, there are few sources of potable water in the monument, so cyclists must transport all drinking water or be prepared to purify it.

4WD EXPLORATION

Without a mountain bike or a pair of hiking boots, the best way to explore the backcountry of the GSENM is with a high-clearance 4WD vehicle; however, the scale of the monument, the primitive quality of many of the roads, and the extreme weather conditions common in the desert mean that you shouldn't head into the backcountry unless you are confident in your skills as a mechanic and driver. Choose roads that match your vehicle's capacity and your

GRAND STAIRCASE

driving ability, and you should be OK. Some of the roads that appear on maps are slowly going back to nature: rather than close some roads, park officials are letting the desert reclaim them. Other roads are being closed, so it's best to check on access and road conditions before setting out. Remember that many of the roads in the monument are very slow going. If you've got somewhere to be in a hurry, these corrugated boulder-dodging roads may not get you there in time. Be sure to take plenty of water—not only for drinking but also for overheated radiators. It's also wise to carry wooden planks or old carpet scraps for help in gaining traction should your wheels get mired in the sand.

RAFTING

Most of the year, shallow water and rocks make boat travel impossible on the Escalante River, but for 2-3 weeks during spring runoff, which peaks in late April-early May, river levels rise high enough to be passable. (In some years there may not be enough water in any season.) Contact the **Escalante Interagency Visitor Center** (755 W. Main St., Escalante, 435/826-5499, 8am-4:30pm daily mid-Mar.-mid-Nov., 8am-4:30pm Mon.-Fri. mid-Nov.-mid-Mar.) for ideas on when to hit the river at its highest. Shallow draft and maneuverability are essential, so inflatable canoes or kayaks work best (also because they are easier to carry out at trip's end or if water levels drop too low for floating). Not recommended are rafts (too wide and bulky) and hard-shelled kayaks and canoes

(they get banged up on the many rocks). The usual launch is the Highway 12 bridge. Coyote Gulch—a 13-mile hike—is a good spot to get out, as is Crack in the Wall, which is a 2.75-mile hike on steep sand from the junction of Coyote and Escalante Canyons to Forty-Mile Ridge Trailhead; a 4WD vehicle is needed, and a rope is required to negotiate the vessel over the canyon rim. Hole-in-the-Rock is another pullout (a 600-foot ascent over boulders; rope suggested). You could also arrange for a friend to pick you up by boat from Halls Crossing or Bullfrog Marina. River boaters must obtain a free backcountry permit from either the BLM or the National Park Service.

OUTFITTERS

There aren't many places to shop for gear in this remote area. The most centrally located shops are in the town of Escalante, where you'll find **Utah Canyons Desert Adventure Store** (325 W. Main St., Escalante, 435/826-4967, www.utahcanyons.com), which stocks books, maps, and some outdoor gear. Right across the street, **Escalante Outfitters** (310 W. Main St., Escalante, 435/826-4266, www.escalanteoutfitters.com) has a little bit of everything, including a small liquor store, and is a good place to pick up a warm jacket or a stylish tank top.

Another shop with a good selection of clothing and gear is in Kanab. **Willow Canyon Outdoor** (263 S. 100 E., Kanab, 435/644-8884 www.willowcanyon.com) also serves good coffee and has an excellent book shop.

Escalante

Escalante (elevation 5,813 feet) is a natural hub for exploration of the Grand Staircase-Escalante National Monument. Even if you don't have the time or the inclination to explore the rugged canyon country that the monument protects, you'll discover

incredible scenery just by traveling Highway 12 through the Escalante area.

At first glance, Escalante looks like a town that time has passed by. Just under 1,000 people live here, in addition to the resident cows, horses, and chickens that you'll meet just one block off Main Street. Yet this little community is the biggest place for scores of miles around and a center for ranchers and travelers. Escalante has the neatly laid-out streets and trim little houses typical of Mormon settlements.

ACCOMMODATIONS

Accommodations in Escalante range from simple to luxurious, but add a hefty 12.5 percent room tax to the listed rates.

Under $50

The seven small but comfy log cabins at **◖Escalante Outfitters** (310 W. Main St., 435/826-4266, www.escalanteoutfitters.com, $45) share men's and women's bathhouses and a common grassy area. Tucked behind the store, which also houses a casual pizza and espresso restaurant and a tiny liquor store, these cabins are convenient to all the action the town has to offer and include wireless Internet access. If you'd rather sleep in your own tent, camping is permitted on the lawn ($16), which is sheltered from the street. Dogs are permitted for a small fee in the cabins and are free if they stay in your tent.

$50-100

The **Prospector Inn** (380 W. Main St., 435/826-4653, www.prospectorinn.com, $62) is Escalante's largest and most modern motel; there's a restaurant and lounge on the premises. If you usually stay at Best Westerns or comparable motels, this is the only standard motel in town that's even close to that level of quality.

The **Padre Motel** (20 E. Main St., 435/826-4276, www.padremotel.com, June-Oct., $69-110) has clean, unfussy guest rooms as well as five mini suites with two bedrooms each. The property is nicely landscaped and maintained, with beautifully green lawns even in the height of summer. One guest room with a kitchen requires a three-day minimum stay. The motel is closed on Sunday, meaning that you can spend Saturday night and leave on Sunday, but you can't check in for Sunday night.

On the west edge of town, the **Circle D Motel** (475 W. Main St., 435/826-4297, www.escalantecircledmotel.com, $69-99) reaches out to bicyclists and hikers with clean basic guest rooms. Pets are welcome in some guest rooms; a restaurant is part of the complex.

Recently remodeled with a fanciful Old West theme, the **Cowboy Country Inn** (75 S. 100 W., 435/826-4250, www.cowboycountry-inn.com, $65-125) is half a block off the highway and offers one two-bedroom suite.

Another pleasant and modern establishment is **Rainbow Country B&B** (586 E. 300 S., 435/826-4567 or 800/252-8824, www.bnbescalante.com, $69-99), with four guest rooms sharing 2.5 baths; guests have the use of a hot tub, a pool table, and a TV lounge.

$100-150

Right in the center of town but tucked back away from the main drag, guest rooms at **Escalante's Grand Staircase B&B Inn** (280 W. Main St., 435/826-4890 or 866/826-4890, www.escalantebnb.com, $145) are some of the nicest in the area. The eight purpose-built B&B guest rooms are individually decorated—several have rather bold murals—and are separate from the main house.

Another downtown Escalante B&B is **◖Canyons B&B** (120 E. Main St., 435/826-4747 or 866/526-9667, www.canyonsbnb.com, Mar.-Nov., $125-135), where a modern three-bedroom "bunkhouse" has been built behind an old farmhouse, which offers its own "lodge" room. There's nothing rustic about the guest rooms; all are attractively decorated and equipped with TV, telephones, and wireless Internet. Minimum stay requirements may apply.

Over $150

Head east from Escalante on Highway 12 to the landmark Kiva Koffeehouse, a quirky hilltop restaurant just east of the Boynton

THE PETRIFIED FOREST

Trees fall into water, are washed downstream, and are buried by mud, silt, and ash. Minerals and elements like silica, from volcanic ash, enter the wood either from water or the ground, filling in its pores. When the pores of the wood have been filled, its color changes, depending on the minerals present. This mineral-loaded wood is resistant to rotting and is often quite beautiful, displaying the original cellular structure and grain of the wood.

Two especially good places to see petrified wood are along Huber Wash, in the western section of Zion National Park just west of Springdale, and at Escalante Petrified Forest State Park, just west of the town of Escalante.

Although it should go without saying that the petrified wood in these places should stay here—and not travel home in a hiker's pack or pocket—this general ethical guideline is backed up by a potent mythology of misfortune befalling people who steal petrified wood. Posted on a bulletin board at the base of the Petrified Forest Trail in the state park are many letters from people who decided to return bits of petrified wood they'd secreted away from the park, and the tales of how their lives went down the tubes after they stole the wood.

Overlook high above the Escalante River, and its beautiful **◖ Kiva Kottage** (milepost 73.86 on Hwy. 12, 435/826-4550, www.kivakofeehouse.com, $170, breakfast included). The two spacious and beautifully decorated guest rooms each include a remarkable view of the surrounding country. The comfortable guest rooms, with their grand views, fireplaces, and big, deep, jetted bathtubs, make this a wonderful place to relax after a day of exploring, and the absence of TVs and phones makes it all the better. The Kiva is just above the spot where

the Escalante River crosses Highway 12 and is a good base for hikers.

The **◖ Slot Canyons Inn B&B** (3680 W. Hwy. 12, 435/826-4901 or 866/889-8375, www.slotcanyonsinn.com, $165-215) is a new and purpose-built lodging about five miles west of Escalante on a dramatically scenic 160-acre ranch. Although the structure has adobe-like features and blends into the rustic environment, the eight guest rooms are very comfortable and modern, some with patios and balconies. There's even a restaurant on the ground floor (dinner Tues.-Sun., reservations required) so you don't have to drive into Escalante for your dinner. This is a very lovely place to stay—think of it not so much as a B&B (although breakfast is included in the rates) but as an exclusive small country inn.

If you're traveling with a family or group of friends, consider renting the architecturally striking solar-heated **La Luz Desert Retreat** (888/305-4705, www.laluz.net, high season $175 for 4 people, 2-night minimum), in a private setting just south of town. The house, designed in the Usonian tradition of Frank Lloyd Wright, can sleep up to six.

Campgrounds

Escalante Petrified Forest State Park (435/826-4466, www.stateparks.utah.gov, reservations 800/322-3770, www.reserveamerica.com, year-round, $16), just northwest of the town of Escalante, is conveniently located and full of attractions of its own, most notably trails passing big chunks of petrified wood. Drinking water and showers are available, as are RV hookups.

In town, you can stay at **Broken Bow RV Camp** (495 W. Main St., 435/826-4959 or 888/241-8785, www.brokenbowrvpark.com, spring-fall), which has simple cabins ($44-59) and sites for tents ($16) and RVs ($28-30), plus showers and laundry services.

Calf Creek Campground (early Apr.-late

Oct., $7) is in a pretty canyon 15.5 miles east of Escalante on Highway 12. Group sites through the BLM at the **Escalante Interagency Visitor Center** (755 W. Main St., 435/826-5499, 8am-4:30pm daily mid-Mar.-mid-Nov., 8am-4:30pm Mon.-Fri. mid-Nov.-mid-Mar.). Lower Calf Creek Falls Trail (5.5 miles round-trip) begins at the campground and follows the creek upstream to the 126-foot-high falls.

Campgrounds at **Posey Lake** (16 miles north of Hwy. 12, 435/676-8608, reservations www.recreation.gov, Memorial Day-mid-Sept., $10) and **Blue Spruce** (19 miles north of Hwy. 12, www.fs.fed.us, Memorial Day-mid-Sept., $8) are atop the Aquarius Plateau in Dixie National Forest. Take the dirt Hell's Backbone Road from the east edge of town.

FOOD

The **Esca-Latte Coffee Shop and Pizza Parlor** (310 W. Main St., 435/826-4266, www.escalanteoutfitters.com, 8am-9pm daily), part of Escalante Outfitters, is a reliable place to eat in this little town. It serves espresso, handmade pizza ($17-21), and microbrew beer. The smoked trout plate ($9) is a special treat. The café has a couple of computers where customers can check email.

The **Trailhead Café** (125 E. Main St., 435/826-4714, 11:30am-4pm Wed.-Mon. Apr.-Nov., $7-12) has the best burgers in town, with an outdoor grill and shady deck seating.

As close as you'll get to fine dining in Escalante is the ◖ **Circle D Eatery** (485 W. Main St., 435/826-4125, www.escalantecircledmotel.com, 7:30am-9:30pm Wed.-Mon., $9-19), which offers local open-range beef and a variety of house-smoked meats and cheeses. Steaks are dependably outstanding, as is the smoked brisket and rainbow trout baked on a bed of peppers and onions.

Another spot for better-than-average food is **Cowboy Blues** (530 W. Main St., 435/826-4577, www.cowboyblues.net, 11:30am-10pm

daily, $8-17), with burgers, pizza, ribs, and steaks in a Western-style log dining room.

Other dining spots are more traditional small-town restaurants. The **Golden Loop Cafe** (39 W. Main St., 435/826-4433, 7am-8pm daily, $6-14) is a typical Main Street diner with plenty of local color and homemade food.

East of town, **Kiva Koffeehouse** (milepost 73.86 on Hwy. 12, 435/826-4550, 8:30am-4:30pm Wed.-Mon. Apr.-Oct., $6-12) is worth a stop for a latte or for a lunch of delicious Southwestern-style food, much of it organic, and for a look at the view.

INFORMATION AND SERVICES

The **Escalante Interagency Visitor Center** (755 W. Main St., 435/826-5499, 8am-4:30pm daily mid-Mar.-mid-Nov., 8am-4:30pm Mon.-Fri. mid-Nov.-mid-Mar.), on the west edge of town, has an information center for visitors to Forest Service, BLM, and National Park Service areas around Escalante; this is also one of the best spots for information on the GSENM. Hikers or bikers headed for overnight trips in the monument system can obtain permits at the information center.

Kazan Memorial Clinic (65 N. Center St., 435/826-4374) offers medical care on Monday, Wednesday, and Friday. The nearest hospital is 70 miles west in Panguitch.

GETTING THERE

Located on Highway 12, Escalante is 38 miles east of Bryce Canyon and 23 miles south of Boulder. A word of warning: Drive slowly through town; the local police seem to have a refined eye for out-of-towners exceeding the speed limit.

AROUND ESCALANTE
Hell's Backbone Scenic Drive

This scenic 38-mile drive climbs high into the pine forests north of Escalante with excellent views of the distant Navajo, Fifty-Mile, and Henry Mountains. The highlight, though, is

GRAND STAIRCASE

© BILL MCRAE

Hell's Backbone Bridge spans a neck of land between two canyons.

the one-lane **Hell's Backbone Bridge,** which vaults a chasm between precipitous Death Hollow and Sand Creek Canyons. You'll want to stop here for photographs of the outstanding vistas—and to quell your vertigo.

Hell's Backbone Road reaches an elevation of 9,200 feet on the slopes of Roger Peak before descending to a bridge. Mule teams used this narrow ridge, with sheer canyons on either side, as a route to Boulder until the 1930s. At that time, a bridge built by the Civilian Conservation Corps allowed the first vehicles to make the trip.

To reach Hell's Canyon Road from Escalante, turn north on 300 East and follow the initially paved road out of town. The bridge is about 25 miles from town. Alternatively, you can turn onto Hell's Backbone Road three miles south of Boulder on Highway 12. From this corner, the bridge is 13 miles.

Cars can usually manage the gravel and dirt road when it's dry. Snows and snowmelt,

however, block the way in winter until about late May. Check with the **Escalante Interagency Visitor Center** (755 W. Main St., Escalante, 435/826-5499, 8am-4:30pm daily mid-Mar.-mid-Nov., 8am-4:30pm Mon.-Fri. mid-Nov.-mid-Mar.) for current conditions. Trails and rough dirt roads lead deeper into the backcountry to more vistas and fishing lakes.

Campgrounds

Amid aspen and ponderosa pines, Posey Lake (elevation 8,700 feet) is stocked with rainbow and brook trout. The adjacent **Posey Lake Campground** (Memorial Day-mid-Sept., $10) has drinking water. A hiking trail (two miles round-trip) begins near space number 14 and climbs 400 feet to an old fire-lookout tower, with good views of the lake and surrounding country. Posey Lake is 14 miles north of Escalante, and then two miles west on a side road.

Blue Spruce Campground ($8) is another pretty spot at an elevation of 7,860 feet, but it has only six sites. Anglers can try for pan-size trout in a nearby stream. The campground, surrounded by blue spruce, aspen, and ponderosa pine, has drinking water Memorial Day-mid-September; go north 19 miles from town, then turn left and drive 0.5 miles.

Boulder

About 180 people live in this farming community at the base of Boulder Mountain. Ranchers began drifting in during the late 1870s, although not with the intent to form a town. By the mid-1890s, Boulder had established itself as a ranching and dairy center. Remote and hemmed in by canyons and mountains, Boulder remained one of the last communities in the country to rely on pack trains for transportation; motor vehicles couldn't drive in until the 1930s. Today Boulder is worth a visit to see an excavated Anasazi village and the spectacular scenery along the way.

ACCOMMODATIONS

You wouldn't expect to find one of Utah's nicest places to stay in tiny Boulder, but the C **Boulder Mountain Lodge** (Hwy. 12, 435/355-7460 or 800/556-3446, www. boulder-utah.com, $130-200, discounts outside high season), along the highway right in town, offers the kinds of facilities and setting that make this one of the few destination lodgings in the state. The lodge's buildings are grouped around the edge of a private 15-acre pond that serves as an ad hoc wildlife refuge. You can sit on the deck or wander paths along the pond, watching and listening to the amazing variety of birds that make this spot their home. The guest rooms and suites are in a handsome and modern Western-style lodge facing the pond; guest rooms are nicely decorated with quality furniture and bedding, and there's a central great room with a fireplace and library and a large outdoor hot tub. One of Utah's best restaurants, Hell's Backbone Grill (435/355-7460

or 800/556-3446, 7am-11:30am and 5:30pm-9:30pm daily), is on the premises.

More modest accommodations are available at **Pole's Place** (435/335-7422 or 800/730-7422, www.boulderutah.com/polesplace, spring-fall, $80), across the road from Anasazi State Park. It has a well-maintained motel, café, and gift shop.

Guest Ranches

Cowboy up at the **Boulder Mountain Guest Ranch** (3621 Hells Backbone Rd., 435/355-7480, http://bouldermountainguestranch. com), seven miles from Boulder on Hell's Backbone Road. Guests have a choice of simple bunk rooms with shared baths ($70) and queen-bed guest rooms with private baths ($80-105) in the main lodge, or in free-standing cabins ($95-115) with basic kitchen facilities and private baths. Also in the lodge is the Sweetwater Café, which offers guests a variety of dining plans; nonguests are welcome at dinner (seatings 6:30, 7:15, and 8pm daily, $16-30) but reservations are required. Recreation options include daily trail rides, fly-fishing, multiday horse-packing trips, and 2-5-day riding and lodging packages based at the ranch.

Campgrounds

The best bet for tent campers is **Deer Creek Campground** (year-round, $4), 6.5 miles from Boulder on Burr Trail Road; bring your own drinking water. During the summer, another alternative is to head north on Highway 12 up Boulder Mountain to a cluster of Fishlake National Forest campgrounds—Singletree (www.recreation.gov, $10), Pleasant Creek ($9), and Oak Creek ($9). In town, RV campers can

GRAND STAIRCASE

GRAND STAIRCASE

© BILL MCRAE

Hell's Backbone Grill, one of southern Utah's finest restaurants

stay at the **Boulder Exchange** (425 N. Hwy. 12, 435/335-7304, Apr.-Nov., $16 tents, $24 RVs), next to Anasazi State Park.

FOOD

The Boulder Mountain Lodge restaurant, 🄲 **Hell's Backbone Grill** (Hwy. 12, 435/355-7460 or 800/556-3446, 7am-11am, noon-2pm, and 5pm-9pm daily mid-Mar.-Nov., noon-2pm daily Dec.-mid-Mar., $17-37) has gained something of a cult following across the West. Run by two American Buddhist women, the restaurant has a menu that changes with the seasons, but you can count on finding fresh fish, chipotle-rubbed meat, outstanding meatloaf, tasty posole, and excellent desserts. For simpler but good fare, the **Burr Trail Grill** (10 N. Hwy 12, 435/335-7432, www.burrtrailgrill.com, 11:30am-9:30pm daily Apr.-Oct. $8-18) is at the intersection of Highway 12 and Burr Trail Road. The atmospheric dining room, sided with weathered wood planking and filled with

whimsical art, offers sophisticated soup and sandwiches for lunch and dinner main courses such as grilled pork loin, steaks, chicken, and trout, all with subtle Southwestern spicing.

INFORMATION AND SERVICES

A good stop for visitor information is the **Anasazi State Park Museum** (460 N. Hwy. 12, 435/335-7308, http://stateparks.utah.gov, 8am-6pm daily Apr.-Oct., 9am-5pm Mon.-Sat. Nov.-Mar.), where there's an info desk for the GSENM. The two gas stations in Boulder sell groceries and snack food; at **Hills and Hollows Mini-Mart** (on the hill above Hwy. 12, 435/335-7349), you'll find provisions as diverse as soy milk and organic cashews.

GETTING THERE

Take paved Highway 12 either through the canyon and slickrock country from Escalante or over the Aquarius Plateau from Torrey, near Capitol Reef National Park. Burr Trail Road connects

Boulder with Capitol Reef National Park's southern district via the Waterpocket Fold and Circle Cliffs. A fourth way in is from Escalante on the dirt Hell's Backbone Road, which comes out three miles west of Boulder at Highway 12.

AROUND BOULDER
Boulder Mountain Scenic Drive

Utah Highway 12 climbs high into forests of ponderosa pine, aspen, and fir on Boulder Mountain between the towns of Boulder and Torrey. Travel in winter is usually possible, although heavy snows can close the road. Viewpoints along the drive offer sweeping panoramas of Escalante canyon country, the Circle Cliffs, the Waterpocket Fold, and the Henry Mountains. Hikers and anglers can explore the alpine country of Boulder Mountain and seek out the 90 or so trout-filled lakes. The Great Western Trail, which was built with ATVs in mind, runs over Boulder Mountain to the west of the highway. The Fishlake National Forest map (Teasdale District) shows the back roads, trails, and lakes.

Campgrounds

The U.S. Forest Service has three developed campgrounds about midway along Boulder Mountain Scenic Drive: **Oak Creek** (18 miles from Boulder, elevation 8,800 feet, $8), **Pleasant Creek** (19 miles from Boulder, elevation 8,600 feet, $9), and **Singletree** (24 miles from Boulder, elevation 8,200 feet, www.recreation.gov, $10)—the largest of the three and the best pick for larger RVs. The season runs about late May-mid-September with water available; the campgrounds may also be open in spring and fall without water. **Lower Bowns Reservoir** (elevation 7,000 feet) has primitive camping (no water, free) and fishing for rainbow and cutthroat trout; turn east and go five miles on a rough dirt road (not recommended for cars) just south of Pleasant Creek Campground.

Contact the **Teasdale Ranger District Office** (138 S. Main St., Loa, 435/425-3702) for information about camping or recreation on Boulder Mountain.

Kanab

Striking scenery surrounds this small town in Utah's far south. The Vermilion Cliffs to the west and east glow with a fiery intensity at sunrise and sunset. Streams have cut splendid canyons into surrounding plateaus. The Paiutes knew the spot as *kanab,* meaning "place of the willows," and the trees still grow along Kanab Creek. Mormon pioneers arrived in the mid-1860s and tried to farm along the unpredictable creek. Irrigation difficulties culminated in the massive floods of 1883, which gouged a section of creek bed 40 feet below its previous level in just two days. Ranching proved better suited to this rugged and arid land.

Hollywood discovered this dramatic scenery in the 1920s and has filmed more than 150 movies and TV series here since. Famous films shot hereabouts include movies as varied as *My Friend Flicka, The Lone Ranger,* and *The Greatest Story Ever Told.* The TV series *Gunsmoke* and *F Troop* were shot locally. Film crews have constructed several Western sets near Kanab, but most are on private land and are difficult to visit. The Paria set, east of town, is on BLM land and open to the public.

While most park visitors see Kanab (population 3,500) as a handy stopover on trips to Bryce, Zion, and Grand Canyon National Parks and the southern reaches of the GSENM, a few interesting sites around town warrant more than a sleep-eat-dash visit. Despite the presence of strongly conservative elements in the area—if, while exploring Kanab, you see what looks like a family reunion, it might be just a

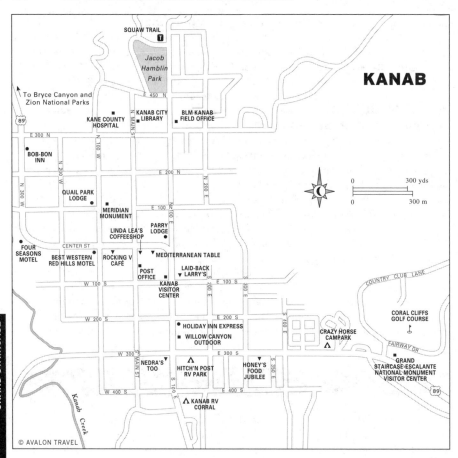

© AVALON TRAVEL

man and his wives from the nearby polygamist settlement of Colorado City or Hildale—there's a pleasantly alternative vibe in the town itself.

SIGHTS
Moqui Cave

The natural Moqui Cave (U.S. 89, 5 miles north of Kanab, 435/644-8525, 9am-7pm Mon.-Sat. Memorial Day-Labor Day, 10am-4pm Mon.-Sat. Labor Day-Memorial Day, $5 adults, $4.50 seniors, $3.50 ages 13-17, $3 ages 6-12) has been turned into a tourist attraction

with a large collection of Native American arti-facts. Most of the arrowheads, pottery, sandals, and burial items on display have been excavated locally. A diorama recreates an Anasazi ruin lo-cated five miles away in Cottonwood Wash. Fossils, rocks, and minerals are exhibited as well, including what's claimed to be one of the largest fluorescent mineral displays in the coun-try. There's even a Prohibition-era speakeasy. The collections and a gift shop are within a spacious cave that stays pleasantly cool even in the hottest weather.

BEST FRIENDS ANIMAL SANCTUARY

If anybody else owned these 35,000 acres in the canyon north of town, there would be expensive McMansions sprawling across the hills. Instead, there are giant octagonal doghouses filled with animals no one else wants: former research animals, aggressive dogs, old dogs, sick dogs, and dogs who have been abused or neglected. There are also plenty of cats, rabbits, birds, pot-bellied pigs, and horses.

Best Friends Animal Sanctuary, the largest no-kill animal shelter in the country, takes in unwanted or abused animals and provides whatever rehabilitation is possible. Many animals are adopted out, but even the unadoptable ones are given homes for life, with plenty of care and attention from the sanctuary's roster of employees and volunteers.

The shelter's origins date back to the 1970s, when a group of animal lovers began trying to prevent unadoptable animals being euthanized. They began rescuing animals that were about to be put to sleep by shelters, rehabilitated them as necessary, and found them homes. In the early 1980s this group of dedicated rescuers bought land in Angel Canyon just north of Kanab and, with their motley crew of unadoptable animals, established this sanctuary. Now some 1,800 animals live here at any given time, and the shelter is the county's largest employer, with more than 200 staff members caring for the animals and the grounds.

But even the large staff can't take care of all of the animals' needs. The shelter's volunteers spend anywhere from a couple of days to a couple of months feeding, walking, petting, and cleaning up after the animals. Volunteers also give the animals the attention and socialization necessary for them to become good companions.

Best Friends (www.bestfriends.org) runs tours several times a day. Call 435/644-2001 for reservations or to learn more about volunteering at the shelter. There's no charge for the tour, although donations are gladly accepted.

HIKING
Squaw Trail

- Distance: 1.5 miles one-way
- Duration: 2 hours
- Elevation change: 800 feet
- Effort: moderate
- Trailhead: north end of 100 East, near the city park

This well-graded trail provides a close look at the geology, plantlife, and animals of the Vermilion Cliffs just north of town. To cut the hike down by one mile and cut the elevation gain in half, turn around at the first overlook, where views to the south take in Kanab, Fredonia, Kanab Canyon, and the vast Kaibab Plateau. At the top, look north to see the White, Gray, and Pink Cliffs of the Grand Staircase. Pick up a trail guide at the **Kanab Visitor Center** (745 E. U.S. 89, Kanab, 435/644-1300, 8am-4:30pm daily). Brochures may also be available at the trailhead. Bring water with you, and in summer, try to get a very early start.

TOURS

Kanab is central to an amazing number of sights, and if you'd like the pros to handle the logistics of your visit, turn to **Dreamland Safari Tours** (435/644-5506, www.dreamlandtours.net).

ENTERTAINMENT AND EVENTS

In summer, free musical concerts are held at the city park gazebo at the center of town. Every Wednesday is an ongoing local talent show. The GSENM office (435/644-4680, www.blm.gov/ut) sponsors regular ranger talks through the spring. A unique Kanab event is the **Greyhound Gathering** (435/644-2903, www.greyhoundgang.com, mid-May most

GRAND STAIRCASE

years), when hundreds of greyhound owners converge on the town. Events include a parade, a race, and a howl-in. The Greyhound Gang, a nonprofit organization dedicated to the rescue, rehabilitation, and adoption of former racing greyhounds, hosts this unlikely festival.

SHOPPING

Find a good selection of books, camping gear, and clothing, along with a little coffee bar, at **Willow Canyon Outdoor** (263 S. 100 E., 435/644-8884, www.willowcanyon.com). **Terry's Cameras** (19 W. Center St., 435/644-5981, www.utahcameras.com) supplies film and camera needs, including repairs for film cameras, beyond what you would expect in a town of this size. The shop almost qualifies as an antique camera museum.

Denny's Wigwam (78 E. Center St., 435/644-2452, www.dennyswigwam.com) is a landmark Old West trading post with a broad selection of Western jewelry, cowboy hats and boots, and souvenirs.

ACCOMMODATIONS

Most of the lodgings in Kanab are in modest family-run motels. Reservations are a good idea during the busy summer months. All of the motels and campgrounds are on U.S. 89, which follows 300 West, Center, 100 East, and 300 South through town.

$50-100

The **Sun-N-Sand Motel** (347 S. 100 E., 435/644-5050 or 800/654-1868, $45-75) has a pool, included continental breakfast, kitchenettes, and very welcoming owners.

The **Bob-Bon Inn** (236 U.S. 89 N., 435/644-5094, http://bobboninn.com, $79-109) is a renovated family-run motel with pleasant log cabin-style guest rooms, fridges and microwaves in all guest rooms, plus an outdoor pool and breakfast included.

One place in Kanab that varies from the usual motor-court formula is the **Parry Lodge** (89 E. Center St., 435/644-2601 or 800/748-4104, www.parrylodge.com, $70-120). Built during Kanab's heyday as a movie-making center, the Parry Lodge was where the stars stayed; 60 years later, this is still a pleasantly old-fashioned place to spend the night, and it has lots of character. At the very least you'll want to stroll through the lobby, where lots of photos of the celebrities who once stayed here are displayed. There are many room types, including two-bedroom units, kitchen suites, a pool, and a restaurant.

A good midrange choice is the **Four Seasons Motel** (36 N. 300 W., 435/644-2635, www.fourseasonskanab.com, $80-110), which has a pool and accepts pets.

North of Kanab, at Mount Carmel Junction, is another Best Western. The **Best Western East Zion Thunderbird Resort** (435/648-2203, www.bestwestern.com, from $107), with a pool, a nine-hole golf course, and a restaurant, is convenient if you're heading to Zion or Bryce Canyon National Parks. All guest rooms have balconies or patios.

$100-150

The guest rooms at **Best Western Red Hills Motel** (125 W. Center St., 435/644-2675 or 800/830-2675, www.bestwesternredhills.com, $90-125) are a step up in comfort from Kanab's lower-priced digs. The motel has balcony rooms and a pool, and it is within a short walk of restaurants.

The **☾ Quail Park Lodge** (125 U.S. 89 N., 435/644-5094 or 866/702-8099, www.quailparklodge.com, $89-149) has a pool and accepts pets. It's one of the nicer budget motels in town, with 50s-era kitsch as well as quality linens and toiletries.

At the center of town is the **Holiday Inn Express** (217 S. 100 E., 435/644-3100, www.hiexpress.com, $139-154), with large, nicely furnished guest rooms, an indoor pool and exercise facility, a business center, and a guest lounge with complimentary continental breakfast.

© PAUL LEVY

With many inexpensive lodging options, Kanab is a good base for exploring the region.

GRAND STAIRCASE

Over $150

Especially nice if you're traveling with a group that plans to spend several nights in Kanab are the **Kanab Garden Cottages** (various locations, 435/644-2020, www.kanabcottages.com). You have a choice of beautifully furnished, fully outfitted studios (3-night minimum, $79) or full-size houses (3-night minimum, $160 for 2 people), which can easily sleep up to eight and are pet-friendly. All are within walking distance of town.

Northwest of Kanab, just a few miles east of Zion National Park, are the very appealing log cabins and lodges of the **Zion Mountain Ranch** (E. Hwy. 9, 435/648-2555 or 866/648-2555, www.zmr.com, $179-374). The cabins all have king beds and private baths plus microwaves and fridges; family lodges offer two or three bedrooms. The setting is great, with expansive views, a buffalo herd, and a decent on-site restaurant, Chez Bison. Horseback riding and other outdoor recreation is offered.

Campgrounds

The campground at **Coral Pink Sand Dunes State Park** (reservations 435/648-2800 or 800/322-3770, www.stateparks.utah.gov, $16) has restrooms with showers, paved pull-through sites, and a dump station. It's a pleasant, shady spot, but it can hum with ATV traffic. It's open year-round, but the water is shut off late October-Easter; winter campers must bring their own. Reservations are recommended for the busy Memorial Day-Labor Day season. The campground is about 10 miles due west of Kanab, but the two are not directly connected by a road. Reach the campground by turning west off U.S. 89 about 10 miles north of Kanab onto Hancock Road, and follow it 12 miles to the campground. The route is well-marked by signs.

Just north of the state park, the BLM maintains **Ponderosa Grove Campground** ($5) on the north edge of the dunes. There's no water here. From Kanab, head eight miles north on U.S. 89, turn west on Hancock Road (between mileposts 72 and 73), and continue 7.3 miles to the campground. The **Kanab RV Corral** (483 S. 100 E., 435/644-5330, www.kanabrvcorral.com, year-round, $27-30) has RV sites (no tents) with hot showers, a pool, and laundry service. The **Hitch'n Post RV Park** (196 E. 300 S., 435/644-2142 or 800/458-3516, www.hitchnpostrvpark.com, May-Oct., $18 tents, $25-27 RVs, $28-32 cabins) has showers. The **Crazy Horse Campark** (625 E. 300 S., 435/644-2782, http://crazyhorservpark.com, mid-Apr.-late Oct., $16 tents, $25 RVs) has a pool, a store, a game room, and showers.

FOOD

Find the best food in town at **(Rocking V Café** (97 W. Center St., 435/644-8001, www.rockingvcafe.com, 11:30am-3pm and 5pm-10pm daily, dinner $18-38). The setting is casual, and the food has a modern Southwestern flair. Rocking V, which caters to both vegans and steak-lovers, pays homage to the "slow food" movement and makes everything from scratch. Be sure to check out the art gallery upstairs.

Drop by **Laid-Back Larry's** (98 S. 100 E., 435/644-3636, 7:30am-7pm Thurs.-Mon.) for an espresso, smoothie, or sandwich ($3-9). Larry's also serves as the local vegan and vegetarian grocer. **Linda Lea's Coffeeshop** (4 E. Center St., 435/644-8191, 7am-2pm Mon.-Fri., 8am-noon Sat.) is another good place for espresso drinks, homemade pastries, bagels, and deli sandwiches.

If you're hankering for a good spinach enchilada or other Mexican food, settle into the friendly **Nedra's Too** (300 S. 100 E., 435/644-2030, www.nedrascafe.com, 7am-9pm Tues.-Thurs., 7am-10pm Fri.-Sat., $6-10). You'll find excellent panini and pita sandwiches at the **(Mediterranean Table** (18 E. Center St., 435/644-3200, 4pm-10pm daily, $7-17), along with a handful of Greek and Italian main courses.

The chef-owner lived in Greece and Italy for over a decade, and the food is authentic and tasty.

Travelers setting out into the GSENM from Kanab should note that this is the best place for many miles around to stock up on groceries. **Honey's Food Jubilee** (260 E. 300 S., 435/644-5877) is a good grocery store on the way out of town to the east.

INFORMATION AND SERVICES

Staff members at the **Kanab Visitor Center** (78 S. 100 E., 435/644-5033, www.visitsouthernutah.com, 8am-8pm Mon.-Sat.) offer literature and advice for services in Kanab and travel in Kane County. The Grand Staircase-Escalante National Monument has a **visitors center** (745 E. U.S. 89, Kanab, 435/644-1300, 8am-4:30pm daily mid-Mar.-mid-Nov., 8am-4:30pm Mon.-Fri. mid-Nov.-mid-Mar.) on the east edge of town.

GETTING THERE

Situated on U.S. 89, Kanab is 15 miles south of Mount Carmel Junction (Hwy. 9 and U.S. 89), a total of 40 miles from Zion National Park, and just 7 miles north of the Arizona-Utah border. From Kanab, U.S. 89 continues southeast, providing access to the southern reaches of Grand Staircase Escalante National Monument and, 74 miles later, Glen Canyon Dam at Page, Arizona.

CORAL PINK SAND DUNES STATE PARK

Churning air currents funneled by surrounding mountains have deposited huge sand dunes in this valley west of Kanab. The ever-changing dunes reach heights of several hundred feet and cover about 2,000 of the park's 3,700 acres. Different areas in Coral Pink Sand Dunes State Park (reservations 435/648-2800 or 800/322-3770, www.stateparks.utah.gov, day-use $6 per vehicle, camping $16 per vehicle) have been set aside for hiking, off-road vehicles, and a campground.

From Kanab, the shortest route is to go north eight miles on U.S. 89 to Hancock Road (between mileposts 72 and 73), turn left, and travel 9.3 miles on the paved road to its end, then turn left (south) and go one mile on a paved road into the park. From the north, you can follow U.S. 89 for 3.5 miles south of Mount Carmel Junction (Hwy. 9 and U.S. 89), then turn right (south) and go 11 miles on a paved road. The back road from Cane Beds in Arizona has about 16 miles of gravel and dirt with some sandy spots; ask a park ranger for current conditions.

The canyon country surrounding the park has good opportunities for hiking and off-road-vehicle travel; the Kanab BLM office (318 N. 100 E., Kanab, 435/644-2672, 8am-4:30pm Mon.-Fri. year-round) can supply maps and information. Drivers with 4WD vehicles can turn south on Sand Springs Road (1.5 miles east of Ponderosa Grove Campground) and go one mile to Sand Springs, and another four miles to the South Fork Indian Canyon Pictograph Site, in a pretty canyon. Visitors may not enter the Kaibab-Paiute Indian Reservation, which is south across the Arizona state line, from this side.

GRAND STAIRCASE

CAPITOL REEF NATIONAL PARK

Although Capitol Reef gets far less attention than the region's other national parks, it is a great place to visit, with excellent hiking and splendid scenery. Wonderfully sculpted rock layers in a rainbow of colors put on a fine show; you'll find these same rocks throughout much of the Four Corners region, but their artistic variety has no equal outside Capitol Reef National Park. About 70 million years ago, gigantic forces within the earth began to uplift, squeeze, and fold more than a dozen rock formations into the central feature of the park today—the Waterpocket Fold, so named for the many small pools of water trapped by the tilted strata. Erosion has since carved spires, graceful curves, canyons, and arches. The Waterpocket Fold extends 100 miles between Thousand Lake Mountain to the north and Lake Powell to the south. (Look for it if you ever fly south from Salt Lake City—we never really grasped its magnitude until we flew over it on the way to Mexico.) The most spectacular cliffs and rock formations of the Waterpocket Fold form Capitol Reef, located north of Pleasant Creek and curving northwest across the Fremont River toward Thousand Lake Mountain. The reef was named by explorers who found the Waterpocket Fold a barrier to travel and likened it to a reef blocking passage on the ocean. One specific rounded sandstone hill reminded them of the Capitol Dome in Washington DC.

Roads and hiking trails in the park provide

© JUDY JEWELL

HIGHLIGHTS

◖ The Scenic Drive: Capitol Reef's 25-mile round-trip Scenic Drive encompasses not only scenery and all its attendant geology, but also human history, pioneer sites, and even free fruit in season (page 142).

◖ Notom-Bullfrog Road: You'll pass nearly 80 miles of the Waterpocket Fold's eastern side while traveling along this road, which exposes the fold's geologic wonders. Distinctive panoramas are your reward, and scenic side canyons beckon hikers (page 144).

◖ Chimney Rock Trail: The trail to Chimney Rock starts right on Highway 24, and even if you weren't meaning to visit Capitol Reef, it's worth taking a couple of hours to hike it. Panoramic views from the top take in the face of Capitol Reef (page 149).

◖ Grand Wash Trail: Hike from the trailhead on Highway 24 into the Narrows, where the canyon walls close in and rise to 200 feet. Grand Wash offers easy hiking, great scenery, and an abundance of wildflowers (page 152).

◖ Capitol Gorge: Hike through another wash past rock art left by the Fremont people and a Mormon "pioneer register" to a turnoff for a spur trail (leading to natural water reservoirs called water pockets). Listen for the lovely song of the canyon wren (page 155).

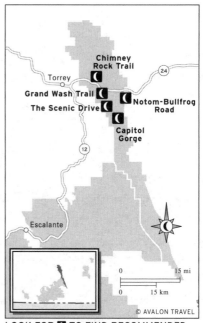

LOOK FOR ◖ TO FIND RECOMMENDED SIGHTS, ACTIVITIES, DINING, AND LODGING.

access to the colorful rock layers and to the plants and wildlife that live here. You'll also see remnants of the area's long human history—petroglyphs and storage bins of the prehistoric Fremont people, a schoolhouse and other structures built by Mormon pioneers, and several small uranium mines from the 20th century. Legends tell of Butch Cassidy and other outlaw members of the Wild Bunch who hid out in these remote canyons in the 1890s.

Even travelers short on time will enjoy a quick look at visitors center exhibits and a drive on Highway 24 through an impressive cross section of Capitol Reef cut by the

Fremont River. You can see more of the park on the Scenic Drive, a narrow paved road that heads south from the visitors center. The drive passes beneath spectacular cliffs of the reef and enters Grand Wash and Capitol Gorge Canyons; allow at least 1.5 hours for the 21-mile round-trip and any side trips. The fair-weather Notom-Bullfrog Road (about half paved, with paved segments at both north and south ends) heads south along the other side of the reef for almost 70 miles, offering fine views of the Waterpocket Fold. Burr Trail Road (dirt inside the park) in the south actually climbs over the fold in a steep set of switchbacks,

CAPITOL REEF

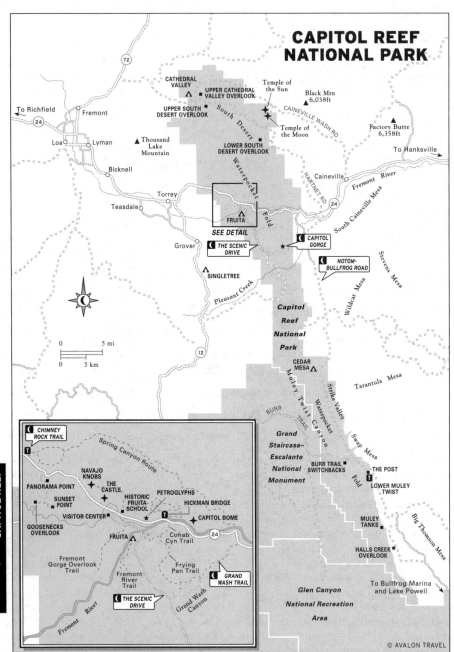

CAPITOL REEF NATIONAL PARK

To Richfield

Fremont

Loa

Lyman

Bicknell

Torrey

Teasdale

Grover

CATHEDRAL VALLEY

UPPER CATHEDRAL VALLEY OVERLOOK

UPPER SOUTH DESERT OVERLOOK

Thousand Lake Mountain

South Desert

LOWER SOUTH DESERT OVERLOOK

Temple of the Sun

Temple of the Moon

Black Mtn 6,038ft

CAINEVILLE WASH RD

Factory Butte 6,358ft

To Hanksville

Caineville

Fremont River

South Caineville Mesa

HARTNET RD

Waterpocket Fold

FRUITA

SEE DETAIL

THE SCENIC DRIVE

SINGLETREE

Pleasant Creek

CAPITOL GORGE

NOTOM-BULLFROG ROAD

Stevens Mesa

Capitol Reef National Park

CEDAR MESA

Muley Twist Canyon

Waterpocket Fold

Strike Valley

BURR TRAIL

Tarantula Mesa

Swap Mesa

Grand Staircase-Escalante National Monument

BURR TRAIL SWITCHBACKS

THE POST

LOWER MULEY TWIST

MULEY TANKS

HALLS CREEK OVERLOOK

Big Thomson Mesa

Glen Canyon National Recreation Area

To Bullfrog Marina and Lake Powell

0   5 mi
0   5 km

Detail

CHIMNEY ROCK TRAIL

Spring Canyon Route

NAVAJO KNOBS

PANORAMA POINT

THE CASTLE

PETROGLYPHS

SUNSET POINT

HISTORIC FRUITA SCHOOL

HICKMAN BRIDGE

VISITOR CENTER

GOOSENECKS OVERLOOK

FRUITA

CAPITOL DOME

Cohab Cyn Trail

Fremont Gorge Overlook Trail

Fremont River Trail

Frying Pan Trail

GRAND WASH TRAIL

THE SCENIC DRIVE

Grand Wash Canyon

Fremont River

© AVALON TRAVEL

connecting Notom Road with Boulder. Only drivers with high-clearance vehicles can explore Cathedral Valley in the park's northern district. All of these roads provide access to viewpoints and hiking trails.

Expect hot summer days (highs in the upper 80s and low 90s) and cool nights. Late-afternoon thunderstorms are common in July-August; be alert for impending storms, which can bring flash flooding. Winter brings cool days (highs in the 40s) and night temperatures in the low 20s and teens. Snow accents the colored rocks while rarely hindering traffic on the main highway. Winter travel on the back roads and trails may be halted by snow, but it soon melts when the sun comes out. Annual precipitation averages only seven inches, peaking in the late-summer thunderstorm season.

PLANNING YOUR TIME

Many southern Utah travelers treat Capitol Reef as a pass-through, and indeed, it's easy to get a feel for the park by taking a short hike off Highway 24, perhaps just the walk out to Goosenecks and Sunset Point. But a short visit here may leave you longing for more. On a one-day visit, be sure to stop at the visitors center for the slide show (it's less schmaltzy than many national-park slide shows and explains the geology quite nicely), hike either Grand Wash or Capitol Gorge, and spend some time exploring the park's human history, from petroglyphs left by the Fremont people to the Fruita blacksmith shop. It's easy to spend 2-3 days camping at the park campground or staying in nearby Torrey and taking day hikes in the park's core district. But if you've got the proper vehicle, after a couple of days you'll want to explore the Notom-Bullfrog Road. If you're just driving, this is easy to do in a day; if you get out of the car to explore every canyon, it can take all the time you have.

Exploring the Park

The most accessible part of Capitol Reef National Park (435/425-3791, www.nps.gov/care, $5 per vehicle, $3 cyclists and pedestrians) is along Highway 24, about 11 miles east of Torrey. In fact, several trails start right off the highway, which means that it's not necessary to pay the admission fee to get a tiny taste of this park.

VISITORS CENTER

At the visitors center (Hwy. 24, 8am-6pm daily June-Sept., 8am-4:30pm daily Oct.-May), start with the good 10-minute slide show, shown on request, introducing Capitol Reef's natural wonders and history. Rock samples and diagrams illustrate the park's geologic formations, and photos identify local plants and birds. Prehistoric Fremont artifacts on display include petroglyph replicas, sheepskin moccasins, pottery, basketry, stone knives, spear and arrow points, and bone jewelry. Other historic exhibits outline exploration and early Mormon settlement.

Hikers can pick up a map of trails that are near the visitors center and of longer routes in the southern areas of the park; naturalists will want the checklists of plants, birds, mammals, and other wildlife, while history buffs can learn more about the area's settlement and the founding of the park. Rangers offer nature walks, campfire programs, and other special events Easter-mid-October; the bulletin board outside the visitors center lists what's on. The visitors center is on Highway 24 at the turnoff for Fruita Campground and the Scenic Drive.

ALONG HIGHWAY 24

From the west, Highway 24 drops from the broad mountain valley near Torrey onto

THE LIFE AND LANDSCAPE OF CAPITOL REEF

Capitol Gorge is one of only five canyons cut through the Waterpocket Fold.

GEOLOGY

Exposed rocks at Capitol Reef reveal windswept deserts, rivers, mud flats, and inland seas of long ago. Nearly all the layers date from the Mesozoic Era (65-230 million years ago), when dinosaurs ruled the earth. Later uplift and twisting of the land, which continues to this day, built up the Colorado Plateau of southern Utah and the Rocky Mountains to the east. Immense forces squeezed the rocks until they bent up and over from east to west in the massive crease of the **Waterpocket Fold.**

FLORA AND FAUNA

Ponderosa pine and other cool-climate vegetation grow on the flanks of **Thousand Lake Mountain** at elevations of 7,000-9,000 feet in the northwest corner of the park. Most of the Waterpocket Fold, however, is at 5,000-7,000 feet, covered with sparse junipers and piñon pines that cling precariously in cracks and thin soils of the slickrock. The soil from each rock type generally determines what will grow. Mancos Shale forms a poor clay soil supporting only saltbush, shadscale, and galleta grass. On Dakota sandstone you'll see mostly sage and rabbitbrush. Clays of the Morrison Formation repel nearly all plants, while its sandstone nurtures mostly juniper, piñon pine, and cliffrose; uranium prospectors discovered that astragalus and prince's plume commonly grow near ore deposits. Sands of the Summerville Formation nourish grasses and four-wing saltbush. The **Fremont River** and several creeks provide a lush habitat of cottonwood, tamarisk, willow, and other water-loving plants.

Streamside residents include beavers, muskrats, mink, tree lizards, Great Basin spadefoot toads, Rocky Mountain toads, and leopard frogs. Spadefoot toads, fairy shrimp, and insects have adapted to the temporary water pockets by completing the aquatic phases of their short life cycles in a hurry. Near water or out in the drier country, you might see mule deer, coyotes, gray foxes, porcupines, spotted and striped skunks, badgers, black-tailed jackrabbits, desert cottontails, yellow-bellied marmots, rock squirrels, Colorado chipmunks, Ord's kangaroo rats, canyon mice, and five known species of bats. With luck, you may sight a relatively rare (and suitably distant) mountain lion or black bear.

Although you can't miss seeing the many small lizards along the trails, snakes tend to be more secretive; those in the park include the striped whipsnake, Great Basin gopher snake, wandering garter snake, and the rarely seen (and quite venomous) midget faded rattlesnake. Some common birds are the sharp-shinned hawk, American kestrel, chukar, mourning dove, white-throated swift, black-chinned and broad-tailed hummingbirds, violet-green swallow, common raven, piñon and scrub jays, canyon and rock wrens, and rufous-sided towhee. Most wildlife, except birds, wait until evening to come out, and they disappear again the following morning.

© BILL MCRAE

CAPITOL REEF

Sulphur Creek, with dramatic rock formations soaring to the horizon. A huge amphitheater of stone rings the basin, with formations such as Twin Rocks, Chimney Rock, and the Castle glowing in deep red and yellow tones. Ahead, the canyon narrows as the Fremont River slips between the cliffs to carve its chasm through the Waterpocket Fold.

Panorama Point

Take in the incredible view from Panorama Point, 2.5 miles west of the visitors center on the south side of Highway 24. Follow signs south for 250 yards to Panorama Point and views of Capitol Reef, the distant Henry Mountains to the east, and looming Boulder Mountain to the west. The large black basalt boulders were swept down from Boulder Mountain to the reef as part of giant debris flows between 8,000 and 200,000 years ago.

Goosenecks Overlook

On a gravel road one mile south of Panorama Point are the Goosenecks of Sulphur Creek. A short trail leads to Goosenecks Overlook (elevation 6,400 feet) on the rim for dizzying views of the creek below. Canyon walls display shades of yellow, green, brown, and red. Another easy trail leads 0.3 miles to **Sunset Point** and panoramic views of the Capitol Reef cliffs and the distant Henry Mountains.

Historic Fruita School

Remnants of the pioneer community of Fruita stretch along the narrow Fremont River Canyon. The Fruita Schoolhouse is just east of the visitors center on the north side of Highway 24. Early settlers completed this one-room log structure in 1896. Teachers struggled at times with rowdy students, but the kids learned their three R's in grades one through eight. Mormon church meetings, dances, town meetings, elections, and other community gatherings took place here. A lack of students caused the school to close in 1941. Rangers are on duty some days in summer; ask at the visitors center. At other times, you can peer inside the windows and take photos.

Fremont Petroglyphs

Farther down the canyon, 1.2 miles east of the visitors center on the north side of Highway 24, are several panels of Fremont petroglyphs; watch for the road signs. Several mountain sheep and human figures with headdresses decorate the cliff. You can see more petroglyphs by walking to the left and right along the cliff face. Stay on the trail, and do not climb the talus slope.

Behunin Cabin

Behunin Cabin is 6.2 miles east of the visitors center on the south side of Highway 24. Elijah Cutlar Behunin used blocks of sandstone to build this cabin in about 1882. For several years, Behunin, his wife, and 11 of their 13 children shared this sturdy but quite small cabin (the kids slept outside). They moved on when flooding made life too difficult. Small openings allow a look inside the dirt-floored structure, but no furnishings remain.

Fremont River Waterfall

Near the end of the narrow sandstone canyon, a small waterfall, created when the Fremont River was rerouted in 1962 to accommodate the highway, attracts photographers. The river twists through a narrow artificial crack in the rock before making its final plunge into a pool below. Take the sandy path from the parking area to where you can safely view the falls from below. The pool beneath the falls used to be a popular swimming hole, but water dynamics have changed over the years; the National Park Service closed it to swimming in 2011, when three people almost drowned because of the extremely heavy flow and strong currents. Parking is 6.9 miles east of the visitors center, near mile marker 86, on the north side of Highway 24. This area is closed during the

CAPITOL REEF

Fremont petroglyphs along Highway 24

© PAUL LEVY

CAPITOL REEF

warmer months and opens again when it's too cold for people to be tempted to swim.

◖ THE SCENIC DRIVE

Turn south from Highway 24 at the visitors center to experience some of the reef's best scenery and to learn more about its geology. A quick tour of this 25-mile out-and-back trip requires about 1.5 hours, but several hiking trails may tempt you to extend your stay. It's worth picking up a brochure at the visitors center for descriptions of geology along the road. The Scenic Drive is paved, although side roads have gravel surfaces. Note that drivers must pay the $5 park entrance fee to travel this road.

Fruita

In the Fruita Historic District, you'll first pass orchards and several of Fruita's buildings. A **blacksmith shop** (0.7 miles from the visitors center, on the right) displays tools, harnesses, farm machinery, and Fruita's first tractor. The tractor didn't arrive until 1940, long after the rest of the country had modernized. In a recording, a rancher tells about living and working in Fruita. The nearby orchards and fields are still maintained using old-time farming techniques.

The **Gifford Farmhouse,** one mile south on the Scenic Drive, is typical of rural Utah farmhouses of the early 1900s. Cultural demonstrations and handmade items are available. A picnic area is just beyond; with fruit trees and grass, this is a pretty spot for lunch. A short trail crosses orchards and the Fremont River to the **Historic Fruita School.**

Grand Wash

The Scenic Drive leaves the Fremont River valley and climbs up a desert slope, with the rock walls of the Waterpocket Fold rising to the east. Turn east to explore Grand Wash, a dry channel etched through the sandstone. A dirt road follows the twisting gulch one mile, with sheer rock walls rising along the sandy streambed. At

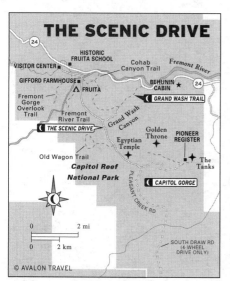

THE SCENIC DRIVE

HISTORIC FRUITA SCHOOL
VISITOR CENTER
GIFFORD FARMHOUSE
Cohab Canyon Trail
Fremont River
BEHUNIN CABIN
△ FRUITA
GRAND WASH TRAIL
Fremont Gorge Overlook Trail
Fremont River Trail
THE SCENIC DRIVE
Grand Wash Canyon
Golden Throne
Egyptian Temple
PIONEER REGISTER
Old Wagon Trail
Capitol Reef National Park
The Tanks
CAPITOL GORGE
PLEASANT CREEK RD

0   2 mi
0   2 km

© AVALON TRAVEL

SOUTH DRAW RD (4-WHEEL DRIVE ONLY)

the road's end, an easy hiking trail follows the wash 2.5 miles to its mouth along Highway 24.

Back on the paved Scenic Drive, continue south past Slickrock Divide to where the rock lining the reef deepens into a ruby red and forms odd columns and spires that resemble statuary. Called the **Egyptian Temple,** this is one of the most striking and colorful areas along the road.

Capitol Gorge

Capitol Gorge is at the end of the Scenic Drive, 10.7 miles from the visitors center. Capitol Gorge is a dry canyon through Capitol Reef, much like Grand Wash. Believe it or not, narrow twisting Capitol Gorge was the route of the main state highway through south-central Utah for 80 years. Mormon pioneers laboriously cleared a path so wagons could get through, a task they repeated every time flash floods rolled in a new set of boulders. Cars bounced their way down the canyon until 1962, when Highway 24 opened, but few traces of the old road remain today. Walking is easy along the gravel riverbed, but don't enter if storms threaten. An easy one-mile saunter

down the gorge will take day hikers past petroglyphs and a "register" rock where pioneers carved their names.

Pleasant Creek Road

The Scenic Drive curves east toward Capitol Gorge and onto Pleasant Creek Road (turn right 8.3 miles from the visitors center), which continues south below the face of the reef. After three miles, the sometimes rough dirt road passes Sleeping Rainbow-Floral Ranch (closed to the public) and ends at Pleasant Creek. A rugged road for 4WD vehicles—South Draw Road—continues on the other side, but it is much too rough for cars. Floral Ranch dates back to the early years of settlement at Capitol Reef. In 1939 it became the Sleeping Rainbow Guest Ranch, from the translation of the Native American name for Waterpocket Fold. Now the ranch belongs to the park and is used as a field research station by students and faculty of Utah Valley University. Pleasant Creek's perennial waters begin high on Boulder Mountain to the west and cut a scenic canyon completely through Capitol Reef. Hikers can head downstream through the three-mile-long canyon and then return the way they went in, or continue another three miles cross-country to Notom Road.

NORTH DISTRICT

Only the most adventurous travelers enter the remote canyons and desert country of the park's northern district. The few roads cannot be negotiated by 4WD vehicles, let alone ordinary cars, in wet weather. In good weather, high-clearance vehicles (good clearance is more important than four-wheel drive) can enter the region from the east, north, and west. The roads lead through stately sandstone monoliths of Cathedral Valley, volcanic remnants, badlands country, many low mesas, and vast sand flats. Foot travel allows closer inspection of these features or lengthy excursions into the canyons of Polk, Deep, and Spring Creeks, which cut deeply into the flanks of Thousand Lake Mountain.

CAPITOL REEF

The Scenic Drive passes historic buildings from the old town of Fruita and provides access to several hiking trails.

Mountain bikers enjoy these challenging roads as well, but they must stay on established roads. Much of the north district is good for horseback riding as well.

The district's two main roads—Hartnett Road and Cathedral Road (a.k.a. Caineville Wash Rd.)—combine with a short stretch of Highway 24 to form a loop, with a campground at their junction. **Cathedral Valley Campground**'s five sites provide a place to stop for the night; rangers won't permit car camping elsewhere in the district. The campground is on the 4WD Cathedral Valley loop road about 36 miles from the visitors center (from the park entrance, head 12 miles east on Highway 24, turn north and ford the Fremont River, and then follow Hartnett Road about 24 miles to the campground); check on road conditions at the visitors center before heading out. The **Upper Cathedral Valley Trail,** just below the campground, is an enjoyable one-mile walk offering

excellent views of the Cathedrals. Backcountry hikers must have a permit and camp at least 0.5 miles from the nearest road. Guides to the area can be purchased at the visitors center.

SOUTH DISTRICT
◖ Notom-Bullfrog Road

Capitol Reef is only a small part of the Waterpocket Fold. By taking the Notom-Bullfrog Road, you'll see nearly 80 miles of the fold's eastern side. This route crosses some of the younger geologic layers, such as those of the Morrison Formation, which form colorful hills. In other places, eroded layers of the Waterpocket Fold jut up at 70-degree angles. The Henry Mountains to the east and the many canyons on both sides of the road add to the memorable panoramas. The northernmost 10 miles of the road have been paved, and about 25 miles are paved on the southern end near Bullfrog, a settlement on the shores of Lake

THE WATERPOCKET FOLD

© BILL MCRAE

The Waterpocket Fold is a vast wrinkle nearly 100 miles long.

About 65 million years ago, well before the Colorado Plateau uplifted, sedimentary rock layers in south-central Utah buckled, forming a steep-sided monocline, a rock fold with one very steep side in an area of otherwise nearly horizontal layers. A monocline is a "step-up" in the rock layers along an underlying fault. The rock layers on the west side of the Waterpocket Fold have been lifted more than 7,000 feet higher than the layers to the east. The 100-mile-long fold was then subjected to millions of years of erosion, which slowly removed the upper layers to reveal the warped sedimentary layers at its base. Continued erosion of the sandstone has left many basins, or "water pockets," along the fold. These seasonal water sources, often called "water tanks," are used by desert animals, and they were a water source for prehistoric people. Erosion of the tilted rock layers continues today, forming colorful cliffs, massive domes, soaring spires, stark monoliths, twisting canyons, and graceful arches. Getting a sense of the Waterpocket Fold requires some off-pavement driving. The best viewpoint is along Burr Trail Road, which climbs up the fold between Boulder and Notom-Bullfrog Road.

Powell. The rest of the road is dirt and gravel, and it can get pretty washboarded and bumpy. Most cars should have no trouble negotiating this road in good weather. Keep an eye on the weather before setting out, though; the dirt-and-gravel surface is usually OK for cars when dry but can be dangerous for any vehicle when wet. Sandy spots and washouts may present a problem for low-clearance vehicles; contact the visitors center to check current conditions. Have a full tank of gas and carry extra water and food; no services are available between Highway 24 and Bullfrog Marina. Purchase a small guide to this area at the visitors center.

© JUDY JEWELL

Notom-Bullfrog Road runs from Highway 24 south to a ferry crossing at Lake Powell; it follows the Waterpocket Fold for much of the way.

CAPITOL REEF

Features and mileage along the drive from north to south include the following:

- **Mile 0.0:** The turnoff from Highway 24 is 9.2 miles east of the visitors center and 30.2 miles west of Hanksville (another turnoff from Highway 24 is three miles east).

- **Mile 2.2:** Pleasant Creek; the mouth of the canyon is 5-6 miles upstream, although it's only about three miles away if you head cross-country from south of Notom. Hikers can follow the canyon three miles upstream through Capitol Reef to Pleasant Creek Road (off the Scenic Drive).

- **Mile 4.1:** Notom Ranch is to the west; once a small town, Notom is now a private ranch.

- **Mile 8.1:** Burrow Wash; hikers can explore the narrow canyon upstream.

- **Mile 9.3:** Cottonwood Wash; another canyon hike just upstream.

- **Mile 10.4:** Five Mile Wash; yet another canyon hike. Pavement ends.

- **Mile 13.3:** Sheets Gulch; a scenic canyon is upstream here.

- **Mile 14.1:** Sandy Ranch Junction; high-clearance vehicles can turn east and go 16 miles to the Henry Mountains.

- **Mile 14.2:** Oak Creek Access Road; the creek cuts a two-mile-long canyon through Capitol Reef and makes a good day hike. Backpackers sometimes start upstream at Lower Bowns Reservoir (off Hwy. 12) and hike the 15 miles to Oak Creek Access Road. The clear waters of Oak Creek flow year-round but are not potable.

- **Mile 14.4:** Oak Creek crossing.

- **Mile 20.0:** Entering Capitol Reef National Park; a small box has information sheets.

- **Mile 22.3:** Cedar Mesa Campground is to the west; the small five-site campground is surrounded by junipers and has fine views of the Waterpocket Fold and the Henry Mountains. Free sites have tables and grills;

there's a pit toilet but no drinking water. Red Canyon Trail (4 miles round-trip) begins here and heads west into a huge box canyon in the Waterpocket Fold.

- **Mile 26.0:** Bitter Creek Divide; streams to the north flow to the Fremont River; Halls Creek on the south side runs through Strike Valley to Lake Powell, 40 miles away.

- **Mile 34.1:** Burr Trail Road Junction; turn west up the steep switchbacks to ascend the Waterpocket Fold and continue to Boulder and Highway 12 (36 miles). Burr Trail is the only road that actually crosses the top of the fold, and it's one of the most scenic in the park. Driving conditions are similar to the Notom-Bullfrog Road—OK for cars when dry. Pavement begins at the park boundary and continues to Boulder. Although paved, the Burr Trail still must be driven slowly because of its curves and potholes. The section of road through Long Canyon has especially pretty scenery.

- **Mile 36.0:** Surprise Canyon Trailhead; a hike into this narrow, usually shaded canyon takes 1-2 hours.

- **Mile 36.6:** Post Corral; a small trading post here once served sheepherders and some cattle ranchers, but today this spot is just a reference point. Park here to hike to Headquarters Canyon. A trailhead for Lower Muley Twist Canyon via Halls Creek is at the end of a 0.5-mile-long road to the south.

- **Mile 37.5:** Leaving Capitol Reef National Park; a small box has information sheets. Much of the road between here and Glen Canyon National Recreation Area has been paved.

- **Mile 45.5:** Road junction; turn right (south) to continue to Bullfrog Marina (25 miles) or go straight (east) for Starr Springs Campground (23 miles) in the Henry Mountains.

- **Mile 46.4:** The road to the right (west) goes to Halls Creek Overlook. This turnoff is poorly signed and easy to miss; look for it 0.9 miles south of the previous junction. Turn in and follow the road three miles, then turn right at a fork and continue 0.4 miles

to the viewpoint. The last 0.3 miles may be too rough for low-clearance vehicles. A picnic table is the only "facility" here. Far below in Grand Gulch, Halls Creek flows south to Lake Powell. Look across the valley for the double Brimhall Bridge in the red sandstone of the Waterpocket Fold. A steep trail descends to Halls Creek (1.2 miles one-way), and it's possible to continue another 1.1 miles up Brimhall Canyon to the bridge. A register box at the overlook has information sheets on this route. Note, however, that the last part of the hike to the bridge requires difficult rock-scrambling and wading or swimming through pools. Hikers looking for another adventure might want to follow Halls Creek 10 miles downstream to the narrows, where convoluted walls as high as 700 feet narrow to little more than arm's length apart. This beautiful area of water-sculpted rock sometimes has deep pools that require swimming.

- **Mile 49.0:** Colorful clay hills of deep red, cream, and gray rise beside the road. This clay turns to goo when wet, providing all the traction of axle grease.

- **Mile 54.0:** Beautiful panorama of countless mesas, mountains, and canyons; Lake Powell and Navajo Mountain can be seen to the south.

- **Mile 65.3:** Junction with paved Highway 276; turn left (north) for Hanksville (59 miles) or right (south) to Bullfrog Marina (5.2 miles).

- **Mile 70.5:** End at Bullfrog Marina in Glen Canyon National Recreation Area.

Lower Muley Twist Canyon

"So winding that it would twist a mule pulling a wagon," said an early visitor. This canyon has some of the best hiking in the southern district of the park. In the 1880s Mormon pioneers used the canyon as part of a wagon route between Escalante and new settlements in southeastern Utah, replacing the even more difficult Hole-in-the-Rock route.

Unlike most canyons of the Waterpocket Fold, Muley Twist runs lengthwise along the crest for about 18 miles before finally turning east and leaving the fold. Hikers starting from Burr Trail Road can easily follow the twisting bends down to Halls Creek, 12 miles away. Two trailheads and the Halls Creek route allow a variety of trips.

Start from Burr Trail Road near the top of the switchbacks (2.2 miles west of Notom-Bullfrog Rd.) and hike down the dry gravel streambed. After four miles, you have the option of returning the same way, taking the Cut Off route east 2.5 miles to the Post Corral trailhead (off Notom-Bullfrog Rd.), or continuing eight miles down Lower Muley Twist Canyon to its end at Halls Creek. On reaching Halls Creek, turn left (north) and travel five miles up the creek bed or the old jeep road beside it to the Post. This section of creek is in an open dry valley. With a car shuttle, the Post would be the end of a good two-day 17-mile hike, or you could loop back to Lower Muley Twist Canyon via the Cut Off route and hike back to Burr Trail Road for a 23.5-mile trip. It's a good idea to check the weather beforehand and avoid the canyon if storms threaten.

Cream-colored sandstone cliffs lie atop the red Kayenta and Wingate Formations. Impressively deep undercuts have been carved into the lower canyon. Spring and fall offer the best conditions; summer temperatures can exceed 100°F. Elevations range from 5,640 feet at Burr Trail Road to 4,540 feet at the confluence with Halls Creek to 4,894 feet at the Post.

An information sheet is available at the visitors center, and the trailheads have a small map and route details. Topographic maps of Wagon Box Mesa, Mount Pennell, and Hall Mesa as well as the 1:100,000-scale Escalante and Hite Crossing maps are sold at the visitors center. You'll also find this hike described in David Day's *Utah's Favorite Hiking Trails* and in the small spiral-bound *Explore Capitol Reef Trails* by the Capitol Reef Natural History Association, available at the visitors center.

Carry all the water you'll need for the trip because natural sources are often dry or polluted.

Upper Muley Twist Canyon

This part of the canyon has plenty of scenery. Large and small natural arches along the way add to its beauty. Upper Muley Twist Road turns north off Burr Trail Road about one mile west from the top of a set of switchbacks. Cars can usually go in 0.5 miles to a trailhead parking area; high-clearance 4WD vehicles can head another three miles up a wash to the end of the primitive road. Look for natural arches on the left along this last section. **Strike Valley Overlook Trail** (0.75 miles round-trip) begins at the end of the road and leads to a magnificent panorama of the Waterpocket Fold and beyond. Return to the canyon, where you can hike as far as 6.5 miles, to the head of Upper Muley Twist Canyon.

Two large arches are a short hike upstream; Saddle Arch, the second one, on the left, is 1.7 miles away. The **Rim Route** begins across from Saddle Arch, climbs the canyon wall, follows the rim (offering good views of Strike Valley and the Henry Mountains), and descends back into the canyon at a point just above the narrows, 4.75 miles from the end of the road. The Rim Route is most easily followed in this direction. Proceed up-canyon to see several more arches. A narrow section of canyon beginning about four miles from the end of the road must be bypassed to continue; look for rock cairns showing the way around to the right. Continuing up the canyon past the Rim Route sign will take you to several small drainages marking the upper end of Muley Twist Canyon. Climb a high tree-covered point on the west rim for great views; experienced hikers with a map can follow the rim back to Upper Muley Road. There is no trail and no markers on this route. Bring all the water you'll need; there are no reliable sources in Upper Muley Twist Canyon.

Recreation

Fifteen trails for day hikes begin within a short drive of the visitors center. Of these, only Grand Wash, Capitol Gorge, and the short paths to Sunset Point and Goosenecks are easy. The others involve moderately strenuous climbs over irregular slickrock. Signs and rock cairns mark the way, but it's all too easy to wander off if you don't pay attention to the route.

Although most hiking trails can easily be done in a day, backpackers and hikers might want to try longer trips in Chimney Rock-Spring Canyons to the north or Muley Twist Canyon and Halls Creek to the south. Obtain the required backcountry permit (free) from a ranger and camp at least 0.5 miles from the nearest maintained road or trail. (Cairned routes like Chimney Rock Canyon, Muley Twist Canyon, and Halls Creek don't count as trails but are backcountry routes.) Bring a stove for cooking; backcountry users are not permitted to build fires. Avoid camping or parking in washes at any time—torrents of mud and boulders can carry away everything.

HIKING FROM HIGHWAY 24

Stop by the visitors center to pick up a map showing hiking trails and trail descriptions. These trailheads are located along the main highway through the park and along the Fremont River. Note that the Grand Wash Trail cuts west through the reef to the Scenic Drive.

◖ Chimney Rock Trail

- Distance: 3.5 miles round-trip
- Duration: 2.5 hours
- Elevation change: 800 feet
- Effort: moderate-strenuous
- Trailhead: 3 miles west of the visitors center, on the north side of Highway 24

Towering 660 feet above the highway, Chimney Rock (elevation 6,100 feet) is a fluted spire of dark red rock (Moenkopi Formation) capped by a block of hard sandstone (Shinarump Member of the Chinle Formation). The trail leads pretty much straight uphill from the parking lot to a ridge overlooking Chimney Rock, and then levels off a bit. Panoramic views take in the face of Capitol Reef. Petrified wood along the trail has been eroded from the Chinle Formation (the same rock layer found in Petrified Forest National Park in Arizona). It is illegal to take any petrified wood.

Spring Canyon Route

- Distance: 10 miles one-way
- Duration: 6 hours
- Elevation change: 540 feet
- Effort: moderate
- Trailhead: Chimney Rock parking lot

Except for its length, this is not a particularly difficult trail. It begins at the top of the Chimney Rock Trail and runs to the Fremont River and Highway 24; since it begins and ends on the highway, a car shuttle can eliminate the need to hike out and back. The wonderfully eroded forms of Navajo sandstone present a continually changing exhibition. The riverbed is normally dry. (Some maps show all or part of this as "Chimney Rock Canyon.") Check with rangers for the weather forecast before setting off, because flash floods can be dangerous, and the Fremont River (which you must wade across) can rise quite high. Normally, the river runs less than knee-deep to Highway 24 (3.7 miles east of the visitors center). With luck, you'll have a car waiting for you. Summer hikers can beat the heat with a crack-of-dawn departure. Carry water, as this section of canyon lacks a reliable source.

From the Chimney Rock parking area, hike

© BILL MCRAE

Chimney Rock

Chimney Rock Trail to the top of the ridge and follow the signs for Chimney Rock Canyon. Enter the unnamed lead-in canyon and follow it downstream. A sign marks Chimney Rock Canyon, which is 2.5 miles from the start. From this point, it's an additional 6.5 miles downstream to reach the Fremont River. A section of narrows requires some rock-scrambling (bring a cord to lower backpacks), or the area can be bypassed on a narrow trail to the left above the narrows. Farther down, a natural arch high on the left marks the halfway point.

Upper Chimney Rock Canyon could be explored on an overnight trip (permit required). A spring (purify the water before drinking it) is located in an alcove on the right side, about one mile up Chimney Rock Canyon from the lead-in canyon. Wildlife uses this water source, so camp at least 0.25 miles away. Chimney Rock Canyon, the longest in the park, begins high on the slopes of Thousand Lake Mountain and descends nearly 15 miles southeast to join the Fremont River.

Sulphur Creek Route

- Distance: 5 miles one-way
- Duration: 3-5 hours
- Elevation change: 540 feet
- Effort: moderate-strenuous
- Trailhead: across Highway 24 from Chimney Rock parking lot

This moderately difficult hike begins by following a wash across the highway from the Chimney Rock parking area, descends to Sulphur Creek, then heads down the narrow canyon to the visitors center; it's five miles if you've arranged a car or bike shuttle, and double that if you have to hike back to your starting point. It's best to hike Sulphur Creek during warm weather, because you'll be wading in the normally shallow creek passing through a slot canyon. Wear sneakers or other shoes that you don't mind getting wet. Before starting out, check to make sure the water level isn't too high for hiking (you can do this by examining the route's endpoint behind the

CAPITOL REEF

DATURA: A PLANT WITH A PAST

As dusk approaches, the huge white flowers of the datura open, and their sweet smell attracts moths, beetles, and wasps. As intoxicating as the datura's fragrance may be, it doesn't hold a candle to the plant itself, which is a potent hallucinogen. It also contains toxic alkaloids, including nerve toxins capable of killing humans and animals.

Nonetheless, datura, also known as jimsonweed has a rich history of folk use. Many indigenous peoples in the Americas, including the Zuni, the Chumash, and even the Aztecs, were familiar with its uses; some regarded it as sacred. It has been used as a shamanic ritual drug as well as a topical analgesic and even as a sort of medieval Mickey Finn. (Pimps in the Middle Ages used datura to make the prostitutes in their employ more compliant.) Accounts from Jamestown, Virginia, one of the earliest British settlements in North America, report a group of soldiers going insane after eating datura in 1676.

Up until 1968 datura was a component of some over-the-counter asthma medicines; it was banned when it gained popularity among American youth, who began using these medications recreationally. Atropine, an anticholinergic substance often used by ophthalmologists to dilate pupils, is datura's main psychoactive component. It's a central nervous system depressant that mostly causes users to feel drowsy—some report vivid dreams—and also increases the heart rate, sometimes to dangerous levels.

In Carlos Castaneda's *The Teachings of Don Juan: A Yaqui Way of Knowledge*, Don Juan warns that datura "is as powerful as the best of allies, but there is something I personally don't like about her. She distorts men. She gives them a taste of power too soon without fortifying their hearts and makes them domineering and unpredictable. She makes them weak in the middle of their great power."

visitors center; it should be ankle-deep or less for a safe and fun hike).

Three small waterfalls are along the route, but it's fairly easy to climb down rock ledges to the side of the water; two falls are just below the goosenecks and the third is about 0.5 miles before the visitors center. Carry water with you.

Hickman Natural Bridge

- Distance: 2 miles round-trip
- Duration: 1.5 hours
- Elevation change: 380 feet
- Effort: easy-moderate
- Trailhead: 2 miles east of the visitors center, on the north side of Highway 24

The graceful Hickman Natural Bridge spans 133 feet across a small streambed. Numbered stops along the self-guided trail correspond to descriptions in a pamphlet available at the trailhead or visitors center. Starting from the parking area (elevation 5,320 feet), the trail follows

the Fremont River's green banks a short distance before climbing to the bridge. The last section of trail follows a dry wash shaded by cottonwoods, junipers, and piñon pines. You'll pass under the bridge (eroded from the Kayenta Formation) at trail's end. Capitol Dome and other sculptured sandstone features surround the site. Joseph Hickman, for whom the bridge was named, served as principal of Wayne County High School and later in the state legislature; he and another local, Ephraim Pectol, led efforts to promote Capitol Reef.

Rim Overlook Trail

- Distance: 4.5 miles round-trip
- Duration: 3-5 hours
- Elevation change: 540 feet
- Effort: moderate-strenuous
- Trailhead: Hickman Natural Bridge Trailhead

A splendid overlook 1,000 feet above Fruita beckons hikers up the Rim Overlook Trail.

CAPITOL REEF

Take the Hickman Natural Bridge Trail from the parking area, turn right at the signed fork, and hike for about two miles. Allow 3.5 hours from the fork for this hike. Panoramic views take in the Fremont River valley below, the great cliffs of Capitol Reef above, the Henry Mountains to the southeast, and Boulder Mountain to the southwest.

Continue another 2.2 miles from the Rim Overlook to reach **Navajo Knobs.** Rock cairns lead the way over slickrock along the rim of the Waterpocket Fold. A magnificent view at trail's end takes in much of southeastern Utah.

◻ Grand Wash Trail

- Distance: 4.5 miles round-trip
- Duration: 2-3 hours
- Elevation change: negligible
- Effort: easy
- Trailhead: 4.7 miles east of the visitors center, on the south side of Highway 24

One of only five canyons cutting completely through the reef, Grand Wash offers easy hiking, great scenery, and an abundance of wildflowers. There's no trail—just follow the dry riverbed. (Flash floods can occur during storms.) Only a short distance from Highway 24, canyon walls rise 800 feet above the floor and narrow to as little as 20 feet in width; this stretch of trail is known as the Narrows. After the Narrows, the wash widens, and wildflowers grow everywhere. Cassidy Arch Trailhead is two miles from Highway 24.

The hike can also be started from a trailhead at the end of Grand Wash Road, off the Scenic Drive. A car or bike shuttle can make it a one-way hike of about 2.5 miles.

HIKING THE SCENIC DRIVE

These hikes begin from trailheads along the Scenic Drive. Drivers must pay the $5 National Park admission fee to travel this road.

Fremont Gorge Overlook Trail

- Distance: 4.5 miles round-trip
- Duration: 2-3 hours
- Elevation change: 1,000 feet
- Effort: moderate-strenuous
- Trailhead: Fruita blacksmith shop

From the start at the Fruita blacksmith shop, the trail climbs a short distance, then crosses Johnson Mesa and climbs steeply to the overlook about 1,000 feet above the Fremont River. The overlook is not a place for the acrophobic—even people who aren't ordinarily afraid of heights might find it a little daunting.

Cohab Canyon Trail

- Distance: 3.5 miles round-trip
- Duration: 2.5 hours
- Elevation change: 400 feet
- Effort: moderate-strenuous
- Trailheads: across the road from Fruita Campground (one mile south of the visitors center) and across Highway 24 from Hickman Natural Bridge trailhead

Cohab is a pretty little canyon overlooking the campground. Mormon polygamists ("cohabitationists") supposedly used the canyon to escape federal marshals during the 1880s. It's possible to hike this trail starting from either trailhead. Starting from the campground, the trail first follows steep switchbacks before continuing along more gentle grades to the top of the reef, 400 feet higher and one mile from the campground. You can take a short trail to viewpoints or continue 0.75 miles down the other side of the ridge to Highway 24.

Another option is to turn right at the top on Frying Pan Trail and head to Cassidy Arch (3.5 miles one-way) and Grand Wash (4 miles one-way). The trail from Cassidy Arch to Grand Wash is steep. All of these interconnecting trails offer many hiking possibilities, especially if you can arrange a car shuttle. For example,

DESERT VARNISH

The dark-colored vertical stripes often seen on sandstone cliff faces across the Colorado Plateau are known as desert varnish. They're mostly composed of very fine clay particles, rich in iron and manganese. It's not entirely known how these streaks are formed, but it seems likely that they're at least partly created by mineral-rich water coursing down the cliffs along the varnished areas and wind-blown clay dust sticking to cliff faces. Bacteria and fungi on the rock's surface may help this process along by absorbing manganese and iron from the atmosphere and precipitating it as a black layer of manganese oxide or reddish iron oxide on the rock surfaces. The clay particles in this thin layer of varnish help shield the bacteria against the drying effects of the desert sun. Prehistoric rock artists worked with desert varnish, chipping away the dark surface to expose the lighter underlying rocks.

© PAUL LEVY

Desert varnish streaks sandstone walls.

CAPITOL REEF

you could start up Cohab Canyon Trail from Highway 24, cross over the reef on Frying Pan Trail, make a side trip to Cassidy Arch, descend Cassidy Arch Trail to Grand Wash, walk down Grand Wash to Highway 24, then walk (or car shuttle) 2.7 miles along the highway back to the start, for 10.5 miles in total.

Hiking the Frying Pan Trail involves an additional 600 feet of climbing from either Cohab Canyon or Cassidy Arch Trail. Once atop Capitol Reef, the trail follows the gently rolling slickrock terrain.

Fremont River Trail

- Distance: 2.5 miles round-trip
- Duration: 2 hours
- Elevation change: 770 feet
- Effort: moderate-strenuous
- Trailhead: Fruita Campground amphitheater

The Cohab Canyon Trail climbs from the tree-shaded Fruita Campground.

The trail starts out quite easy, passing orchards along the Fremont River (elevation 5,350 feet). This part of the trail is wheelchair accessible. After 0.5 miles, it begins a climb up sloping rock to a Miners Mountain viewpoint overlooking Fruita, Boulder Mountain, and Capitol Reef. Bring $0.50 for a trail brochure describing traditional agricultural practices in the valley and the geological formations visible at the top of the trail.

Cassidy Arch

- Distance: 3.5 miles round-trip
- Duration: 3 hours
- Elevation change: 670 feet
- Effort: moderate-strenuous
- Trailhead: end of drivable section of Grand Wash Road
- Directions: Turn left off the Scenic Drive, 3.6 miles from the visitors center, and follow Grand Wash Road to the trailhead.

Cassidy Arch Trail begins near the end of Grand Wash Road, ascends the north wall of Grand Wash, and then winds across slickrock to a vantage point close to the arch. Energetic hikers will enjoy good views of Grand Wash, the great domes of Navajo sandstone, and the arch itself. The notorious outlaw Butch Cassidy may have traveled through Capitol Reef and seen this arch. Frying Pan Trail branches off Cassidy Arch Trail at the one-mile mark, and then wends its way across three miles of slickrock to Cohab Canyon.

Old Wagon Trail Loop

- Distance: 3.5 miles round-trip
- Duration: 3 hours
- Elevation change: 1,000 feet
- Effort: moderate-strenuous
- Trailhead: on the Scenic Drive, 6 miles south of visitors center, between Grand Wash and Capitol Gorge

Wagon drivers once used this route as a

The Fremont River Trail starts out level, then climbs to provide good views of the valley and the local geology.

shortcut between Grover and Capitol Gorge. The old trail crosses a wash to the west, and then ascends steadily through piñon and juniper woodland on Miners Mountain. After 1.5 miles, the trail leaves the wagon road and continues north for 0.5 miles to a high knoll and the best views of the Capitol Reef area.

◖ Capitol Gorge

- Distance: 2 miles round-trip
- Duration: 1-2 hours
- Elevation change: 100 feet
- Effort: easy-moderate
- Trailhead: Capitol Gorge parking area

Follow the well-maintained dirt road to the parking area in Capitol Gorge to begin this hike. The first mile downstream is the most scenic: Fremont petroglyphs (in poor condition) appear on the left after 0.1 miles; narrows of Capitol Gorge close in at 0.3 miles; a

"pioneer register" on the left soon after consists of names and dates of early travelers and ranchers scratched in the canyon wall. If you're able to, scramble up some rocks and follow a cairn-marked trail across the slickrock, then head up out of the wash at the trail marker to see natural water tanks, about 0.8 miles from the trail. These depressions in the rock collect water and give the Waterpocket Fold its name. Back in the wash, listen for canyon wrens—their song starts on a high note and then trills down the scale. From the turnoff to the water tanks, hikers can continue another three miles downstream to Notom Road.

Golden Throne Trail

- Distance: 4 miles round-trip
- Duration: 3 hours
- Elevation change: 1,100 feet
- Effort: strenuous

CAPITOL REEF

© JUDY JEWELL

Fruita Campground provides easy access to a couple of good hiking trails.

• Trailhead: Capitol Gorge parking area

The Golden Throne Trail begins at the trailhead at the end of the drivable part of Capitol Wash. Instead of heading down Capitol Gorge from the parking area, turn left up this trail for a steady climb to dramatic views of the reef and surrounding area. The Golden Throne is a massive monolith of yellow-hued sandstone capped by a thin layer of red rock. This is a good hike to take around sunset, when the rocks take on a burnished glow.

MOUNTAIN BIKING

Ditch the car and really get to know this country with a big loop tour. For a strenuous ride with steep grades, take the **Boulder Mountain Loop.** Start from Highway 24 near Capitol Reef, take the Notom-Bullfrog Road to Burr Trail Road, and then take Highway 12 over Boulder Mountain to Highway 24 and back to Capitol Reef. This is definitely the sort of

trip that requires some touring experience and a decent level of training (Boulder Mountain is quite a haul). This route can run 80-125 miles over several days.

In the remote northern section of the park, cyclists can ride the challenging **Cathedral Valley Loop.** The complete loop is more than 60 miles long. Little water is available along the route, so it's best ridden in spring or fall, when temperatures are low. Access the loop on either Hartnett Road (11.7 miles east of the visitors center) or Caineville Wash Road (18.6 miles east of the visitors center). A small campground is located about 36 miles into the loop.

Although the Scenic Drive doesn't have much of a shoulder, it's not a bad bicycling road, especially early in the morning before car traffic has picked up. Dirt spur roads off the Scenic Drive lead up Grand Wash, into Capitol Gorge, and up South Draw to Pleasant Creek.

Contact the visitors center for more information on these and other routes.

CLIMBING

Rock climbing is allowed in the park. Climbers should check with rangers to learn about restricted areas, but registration is voluntary. Permits are not required unless climbers plan to camp overnight. Climbers must use "clean" techniques (no pitons or bolts) and keep at least 100 feet from rock-art panels and prehistoric structures. Because of the abundance of prehistoric rock art found there, the rock wall north of Highway 24—between the Fruita School and the east end of Kreuger Orchard (mile 81.4)—is closed to climbing. Other areas closed to climbing include Hickman Natural Bridge and all other arches and bridges, Temple of the Moon and Temple of the Sun, and Chimney Rock.

The harder, fractured sandstone of the Wingate Formation is better suited to climbing than the more crumbly Entrada sandstone. The rock is given to flaking, however, so climbers should use caution. Be sure that your chalk matches the color of the rock; white chalk is prohibited.

CAPITOL REEF

THE ORCHARDS OF CAPITOL REEF

Capitol Reef was one of the last places in the West to be found by settlers. The first reports came in 1866 from a detachment of Mormon militia pursuing insurgent Utes. In 1872, Professor Almon H. Thompson of the Powell Expedition led the first scientific exploration in the fold country and named several park features along the group's Pleasant Creek route. Mormons, expanding their network of settlements, arrived in the upper Fremont Valley in the late 1870s and spread downriver to Hanksville. Junction (renamed Fruita in 1902) and nearby Pleasant Creek (Sleeping Rainbow-Floral Ranch) were settled about 1880. Floods, isolation, and transportation difficulties forced many families to move on, especially downstream from Capitol Reef. Irrigation and hard work paid off with prosperous fruit orchards and the sobriquet "The Eden of Wayne County." The aptly named Fruita averaged about 10 families, who grew alfalfa, sorghum (for syrup), vegetables, and a wide variety of fruit. Getting the produce to market required long and difficult journeys by wagon. The region remained one of the most isolated in Utah until after World War II.

Although Fruita's citizens have departed, the National Park Service still maintains the old orchards. They are lovely in late April, when the trees are in bloom beneath the towering canyon walls. Visitors are welcome to pick and carry away the cherries, apricots, peaches, pears, and apples during harvest seasons. Harvest begins in late June-early July and ends in October. You'll be charged about the same as in commercial pick-your-own orchards. You can also wander through any orchard and eat all you want on the spot for free before and during the designated picking season.

CAMPGROUNDS

Fruita Campground (year-round, $10), one mile south of the visitors center on the Scenic Drive, has 71 sites for tents and RVs with drinking water and heated restrooms, but no showers or hookups. Campers must get their water from the visitors center November-April. The surrounding orchards and lush grass make this an attractive spot. Sites are first-come, first-served and often fill by early afternoon in the busy May-October season. One group campground (reservations required, $3 pp, $50 minimum) and a picnic area are nearby. Submit written reservation requests for the group site to Group Campsite Reservations, Capitol Reef National Park, HC 70, Box 15, Torrey, UT, 84775.

Two campgrounds offer first-come, first-served primitive sites with no water. The five-site **Cedar Mesa Campground** (year-round, free) is in the park's southern district, just off Notom-Bullfrog Road (dirt); campers enjoy fine views of the Waterpocket Fold and the Henry Mountains. From the visitors center, go east 9.2 miles on Highway 24, then turn right and go 22 miles on Notom-Bullfrog Road (avoid this road if it's wet). **Cathedral Valley Campground** (year-round, free) serves the park's northern district; it has six sites near the Hartnett Junction, about 30 miles north of Highway 24. Take either Caineville Wash Road or Hartnett Road. Both roads are dirt and should be avoided when wet. Hartnett has a river ford.

If you're just looking for a place to park for the night, check out the public land east of the park boundary, off Highway 24. Areas on both sides of the highway (about nine miles east of the visitors center) can be used for free primitive camping.

Backcountry camping is allowed in the park; obtain a free backcountry permit at the visitors center.

CAPITOL REEF

Torrey

Torrey (population 179) is an attractive little village with a real Western feel. Only 11 miles west of the Capitol Reef National Park visitors center, at the junction of Highways 12 and 24, it's a friendly and convenient place to stay, with several excellent lodgings and a good restaurant.

There are other little towns along the Fremont River, which drains this steep-sided valley. Teasdale is a small community just four miles west, situated in a grove of piñon pines. Bicknell, a small farm and ranch town, is eight miles west of Torrey.

OUTFITTERS

You can rent mountain bikes at **Backcountry Outfitters** (Hwy. 12 and Hwy. 24, 435/425-2010, www.ridethereef.com); their main business is guiding people on hiking, canyoneering, 4WD, or horseback trips.

Hondoo Rivers and Trails (435/425-3519 or 800/332-2696, www.hondoo.com), run by longtime locals, offers guide services for both day trips and multiday backcountry excursions; for a real treat, check out the inn-to-inn trail rides. They also provide shuttle services.

ENTERTAINMENT AND EVENTS

The **Entrada Institute** (www.entradainstitute.org), a nonprofit organization that seeks to further understanding and appreciation of the natural, historical, cultural, and scientific heritage of the Colorado Plateau, sponsors a cultural event as part of their **Saturday Sunset Series** (7:30pm Sat. late May-late Oct., usually free). Events range from talks by local ranchers on the cattle industry to musical performances. These events are held at **Robber's Roost Bookstore** (185 W. Main St., 435/425-3265, www.robbersroostbooks.com), which is a good place to visit any time of day.

ACCOMMODATIONS
Under $50

There are a few small bunkhouse cabins at the center of town, at the **Torrey Trading Post** (75 W. Main St., 435/425-3716, www.torreytradingpost.com, $35). They aren't loaded with frills—the toilets and showers are in men's and women's bathhouses—but the price is right, pets are permitted, and there's a place to do laundry.

$50-100

The **Capitol Reef Inn and Cafe** (360 W. Main St., 435/425-3271, www.capitolreefinn.com, $53, spring-fall) has homey motel rooms and a good café serving breakfast, lunch, and dinner. In the front yard, the motel's owner and his brother have built a kiva resembling those used by Native Americans. It's obviously a labor of love, and a pretty cool place to explore.

At the east end of Torrey, the **Rim Rock Inn** (2523 E. Hwy. 24, 435/425-3388 or 888/447-4676, www.therimrock.net, $59-69, Mar.-Dec.) does indeed perch on a rim of red rock; it's just about as close as you can get to the park. The motel and its two restaurants are part of a 120-acre ranch, so the views are expansive.

Another Torrey hotel with good views is the **Howard Johnson** (877 N. Hwy. 24, 435/425-3866 or 800/221-5801, www.hojo.com, $89-109), located toward the east end of town. A decent Mexican restaurant is right next door.

In a grove of trees immediately behind downtown Torrey's old trading post and country store is **Austin's Chuck Wagon Lodge** (12 W. Main St., 435/425-3335 or 800/863-3288, www.austinschuckwagonmotel.com, rooms $49-79, cabins $135, Mar.-Dec.), with guest rooms in an older motel ($49), a newer lodge-like building, or newer two-bedroom cabins. There's also a pool and a hot tub.

In a pretty setting three miles south of

town, **Cowboy Homestead Cabins** (Hwy. 12, 435/425-3414 or 888/854-5871, www.cowboy-homesteadcabins.com, $79) has attractive one- and two-bedroom cabins with private baths, kitchenettes, and outdoor gas barbecue grills.

In Teasdale, four miles west of Torrey, **Pine Shadows** (125 S. 200 W., Teasdale, 435/425-3939 or 800/708-1223, www.pineshadowcab-ins.net, $98) offers spacious, modern cabins, equipped with two queen beds plus full baths and kitchens, in a piñon forest.

Head five miles down the Notom-Bullfrog Road to find accommodations at the **Notom Ranch Bed & Breakfast** (Notom Rd., 435/456-9153, www.notomranchbandb.com, $75), a working ranch on the edge of the park with Western-themed guest rooms and expansive views. Guests can arrange to have a home-cooked dinner ($10) at the ranch, which beats driving to and from Torrey for an evening meal. Breakfast is also served.

$100-150

The lovely **SkyRidge Inn Bed and Breakfast** (950 W. Hwy. 24, 435/425-3222 or 800/448-6990, www.skyridgeinn.com, $99-149) is one mile east of downtown Torrey. The modern inn has been decorated with high-quality Southwestern art and artifacts; all six guest rooms have private baths. SkyRidge sits on a bluff amid 75 acres, and guests are invited to explore the land on foot or bike.

Muley Twist Inn (off 125 S., outside Teasdale, 435/425-3640 or 800/530-1038, www.muleytwistinn.com, $99-140), an elegantly decorated five-bedroom B&B, is on a 30-acre parcel with great views. One guest room is fully accessible to wheelchair users. It's another really wonderful place to come home to at the end of a day of driving or hiking.

Stay in a renovated 1914 schoolhouse: The **Torrey Schoolhouse Bed and Breakfast** (150 N. Center St., 435/491-0230, $115-145) has been renovated but retains many period touches and an old-fashioned atmosphere, but with modern amenities such as a shiatsu massage chair in every room, memory foam mattress toppers, flat-screen TVs, and a wheelchair-accessible suite.

Over $150

If you're looking for comfortable motel rooms with perks like an in-room coffeemaker and ironing board and an outdoor pool, a good choice is the **Best Western Capitol Reef Resort** (2600 E. Hwy. 24, 435/425-3761, www.bestwestern.com, $150-170).

The ◖ **Lodge at Red River Ranch** (2900 W. Hwy. 24, 435/425-3322 or 800/205-6343, www.redriverranch.com, $160-245) is between Bicknell and Torrey beneath towering cliffs of red sandstone on the banks of the Fremont River. This wonderful wood-beamed lodge sits on a 2,200-acre working ranch, but there's nothing rustic or unsophisticated about the accommodations. The three-story structure is newly built, although in the same grand architectural style as old-fashioned mountain lodges. The great room has a massive stone fireplace, cozy chairs and couches, and a splendid Old West atmosphere. There are 15 guest rooms, most decorated according to a theme, and all have private baths. Guests are welcome to wander ranch paths, fish for trout, or meander in the gardens and orchards. Breakfast and dinner are served in the lodge restaurant but are not included in the price of lodgings; box lunches can be ordered.

Campgrounds

Although most campers will try for a site at Capitol Reef National Park, the campground there does not take reservations and fills up quickly. Torrey has a couple of private campgrounds that cater to both RV and tent campers. **Thousand Lakes RV Park** (Hwy. 24, 1 mile west of Torrey, 435/425-3500 or 800/355-8995, www.thousandlakesrvpark.com, Apr.-late Oct., $18 tents, $28 RVs with full hookups)

© JUDY JEWELL

Head into Torrey for dinner at Cafe Diablo.

has sites with showers, wireless Internet, a laundry room, and a store. Thousand Lakes also has cabins, ranging from Spartan (no linens, $35) to deluxe (sleeps 8, linens provided, $95), as well as Western-style cookouts on summer weeknights ($15-23). Right in town, the **Sand Creek RV Park** (540 W. Hwy. 24, 435/425-3577, www.sandcreekrv.com, Apr.-mid-Oct., $15 tents, $22-27 RVs, $30 camping cabins) has shaded tent spaces in a pleasant grassy field. Showers ($5 for nonguests) and laundry facilities ($5 to wash and dry) are available.

The U.S. Forest Service's **Sunglow Campground** (Forest Rd. 143, east of Bicknell, 435/836-2811, $8) is just east of Bicknell at an elevation of 7,200 feet. The seven first-come, first-served sites are open and have water mid-May-late October. The surrounding red cliffs really light up at sunset, hence the name. Several other Forest Service campgrounds are on the slopes of Boulder Mountain along Highway 12 between Torrey and Boulder.

These places are all above 8,600 feet and usually don't open until late May-early June.

FOOD

Torrey's restaurant of note is **Cafe Diablo** (599 W. Main St., 435/425-3070, www.cafediablo.net, 11:30am-10pm daily Apr.-Oct., dinner entrées $22-32). The specialty is zesty Southwestern cuisine, with excellent dishes like fire-roasted pork tenderloin, eggplant- and poblano-stuffed tamales, and pumpkinseed trout. This is one of the few places you can order free-range rattlesnake meat, cooked into crab cake-like patties. Because there aren't many restaurants this good in rural Utah, this place is worth a detour, though it must be said that it's not the place for a quiet romantic dinner—it's a high-volume, fast-paced, high-energy dining experience. Lunchtime, which features a Cuban sandwich ($12), crab chalupas ($12), turkey *picadillo* ($12), and more, tends to be a bit quieter.

Another pleasant surprise in this small town is the **Capitol Reef Inn and Cafe** (360 W. Main St., 435/425-3271, www.capitolreefinn.com, 7am-9pm daily, $10-15), where there's an emphasis on healthy and, when possible, locally grown food. It's easy to eat your veggies here—the 10-vegetable salad will make up for some of the less nutritious meals you've had on the road.

For something a little less elevated, try the burgers and milk shakes at **Slacker's Burger Joint** (165 E. Main St., 435/425-3710, noon-8pm Mon.-Thurs., noon-9pm Fri.-Sat., noon-5pm Sun., $6-12), in the center of Torrey. The pastrami burger is rightfully famous, and an afternoon milk shake hits the spot after a day of hiking.

About 12 miles east of Capitol Reef, stop by the tiny **☾Mesa Market** (Hwy. 24, Caineville, 435/487-9711, www.mesafarmmarket.com, 7am-7pm daily late Mar.-Oct., $3-17) for artisanal cheese and yogurt, sourdough bread baked in a wood-fired oven, and whatever produce is growing in the back 40. You won't find better picnic makings anywhere in southeastern Utah, and if he has a minute to spare, the owner will explain the sustainable nature of his farm and dairy.

INFORMATION AND SERVICES

The **Fremont River Ranger District** (138 S. Main St., Loa, 435/836-2800, www.fs.fed.us/r4/fishlake, 8am-4:30pm Mon.-Fri.) of the Fishlake National Forest has information about hiking, horseback riding, and road conditions in the northern and eastern parts of Boulder Mountain and the Aquarius Plateau.

CAPITOL REEF

CANYONLANDS NATIONAL PARK

The canyon country of southeastern Utah puts on its supreme performance in this vast park, which spreads across 527 square miles. The deeply entrenched Colorado and Green Rivers meet in its heart, and then continue south, as the mighty Colorado, through tumultuous Cataract Canyon Rapids. The park is divided into four districts and a separate noncontiguous unit. The Colorado and Green Rivers form the River District and divide Canyonlands National Park into three other regions. Island in the Sky is north, between the rivers; the Maze is to the west; and Needles is to the east. The Horseshoe Canyon Unit is farther to the west. This small parcel of land preserves a canyon on Barrier Creek, a tributary of the Green River, in which astounding petroglyphs and other ancient rock paintings are protected.

Each district has its own distinct character. No bridges or roads directly connect the three land districts and the Horseshoe Canyon Unit, so most visitors have to leave the park to go from one region to another. The huge park can be seen in many ways and on many levels. Paved roads reach a few areas, 4WD roads go to more places, and hiking trails reach still more, but much of the land shows no trace of human passage. To get the big picture, you can fly over this incredible complex of canyons on an air tour; however, only a river trip or a hike lets you experience the solitude and detail of the land.

The park can be visited in any season of the

© JUDY JEWELL

HIGHLIGHTS

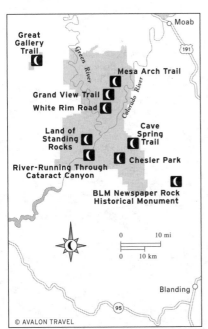

© AVALON TRAVEL

LOOK FOR ⟨ TO FIND RECOMMENDED SIGHTS, ACTIVITIES, DINING, AND LODGING.

⟨ **White Rim Road:** Take a few days to drive or bike this trail at the base of the Island in the Sky. Only high-clearance 4WD rigs or sturdy mountain bikes can make it on this scenic drive along the Colorado and Green Rivers (page 172).

⟨ **Mesa Arch Trail:** This easy trail leads to a dramatic cliff-side arch. The sun rising through the arch is a sight to behold—if you have time and energy for just one hike in Canyonlands, this should be it (page 173).

⟨ **Grand View Trail:** This short hike along slickrock cliffs captures the essence of the

"Island in the Sky." A sheer mile below the trail, the gorges of the Colorado and Green Rivers join to form Cataract Canyon, and in the distance, the odd promontories of the Needles District punctuate the skyline (page 175).

⟨ **BLM Newspaper Rock Historical Monument:** This is one of Utah's foremost prehistoric rock-art sites and also one of the most easily accessible. The distinctive petroglyphs span 2,000 years of human history (page 177).

⟨ **Cave Spring Trail:** The Cave Spring Trail in the Needles District introduces the geology and ecology of the park and passes an old cowboy line camp. It's also a good introduction to slickrock hiking; rock cairns mark the way and ladders assist hikers on the steep sections (page 179).

⟨ **Chesler Park:** A lovely desert meadow contrasts with the characteristic red and white spires of the Needles District. The trail winds through sand and slickrock before ascending a small pass through the Needles to Chesler Park; the park itself is encircled by a loop trail (page 182).

⟨ **Land of Standing Rocks:** Rock spires stand guard over myriad canyons in the Maze District. Land of Standing Rocks is a good place to camp, hike, and generally explore, but it's remote. Be sure to have a high-clearance 4WD vehicle, a compass, and some good maps (page 187).

⟨ **Great Gallery Trail:** Ghostly life-size pictographs in the Great Gallery are in remote Horseshoe Canyon, just west of the main part of Canyonlands. The hike in to the Gallery offers pleasant scenery and spring wildflowers (page 190).

⟨ **River-Running Through Cataract Canyon:** Downstream from its confluence with the Green River, the Colorado River enters Cataract Canyon and picks up speed. The rapids begin four miles downstream and extend for the next 14 miles to Lake Powell. Especially in spring, the 26 or more rapids give a wild ride equal to the best in the Grand Canyon (page 193).

CANYONLANDS

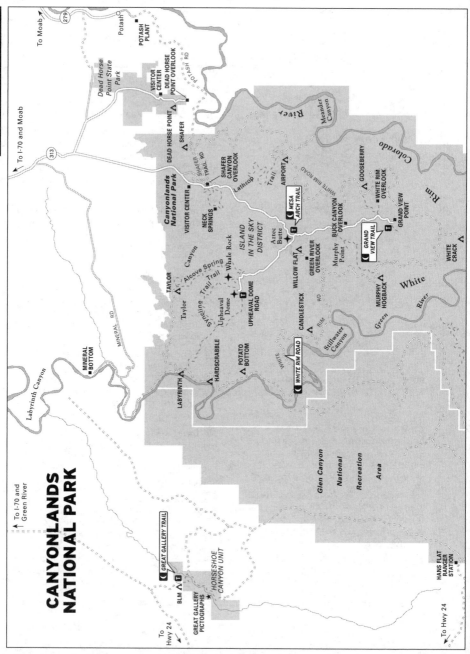

CANYONLANDS NATIONAL PARK

To Moab
279
Potash
POTASH PLANT
POTASH RD

Dead Horse Point State Park
VISITOR CENTER
DEAD HORSE POINT OVERLOOK

To I-70 and Moab
313
DEAD HORSE POINT
SHAFER

Canyonlands National Park

River
Meander Canyon

SHAFER TRAIL RD
SHAFER CANYON OVERLOOK
Lathrop Trail
AIRPORT

Colorado River
GOOSEBERRY
WHITE RIM OVERLOOK
WHITE RIM ROAD

VISITOR CENTER
NECK SPRINGS
MESA ARCH TRAIL
ISLAND IN THE SKY DISTRICT
Aztec Butte
BUCK CANYON OVERLOOK
GRAND VIEW POINT
GRAND VIEW TRAIL

Rim
TAYLOR
Taylor Canyon
Alcove Spring Trail
Whale Rock
WILLOW FLAT
GREEN RIVER OVERLOOK
Murphy Point
WHITE CRACK

Syncline Trail
Upheaval Dome
UPHEAVAL DOME ROAD
White River
MURPHY HOGBACK

MINERAL RD
HARDSCRABBLE
POTATO BOTTOM
WHITE RIM RD
Stillwater Canyon
Green River

Labyrinth Canyon
MINERAL BOTTOM
LABYRINTH
WHITE RIM ROAD
CANDLESTICK

Glen Canyon National Recreation Area

To I-70 and Green River

GREAT GALLERY TRAIL
BLM
HORSESHOE CANYON UNIT
GREAT GALLERY PICTOGRAPHS

HANS FLAT RANGER STATION

To Hwy 24

To Hwy 24

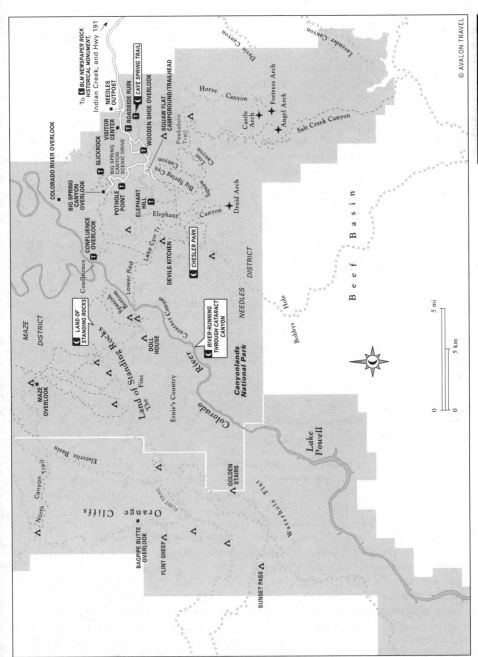

© AVALON TRAVEL

year, with spring and autumn the best choices. Summer temperatures can climb over 100°F; carrying and drinking lots of water becomes critical then (bring at least one gallon per person per day). Arm yourself with insect repellent late spring-midsummer. Winter days tend to be bright and sunny, although nighttime temperatures can dip into the teens or even below zero Fahrenheit. Winter visitors should inquire about travel conditions, as snow and ice occasionally close roads and trails at higher elevations.

PLANNING YOUR TIME

Unless you have a great deal of time, you can't really "do" the entire park in one trip. It's best to pick one section and concentrate on it.

Island in the Sky District

The mesa-top Island in the Sky District has paved roads on its top to impressive belvederes such as Grand View Point and the strange Upheaval Dome. If you're short on time or don't want to make a rigorous backcountry trip, you'll find this district the best choice. It is easily visited as a day trip from Moab. The "Island," which is actually a large mesa, is much like nearby Dead Horse Point on a giant scale; a narrow neck of land connects the north side with the "mainland."

If you're really on a tight schedule, it's possible to spend a few hours exploring Arches National Park, then head to Island in the Sky for a drive to the scenic Grand View overlook and a brief hike to Mesa Arch or the Upheaval Dome viewpoint. A one-day visit should include these elements, plus a hike along the Neck Spring Trail. For a longer visit, hikers, mountain bikers, and those with suitable high-clearance 4WD vehicles can drop off the Island in the Sky and descend about 1,300 feet to White Rim Road, which follows the cliffs of the White Rim around most of the island. Plan to spend at least 2-3 days exploring this 100-mile-long road.

Needles District

Colorful rock spires prompted the name of the Needles District, which is easily accessed from Highway 211 and U.S. 191 south of Moab. Splendid canyons contain many arches, strange rock formations, and archaeological sites. Overlooks and short nature trails can be enjoyed from the paved scenic drive in the park; if you are only here for a day, hike the Cave Spring and Pothole Point Trails. On a longer visit, make a loop of the Big Spring and Squaw Canyon Trails, and hike to Chesler Park. A 10-mile round-trip hike will take you to the Confluence Overlook, a great view of the junction of the Green and Colorado Rivers.

Drivers with 4WD vehicles have their own challenging roads through canyons and other highly scenic areas.

Maze District

Few visitors make it over to the Maze District, which is some of the wildest country in the United States. Only the rivers and a handful of 4WD roads and hiking trails provide access. Experienced hikers can explore the maze of canyons on unmarked routes. Plan to spend at least 2-3 days in this area; even if you're only taking day hikes, it can take a long time to get to any destination here. That said, a hike from the Maze Overlook to the Harvest Scene pictographs is a good bet if you don't have a lot of time. If you have more than one day, head to the Land of Standing Rocks area and hike north to the Chocolate Drops.

Horseshoe Canyon Unit

Horseshoe Canyon Unit, a detached section of the park northwest of the Maze District, is equally remote. It protects the Great Gallery, a group of pictographs left by prehistoric Native Americans. This ancient artwork is reached at the end of a series of long unpaved roads and down a canyon on a moderately challenging hiking trail. Plan to spend a full day exploring this area.

River District

The River District includes long stretches of the Green and the Colorado Rivers. River-running is one of the best ways to experience the inner depths of the park. Boaters can obtain helpful literature and advice from park rangers. Groups planning their own trip through Cataract Canyon need a river-running permit. Flat-water permits are also required. River outfitters based in Moab offer trips ranging from half a day to several days in length.

Exploring the Park

There are four districts and a noncontiguous unit in Canyonlands National Park (www.nps.gov/cany, $10 per vehicle, $5 bicyclists, motorcyclists, and pedestrians, good for one week in all districts, no fee to enter Maze or Horseshoe Canyon), each affording great views, spectacular geology, a chance to see wildlife, and endless opportunities to explore. You won't find crowds or elaborate park facilities because most of Canyonlands remains a primitive backcountry park. If your plans include visiting Arches National Park plus Hovenweep and Natural Bridges National Monuments, consider the so-called Local Passport ($25), which allows entry to each of these federal preserves. Purchase the pass at any park or national monument entrance.

Front-country camping is allowed only in established campgrounds at Willow Flat (Island in the Sky) and Squaw Flat (Needles).

Rock climbing is allowed in the park, and permits are not required, unless the trip involves overnight camping; however, it's always a good idea to check in at district visitors centers for advice and information and to learn where climbing is restricted. Climbing is not allowed within 300 feet of cultural sites.

Pets aren't allowed on trails and must be leashed in campgrounds. No firewood collecting is permitted in the park; backpackers must use gas stoves for cooking. Vehicle and boat campers can bring in firewood but must use grills or fire pans.

The best maps for the park are a series of topographic maps by National Geographic/Trails Illustrated; these have the latest trail and road information. For most day hikes, the simple maps issued by park visitors centers will suffice.

VISITORS CENTERS

Since Canyonlands covers so much far-flung territory, separate visitors centers serve each district. One website (www.nps.gov/cany) serves the whole park and is a good source for current information and permit applications. There are visitors centers at the entrances to the **Island in the Sky District** (435/259-4712, 9am-4pm daily winter, longer hours daily spring-fall) and the **Needles District** (435/259-4711, 9am-4pm daily mid-Feb.-early Dec., longer hours mid-Feb.-Nov.). The **Hans Flat Ranger Station** (435/259-2652, 8am-4:30pm daily year-round) is on a remote plateau above the even more isolated canyons of the Maze District and the Horseshoe Canyon Unit. The River District is administered out of the **National Park Service Office** (2282 SW Resource Blvd., Moab, 435/719-2313, 8am-4pm Mon.-Fri.). This office can generally handle inquiries for all districts of the park. For backcountry information, or to make backcountry reservations, call 435/259-4351. Handouts from the ranger offices describe natural history, travel, and other aspects of the park.

If you are in Moab, it is most convenient to stop at the **Moab Information Center** (Main St. and Center St., 435/259-8825 or 800/635-6622), where a national park ranger is often on duty. All visitors centers have brochures, maps, and books, as well as someone to answer your questions.

CANYONLANDS

EARLY EXPLORATION OF THE COLORADO RIVER CANYON

The Dominguez-Escalante Expedition skirted the east edge of the Colorado River Canyon in 1776 in an unsuccessful attempt to find a route west to California. Retreating back to New Mexico, the Spanish explorers encountered great difficulties in the canyons of southern Utah before finding a safe ford across the Colorado River. This spot, known as the "Crossing of the Fathers," now lies under Lake Powell. Later explorers established the Old Spanish Trail through Utah to connect New Mexico with California. The route crossed the Colorado River near present-day Moab and was used 1829-1848, when the United States acquired the western territories. Fur trappers also traveled the canyons in search of beaver and other animals during the early 1800s; inscriptions carved into the sandstone record their passage.

Major John Wesley Powell led the first scientific expedition by boat through the Green River and lower Colorado River canyons in 1869, then repeated most of the journey in 1871-1872. Cowboys brought in cattle during the 1870s. Some of their camps, corrals, and inscriptions still survive, although grazing no longer takes place in the park. Uranium prospectors swarmed through the area with Geiger counters during the 1950s, staking thousands of claims and opening some mines. Most of the jeep roads in use today date from that time.

TOURS

Rangers lead interpretive programs in the Island in the Sky and Needles Districts (Mar.-Oct.), and they guide hikers into Horseshoe Canyon (Sat.-Sun. spring and fall), weather permitting. Call the Hans Flat Ranger Station (435/259-2652) for details.

OUTFITTERS

Outfitters must be authorized by the National Park Service to operate in Canyonlands. Most guides concentrate on river trips, but some can take you on mountain bike trips, including vehicle-supported tours of the White Rim 4WD Trail. Most of the guides operating in Canyonlands are based in Moab. For a complete list of authorized outfitters, visit the park website (www.nps.gov/cany).

Biking

• **Escape Adventures** (at Moab Cyclery, 391 S. Main St., Moab, 435/259-7423 or 800/596-2953, www.escapeadventures.com)
• **Rim Tours** (1233 S. U.S. 191, Moab, 435/259-5223 or 800/626-7335, www.rimtours.com)

• **Western Spirit Cycling** (478 Mill Creek Dr., Moab, 435/259-8732 or 800/845-2453, www.westernspirit.com)

Rafting

• **Adrift Adventures** (378 N. Main St., Moab, 435/259-8594 or 800/874-4483, www.adrift.net)
• **Navtec Expeditions** (321 N. Main St., Moab, 435/259-7983 or 800/833-1278, www.navtec.com)
• **Sheri Griffith Expeditions** (503/259-8229 or 800/332-2439, www.griffithexp.com)
• **Tag-A-Long Expeditions** (452 N. Main St., Moab, 435/259-8946 or 800/453-3292, www.tagalong.com)
• **Western River Expeditions** (225 S. Main St., Moab, 435/259-7019 or 866/904-1163, www.westernriver.com)

BACKCOUNTRY EXPLORATION

A complex system of fees is charged for backcountry camping, 4WD exploration, and river rafting. Except for the main campgrounds at Willow Flat (Island in the Sky) and Squaw Flat (Needles), you'll need a permit for backcountry camping. There is a $30 fee for a backpacking permit and, in the Needles District, a $10 day-use fee for a 4WD vehicle. Each of the three major districts has a different policy for backcountry vehicle camping, so it's a good idea to make sure that you understand the details. Backcountry permits are also needed for any trips with horses or stock; check with a ranger for details.

It's possible to reserve a backcountry permit in advance; for spring and fall travel to popular areas like Island in the Sky's White Rim Trail or the Needles backcountry, this is an extremely good idea. Find application forms on the Canyonlands website (www.nps.gov/cany). Forms should be completed and returned at least two weeks in advance of your planned trip. Telephone reservations are not accepted.

Back-road travel is a popular method of exploring the park. Canyonlands National Park offers hundreds of miles of exceptionally scenic jeep roads, favorites both with mountain bikers and 4WD enthusiasts. Park regulations require all motorized vehicles to have proper registration and licensing for highway use, and all-terrain vehicles are prohibited in the park; drivers must also be licensed. Normally you must have a vehicle with both 4WD and high clearance. It's essential for both motor vehicles

and bicycles to stay on existing roads to prevent damage to the delicate desert vegetation. Carry tools, extra fuel, water, and food in case you break down in a remote area.

Before making a trip, drivers and cyclists should talk with a ranger to register and to check on current road conditions, which can change drastically from one day to the next. The rangers can also tell you where to seek help if you get stuck. Primitive campgrounds are provided on most of the roads, but you'll need a backcountry permit from a ranger. Books on backcountry exploration include Charles Wells's *Guide to Moab, UT Backroads & 4-Wheel Drive Trails,* which includes Canyonlands, and Damian Fagan and David Williams's *A Naturalist's Guide to the White Rim Trail.*

One more thing about backcountry travel in Canyonlands: You may need to pack your poop out of the backcountry. Because of the abundance of slickrock and the desert conditions, it's not always possible to dig a hole, and you can't just leave your waste on a rock until it decomposes (decomposition is a very slow process in these conditions). Check with the ranger when you pick up your backcountry permit for more information.

Island in the Sky District

The main part of this district sits on a mesa high above the Colorado and Green Rivers. It is connected to points north by a narrow land bridge just wide enough for the road, known as "the neck," which forms the only vehicle access to the 40-square-mile Island in the Sky. Panoramic views from the "Island" can be enjoyed from any point along the rim; you'll see much of the park and southeastern Utah.

Short hiking trails lead to overlooks and to Mesa Arch, Aztec Butte, Whale Rock, Upheaval Dome, and other features. Longer trails make steep, strenuous descents from the Island to

the White Rim Road below. Elevations on the Island average about 6,000 feet.

Although the massive cliffs in the area look to be perfect for rock climbing, in fact much of the rock is not suitable for climbing, and the remoteness of the area means that few routes have been explored. One exception is Taylor Canyon, in the extreme northwest corner of the park, which is reached by lengthy and rugged 4WD roads.

Bring water for all hiking, camping, and travel in Island in the Sky. Except for the bottled water sold at the visitors center, there is no water available in this district of the park.

CANYONLANDS

THE LIFE AND LANDSCAPE OF CANYONLANDS

GEOLOGY

Deep canyons of the Green and Colorado Rivers have sliced through rocks representing 150 million years of deposition. The Paradox Formation, exposed in Cataract Canyon, contains salt and other minerals responsible for some of the folded and faulted rock layers in the region. Under the immense pressure of overlying rocks, the Paradox flows plastically, forming domes where the rock layers are thinnest and causing cracks or faults as pressures rise and fall. Each of the overlying formations has a different color and texture; they're the products of ancient deserts, rivers, and seas that once covered this land. Views from any of the overlooks reveal that an immense quantity of rock has already been washed downriver toward California. Not so evident, however, is the 10,000 vertical feet of rock that geologists say once lay across the high mesas. The dry climate and sparse vegetation allow clear views of the remaining rock layers and the effects of erosion and deformation. You can read the geologic story at Canyonlands National Park in the 3,500 feet of strata that remain, from the bottom of **Cataract Canyon** to the upper reaches of **Salt Creek** in the **Needles District.**

FLORA AND FAUNA

Extremes of flash flood and drought, hot summers, and cold winters discourage all but the most hardy and adaptable life. Desert grasses, small flowering plants, cacti, and shrubs like blackbrush and saltbush survive on the mostly thin soils and meager 8-9 inches of annual precipitation. Trees either grow in cracks that concentrate rainfall and nutrients or rely on springs or canyon streams for moisture. Piñon pine and juniper prefer the higher elevations

of the park, while cottonwoods live in the canyon bottoms that have permanent subsurface water. Tamarisk, an exotic and invasive streamside plant, and willows often form dense thickets on sandbars along the Green and Colorado Rivers. The hanging gardens of lush vegetation that surround cliff-side springs or seeps seem oblivious to the surrounding desert.

The fragile desert ecology can easily be upset. Cattle, especially in the Needles District, once overgrazed the grasslands and trampled cryptobiotic crusts and other vegetation. Increased erosion and growth of undesirable exotic plants like cheatgrass have been the result. Scars left by roads and mines during the uranium frenzy of the 1950s can still be seen, most commonly in the Island in the Sky District.

Fewer than 10 species of fish evolved in the canyons of the Colorado and the Green Rivers. These fish developed streamlined bodies and strange features, such as humped backs, to cope with the muddy and varying river waters. Species include Colorado pikeminnow, humpback chub, bonytail chub, and humpback sucker; most of these live nowhere else. All have suffered greatly reduced populations and restricted ranges as a result of dam building.

Of the approximately 65 mammal species living in the park, about one-third are rodents, and another third are bats. You're most likely to see chipmunks, antelope ground squirrels, and rock squirrels, which are often active during the day. Most other animals wait until evening to come out and feed; in the morning, look for tracks of mule deer, bighorn sheep, coyotes, gray foxes, badgers, porcupines, spotted skunks, beavers, black-tailed jackrabbits, wood rats, kangaroo rats, and many species of mice.

VISITORS CENTER

Stop here for information about Island in the Sky and to see exhibits on geology and history; books and maps are available for purchase. The visitors center (435/259-4712, 9am-4pm daily winter, longer hours spring-fall) is located just

before the neck crosses to Island in the Sky. From Moab, go northwest 10 miles on U.S. 191, then turn left and drive 15 miles on Highway 313 to the junction for Dead Horse Point State Park. From here, continue straight for seven miles. Many of the park's plants grow and are identified outside the visitors center; look also at the display of pressed plants inside the center.

SHAFER CANYON OVERLOOK

Half a mile past the visitors center is the Shafer Canyon Overlook (on the left, just before crossing the neck). The overlook has good views east down the canyon and onto the incredibly twisting **Shafer Trail Road.** Cattlemen Frank and John Schafer built the trail in the early 1900s to move stock to additional pastures (the *c* in their name was later dropped by mapmakers). Uranium prospectors upgraded the trail to a 4WD road during the 1950s so that they could reach their claims at the base of the cliffs. Today, Shafer Trail Road connects the mesa top with White Rim Road and Potash Road, four miles and 1,200 vertical feet below. High-clearance vehicles should be used on the Shafer. It's also fun to ride this road on a mountain bike. Road conditions can vary considerably, so contact a ranger before starting. Shafer Trail Viewpoint, across the neck, provides another perspective 0.5 miles farther.

Back on top of the Island, the paved park road leads south from the neck six miles across Gray's Pasture to a junction. The Grand View Point Overlook road continues south while the road to Upheaval Dome turns west.

BUCK CANYON OVERLOOK

As the park road continues south, a series of incredible vistas over the canyons of the Green and Colorado Rivers peek into view. The first viewpoint is Buck Canyon Overlook, which looks east over the Colorado River Canyon. Two miles farther is the **Grand View Picnic Area,** a handy lunch stop.

GRAND VIEW POINT

At the end of the main road, one mile past the Grand View Picnic Area, is Grand View Point, perhaps the most spectacular panorama from Island in the Sky. Monument Basin lies directly

below, and countless canyons, the Colorado River, the Needles, and mountain ranges are in the distance. The easy 1.5-mile **Grand View Trail** continues past the end of the road for other vistas from the point.

Return to the main road to explore more overlooks and geological curiosities in the western portion of Island in the Sky.

GREEN RIVER OVERLOOK

The Green River Overlook is just west of the main junction on an unpaved road. From the overlook, Soda Springs Basin and a section of the Green River (deeply entrenched in Stillwater Canyon) can be seen below. Small Willow Flat Campground is on the way to the overlook.

UPHEAVAL DOME ROAD

At the end of the road, 5.3 miles northwest of the junction, is **Upheaval Dome.** This geologic oddity is a fantastically deformed pile of rock sprawled across a crater about three miles wide and 1,200 feet deep. For many years, Upheaval Dome has kept geologists busy trying to figure out its origins. They once assumed that salt of the Paradox Formation pushed the rock layers upward to form the dome. Now, however, strong evidence suggests that a meteorite impact created the structure. The surrounding ring depression, caused by collapse, and the convergence of rock layers upward toward the center correspond precisely to known impact structures. Shatter cones and microscopic analysis also indicate an impact origin. When the meteorite struck, sometime in the last 150 million years, it formed a crater up to five miles across. Erosion removed some of the overlying rock—perhaps as much as a vertical mile. The underlying salt may have played a role in uplifting the central section.

The easy **Crater View Trail** leads to overlooks on the rim of Upheaval Dome; the first viewpoint is 0.5 miles round-trip, and the second is one mile round-trip. There's also a small **picnic area** here.

WHITE RIM ROAD

This driving adventure follows the White Rim below the sheer cliffs of Island in the Sky. A close look at the light-colored surface reveals ripple marks and cross beds laid down near an ancient coastline. The plateau's east side is about 800 feet above the Colorado River. On the west side, the plateau meets the bank of the Green River.

Travel along the winding road presents a constantly changing panorama of rock, canyons, river, and sky. Keep an eye out for desert bighorn sheep. You'll see all three levels of Island in the Sky District, from the high plateaus to the White Rim to the rivers.

Only 4WD vehicles with high clearance can make the trip. With the proper vehicle, driving is mostly easy but slow and winding; a few steep or rough sections have to be negotiated. The 100-mile trip takes 2-3 days. Allow an extra day to travel all the road spurs.

Mountain bikers find this a great trip too; most cyclists arrange an accompanying 4WD vehicle to carry water and camping gear. Primitive campgrounds along the way provide convenient stopping places. Both cyclists and 4WD drivers must obtain reservations and a backcountry permit ($30) for the White Rim campsites from the Island in the Sky visitors center. Find application forms on the Canyonlands website (www.nps.gov/cany); return the completed application at least two weeks in advance of your planned trip. Questions can be fielded via telephone (435/259-4351, 8am-12:30pm Mon.-Fri.), but no telephone reservations are accepted. Demand exceeds supply during the popular spring and autumn seasons, when you should make reservations as far in advance as possible. No services or developed water sources exist anywhere on the drive, so be sure to have plenty of fuel and water with some to spare. Access points are Shafer Trail Road (from near Island in the Sky) and Potash Road (Hwy. 279 from Moab) on the east and Mineral Bottom Road on the west. White Rim sandstone forms the distinctive plateau crossed on the drive.

HIKING
Neck Spring Trail

• Distance: 5.8-mile loop

• Duration: 3-4 hours

• Elevation change: 300 feet

• Effort: moderate

• Trailhead: Shafer Canyon Overlook

The trail begins near the Shafer Canyon Overlook and loops down Taylor Canyon to Neck and Cabin Springs, formerly used by ranchers (look for the remains of the old cowboy cabin near Cabin Springs), then climbs back to Island in the Sky Road at a second trailhead 0.5 miles south of the start. A brochure should be available at the trailhead. Water at the springs supports maidenhair fern and other plants. Also watch for birds and wildlife attracted to this spot. Bring water with you, as the springs are not potable.

Lathrop Trail

• Distance: 10.5 miles one-way to the Colorado River

• Duration: overnight

• Elevation change: 2,000 feet

• Effort: strenuous

• Trailhead: on the left, 1.3 miles past the neck

This is the only marked hiking route going all the way from Island in the Sky to the Colorado River. The first 2.5 miles cross Gray's Pasture to the rim, which affords fantastic vistas over the Colorado River. From here, the trail descends steeply, dropping 1,600 feet over the next 2.5 miles, to White Rim Road, a little less than seven miles from the trailhead. Part of this section follows an old mining road past several abandoned mines, all relics of the uranium boom. Don't enter the shafts; they're in

FOUR-WHEELING IN CANYONLANDS

© BILL MCRAE

The 4WD White Rim Road snakes along the base of the Island in the Sky.

For people who think that just as a dog needs to run free every once in a while, sport-utility vehicles need to occasionally escape the home-to-work loop, Canyonlands is a tonic.

Each of the park's three main districts has a focal point for 4WD travel. In the Island in the Sky, it's the 100-mile-long White Rim Road. Four-wheelers in the Needles head to Elephant Rock for the challenging climb to a network of roads. The Maze's Flint Trail traverses clay slopes that are extremely slippery when wet. Though all of the park's 4WD roads are rugged, those in the Maze are especially challenging, and this area is by far the most remote.

Drivers should note that ATVs are not permitted in national parks. All vehicles must be street-legal. The most commonly used vehicles are jeeps. Four-wheel drivers should be pre-pared to make basic road or vehicle repairs and should carry the following items:

- at least one full-size spare tire

- extra gas

- extra water

- a shovel

- a high-lift jack

- chains for all four tires, especially October-April

Also note that towing from any backcountry area of Canyonlands is very expensive: It's not uncommon for bills to top $1,000.

Permits are required for overnight trips; camping is only in designated sites.

danger of collapse and may contain poisonous gases. From the mining area, the route descends through a wash to White Rim Road, follows the road a short distance south, then goes down Lathrop Canyon Road to the Colorado River, another four miles and 500 vertical feet. The trail has little shade and can be very hot. Vehicular traffic may be encountered along the White Rim Road portion of the trail. For a long day hike (13.6 miles round-trip), turn around when you reach the White Rim Road and hike back up to the top of the mesa.

◖ Mesa Arch Trail

- Distance: 0.25 miles one-way
- Duration: 30 minutes
- Elevation change: 80 feet
- Effort: easy
- Trailhead: on the left, 5.5 miles from the neck

A short hike leads to the clifftop Mesa Arch.

This easy trail leads to a spectacular arch on the rim of the mesa. On the way, the road crosses the grasslands and scattered juniper trees of Gray's Pasture. A trail brochure available at the start describes the ecology of the mesa. The sandstone arch frames views of rock formations below and the La Sal Mountains in the distance. Photographers come here to catch the sun rising through the arch.

Murphy Point

- Distance: 11-mile loop
- Duration: 5-7 hours
- Elevation change: 1,100 feet
- Effort: strenuous
- Trailhead: Murphy Point
- Directions: From the Upheaval Dome junction on the main park road, head three miles south. Turn right onto a rough dirt road and follow it 1.7 miles to Murphy Point.

Murphy Trail starts as a jaunt across the mesa, then drops steeply from the rim down to White Rim Road. This strenuous route forks partway down; one branch follows Murphy

Hogback (a ridge) to Murphy Campground on the 4WD road, and the other follows a wash to the road one mile south of the campground.

White Rim Overlook Trail

- Distance: 0.75 miles one-way
- Duration: 1 hour
- Elevation change: 25 feet
- Effort: easy
- Trailhead: Grand View Picnic Area

Hike east along a peninsula to an overlook of Monument Basin and beyond. There are also good views of White Rim Road and potholes.

Gooseberry Trail

- Distance: 2.5 miles one-way
- Duration: 5 hours
- Elevation change: 1,400 feet
- Effort: strenuous
- Trailhead: Grand View Picnic Area

Gooseberry Trail drops off the mesa and makes an extremely steep descent to White Rim Road,

© BILL MCRAE

just north of Gooseberry Campground. The La Sal Mountains are visible from the trail.

◆ Grand View Trail

- Distance: 1 mile one-way
- Duration: 2 hours
- Elevation change: 50 feet
- Effort: easy
- Trailhead: Grand View Point Overlook

At the overlook, Grand View Trail continues past the end of the road for other vistas from the point, which is the southernmost tip of Island in the Sky. This short hike across the slickrock will really give you a feel for the entire Canyonlands National Park. From the mesa-top trail, you'll see the gorges of the Colorado and Green Rivers come together; across the chasm is the Needles District. Look down to spot vehicles traveling along the White Rim Trail at the base of the mesa.

Aztec Butte Trail

- Distance: 1 mile one-way
- Duration: 1.5 hours
- Elevation change: 200 feet
- Effort: moderate
- Trailhead: Aztec Butte parking area, 1 mile northwest of road junction on Upheaval Dome Road

It's a bit of a haul up the slickrock to the top of this sandstone butte, but once you get here, you'll be rewarded with a good view of the Island and Taylor Canyon. Atop the butte a loop trail passes several Anasazi granaries. Aztec Butte is one of the few areas in Island in the Sky with Native American ruins; the shortage of water in this area prevented permanent settlement.

Whale Rock Trail

- Distance: 0.5 miles one-way
- Duration: 1 hour
- Elevation change: 100 feet
- Effort: easy-moderate

- Trailhead: Upheaval Dome Road, on the right, 4.4 miles northwest of the road junction

A relatively easy trail climbs Whale Rock, a sandstone hump near the outer rim of Upheaval Dome. In a couple of places you'll have to do some scrambling up the slickrock, which is made easier and a bit less scary thanks to handrails. From the top of the rock, there are good views of the dome.

Upheaval Dome Viewpoint Trail

- Distance: 1 mile one-way
- Duration: 1.5 hours
- Elevation change: 150 feet
- Effort: easy
- Trailhead: Upheaval Dome parking area

The trail leads to Upheaval Dome overviews; it's about 0.5 miles to the first overlook and a mile to the second. The shorter trail leads to the rim with a view about 1,000 feet down into the jumble of rocks in the craterlike center of Upheaval Dome. The longer trail descends the slickrock and offers even better views. Energetic hikers can explore this formation in depth by circling it on the Syncline Loop Trail or from White Rim Road below.

Syncline Loop Trail

- Distance: 8-mile loop
- Duration: 5-7 hours
- Elevation change: 1,200 feet
- Effort: strenuous
- Trailhead: Upheaval Dome parking area

Syncline Loop Trail makes a circuit completely around Upheaval Dome. The trail crosses Upheaval Dome Canyon about halfway around from the overlook; walk east 1.5 miles up the canyon to enter the crater itself. This is the only nontechnical route into the center of the dome. A hike around Upheaval Dome with a side trip to the crater totals 11 miles, and it is best done as an overnight trip. Carry plenty of water for the entire trip; this dry country can be very hot in summer. The Green River is the only reliable source of water. An alternate approach is to start near Upheaval Campsite on White Rim Road; hike four miles southeast on through Upheaval Canyon to a junction with the Syncline Loop Trail, then another 1.5 miles into the crater. The elevation gain is about 600 feet.

Alcove Spring Trail

- Distance: 10 miles one-way
- Duration: overnight
- Elevation change: 1,500 feet
- Effort: strenuous
- Trailhead: 1.5 miles southeast of the Upheaval Dome parking area

Alcove Spring Trail connects with White Rim Road in Taylor Canyon. Five miles of the 10-mile distance is on the steep trail down through Trail Canyon and five miles is on a jeep road in Taylor Canyon. One downside of this trail is the 4WD traffic, which can be pretty heavy during the spring and fall. From the Taylor Canyon end of the trail, it is not far to the Upheaval Trail, which heads southeast to its junction with the Syncline Trail, which in turn leads to the Upheaval Dome parking area. Allow at least one overnight if you plan to hike this full loop. Day hikers should plan to turn around after the first five-mile section; this is still a very full day of hiking. Carry plenty of water—the trail is hot and dry.

CAMPGROUNDS

There is only one developed campground in the Island in the Sky District. **Willow Flat Campground** on Murphy Point Road has only 12 sites ($10), available on a first-come, first-served basis; sites tend to fill up in all seasons except winter. No water or services are available.

Camping is available outside the park at **Dead Horse Point State Park** (reservations 800/322-3770, www.reserveamerica.com, $20 plus $9 reservations fee), which is also very popular, so don't plan on getting a spot without reserving ahead. There are also primitive Bureau of Land Management (BLM) campsites along Highway 313.

Needles District

The Needles District, named for the area's distinctive sandstone spires, showcases some of the finest rock sculptures in Canyonlands National Park. Spires, arches, and monoliths appear in almost every direction. Prehistoric ruins and rock art exist in greater variety and quantity here than elsewhere in the park. Perennial springs and streams bring greenery to the desert.

While a scenic paved road leads to the district, this area of the park has only about a dozen miles of paved roads. Needles doesn't have a lot to offer travelers who are unwilling to get out of their vehicles and hike; however, it's the best section of the park for a wide variety of day hikes. Even a short hike opens up the landscape and leads to remarkable vistas and prehistoric sites.

To reach the Needles District, go 40 miles south from Moab (or 14 miles north of Monticello) on U.S. 191, turn west on Highway 211, and continue for 38 miles.

VISITORS CENTER

Stop at the visitors center (west end of Hwy. 211, 435/259-4711, 8am-4:30pm daily Nov.-Feb., longer hours Mar.-Oct.) for information on hiking, back roads, and other aspects of travel in the Needles, as well as backcountry permits, required for all overnight stays in the backcountry, and maps, brochures, and books. Take a moment to look at the little computer-animated slide show on the region's geology—its graphics make it all become clear. When the office isn't open, you'll find information posted outside on the bulletin board.

© PAUL LEVY

Newspaper Rock preserves some of the richest, most fanciful prehistoric rock art in Utah.

◖ BLM NEWSPAPER ROCK HISTORICAL MONUMENT

Although not in the park itself, Newspaper Rock lies just 150 feet off Highway 211 on Bureau of Land Management (BLM) land on the way to the Needles District. At Newspaper Rock, a profusion of petroglyphs depict human figures, animals, birds, and abstract designs. These represent 2,000 years of human history during which prehistoric people and Anasazi, Fremont, Paiute, Navajo, and Anglo travelers passed through Indian Creek Canyon. The patterns on the smooth sandstone rock face stand out clearly, thanks to a coating of dark desert varnish. A short nature trail introduces you to the area's desert and riparian vegetation.

The cracks in the rock walls around **Indian Creek** offer world-class rock climbing; climbers should track down a copy of *Indian Creek: A Climbing Guide,* by David Bloom, for details and lots of pictures. **Moab Desert Adventures** (415 N. Main St., Moab, 435/260-2404 or 877/765-4273, www.moabdesertadventures. com) offers guided climbing at Indian Creek.

From U.S. 191 between Moab and Monticello, turn west on Highway 211 and travel 12 miles to Newspaper Rock. Indian Creek's climbing walls start about three miles west of Newspaper Rock.

NEEDLES AND ANTICLINE OVERLOOKS

Although outside the park, these viewpoints atop the high mesa east of Canyonlands National Park offer magnificent panoramas of the surrounding area. Part of the BLM's **Canyon Rims Recreation Area** (www.blm.gov), these easily accessed overlooks provide the kind of awe-inspiring vistas over the Needles District that would otherwise require a hike in the park. The turnoff for both overlooks is at milepost 93 on U.S. 191, which is 32 miles south of Moab and 7 miles north of Highway 211. There are also two campgrounds along the access road.

For the Needles Overlook, follow the paved road 22 miles west to its end (turn left at the junction 15 miles in). The BLM maintains a picnic area and interpretive exhibits here. A fence protects visitors from the sheer cliffs that drop off more than 1,000 feet. You can see much of Canyonlands National Park and southeastern Utah. Look south for the Six-shooter Peaks and the high country of the Abajo Mountains; southwest for the Needles (thousands of spires reaching for the sky); west for the confluence area of the Green and Colorado Rivers, the Maze District, the Orange Cliffs, and the Henry Mountains; northwest for the lazy bends of the Colorado River Canyon and the sheer-walled mesas of Island in the Sky and Dead Horse Point; north for the Book Cliffs; and northeast for the La Sal Mountains. The changing shadows and colors of the canyon country make for a continuous show throughout the day.

For the Anticline Overlook, continue straight north at the junction with the Needles road and drive 17 miles on a good gravel road to the fenced overlook at road's end. You'll be standing 1,600 feet above the Colorado River. The sweeping panorama over the canyons, the river, and the twisted rocks of the Kane Creek Anticline is nearly as spectacular as that from Dead Horse Point, only 5.5 miles west as the crow flies. Salt and other minerals of the Paradox Formation pushed up overlying rocks into the dome visible below. Down-cutting by the Colorado River has revealed the twisted rock layers. The Moab Salt Mine across the river to the north uses a solution technique to bring up potash from the Paradox Formation several thousand feet underground. Pumps then transfer the solution to the blue-tinted evaporation ponds. Look carefully at the northeast horizon to see an arch in the Windows Section of Arches National Park, 16 miles away.

The BLM operates two campgrounds in the Canyon Rims Recreational Area. **Hatch Point Campground** (10 sites, water early May-mid-Sept., $12) has a scenic mesa-top setting just off the road to the Anticline Overlook, about nine miles north of the road junction. Closer to the highway is **Windwhistle Campground** (water early May-late Sept., $12); it's six miles west of U.S. 191 on the Needles Overlook road.

NEEDLES OUTPOST

A general store just outside the park boundary offers a campground (435/979-4007, www.canyonlandsneedlesoutpost.com, mid-Mar.-late Oct., $20 tent or RV, no hookups), groceries, ice, gas, propane, a café, showers ($3 campers, $7 noncampers), and pretty much any camping supply you might have left at home. The campground is a great alternative to the park; sites have a fair amount of privacy and great views onto the park's spires. The turnoff from Highway 211 is one mile before the Needles visitors center.

BIG SPRING CANYON SCENIC DRIVE

The main paved park road continues 6.5 miles past the visitors center to Big Spring Canyon Overlook. On the way, you can stop at several nature trails or turn onto 4WD roads. The overlook takes in a view of slickrock-edged canyons dropping away toward the Colorado River.

HIKING

The Needles District includes about 60 miles of backcountry trails. Many interconnect to provide all sorts of day-hike and overnight opportunities. Cairns mark the trails, and signs point the way at junctions. You can normally find water in upper Elephant Canyon and canyons to the east in spring and early summer, although whatever remains is often stagnant by midsummer. Always ask the rangers about sources of water, and don't depend on its availability. Treat water from all sources, including springs, before drinking it. Chesler Park and other areas west of Elephant Canyon are very dry; you'll need to bring all your water. Mosquitoes, gnats, and deer flies can be pesky late spring-midsummer, especially in the wetter places, so be sure to bring insect repellent. To plan your trip, obtain the small hiking map available from the visitors center, the National Geographic/Trails Illustrated's

© BONYU CHU/FLICKR.COM

Cave Spring Trail

Needles District map, or USGS topographic maps. Overnight backcountry hiking requires a permit ($30 per group). Permits can be hard to get at the last minute during the busy spring hiking season, but you can apply for your permit any time after mid-July for the following spring. Find permit applications on the Canyonlands website (www.nps.gov/cany).

Roadside Ruin Trail

- Distance: 0.3 miles round-trip
- Duration: 20 minutes
- Elevation change: 20 feet
- Effort: easy
- Trailhead: on the left, 0.4 miles past the visitors center

This is one of two easy hikes near the visitors center. It passes near a well-preserved Anasazi granary. A trail guide available at the start tells about the Anasazi and the local plants.

◀ Cave Spring Trail

- Distance: 0.6 miles round-trip
- Duration: 45 minutes
- Elevation change: 50 feet
- Effort: easy
- Trailhead: Cave Spring
- Directions: Turn left 0.7 miles past the visitors center and follow signs about 1 mile to the trailhead.

Don't miss the Cave Spring Trail, which introduces the geology and ecology of the park and leads to an old cowboy line camp. Pick up the brochure at the beginning. The loop goes clockwise, crossing some slickrock; two ladders assist hikers on the steep sections. Native Americans first used these rock overhangs for shelter, and faint pictographs still decorate the rock walls. Much later—from the late 1800s until the park was established in 1964—cowboys used these open caves as a line camp. The park service has recreated the line camp, just

POTHOLE ECOSYSTEMS

At Canyonlands it's easy to be in awe of the deep canyons and big desert rivers. But the little details of Canyonlands geology and ecology are pretty wonderful too. Consider the potholes: shallow depressions dusted with windblown dirt. These holes, which range from less than an inch to several feet deep, fill after rainstorms and bring entire little ecosystems to life.

Pothole dwellers must be able to survive long periods of dryness, then pack as much living as possible into the short wet periods. Some creatures, like the tadpole shrimp, live only for a couple of weeks. Others, like the spadefoot toad, hatch from drought-resistant eggs when water is present, quickly pass through the critical tadpole stage, then move onto dry land, returning to mate and lay eggs in potholes.

Although pothole dwellers are tough enough to survive in a dormant form during the long dry spells, most are very sensitive to sudden water-chemistry changes, temperature changes, sediment input, being stepped on, and being splashed out onto dry land. Humans should never use pothole water for swimming, bathing, or drinking, as this can drastically change the salinity or pH of a pool. Organisms are unable to adapt to these human-generated changes, which occur suddenly, unlike slow, natural changes. While the desert pothole ecosystems may seem unimportant, they act as an indicator of the health of the larger ecosystems in which they occur.

---

50 yards in from the trailhead, with period furnishings and equipment. If you're not up for the full hike, or would rather not climb ladders, the cowboy camp and the pictographs are just a five-minute walk from the trailhead.

This trail is a good introduction to hiking on slickrock and using rock cairns to find your way. Signs identify plants along the way.

Pothole Point Nature Trail

- Distance: 0.6 miles round-trip
- Duration: 40 minutes
- Elevation change: 20 feet
- Effort: easy
- Trailhead: parking area on the left side of Big Spring Canyon Overlook Scenic Drive, five miles past the visitors center

Highlights of this hike across the slickrock are the many potholes dissolved in the Cedar Mesa sandstone. A brochure illustrates the fairy shrimp, tadpole shrimp, horsehair worms, snails, and other creatures that spring to life when rain fills the potholes. Desert varnish rims the potholes; it forms when water evaporates,

leaving mineral residues on the surface of the rocks. In addition to the potholes, you'll enjoy fine views of distant buttes from the trail.

Slickrock Trail

- Distance: 2.4 miles round-trip
- Duration: 2 hours
- Elevation change: 150 feet
- Effort: easy-moderate
- Trailhead: parking area on the right side of Big Spring Canyon Overlook Scenic Drive, 6.2 miles past the visitors center

The Slickrock Trail leads north to a series of four viewpoints, including a panoramic view over much of southeastern Utah, and overlooks of Big Spring and Little Spring Canyons. As its name indicates, much of the trail is across slickrock, but there are enough pockets of soil to support a good springtime display of wildflowers. The trailhead is almost at the end of the paved road, where **Big Spring Canyon Overlook,** 6.5 miles past the visitors center, marks the end of the scenic drive but not the scenery.

CANYONLANDS

© PAUL LEVY

The Slickrock Trail has several great viewpoints.

Confluence Overlook Trail

- Distance: 5.5 miles one-way
- Duration: 5 hours
- Elevation change: 1,250 feet
- Effort: moderate-strenuous
- Trailhead: Big Spring Canyon Overlook

The Confluence Overlook Trail begins at the end of the paved road and winds west to an overlook of the Green and Colorado Rivers 1,000 feet below; there's no trail down to the rivers. The trail starts with some ups and downs, crossing Big Spring and Elephant Canyons, and follows a jeep road for a short distance. Much of the trail is through open country, so it can get quite hot. Higher points have good views of the Needles to the south. You might see rafts in the water or bighorn sheep on the cliffs. Except for a few short steep sections, this trail is level and fairly easy; it's the length of this 10-mile round-trip to the confluence as well as the hot sun that make it challenging. A very early start is recommended in summer

because there's little shade. Carry water even if you don't plan to go all the way. This enchanting country has lured many a hiker beyond his or her original goal.

Peekaboo Trail

- Distance: 5 miles one-way
- Duration: 5-6 hours
- Elevation change: 550 feet
- Effort: strenuous
- Trailhead: Squaw Flat trailhead
- Directions: A road to Squaw Flat Campground and Elephant Hill turns left 2.7 miles past the ranger station. The Squaw Flat trailhead sits a short distance south of the campground and is reached by a separate signed road. You can also begin from a trailhead in the campground itself.

Peekaboo Trail winds southeast over rugged up-and-down terrain, including some steep sections of slickrock (best avoided when wet, icy, or covered with snow) and a couple of ladders.

There's little shade, so carry water. The trail follows Squaw Canyon, climbs over a pass to Lost Canyon, then crosses more slickrock before descending to Peekaboo Campground on Salt Creek Road (accessible by 4WD vehicles). Look for Anasazi ruins on the way and rock art at the campground. A rockslide took out Peekaboo Spring, which is still shown on some maps. Options on this trail include a turnoff south through Squaw or Lost Canyon to make a loop of 8.75 miles or more.

Squaw Canyon Trail

- Distance: 3.75 miles one-way
- Duration: 4 hours
- Elevation change: 700 feet
- Effort: moderate
- Trailhead: parking area on the left of the main road, 5 miles past the visitors center
- Directions: A road to Squaw Flat Campground and Elephant Hill turns left 2.7 miles past the ranger station. The Squaw Flat Trailhead is a short distance south of the campground and is reached by a separate signed road. You can also begin from a trailhead in the campground itself.

Squaw Canyon Trail follows the canyon south. Intermittent water can often be found until late spring. You can take a connecting trail (Peekaboo, Lost Canyon, or Big Spring Canyon) or cross a slickrock pass to Elephant Canyon.

Lost Canyon Trail

- Distance: 3.25 miles one-way
- Duration: 4-5 hours
- Elevation change: 360 feet
- Effort: moderate-strenuous
- Trailhead: parking area on the left of the main road, 5 miles past the visitors center
- Directions: A road to Squaw Flat Campground and Elephant Hill turns left 2.7 miles past the ranger station. The Squaw

Flat trailhead sits a short distance south of the campground and is reached by a separate signed road. You can also begin from a trailhead in the campground itself.

Lost Canyon Trail is reached via Peekaboo or Squaw Canyon Trails and makes a loop with them. Lost Canyon is surprisingly lush, and you may be forced to wade through water. Most of the trail is in the wash bottom, except for a section of slickrock to Squaw Canyon.

Big Spring Canyon Trail

- Distance: 3.75 miles one-way
- Duration: 4 hours
- Elevation change: 370 feet
- Effort: moderate-strenuous
- Trailhead: parking area on the left of the main road, 5 miles past the visitors center
- Directions: A road to Squaw Flat Campground and Elephant Hill turns left 2.7 miles past the ranger station. The Squaw Flat trailhead is a short distance south of the campground and is reached by a separate signed road. You can also begin from a trailhead in the campground itself.

Big Spring Canyon Trail crosses an outcrop of slickrock from the trailhead, then follows the canyon bottom to the head of the canyon. It's a lovely springtime hike with lots of flowers, including the fragrant cliffrose. Except in summer, you can usually find intermittent water along the way. At canyon's end, a steep slickrock climb leads to Squaw Canyon Trail and back to the trailhead for a 7.5-mile loop. Another possibility is to turn southwest to the head of Squaw Canyon, then hike over a saddle to Elephant Canyon, for a 10.5-mile loop.

◖ Chesler Park

- Distance: 3 miles one-way
- Duration: 3-4 hours
- Elevation change: 920 feet

- Effort: moderate
- Trailhead: Elephant Hill parking area or Squaw Flat trailhead (increases the distance slightly)
- Directions: Drive west 3 miles past the Squaw Flat campground turnoff (on passable dirt roads) to the Elephant Hill picnic area and trailhead at the base of Elephant Hill.

The Elephant Hill parking area doesn't always inspire confidence: Sounds of racing engines and burning rubber can often be heard from above as vehicles attempt the difficult 4WD road that begins just past the picnic area. However, the noise quickly fades as you hit the trail. Chesler Park is a favorite hiking destination. A lovely desert meadow contrasts with the red and white spires that give the Needles District its name. An old cowboy line camp is on the west side of the rock island in the center of the park. The trail winds through sand and slickrock before ascending a small pass through the Needles to Chesler Park. Once inside, you can take the Chesler Park Loop Trail (5 miles) completely around the park. The loop includes the unusual 0.5-mile Joint Trail, which follows the bottom of a very narrow crack. Camping in Chesler Park is restricted to certain areas; check with a ranger.

Druid Arch

- Distance: 5.5 miles one-way
- Duration: 5-7 hours
- Elevation change: 1,000 feet
- Effort: strenuous
- Trailhead: Elephant Hill parking area or Squaw Flat trailhead (increases the round-trip distance by 2 miles)
- Directions: Drive west 3 miles past the Squaw Flat campground turnoff (on passable dirt roads) to the Elephant Hill picnic area and trailhead at the base of Elephant Hill.

Druid Arch reminds many people of the massive slabs at Stonehenge in England, which are popularly associated with the druids. Follow the Chesler Park Trail two miles to Elephant Canyon, turn up the canyon for 3.5 miles, and then make a steep 0.25-mile climb, which includes a ladder and some scrambling, to the arch. Upper Elephant Canyon has seasonal water but is closed to camping.

Lower Red Lake Canyon Trail

- Distance: 9.5 miles one-way
- Duration: 2 days
- Elevation change: 1,000 feet
- Effort: strenuous
- Trailhead: Elephant Hill parking area or Squaw Flat trailhead (increases the distance by 2 miles)
- Directions: Drive west 3 miles past the Squaw Flat campground turnoff (on passable dirt roads) to the Elephant Hill picnic area and trailhead at the base of Elephant Hill.

Lower Red Lake Canyon Trail provides access to the Colorado River's Cataract Canyon. This long, strenuous trip is best suited for experienced hikers and is ideally completed in two days. Distance from the Elephant Hill trailhead is 19 miles round-trip; you'll be walking on 4WD roads and trails. If you can drive Elephant Hill 4WD Road to the trail junction in Cyclone Canyon, the hike is only eight miles round-trip. The most difficult trail section is a steep talus slope that drops 700 feet in 0.5 miles into the lower canyon. The canyon has little shade and lacks any water source above the river. Summer heat can make the trip grueling; temperatures tend to be 5-10°F hotter than on other Needles trails. The river level drops between midsummer and autumn, allowing hikers to go along the shore both downstream to see the rapids and upstream to the confluence. Undertows and strong currents make the river dangerous to cross.

Upper Salt Creek Trail

- Distance: 12 miles one-way
- Duration: 2 days

- Elevation change: 1,650 feet
- Effort: strenuous
- Trailhead: end of Salt Creek Road
- Directions: Drive to the end of the rugged 13.5-mile 4WD road up Salt Creek to start this hike.

Several impressive arches and many inviting side canyons attract adventurous hikers to the extreme southeast corner of the Needles District. The trail goes south 12 miles up-canyon to Cottonwood Canyon and Beef Basin Road near Cathedral Butte, just outside the park boundary. The trail is nearly level except for a steep climb at the end. Water can usually be found. Some wading and bushwhacking may be necessary. The famous "All-American Man" pictograph, shown on some topographic maps (or ask a ranger), is in a cave a short way off to the east at about the midpoint of the trail; follow your map and unsigned paths to the cave, but don't climb in—it's dangerous to you, the ruins, and the pictograph inside. Many more archaeological sites are near the trail, but they're all fragile, and great care should be taken when visiting them.

MOUNTAIN BIKING AND 4WD EXPLORATION

Visitors with bicycles or 4WD vehicles can explore the many backcountry roads that lead to the outback. More than 50 miles of challenging roads link primitive campsites, remote trailheads, and sites with ancient cultural remnants. Some roads in the Needles District are rugged and require previous experience in handling 4WD vehicles on steep inclines and in deep sand. Be aware that towing charges from this area commonly run over $1,000.

The best route for mountain bikers is the seven-mile-long Colorado Overlook Road, which starts near the visitors center. Although very steep for the first stretch and busy with 4WD vehicles spinning their wheels on the hill, Elephant Hill Road is another good bet,

with just a few sandy parts. Start here and do a combination ride and hike to the Confluence Overlook. It's about eight miles from the Elephant Hill parking area to the confluence; the final 0.5 miles is on a trail, so you'll have to lock up your bike and walk this last bit. Horse Canyon and Lavender Canyon are too sandy for pleasant biking.

All motor vehicles and bicycles must purchase a $10 day-use permit and remain on designated roads. Overnight backcountry trips with bicycles or motor vehicles require a permit ($30 per group).

Salt Creek Canyon 4WD Road

This rugged route begins near Cave Spring Trail, crosses sage flats for the next 2.5 miles, and then terminates at Peekaboo campground. Hikers can continue south into a spectacular canyon on Upper Salt Creek Trail.

Horse Canyon 4WD Road turns off to the left shortly before the mouth of Salt Canyon. The round-trip distance, including a side trip to Tower Ruin, is about 13 miles; other attractions include Paul Bunyan's Potty, Castle Arch, Fortress Arch, and side canyon hiking. Salt and Horse Canyons can easily be driven in 4WD vehicles. Salt Canyon is usually closed in summer because of quicksand after flash floods and in winter due to shelf ice.

Davis and Lavender Canyons

Both canyons are accessed via Davis Canyon Road off Highway 211; contain great scenery, arches, and Native American historic sites; and are easily visited with high-clearance vehicles. Davis is about 20 miles round-trip, while sandy Lavender Canyon is about 26 miles round-trip. Try to allow plenty of time in either canyon, because there is much to see and many inviting side canyons to hike. You can camp on BLM land just outside the park boundaries, but not in the park itself.

Colorado Overlook 4WD Road

This popular route begins beside the visitors

© JUDY JEWELL

camping in style at Needles Outpost

center and follows Salt Creek to Lower Jump Overlook. It then bounces across slickrock to a view of the Colorado River, upstream from the confluence. Driving, for the most part, is easy-moderate, although it's very rough for the last 1.5 miles. Round-trip distance is 14 miles. This is also a good mountain bike ride.

Elephant Hill 4WD Loop Road

This rugged backcountry road begins three miles past the Squaw Flat Campground turnoff. Only experienced drivers with stout vehicles should attempt the extremely rough and steep climb up Elephant Hill (coming up the back side of Elephant Hill is even worse). The loop is about 10 miles round-trip. Connecting roads go to the Confluence Overlook trailhead (the viewpoint is one mile round-trip on foot), the Joint trailhead (Chesler Park is two miles round-trip on foot), and several canyons. Some road sections on the loop are one-way. The parallel canyons in this area are grabens caused by faulting, where a layer of salt has shifted deep

underground. In addition to Elephant Hill, a few other difficult spots must be negotiated.

This area can also be reached by a long route south of the park using Cottonwood Canyon and Beef Basin Road from Highway 211, about 60 miles one-way. You'll enjoy spectacular vistas from the Abajo Highlands. Two very steep descents from Pappys Pasture into Bobbys Hole effectively make this section one-way; travel from Elephant Hill up Bobbys Hole is possible but much more difficult than going the other way, and it may require hours of road-building. The Bobbys Hole route may be impassable at times; ask about conditions at the BLM office in Monticello or at the Needles visitors center.

CAMPGROUNDS

The **Squaw Flat Campground** (year-round, no reservations, $15) about six miles from the visitors center, has 26 sites, many snuggled under the slickrock, and has water. RVs must be less than 28 feet long. Rangers present evening programs at the campfire circle on Loop A spring through autumn.

If you can't find a space at Squaw Flat, a common occurrence in spring and fall, the private campground at **Needles Outpost** (435/979-4007, www.canyonlandsneedlesout-post.com, mid-Mar.-late Oct., $20 tents or RVs, no hookups, showers $3), just outside the park entrance, is a good alternative.

Nearby BLM land also offers a number of places to camp. A string of campsites along **Lockhart Basin Road** are convenient and inexpensive. Lockhart Basin Road heads north from Highway 211 about five miles east of the entrance to the Needles District. **Hamburger Rock Campground** (no water, $6) is about one mile up the road. North of Hamburger Rock, camping is dispersed, with many small (no water, free) campsites at turnoffs from the road. Not surprisingly,

the road gets rougher the farther north you travel; beyond Indian Creek Falls, it's best to have 4WD. These campsites are very popular with climbers who are here to scale the walls at Indian Creek.

There are two first-come, first-served campgrounds ($12) in the Canyon Rims Special Recreation Management Area (www.blm.gov). **Windwhistle Campground,** backed by cliffs to the south, has fine views to the north and a nature trail; follow the main road from U.S. 191 for six miles and turn left. At **Hatch Point Campground,** in a piñon-juniper woodland, you can enjoy views to the north. Go 24 miles in on the paved and gravel roads toward Anticline Overlook, then turn right and continue for one mile. Both campgrounds have water mid-April–mid-October, tables, grills, and outhouses.

The Maze District

Only adventurous and experienced travelers will want to visit this rugged land west of the Green and Colorado Rivers. Vehicle access wasn't even possible until 1957, when mineral-exploration roads first entered what later became Canyonlands National Park. Today, you'll need a high-clearance 4WD vehicle, a horse, or your own two feet to get around, and most visitors spend at least three days in the district. The National Park Service plans to keep this district in its remote and primitive condition. An airplane flight, which is recommended if you can't come overland, provides the only easy way to see the scenic features.

The names of erosional forms describe the landscape—Orange Cliffs, Golden Stairs, the Fins, Land of Standing Rocks, Lizard Rock, the Doll House, Chocolate Drops, the Maze, and Jasper Canyon. The many-fingered canyons of the Maze gave the district its name; although it is not a true maze, the canyons give that impression. It is extremely important to have a good map before entering this part of Canyonlands.

National Geographic/Trails Illustrated makes a good one, called *Canyonlands National Park Maze District, NE Glen Canyon NRA.*

Getting to the Maze District

Dirt roads to the **Hans Flat Ranger Station** (435/259-2652, 8am-4:30pm daily) and Maze District branch off from Highway 24 (across from the Goblin Valley State Park turnoff) and Highway 95 (take the usually unmarked Hite-Orange Cliffs Road between the Dirty Devil and Hite Bridges at Lake Powell). The easiest way in is the graded 46-mile road from Highway 24; it's fast, although sometimes badly corrugated. The 4WD Hite Road (also called Orange Cliffs Rd.) is longer, bumpier, and, for some drivers, tedious; it's 54 miles from the turnoff at Highway 95 to the Hans Flat Ranger Station via the Flint Trail. All roads to the Maze District cross Glen Canyon National Recreation Area. From Highway 24, two-wheel-drive vehicles with good clearance can travel to Hans Flat Ranger Station and other areas near, but not actually in, the Maze District. From the ranger station it takes at least three hours of skillful four-wheeling to drive into the canyons of the Maze.

One other way of getting to the Maze District is by river. **Tex's Riverways** (435/259-5101 or 877/662-2839, www.texsriverways.com, about $110 pp) can arrange a jet-boat shuttle on the Colorado River from Moab to the Spanish Bottom. After the two-hour boat ride, it's 1,260 vertical feet uphill in a little over one mile to the Doll House via the Spanish Bottom Trail.

Planning an Expedition

Maze District explorers need a backcountry permit ($30) for overnight trips. Note that a backcountry permit in this district is not a reservation. You may have to share a site, especially in the popular spring months. As in the rest of the park, only designated sites can be used for vehicle camping. You don't need a permit to camp in the adjacent Glen Canyon National Recreation Area (NRA) or on BLM land.

There are no developed sources of water in the Maze District. Hikers can obtain water from springs in some canyons (check with a ranger to find out which are flowing) or from the rivers; purify all water before drinking. The Maze District has nine camping areas (two at Maze Overlook, seven at Land of Standing Rocks), each with a 15-person, three-vehicle limit.

The National Geographic/Trails Illustrated topographic map of the Maze District describes and shows the few roads and trails here; some routes and springs are marked on it too. Agile hikers experienced in desert and canyon travel may want to take off on cross-country routes, which are either unmarked or lightly cairned.

Extra care and preparation must be undertaken for travel in both Glen Canyon NRA and the Maze. Always ask rangers beforehand for current conditions. Be sure to leave an itinerary with someone reliable who can contact the rangers if you're overdue returning. Unless the rangers know where to look for you in case of breakdown or accident, a rescue could take weeks.

◖ LAND OF STANDING ROCKS

Here in the heart of the Maze District, strangely shaped rock spires stand guard over myriad canyons. Six camping areas offer scenic places to stay (permit required). Hikers have a choice of many ridge and canyon routes from the 4WD road, a trail to a confluence overlook, and a trail that descends to the Colorado River near Cataract Canyon.

Getting to the Land of Standing Rocks takes some careful driving, especially on a three-mile stretch above Teapot Canyon. The many washes and small canyon crossings here make for slow going. Short-wheelbase vehicles have the easiest time, of course. The turnoff for Land of Standing Rocks Road is 6.6 miles from the junction at the bottom of the Flint Trail via a wash shortcut (add about three miles if driving via the four-way intersection). The lower end of the Golden Stairs foot trail is 7.8 miles in; the western end of the Ernies Country route trailhead is 8.6 miles in; the Wall is 12.7 miles in; Chimney Rock is 15.7 miles in; and the Doll House is 19 miles in, at the end of the road. If you drive from the south on Hite-Orange Cliffs Road, stop at the self-registration stand at the four-way intersection, about 31 miles in from Highway 95; you can write your own permit for overnights in the park.

Tall, rounded rock spires near the end of the road reminded early visitors of dolls, hence the name Doll House. The Doll House is a great place to explore, or you can head out on nearby routes and trails.

NORTH POINT

Hans Flat Ranger Station and this peninsula, which reaches out to the east and north, are at an elevation of about 6,400 feet. Panoramas from North Point take in the vastness of Canyonlands, including the Maze, Needles, and Island in the Sky Districts. From **Millard Canyon Overlook,** just 0.9 miles past the ranger station, you can see arches, Cleopatra's Chair, and features as distant as the La Sal Mountains and Book Cliffs. For the best views, drive out to Panorama Point, about 10.5 miles one-way from the ranger station. A spur road to the left goes two miles to Cleopatra's Chair, a massive sandstone monolith and area landmark.

HIKING
North Canyon Trail

- Distance: 7 miles one-way
- Duration: overnight
- Elevation change: 1,000 feet
- Effort: strenuous
- Trailhead: on North Point Road
- Directions: From Hans Flat Ranger Station, drive 2.5 miles east, turn left onto North Point Road, and continue about 1 mile to the trailhead.

This is just about the only trailhead in the Maze District that two-wheel-drive vehicles can usually reach. The trail leads down through the Orange Cliffs. At the eastern end of the trail, ambitious hikers can follow 4WD roads an additional six miles to the Maze Overlook Trail, then one more mile into a canyon of the Maze. Because North Point belongs to the Glen Canyon NRA, you can camp here without a permit.

Maze Overlook Trail

- Distance: 3 miles one-way (to Harvest Scene)
- Duration: 3-4 hours
- Elevation change: 550 feet
- Effort: strenuous
- Trailhead: at the end of the road in the Maze District

Here, at the edge of the sinuous canyons of the Maze, the Maze Overlook Trail drops one mile into the South Fork of Horse Canyon; bring a 25-foot-long rope to help lower backpacks through one difficult section. Once in the canyon, you can walk around to the Harvest Scene, a group of prehistoric pictographs, or do a variety of day hikes or backpacking trips. These canyons have water in some places; check with the ranger when you get your permit. At least four routes connect with the 4WD road in Land of Standing Rocks, shown on the Trails Illustrated map. Hikers can also climb Petes Mesa from the canyons or head downstream to explore Horse Canyon, but a dry fall blocks access to the Green River. You can stay at primitive camping areas (backcountry permit required) and enjoy the views.

The Golden Stairs

- Distance: 2 miles one-way
- Duration: 3 hours
- Elevation change: 800 feet
- Effort: moderate
- Trailhead: bottom of Flint Trail, at Golden Stairs camping area
- Directions: Drive the challenging Flint Trail, a 4WD route, to its bottom. The top of the Golden Stairs is 2 miles east of the road junction at the bottom of the Flint Trail.

Hikers can descend this steep foot trail to the Land of Standing Rocks Road in a fraction of the time it takes for drivers to follow the roads. The trail offers good views of Ernies Country, the vast southern area of the Maze District, but it lacks shade or water. The eponymous stairs are not actual steps carved into the rock, but a series of natural ledges.

Chocolate Drops Trail

- Distance: 4.5 miles one-way
- Duration: 5 hours
- Elevation change: 550 feet
- Effort: strenuous
- Trailhead: Chocolate Drops

- Directions: The Land of Standing Rocks turnoff is 6.6 miles from the junction at the bottom of the Flint Trail. The trailhead is just east of the Wall camping area.

The well-named Chocolate Drops can be reached by a trail from the Wall near the beginning of the Land of Standing Rocks. A good day hike makes a loop from Chimney Rock to the Harvest Scene pictographs; take the ridge route (toward Petes Mesa) in one direction and the canyon fork northwest of Chimney Rock in the other. Follow your topographic map through the canyons and the cairns between the canyons and ridge. Other routes from Chimney Rock lead to lower Jasper Canyon (no river access) or into Shot and Water Canyons and on to the Green River.

Spanish Bottom Trail

- Distance: 1.2 miles one-way
- Duration: 3 hours
- Elevation change: 1,260 feet
- Effort: strenuous
- Trailhead: Doll House, near Camp 1, just before the end of the Land of Standing Rocks Road

This trail drops steeply to Spanish Bottom beside the Colorado River; a thin trail leads downstream into Cataract Canyon and the first of a long series of rapids. **Surprise Valley Overlook Trail** branches to the right off the Spanish Bottom Trail after about 300 feet and winds south past some dolls to a T junction (turn right for views of Surprise Valley, Cataract Canyon, and beyond); the trail ends at some well-preserved granaries, after 1.5 miles one-way. From the same trailhead, the **Colorado-Green River Overlook Trail** heads north five miles one-way from the Doll House to a viewpoint of the confluence. See the area's Trails Illustrated map for routes, trails, and roads.

4WD EXPLORATION
Flint Trail 4WD Road

This narrow, rough 4WD road connects the Hans Flat area with the Maze Overlook, Doll House, and other areas below. The road, driver, and vehicle should all be in good condition before attempting this route. Winter snow and mud close the road late December-March, as can rainstorms anytime. Check on conditions with a ranger before you go. If you're starting from the top, stop at the signed overlook just before the descent to scout for vehicles headed up (the Flint Trail has very few places to pass). The top of the Flint Trail is 14 miles south of Hans Flat Ranger Station; at the bottom, 2.8 nervous miles later, you can turn left and go two miles to the Golden Stairs Trailhead or 12.7 miles to the Maze Overlook; keep straight 28 miles to the Doll House or 39 miles to Highway 95.

Horseshoe Canyon Unit

This canyon contains exceptional prehistoric rock art in a separate section of Canyonlands National Park. Ghostly life-size pictographs in the Great Gallery provide an intriguing look into the past. Archaeologists think that the images had religious importance, although the meaning of the figures remains unknown. The Barrier Canyon Style of these drawings has been credited to an archaic culture beginning at least 8,000 years ago and lasting until about AD 450. Horseshoe Canyon also contains rock art left by the subsequent Fremont and Anasazi people. The relationship between the earlier and later prehistoric groups hasn't been determined.

Call the **Hans Flat Ranger Station** (435/259-2652) to inquire about ranger-led hikes to the Great Gallery (Sat.-Sun. spring); when staff are available, additional walks may

© TERRY WOOD/FLICKR.COM

some of the figures in the Great Gallery, the largest panel of pictographs and petroglyphs in the Horseshoe Canyon Unit

be scheduled. In-shape hikers will have no trouble making the hike on their own, however.

HIKING
◖ Great Gallery Trail

- Distance: 3.25 miles one-way
- Duration: 4-6 hours
- Elevation change: 800 feet
- Effort: moderate-strenuous
- Trailhead: parking area on the canyon's west rim
- Directions: From Highway 24, turn east across from the Goblin Valley State Park turnoff, then continue east 30 miles on a dirt road; keep left at the Hans Flat Ranger Station and Horseshoe Canyon turnoff 25 miles in.

Horseshoe Canyon is northwest of the Maze District. The easiest and most common way to reach Horseshoe Canyon is from the west and Highway 24. In dry weather, cars with good clearance can reach a trailhead on the canyon's west rim. From the rim and parking area, the trail descends 800 feet in one mile on an old jeep road, which is now closed to vehicles. At the canyon bottom, turn right and go two miles upstream to the Great Gallery. The sandy canyon floor is mostly level; trees provide shade in some areas.

Look for other rock art along the canyon walls on the way to the Great Gallery. Take care not to touch any of the drawings, because they're fragile and irreplaceable. The oil from your hands will remove the paints. Horseshoe Canyon also offers pleasant scenery and spring wildflowers. Carry plenty of water. Neither camping nor pets are allowed in the canyon, although horses are OK, but you can camp on the rim. Contact the Hans Flat Ranger Station or the Moab office for road and trail conditions.

Horseshoe Canyon can also be reached via primitive roads from the east. A 4WD road runs north 21 miles from Hans Flat Ranger Station and drops steeply into the canyon from the east side. The descent on this road is so rough that most people prefer to park on the rim and hike the last mile of road. A vehicle barricade prevents driving right up to the rock-art panel, but the 1.5-mile walk is easy. A branch off the jeep road goes to the start of **Deadman's Trail** (1.5 miles one-way), which is less used and more difficult.

The River District

The River District is the name of the administrative unit of the park that oversees conservation and recreation for the Green and Colorado Rivers.

Generally speaking, there are two boating experiences on offer in the park's River District. First are the relatively gentle paddling and rafting experiences on the Colorado and Green Rivers above their confluence. After these rivers meet, deep in the park, the resulting Colorado River then tumbles into Cataract Canyon, a white-water destination par excellence with abundant Class III-V rapids.

While rafting and canoeing enthusiasts can plan their own trips to any section of these rivers, by far the vast majority of people sign on with outfitters, often located in Moab, and let them do the planning and work. Do-it-yourselfers must start with the knowledge that permits are required for most trips but are not always easily procured; because these rivers flow through rugged and remote canyons, most trips require multiple days and can be challenging to plan.

No matter how you execute a trip through the River District, there are several issues to think about beforehand. There are no designated campsites along the rivers in Canyonlands. During periods of high water, camps can be difficult to find, especially for large groups. During late summer and fall, sandbars are usually plentiful and make ideal

© BILL MCRAE

Rafters set out on the Colorado River.

camps. There is no access to potable water along the river, so river runners either need to bring along their own water or be prepared to purify river water.

While it's possible to fish in the Green and Colorado Rivers, these desert rivers don't offer much in the way of species that most people consider edible. You'll need to bring along all your foodstuffs.

The park requires all river runners to pack out their solid human waste. Specially designed portable toilets that fit into rafts and canoes can be rented from most outfitters in Moab.

RIVER-RUNNING ABOVE THE CONFLUENCE

The Green and Colorado Rivers flow smoothly through their canyons above the confluence of the two rivers. Almost any shallow-draft boat can navigate these waters: Canoes, kayaks, rafts, and powerboats are commonly used. Any travel requires advance planning because of the remoteness of the canyons and the scarcity of river access points. No campgrounds, supplies, or other facilities exist past Moab on the Colorado River or the town of Green River on the Green River. All river runners must follow park regulations, which include carrying life jackets, using a fire pan for fires, and packing out all garbage and solid human waste. The river flow on both the Colorado and the Green Rivers averages a gentle 2-4 mph (7-10 mph at high water). Boaters typically do 20 miles per day in canoes and 15 miles per day on rafts.

The Colorado has one modest rapid, called the Slide (1.5 miles above the confluence), where rocks constrict the river to one-third of its normal width; the rapid is roughest during high water levels in May-June. This is the only difficulty on the 64 river miles from Moab. Inexperienced canoeists and rafters may wish to portage around it. The most popular launch points on the Colorado are the Moab Dock (just upstream from the U.S. 191 bridge near

town) and the Potash Dock (17 miles downriver on Potash Rd./Hwy. 279).

On the Green River, boaters at low water need to watch for rocky areas at the mouth of Millard Canyon (33.5 miles above the confluence, where a rock bar extends across the river) and at the mouth of Horse Canyon (14.5 miles above the confluence, where a rock and gravel bar on the right leaves only a narrow channel on the left side). The trip from the town of Green River through Labyrinth and Stillwater Canyons is 120 miles. Launch points include Green River State Park (in the town of Green River) and Mineral Canyon (52 miles above the confluence and reached on a fairweather road from Hwy. 313). Boaters who launch at Green River State Park pass through Labyrinth Canyon; a free interagency permit is required for travel along this stretch of the river. Permits are available from the BLM office (82 Dogwood Ave., Moab, 435/259-2100, 7:45am-noon Mon.-Fri.), the Canyonlands National Park Headquarters (2282 SW Resource Blvd., Moab, 435/719-2313, 8am-4pm Mon.-Fri.), Green River State Park in Green River, or the John Wesley Powell River History Museum (1765 E. Main St., Green River, 435/564-3427, 8am-7pm daily). A permit can also be downloaded from the BLM website (www.blm.gov).

No roads go to the confluence. The easiest return to civilization for nonmotorized craft is a pickup by jet boat from Moab by **Tex's Riverways** (435/259-5101, www.texsriverways. com) or **Tag-A-Long Tours** (800/453-3292, www.tagalong.com). A far more difficult way out is hiking either of two trails just above the Cataract Canyon Rapids to 4WD roads on the rim. Don't plan to attempt this unless you're a very strong hiker and have a packable watercraft.

National park rangers require that boaters above the confluence obtain a backcountry permit ($30) either in person from the Moab National Park Service office (2282 SW

ENDANGERED FISH OF THE COLORADO RIVER BASIN

Colorado pikeminnow (*Ptychocheilus lucius*): Native only to the Colorado and its tributaries, this species is the largest minnow in North America. It has been reported to weigh up to 100 pounds and measure six feet long. Loss of habitat caused by dam construction has greatly curtailed its size and range. Fishers often confuse the smaller, more common roundtail chub (*Gila robusta*) with the Colorado pikeminnow; the chub is distinguished by a smaller mouth extending back only to the front of the eye.

Humpback chub (*Gila cypha*): Scientists first described this fish only in 1946 and know little about its life. This small fish usually weighs less than two pounds and measures less than 13 inches. Today the humpback chub hangs on the verge of extinction; it has retreated to a few small areas of the Colorado River where the water still runs warm, muddy, and swift. The bonytail chub (*Gila elegans*) has a similar size and shape, but without a hump; its numbers are also rapidly declining.

Humpback or razorback sucker (*Xyrauchen texanus*): This large sucker grows to weights of 10-16 pounds and lengths of about three feet. Its numbers have been slowly decreasing, especially above the Grand Canyon. It requires warm, fast-flowing water to reproduce. Mating is a bizarre ritual in the spring: When the female has selected a suitable spawning site, two male fish press against the sides of her body. The female begins to shake her body until the eggs and spermatozoa are expelled simultaneously. One female can spawn three times, but she uses a different pair of males each time.

Resource Blvd., Moab, 435/719-2313, 8am-4pm Mon.-Fri.) or by mail (National Park Service Reservation Office, 2282 SW Resource Blvd., Moab, UT 84532-3298) or fax (435/259-4285) at least two weeks in advance.

Notes on boating the Green and Colorado Rivers are available on request from the National Park Service's Moab office (435/259-3911). Bill and Buzz Belknap's *Canyonlands River Guide* has river logs and maps pointing out items of interest on the Green River below the town of Green River and all of the Colorado River from the upper end of Westwater Canyon to Lake Powell.

◖ RIVER-RUNNING THROUGH CATARACT CANYON

The Colorado River enters Cataract Canyon at the confluence and picks up speed. The rapids begin four miles downstream and extend for the next 14 miles to Lake Powell. Especially in spring, the 26 or more rapids give a wild ride equal to the best in the Grand Canyon. The current zips along at up to 16 mph and forms waves more than seven feet high. When the excitement dies down, boaters have a 34-mile trip across Lake Powell to Hite Marina; most people either carry a motor or arrange for a powerboat to pick them up. Depending on water levels, which can vary wildly from year to year, the dynamics of this trip and the optimal take-out point can change. Depending on how much motoring is done, the trip through Cataract Canyon takes 2-5 days.

Because of the real hazards of running the rapids, the National Park Service requires boaters to have proper equipment and a permit ($30). Many people go on commercial trips with Moab outfitters on which everything has been taken care of. Private groups must contact the Canyonlands River Unit of the National Park Service far in advance for permit details (435/259-3911, www.nps.gov/cany).

ARCHES NATIONAL PARK

A concentration of rock arches of marvelous variety has formed within the maze of sandstone fins at Arches National Park, one of the most popular national parks in the United States. Balanced rocks and tall spires add to the splendor. Paved roads and short hiking trails provide easy access to some of the more than 1,500 arches in the park. If you're short on time, a drive through the Windows Section (23.5 miles round-trip) affords a look at some of the largest and most spectacular arches. To visit all the stops and hike a few short trails takes a full day.

Most of the early settlers and cowboys who passed through the Arches area paid little attention to the scenery. In 1923, however, a prospector by the name of Alexander Ringhoffer interested officials of the Rio Grande Railroad in the scenic attractions at what he called Devils Garden, now known as Klondike Bluffs. The railroad people liked the area and contacted Stephen Mather, the first director of the National Park Service. Mather started the political process that led to designating two small areas as a national monument in 1929, but Ringhoffer's Devils Garden wasn't included until later. The monument grew in size over the years and became Arches National Park in 1971. The park now comprises 76,519 acres—small enough to be appreciated in one day, yet large enough to warrant extensive exploration.

© JUDY JEWELL

HIGHLIGHTS

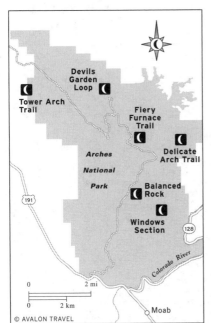

LOOK FOR ◖ TO FIND RECOMMENDED SIGHTS, ACTIVITIES, DINING, AND LODGING.

◖ **Balanced Rock:** An unbelievable spire-upon-spire balancing act rising 128 feet from the desert, Balanced Rock is sure to give your camera a warm-up (page 198).

◖ **Windows Section:** Some of the park's largest arches are here—so are some of its largest crowds. But you have to go: Make it past the first arch and the crowds thin out (page 199).

◖ **Delicate Arch Trail:** Delicate Arch is beautiful when seen from the easily reached viewpoint. It's mystical when seen close up, after a tough 1.5-mile hike to its base. If you're not up to the hike, at least follow the trail across the Salt Wash footbridge and turn left to find a striking but often overlooked rock art panel, carved by Ute artists about 400 years ago (page 204).

◖ **Fiery Furnace Trail:** To reach this unusual wonderland of rock mazes, fins, and turrets, hikers should join a ranger-led tour. Hikes into this red-rock landscape are popular, so go online and book your tour in advance (page 204).

◖ **Devils Garden Loop:** This 7.2-mile loop trail, leading to eight named arches and through a landscape of bizarre rock fins, offers the park's best day hiking (page 205).

◖ **Tower Arch Trail:** This spire, with an arch at its base, is one of the park's most beautiful but neglected sights. The formation in Arches' backcountry is off-limits to the RV set—you'll need a high-clearance vehicle (page 207).

ARCHES NATIONAL PARK

Thanks to unrelenting erosion, the arches themselves are constantly changing. Every so often there's a dramatic change, as there was during the summer of 2008 when Wall Arch, a 71-foot span on the Devils Garden Trail, collapsed.

PLANNING YOUR TIME

If you only have part of the day to explore, drive the 18-mile length of the main park road with brief stops at Balanced Rock and the Delicate Arch viewpoint. At the road's end, set out on the Devils Garden Trail, but take only the trip to Tunnel and Pine Tree Arches. If you still have some time, stop on the way back out of the park and take a stroll on the Park Avenue Trail.

A full day in the park allows plenty of time to stop at the visitors center and then hike the full Delicate Arch Trail and explore Devils Garden. Energetic hikers may want to do the entire 7.2-mile loop in Devils Garden; those who want less of a workout can walk the one-mile-long trail to Landscape Arch.

If you have more than one day to spend, plan ahead and register online for a ranger-led

ARCHES NATIONAL PARK

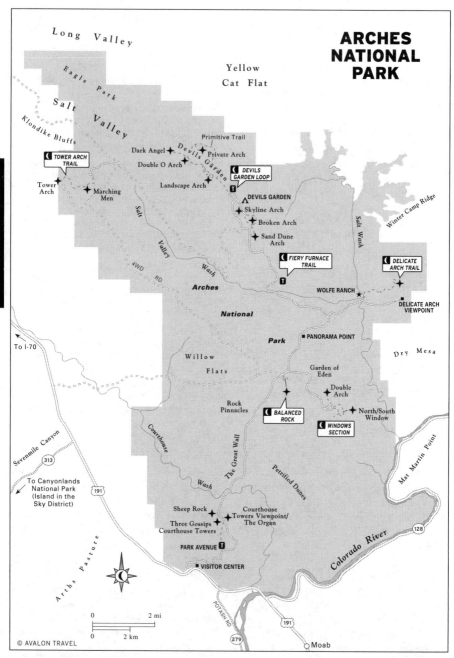

ARCHES NATIONAL PARK

Long Valley

Yellow Cat Flat

Eagle Park

Salt Valley

Klondike Bluffs

Primitive Trail

Dark Angel   Devils Garden   Private Arch

Double O Arch

🌙 TOWER ARCH TRAIL

Tower Arch   Marching Men

Landscape Arch

🌙 DEVILS GARDEN LOOP

DEVILS GARDEN

Skyline Arch

Broken Arch

Sand Dune Arch

Salt Valley Wash

🌙 FIERY FURNACE TRAIL

🌙 DELICATE ARCH TRAIL

Salt Wash

Winter Camp Ridge

4WD RD

Arches

National

Park

WOLFE RANCH

DELICATE ARCH VIEWPOINT

To I-70

PANORAMA POINT

Willow Flats

Dry Mesa

Garden of Eden

Double Arch

Courthouse Wash

Rock Pinnacles

🌙 BALANCED ROCK

North/South Window

🌙 WINDOWS SECTION

Sevenmile Canyon

313

To Canyonlands National Park (Island in the Sky District)

191

The Great Wall

Petrified Dunes

Mat Martin Point

Sheep Rock   Courthouse Towers Viewpoint/ The Organ

Three Gossips Courthouse Towers

PARK AVENUE

Colorado River

128

Arches Pasture

VISITOR CENTER

POTASH RD

279

191

Moab

0   2 mi

0   2 km

© AVALON TRAVEL

EDWARD ABBEY: "RESIST MUCH, OBEY LITTLE"

Edward Abbey spent two summers in the late 1950s living in a trailer in Arches National Park. From this experience, he wrote *Desert Solitaire*, which, when it was published in 1968, introduced many readers to the beauties of Utah's slickrock country and to the need to preserve it. In the introduction to this book, he gives a word of caution to slickrock pilgrims:

> Do not jump into your automobile next June and rush out to the Canyon country hoping to see some of that which I have attempted to evoke in these pages. In the first place you can't see anything from a car; you've got to get out of the goddamned contraption and walk, better yet crawl, on hands and knees, over the sandstone and through the...cactus. When traces of blood begin to mark your trail you'll see something, maybe.

This sense of letting the outdoors affect you—right down to the bone—pervades Abbey's writing. He advocated responding to assaults on the environment in an equally raw, gutsy way. Convinced that the only way to confront rampant development in the American West was by preserving its wilderness, he was a pioneer of radical environmentalism, a "desert anarchist." Long before Earth First!, Abbey's fictional characters blew up dams and created a holy environmentalist ruckus in *The Monkey Wrench Gang*. Some of his ideas were radical, others reactionary, and he seemed deeply committed to raising a stir. Abbey's writing did a lot to change the way people think about the American West, its development, and staying true to values derived from the natural world.

Two biographies, *Edward Abbey: A Life*, by James M. Cahalan (Tucson: University of Arizona Press, 2001), and the less academic *Adventures with Ed*, by Abbey's good friend Jack Loeffler (Albuquerque: University of New Mexico Press, 2002), help readers see the person behind the icon.

hike into the Fiery Furnace area of the park. This takes about half a day; for the other half, head out via car or mountain bike to Tower Arch Trail.

Although Arches is known more for day hiking than backpacking, park rangers can help you put together a backpacking trip and issue the required backcountry permit.

Exploring the Park

The entrance to Arches National Park (435/719-2299, www.nps.gov/arch, $10 per vehicle, $5 bicyclists, motorcyclists, and pedestrians) is five miles north of downtown Moab on U.S. 191.

VISITORS CENTER

Located just past the park entrance booth, the expansive visitors center (7:30am-6:30pm daily Apr.-Oct., 8am-4:30pm daily Nov.-Mar.) provides a good introduction to what you can expect ahead. Exhibits identify the rock layers, describe

the geologic and human history, and illustrate some of the wildlife and plants of the park. A large outdoor plaza is a good place to troll for information when the visitors center is closed.

A short slide program runs regularly, and staff members are available to answer your questions, issue backcountry permits, and check you in for a ranger-led tour in the Fiery Furnace area of the park. Look for the posted list of special activities; rangers host campfire programs and lead a wide variety of guided walks April-September. You'll also find checklists, pamphlets, books, maps, posters, postcards, and film for purchase. See the rangers for advice and the free backcountry permit required for overnight trips. The easy 0.2-mile **Desert Nature Trail** begins near the visitors center and identifies some of the native plants. Picnic areas are outside the visitors center and at Balanced Rock and Devils Garden.

Desert bighorn sheep frequent the area around the visitors center and can sometimes be seen from U.S. 191 just south of the park entrance. A sheep crossing about three miles north of the visitors center is also a good place to scan the steep talus slopes for these nimble animals.

A road guide to Arches National Park, available at the visitors center, has detailed descriptions that correspond to place-names along the main road. Be sure to stop only in parking lots and designated pullouts. Watch out for others who are sightseeing in this popular park. With less than 30 miles of paved road, the traffic can be surprisingly heavy in the summer high season.

The aptly named Balanced Rock only looks precarious.

© BILL MCRAE

If your plans include visiting Canyonlands National Park plus Hovenweep and Natural Bridges National Monuments, consider the so-called Local Passport ($25), which buys entry to all of these federal preserves. Purchase the pass at any of the park or national monument entrances.

MOAB FAULT

The park road begins a long but well-graded climb from the visitors center up the cliffs to the northeast. A pullout on the right after 1.1 miles offers a good view of Moab Canyon and its geology. The rock layers on this side of the canyon have slipped down more than 2,600 feet in relation to the other side. Movement took place about six million years ago along the Moab Fault, which follows the canyon floor. Rock layers at the top of the far cliffs are nearly the same age as those at the bottom on this side. If you could stack the rocks of this side on top of rocks on the other side, you'd have a complete stratigraphic column of the Moab area—more than 150 million years' worth.

PARK AVENUE

South Park Avenue overlook and trailhead are on the left 2.1 miles from the visitors center. Great sandstone slabs form a skyline on each side of this dry wash. A trail goes north one mile down the wash to the North Park Avenue trailhead (1.3 miles ahead by road). Arrange to be picked up there, or backtrack to your starting point. The large rock monoliths of Courthouse Towers rise north of Park Avenue. Only a few small arches exist now, although major arches may have formed there in the past.

◖ BALANCED ROCK

This gravity-defying formation is on the right, 8.5 miles from the visitors center. A boulder more than 55 feet high rests precariously atop a 73-foot pedestal. Chip Off the Old Block, a much smaller version of Balanced Rock, stood nearby until it collapsed in the winter of

© JUDY JEWELL

The Windows Section is a good place for a short hike.

1975-1976. For a closer look at Balanced Rock, take the 0.3-mile trail encircling it. There's a picnic area across the road. Author Edward Abbey lived in a trailer near Balanced Rock for a season as a park ranger in the 1950s; his journal became the basis for the classic *Desert Solitaire.*

◖ WINDOWS SECTION

The Windows Section of Arches is located 2.5 miles past Balanced Rock, on a paved road to the right. Short trails (0.25-1 mile one-way) lead from the road's end to some massive arches. Windows trailhead is the start for North Window (an opening 51 feet high and 93 feet wide), South Window (66 feet high and 105 feet wide), and Turret Arch (64 feet high and 39 feet wide). Double Arch, a short walk from a second trailhead, is an unusual pair of arches; the larger opening—105 feet high and 163 feet wide—is best appreciated by walking inside. The smaller opening is 61 feet high and

60 feet wide. Together, the two arches frame a large opening overhead.

Garden of Eden Viewpoint, on the way back to the main road, promises a good panorama of Salt Valley to the north. Under the valley, the massive body of salt and gypsum that's responsible for the arches comes close to the surface. Far-off Delicate Arch can be seen across the valley on a sandstone ridge. Early visitors to the Garden of Eden saw rock formations resembling Adam (with an apple) and Eve. Two other viewpoints of the Salt Valley area lie farther north on the main road.

DELICATE ARCH AND WOLFE RANCH

A bit of pioneer history survives at Wolfe Ranch, 2.5 miles north on the main road from the Windows junction (turn right and drive 1.8 miles to the parking area). John Wesley Wolfe came to this spot in 1888, hoping the desert climate would provide relief for health problems

ARCHES NATIONAL PARK

Sign up in advance for a ranger-led hike through the Fiery Furnace.

The span is 45 feet high and 33 feet wide. A moderately strenuous three-mile round-trip hike leads to the arch. Another perspective on Delicate Arch can be obtained by driving 1.2 miles beyond Wolfe Ranch. Look for the small arch high above. A short, steep trail (0.5 miles round-trip) climbs a hill for the best view.

FIERY FURNACE

The Fiery Furnace Viewpoint and trailhead are three miles from the Wolfe Ranch junction, on the right side of the main road. The Fiery Furnace gets its name from sandstone fins that turn flaming red on occasions when thin cloud cover at the horizon reflects the warm light of sunrise or sunset. The shady recesses beneath the fins provide a cool respite from the hot summer sun.

Closely packed sandstone fins form a maze of deep slots, with many arches and at least one natural bridge inside. Both for safety reasons and to reduce human impact on this sensitive area, which harbors several species of rare plants, hikers are encouraged to join a ranger-led hike. The hike is moderately strenuous and involves steep ledges, squeezing through narrow cracks, a couple of jumps, and hoisting yourself up off the ground. There is no turning back once the hike starts, so make sure you're physically prepared and properly equipped.

Rangers lead three-hour hikes (Mar.-Oct., $10 adults, $5 ages 5-12 and Interagency Senior Pass holders) into the Fiery Furnace twice each day. Unlike most ranger-led activities, a fee is charged for these hikes. Group size is limited to about 20 people, and it is not recommended for children under age five. Walks often fill weeks in advance. Make reservations online at www.recreation.gov or in person at the visitors center up to seven days in advance. To visit the Fiery Furnace without a ranger, visitors must obtain a permit ($5 pp) at the visitors center. A couple of Moab outfitters also lead hikes into the Fiery Furnace; these cost considerably more, but there's usually space available.

related to a Civil War injury. He found a good spring high in the rocks, grass for cattle, and water in Salt Wash to irrigate a garden. The ranch that he built provided a home for him and some of his family for more than 20 years, and cattlemen later used it as a line ranch. Then sheepherders brought in their animals, which so overgrazed the range that the grass has yet to recover. A trail guide available at the entrance tells about the Wolfe family and the features of their ranch. The weather-beaten cabin built in 1906 still survives. A short trail leads to petroglyphs above Wolfe Ranch; figures of horses indicate that Ute people, rather than earlier inhabitants, did the artwork. Park staff can give directions to other rock-art sites; great care should be taken not to touch the fragile artwork.

Delicate Arch stands in a magnificent setting atop gracefully curving slickrock. Distant canyons and the La Sal Mountains lie beyond.

WHY ARE THERE ARCHES?

The park's distinctive arches are formed by an unusual combination of geologic forces. About 300 million years ago, evaporation of inland seas left behind a salt layer more than 3,000 feet thick in the Paradox Basin of this region. Sediments, including those that later became the arches, then covered the salt. Unequal pressures caused the salt to gradually flow upward in places, bending the overlying sediments as well. These upfolds, or anticlines, later collapsed when ground water dissolved the underlying salt.

The faults and joints caused by the uplift and collapse opened the way for erosion to carve hundreds of freestanding fins. Alternate freezing and thawing action and exfoliation (flaking caused by expansion when water or frost penetrates the rock) continued to peel away more rock until holes formed in some of the fins. Rockfalls in the holes helped enlarge the arches. Nearly all arches in the park eroded out of Entrada sandstone.

Eventually all the present arches will collapse, as Wall Arch did in 2008, but there should be plenty of new ones by the time that happens. The fins' uniform strength and hard upper surfaces have proved ideal for arch formation. Not every hole in the rock is an arch. To qualify, the opening must be at least three feet in one direction, and light must be able to pass through. Although the term *windows* often refers to openings in large walls of rock, windows and arches are really the same.

Water seeping through the sandstone from above has created a second type of arch—the pothole arch. You may also come across a few natural bridges cut from the rock by perennial water runoff.

A succession of rock layers is on display at Arches. The rocks on top of the salt beds—the rocks you actually see at Arches—are mostly Entrada sandstone, which is a pretty general category of rock. Within this Entrada Formation are three distinct types of sandstone. The formation's dark red base layer is known as the Dewey Bridge member. It's softer than the formation's other sandstones and erodes easily. Dewey Bridge rocks are topped by the pinkish orange Slick Rock member, the park's most visible rocks. The Slick Rock layer is much harder than the Dewey Bridge, and the combination of the two layers—softer rocks overlaid by harder—is responsible for the differential erosion that forms hoodoos and precariously balanced rocks. The thin top layer of Entrada sandstone, a white rock similar to Navajo sandstone, is called the Moab Tongue.

SKYLINE ARCH

This arch is on the right, one mile past the Sand Dune/Broken Arch trailhead. In desert climates, erosion can proceed imperceptibly for centuries until a cataclysmic event happens. In 1940 a giant boulder fell from the opening of Skyline Arch, doubling the size of the arch in seconds. The hole is now 45 feet high and 69 feet wide. A short trail leads to the base of the arch.

DEVILS GARDEN

The Devils Garden trailhead, picnic area, and campground are all near the end of the main park road. Devils Garden offers fine scenery and more arches than any other section of the park. The hiking trail leads past large sandstone fins to Landscape and six other named arches. Carry water if the weather is hot or if you might want to continue past the one-mile point at Landscape Arch. Adventurous hikers could spend days exploring the maze of canyons among the fins.

KLONDIKE BLUFFS AND TOWER ARCH

Relatively few visitors come to the spires, high bluffs, and fine arch in this northwestern section of the park. A fair-weather dirt road turns off the main drive 1.3 miles before Devils Garden trailhead, winds down into Salt Valley, and heads northwest. After 7.5 miles, turn left on the road to Klondike Bluffs and proceed one mile to the Tower Arch trailhead. These roads may have washboards, but they are usually passable by cars in dry weather; don't drive on them if storms threaten. The trail to Tower Arch winds past the Marching Men and other rock formations (3 miles round-trip). Alexander Ringhoffer, who discovered the arch in 1922, carved an inscription on the south column. The area can also be fun to explore off-trail with a map and compass or a GPS receiver. Those with 4WD vehicles can drive close to the arch on a separate jeep road. Tower Arch has an opening 34 feet high by 92 feet wide. A tall monolith nearby gave the arch its name.

4WD ROAD

A rough road near Tower Arch in the Klondike Bluffs turns southeast past **Eye of the Whale Arch** in Herdina Park to Balanced Rock on the main park road, 10.8 miles away. The road isn't particularly difficult for 4WD enthusiasts, although normal backcountry precautions should be taken. A steep sand hill north of Eye of the Whale Arch is difficult to climb for vehicles coming from Balanced Rock; it's better to drive from the Tower Arch area instead.

Recreation

Because of its great popularity and proximity to Moab, Arches sees a lot of visitors. Most are content, however, to drive the parkways and perhaps saunter to undemanding viewpoints. You can quickly leave the crowds behind by planning a hike to more outlying destinations. Arches' outback offers magnificent rewards for hikers willing to leave the pavement behind and get dusty on a backcountry trail.

HIKING

Established hiking trails lead to many fine arches and overlooks that can't be seen from the road. You're free to wander cross-country, too, but stay on rock or in washes to avoid damaging the fragile cryptobiotic soils. Wear good walking shoes with rubber soles for travel across slickrock. The summer sun can be especially harsh on the unprepared hiker—don't forget water, a hat, and sunscreen. The desert rule is to carry at least one gallon of water per person for an all-day hike. Take a map and compass or a map and GPS unit for off-trail hiking. Be cautious on the slickrock, as the soft sandstone can crumble easily. Also, remember that it's easier to go up a steep slickrock slope than it is to come back down.

You can reach almost any spot in the park on a day hike, although you'll also find some good overnight camping possibilities. Areas for longer trips include Courthouse Wash in the southern part of the park and Salt Wash in the eastern part. All backpacking is done off-trail. A backcountry permit must be obtained from a ranger before camping in the backcountry.

Backcountry regulations prohibit fires and pets, and they allow camping only out of sight of any road, at least one mile away, or trail, at least 0.5 miles away, and at least 300 feet from a recognizable archaeological site or nonflowing water source.

Park Avenue

- Distance: 1 mile one-way
- Duration: 1 hour round-trip
- Elevation change: 320 feet
- Effort: easy-moderate
- Trailheads: Park Avenue or North Park Avenue trailhead

Get an eyeful of massive stone formations and a feel for the natural history of the park on the easy-moderate Park Avenue trail. The

MORMON TEA

Although it's not the showiest wildflower in the desert, Mormon tea (*Ephedra viridis*) is widespread across southern Utah, and it's very common in Arches. This broom-like plant is remarkably well adapted to the desert, and many desert-dwelling humans have adapted themselves to enjoy drinking it as a tea.

The plant's branches contain chlorophyll and are able to conduct photosynthesis. The leaves are like tiny scales or bracts; their small size reduces the amount of moisture the plant loses to transpiration. Male and female flowers grow on separate plants.

Native Americans used this plant medicinally as a tea for stomach and bowel disorders as well as for colds, fever, and headaches. Some used it to control bleeding and as a poultice for burns.

Mormon tea is related to ma huang, a Chinese herb that is traditionally used to treat hay fever. All parts of the plant contain a small amount of ephedrine, a stimulant that in large concentrations can be quite harmful. Pioneers in southern Utah were mostly Mormons, who are forbidden to drink coffee or similar stimulants. When they learned that drinking the boiled stems of *Ephedra viridis* gave them a mild lift, they approached Brigham Young, the head of the Latter-Day Saints. Young gave the tea his stamp of approval, and the plant's common name grew out of its widespread use by Mormons. In Utah it's also sometimes called Brigham tea.

The tea itself is yellowish and, as one local puts it, tastes something like what she imagines boiled socks would taste like. To increase the tea's palatability, it's often mixed with mint, lemon, and sugar or honey. Pioneers liked to add strawberry jam to their Mormon tea.

If you are tempted to try this tea for yourself, make certain not to harvest plants in a national park. Women who are pregnant or nursing and people with high blood pressure, heart disease, diabetes, glaucoma, or other health problems should definitely avoid even the small amounts of ephedra present in Mormon tea.

Park Avenue trailhead, just past the crest of the switchbacks that climb up into the park, is the best place to start. The vistas from here are especially dramatic: Courthouse Towers, the Three Gossips, and other fanciful rock formations loom above a natural amphitheater. The trail drops into a narrow wash before traversing the park highway at the North Park Avenue trailhead. Hikers can be dropped off at one trailhead and picked up 30 minutes later at the other.

The Windows

- Distance: 1 mile round-trip
- Duration: 1 hour
- Elevation change: 140 feet
- Effort: easy
- Trailhead: end of Windows Road

Ten miles into the park, just past the impossible-to-miss Balanced Rock, follow signs and a paved road to the Windows Section. A one-mile round-trip loop along a sandy trail leads to the Windows—a cluster of enormous arches that are impossible to see from the road. Highlights include the **North** and **South Windows** and **Turret Arch.** Unmarked trails lead to vistas and scrambles along the stone faces that make up the ridge. If this easy loop leaves you eager for more exploration in the area, a second trail starts from just past the Windows parking area and goes to **Double Arch.** This 0.5-mile trail leads to two giant spans that are joined at one end. These easy trails are good for family groups because younger or more ambitious hikers can scramble to their hearts' content along rocky outcrops.

Delicate Arch Viewpoint

- Distance: 0.5 miles round-trip
- Duration: 15-30 minutes
- Elevation change: 100 feet
- Effort: easy-moderate

ARCHES NATIONAL PARK

© PAUL LEVY

Delicate Arch is at the end of a 1.5-mile trail.

- Trailhead: 1 mile past Wolfe Ranch, at the end of Wolfe Ranch Road

If you don't have the time or the endurance for the relatively strenuous hike to Delicate Arch, you can view the astonishing arch from a distance at the Delicate Arch Viewpoint. From the viewing area, hikers can scramble up a steep trail to a rim with views across Cache Valley. Even though this is a short hike, it's a good place to wander around the slickrock for a while. It's especially nice to linger around sunset, when the arch captures the light and begins to glow. If you'd rather not scramble around on the slickrock, a short path leads about 100 yards from the parking area to a decent view of the arch.

◖ Delicate Arch Trail

- Distance: 3 miles round-trip
- Duration: 2 hours
- Elevation change: 500 feet
- Effort: moderate-strenuous

- Trailhead: Wolfe Ranch

For those who are able, the hike to the base of Delicate Arch is one of the park's highlights. Shortly after the trail's start at Wolfe Ranch, a spur trail leads to some petroglyphs depicting horses and their riders and a few bighorn sheep. Horses didn't arrive in the area until the mid-1600s, so these petroglyphs are believed to be the work of the Ute people.

The first stretch of the main trail is broad, flat, and not especially scenic, except for a good display of spring wildflowers. After about half an hour of hiking, the trail climbs steeply up onto the slickrock and the views open up across the park to the La Sal Mountains in the distance.

Just before the end of the trail, walk up to the small, decidedly indelicate Frame Arch for a picture-perfect view of the final destination. The classic photo of Delicate Arch is taken late in the afternoon when the sandstone glows with golden hues. Standing at the base of Delicate Arch is a magical moment: The arch rises out of the barren, almost lunar, rock face, yet it seems ephemeral. Views from the arch over the Colorado River valley are amazing.

◖ Fiery Furnace Trail

- Distance: 2 miles round-trip
- Duration: 3 hours
- Elevation change: 250 feet
- Effort: moderate-strenuous
- Trailhead: Fiery Furnace viewpoint

The Fiery Furnace area is open only to hikers with permits ($5 pp) or to those joining a ranger-led hike. During summer, rangers offer two daily hikes (mid-Mar.-Oct., $10 adults, $5 ages 7-12 and Interagency Senior Pass holders) into this unique area; tickets are required. These hikes are popular and are often booked weeks in advance, so make reservations online at www.recreation.gov or in person at the visitors' center up to one week ahead.

Hiking in the Fiery Furnace is not along a

© PAUL LEVY

A little scrambling is required when exploring the Fiery Furnace.

trail; hikers navigate a maze of narrow sandstone canyons. The route through the area is sometimes challenging, requiring hands-and-knees scrambling up cracks and ledges. Navigation is difficult: Route-finding can be tricky because what look like obvious paths often lead to dead ends. Drop-offs and ridges make straight-line travel impossible. It's easy to become disoriented. Even if you're an experienced hiker, the ranger-led hikes provide the best introduction to the Fiery Furnace.

If you're not able to get in on a ranger-led hike and aren't strapped for cash, several Moab outfitters, including **Canyonlands By Night** (1861 N. U.S. 191, Moab, 435/259-5361 or 800/394-9978, www.canyonlandsbynight, $81 adults) offer guided tours in the Fiery Furnace.

Broken and Sand Dune Arches

- Distance: 1 mile round-trip
- Duration: 45 minutes
- Elevation change: 140 feet
- Effort: easy

- Trailhead: on the right side of the road, 2.4 miles past the Fiery Furnace turnoff

A short sandy trail leads to small Sand Dune Arch (its opening is 8 feet high and 30 feet wide), tucked within fins. A longer trail (1 mile round-trip) crosses a field to Broken Arch, which you can also see from the road. The opening in this arch is 43 feet high and 59 feet wide. Up close, you'll see that the arch isn't really broken. These arches can also be reached by a trail across from campsite 40 at Devils Garden Campground. Another beautiful arch, **Tapestry Arch,** requires a short detour off the trail between the campground and Broken Arch.

Look for low-growing Canyonlands biscuit root, found only in areas of Entrada sandstone, colonizing the sand dunes. Hikers can protect the habitat of the biscuit root and other fragile plants by keeping to washes or rock surfaces.

◖ Devils Garden Loop

- Distance: 7.2 miles round-trip
- Duration: 4 hours
- Elevation change: 350 feet

© PAUL LEVY

Broken Arch is not really broken – yet.

- Effort: strenuous
- Trailhead: Devils Garden

From the end of the paved park road, a full tour of Devils Garden leads to eight named arches and a vacation's worth of scenic wonders. This is one of the park's most popular areas, with several shorter versions of the full loop hike that make the area accessible to nearly every hiker. Don't be shocked to find quite a crowd at the trailhead—it will most likely dissipate after the first two or three arches.

The first two arches are an easy walk from the trailhead and are accessed via a short side trail to the right. **Tunnel Arch** has a relatively symmetrical opening 22 feet high and 27 feet wide. The nearby **Pine Tree Arch** is named for a piñon pine that once grew inside; the arch has an opening 48 feet high and 46 feet wide. Continue on the main trail to **Landscape Arch.** The trail narrows past Landscape Arch and continues to the remains of **Wall Arch,** which collapsed in August 2008. A short side trail branches off to the left beyond the stubs of Wall Arch to **Partition Arch** and **Navajo Arch.** Partition was so named because a piece of rock

divides the main opening from a smaller hole. Navajo Arch is a rock-shelter type; prehistoric Native Americans may have camped here.

The main trail climbs up slickrock, offering great views of the La Sal mountains and Fin Canyon. At the Fin Canyon viewpoint, the trail curves left (watch for rock cairns) and continues northwest, ending at **Double O Arch** (4 miles round-trip from the trailhead). Double O has a large oval-shaped opening (45 feet high and 71 feet wide) and a smaller hole underneath. **Dark Angel** is a distinctive rock pinnacle 0.25 miles northwest; cairns mark the way. Another primitive trail loops back to Landscape Arch via **Fin Canyon.** This route goes through a different part of Devils Garden but adds about one mile to your trip (3 miles back to the trailhead instead of two). Pay careful attention to the trail markers to avoid getting lost.

Landscape Arch

- Distance: 2 miles round-trip
- Duration: 1 hour
- Elevation change: 60 feet

- Effort: easy
- Trailhead: Devils Garden trailhead

Landscape Arch, with an incredible 306-foot span—six feet longer than a football field—is one of the longest unsupported rock spans in the world. It's also one of the park's more precarious arches to observe up close. The thin arch looks ready to collapse at any moment. Indeed, a spectacular rockfall from the arch on September 1, 1991, accelerated its disintegration, which is the eventual fate of every arch. Now the area directly underneath the arch is fenced off; when you look at the photos of the 1991 rockfall, you'll be happy to stand back a ways.

On the way to Landscape Arch, be sure to take the short side trails to Tunnel and Pine Tree Arches.

◖ Tower Arch Trail

- Distance: 3.4 miles round-trip
- Duration: 2.5 hours
- Elevation change: 450 feet
- Effort: moderate-strenuous
- Trailhead: Klondike Bluffs parking area
- Directions: From the main park road, take Salt Valley Road (a dirt road, but usually fine for passenger cars) west 7.7 miles to the Klondike Bluffs turnoff.

Most park visitors don't venture into this area of sandstone fins and big dunes. It's a bit like Devils Garden, but without the crowds.

After a short but steep climb, the trail levels out and opens up to views of Arches' distinctive sandstone fins and, in the distance, the La Sal and Abajo Mountains. The trail drops down to cross a couple of washes, then climbs onto the fin-studded slickrock Klondike Bluffs. Tower Arch is actually both an arch and a tower, and there's no mistaking the tower for just another big sandstone rock.

Because of the dirt-road access to this hike, it's best to skip it if there's been recent rain or if rain is threatening.

BIKING

Cyclists are required to keep to established roads in the park; there is no single-track or trail riding allowed. You'll also have to contend with heavy traffic on the narrow paved roads and dusty washboard surfaces on the dirt roads. Beware of deep sand on the 4WD roads, traffic on the main park road, and summertime heat wherever you ride.

One good, not-too-hard ride is along the Willow Springs Road. Allow 2-3 hours for an out-and-back, starting from the Balanced Rock parking area and heading west.

Perhaps the best bet for relatively fit mountain bikers is the 24-mile ride to Tower Arch and back. From the Devils Garden parking area, ride out the **Salt Valley Road,** which can be rough. After about 7.5 miles, turn left onto a jeep road that leads to the "back door" to Tower Arch.

Nearby, Bureau of Land Management and Canyonlands National Park areas offer world-class mountain biking.

CLIMBING

Rock climbers don't need a permit in Arches, although you should first discuss your plans with a ranger. All features named on U.S. Geological Survey maps are closed to climbing: That means any of the arches and many of the most distinctive towers are off limits. Slacklining is also prohibited in the park. There are still plenty of long-standing routes for advanced climbers to enjoy, although the rock in Arches is sandier and softer than in other areas around Moab.

Several additional climbing restrictions are in place. No new permanent climbing hardware may be installed in any fixed location. If an existing bolt or other hardware item is unsafe, it may be replaced. This effectively limits all technical climbing to existing routes or new routes not requiring placement of fixed anchors. Other restrictions are detailed on the park's website.

The most commonly climbed areas are along the sheer stone faces of **Park Avenue.**

© PAUL LEVY

Be sure to reserve ahead if you want to camp at Arches.

Another popular destination is **Owl Rock,** the owl-shaped small tower located in the Windows Section of the park. For more information on climbing in Arches, consult the bible of Moab-area climbing, *Desert Rock* by Eric Bjørnstad, or ask for advice at **Pagan Mountaineering** (59 S. Main St., Moab, 435/259-1117, www.paganclimber.com), a climbing and outdoor-gear store that also offers a climbing guide service.

CAMPGROUNDS

Devils Garden Campground (elevation 5,355 feet, with water, year-round, $20) is near the end of the 18-mile scenic drive. It's an excellent place to camp, with some sites tucked under rock formations and others offering great views, but it's extremely popular. The well-organized traveler must plan accordingly and reserve a site in advance for March-October. Reservations

(www.recreation.gov, $9 booking fee plus $20 camping fee) must be made no less than four days and no more than 240 days in advance. All campsites can be reserved, so during the busy spring, summer, and fall seasons, campers without reservations are pretty much out of luck. In winter, sites 1-24 are available as first-come, first-served. A camp host is on-site and firewood is available ($5), but there are no other services or amenities.

If you aren't able to score a coveted Arches campsite, all is not lost. There are many Bureau of Land Management (BLM) campsites within an easy drive of the park. Try the primitive BLM campgrounds on Highway 313, just west of U.S. 191 and on the way to Canyonlands National Park's Island in the Sky District. Another cluster of BLM campgrounds is along the Colorado River on Highway 128, which runs northeast from U.S. 191 at the north end of Moab.

MOAB

By far the largest town in southeastern Utah, Moab (population 5,150, elevation 4,025 feet) makes an excellent base for exploring Arches and Canyonlands National Parks and the surrounding canyon country. Moab is near the Colorado River in a green valley enclosed by high red sandstone cliffs. The biblical Moab was a kingdom at the edge of Zion, and early settlers must have felt themselves at the edge of their world too, being so isolated from Salt Lake City—the Mormon version of Zion. Moab's existence on the fringe of Mormon culture and the sizable young non-Mormon population give the town a unique character.

Moab's first boom came during the 1950s, when vast deposits of uranium, important fuel for the atomic age, were discovered. By the 1970s the uranium mines were largely abandoned, but all the rough roads that had been built to access the mines set the stage for exploration with jeeps, ATVs, and mountain bikes. Another legacy of the uranium boom can be seen along the highway at the north end of town, where the area around the Colorado River bridge is the site of a massive environmental cleanup, slated to take years to complete.

In recent years Moab has become nearly synonymous with mountain biking. The slickrock canyon country seems made for exploration by bike, and people come from all over the world to pedal the backcountry. River trips on the Colorado River are nearly as popular, and a

© JUDY JEWELL

HIGHLIGHTS

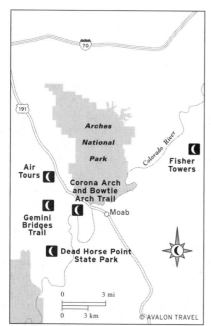

LOOK FOR ◖ TO FIND RECOMMENDED SIGHTS, ACTIVITIES, DINING, AND LODGING.

◖ **Dead Horse Point State Park:** Thirty minutes northwest of Moab, this peninsula of land perched 2,000 feet above the Colorado River has spectacular viewpoints, great camping, and mountain bike trails suitable for the whole family (page 213).

◖ **Corona Arch and Bowtie Arch Trail:** This hike doesn't require a lot of exertion, but there's plenty of payback. Three arches are visible from the short trail, including 140-foot-wide Corona Arch, larger than many in Arches National Park (page 223).

◖ **Fisher Towers:** These thin rock columns reach nearly 1,000 feet into the desert sky just south of Highway 128, northeast of Moab. Hiking trails loop through the unworldly landscape, ringing the mast-like formations and leading to overlooks of rugged Onion Creek Canyon (page 225).

◖ **Gemini Bridges Trail:** Skip the pros and posers at the Slickrock Trail and have some real fun on the mostly downhill ride from the trailhead near Dead Horse Point State Park to U.S. 191. Most cyclists do this 14-mile one-way ride with a shuttle vehicle (page 227).

◖ **Air Tours:** It's hard to grasp the scale of Moab's canyon country without getting up above it. Local aviators offer flightseeing trips, providing the chance to see this amazing landscape from the viewpoint of an eagle (page 233).

host of other outdoor recreational diversions—from horseback riding to 4WD jeep exploring to hot-air ballooning—combine to make Moab one of the most popular destinations in Utah.

As Moab's popularity has grown, so have concerns that the town and the surrounding countryside are simply getting loved to death. On a busy day, hundreds of mountain bikers form queues to negotiate the trickier sections of the famed Slickrock Trail, and more than 20,000 people crowd into town on busy weekends to bike, hike, float, and party. As noted in an article in *Details* magazine, "Moab is pretty much the Fort Lauderdale of the intermountain West." Whether this old Mormon town and the delicate desert environment can endure such an onslaught of popularity is a question of increasing concern.

PLANNING YOUR TIME

While many people come to Moab because of what it's near, there's certainly enough to do in the town to justify adding an extra day to a park-focused itinerary just for exploring Moab and environs. It's easy to spend a few hours lounging by the hotel pool or shopping for books, crafts, and gifts, and the quality of

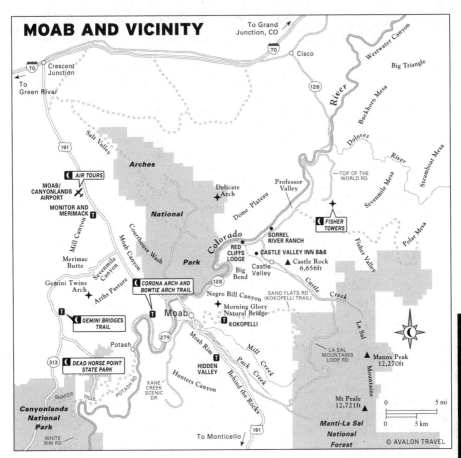

the food and locally brewed beer has its own appeal, particularly after several days of hiking or driving the Utah outback.

Moab is also central for expeditions into the less regulated red-rock canyon country not included in the national parks. Take a break from exploring the parks themselves and devote a day to nonpark adventures, such as jet-boat tours on the Colorado River, horseback rides in Castle Valley, ATV tours into the backcountry, hikes with your dog, or even tasting local vintages.

Moab is the most hospitable town in this part of Utah, so don't blow right through. Take time to stop and enjoy its quirky charms. However, be forewarned that the adrenaline (or is it testosterone?) level reaches a fever pitch here during spring break, so don't plan a quiet weekend in Moab anytime around Easter.

Sights

It's fair to say that Moab doesn't tempt travelers with a lot of traditional tourism establishments, but all you have to do is raise your eyes to the horizon. The locale is so striking that you'll want to get outdoors and explore, and the astonishing sights of Canyonlands and Arches National Parks are just minutes from town. But there's nothing wrong with just enjoying the enthusiastic vibe of the town.

MUSEUM OF MOAB

The regional Museum of Moab (118 E. Center St., 435/259-7985, www.moabmuseum.org, 10am-5pm Mon.-Fri., noon-5pm Sat. Mar.-Oct., noon-5pm Mon.-Sat. Nov.-Feb., $5 over age 17, $10 families) tells the story of Moab's and Grand County's past, from prehistoric and Ute artifacts to the explorations of Spanish missionaries. Photos and tools show pioneer Moab life, much of which centered on ranching or mining. You'll also find displays of rocks and minerals as well as the bones of huge dinosaurs, including the backbone of a sauropod found by a rancher just outside town.

HOLE 'N THE ROCK

Fifteen miles south of Moab, Albert Christensen worked 12 years to excavate his dream home within a sandstone monolith south of town. When he died in 1957, his wife, Gladys, worked another eight years to complete the 5,000-square-foot house, called Hole 'n the Rock (11037 S. U.S. 191, 435/686-2250, www.theholeintherock.com, 9am-5pm daily, $5 adults, $3.50 ages 5-10). It's now a full-on roadside attraction. The interior has notable touches like a 65-foot chimney drilled through the rock ceiling, paintings, taxidermy exhibits, and a lapidary room. The 14-room home is open for 12-minute-long guided tours and offers a gift shop, petting zoo, picnic area, and snack bar.

MILL CANYON DINOSAUR TRAIL

The 0.5-mile Mill Canyon Dinosaur Trail, with numbered stops, identifies the bones of dinosaurs that lived in the wet climate that existed here 150 million years ago. You'll see fossilized wood and dinosaur footprints too. Pick up the brochure from the Moab Information Center (25 E. Center St., at Main St., 435/259-8825 or 800/635-6622, www.discovermoab.com) or at the trailhead.

To reach the dinosaur site, drive 15 miles north of Moab on U.S. 191, then turn left (west) at an intersection just north of milepost 141. Cross the railroad tracks and continue two miles on a rough dirt road (impassable when wet) to the trailhead.

You'll find many other points of interest nearby. A copper mill and tailings dating from the late 1800s are across the canyon. The ruins of Halfway Stage Station, where travelers once stopped on the Thompson-Moab run, are a short distance down the other road fork. Jeepers and mountain bikers can do a 13-14-mile loop to Monitor and Merrimac Buttes; a sign just off U.S. 191 has a map and details.

COPPER RIDGE SAUROPOD TRACKS

Apatosaurus, a.k.a. brontosaurus, and theropod tracks crisscross an ancient riverbed at the Copper Ridge Sauropod Tracks site. It's easy to make out the two-foot-wide hind footprints of the brontosaurus, but its small front feet didn't leave much of a dent in the sand. Three-toed tracks of the carnivorous theropods, possibly allosaurus, are 8-15 inches long, and some show an irregular gait—perhaps indicating a limp.

The Copper Ridge tracks are 23 miles north of Moab on U.S. 191; turn right (east) 0.75 miles north of milepost 148. Cross the railroad tracks and turn south, following signs two miles to the tracks.

THE ELK MOUNTAIN MISSION

The Old Spanish Trail, which opened in 1829 between New Mexico and California, ran north from Santa Fe into Utah, crossing the Colorado River near present-day Moab. The Mormons under Brigham Young reached Utah in 1847, and by the 1850s they were establishing settlements across Utah. Young determined that a Mormon outpost was needed at the Colorado River crossing to control settlement and to proselytize the local Ute people.

In 1855, a group of 41 missionaries left the Wasatch Front to explore and build settlements in the Spanish Valley, home to present-day Moab. In those days, travel in roadless Utah was challenging—entering Moab Canyon required that wagons be taken apart and lowered by rope down a precipice near today's entry gate to Arches National Park.

By July 15, 1855, the missionaries and 75 head of cattle had arrived in Spanish Valley, and construction began on a 4,100-square-foot stone fort called the Elk Mountain Mission. The fort's walls were north of today's downtown Moab, near the edge of the current Motel 6 parking lot. They also built a corral, planted various crops, and tried to establish friendships with the Ute people, who controlled a large part of southern Utah. The Spanish Valley area had traditionally been used as a shared common ground for

gathering and trading among the Native Americans, particularly the Utes and the Navajo.

Initially the Mormon missionaries found success, tending their abundant gardens and baptizing more than a dozen Utes. Some of the Utes became concerned about the motives of the new settlers, however, and tensions between them and the missionaries grew. By early fall, it had become increasingly difficult to keep the peace.

After the Utes started helping themselves to the Mormons' garden produce, such as melons and squash, events quickly escalated. On September 23, 1855, one of the Mormon missionaries was shot by a Ute and a fierce gun battle ensued at the fort. At least two Utes were killed and many more wounded during the hostilities. Two other Mormons, who were returning from a hunting trip, were ambushed and killed. The hay and cornfields surrounding the fort were set ablaze by the Utes.

The next morning, the remaining missionaries abandoned the fort, packing what they could and leaving behind five horses and 25 head of cattle. The three dead missionaries were buried within the walls of the fort.

The Elk Mountain Mission marked one of the rare failures of a Mormon settlement during the church's colonization of the West under Brigham Young. For more than two decades afterward, no permanent settlers lived in the Moab area.

MOAB

◖ DEAD HORSE POINT STATE PARK

Just east of Canyonlands National Park's Island in the Sky District and a short drive northwest of Moab is one of Utah's most spectacular state parks. At Dead Horse Point (435/259-2614, www.stateparks.utah.gov, day-use $10 per vehicle), the land drops away in sheer cliffs, and 2,000 feet below the Colorado River twists through a gooseneck on its long journey to the sea. The river and its tributaries have carved canyons that reveal a geologic layer cake of colorful rock formations. Even in a region with impressive views around nearly every corner, Dead

Horse Point stands out for its exceptionally breathtaking panorama. You'll also see below you, along the Colorado River, the result of powerful underground forces: Salt, under pressure, has pushed up overlying rock layers into an anticline. This formation, the Shafer Dome, contains potash that is being processed by the Moab Salt Plant. You can see the mine buildings, processing plant, and evaporation ponds, which are tinted blue to hasten evaporation.

A narrow neck of land only 30 yards wide connects the point with the rest of the plateau. Cowboys once herded wild horses onto the point, then placed a fence across the neck to

MOAB

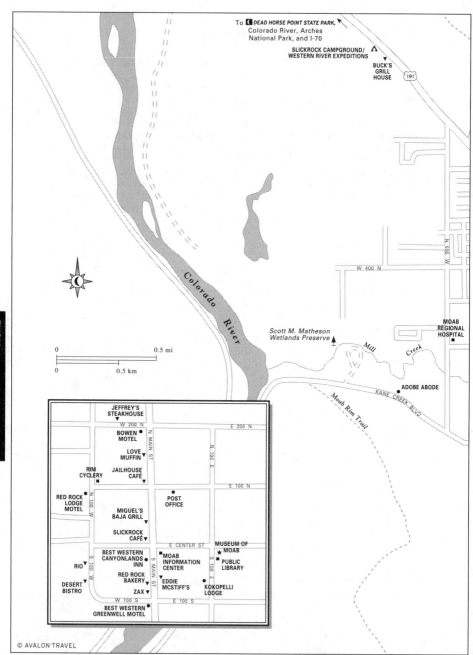

To [C] *DEAD HORSE POINT STATE PARK,*
Colorado River, Arches
National Park, and I-70

SLICKROCK CAMPGROUND/
WESTERN RIVER EXPEDITIONS

BUCK'S
GRILL
HOUSE

191

Colorado River

W 400 N

N 500 W

MOAB
REGIONAL
HOSPITAL

*Scott M. Matheson
Wetlands Preserve*

Mill

Creek

ADOBE ABODE

KANE CREEK BLVD

Moab Rim Trail

0   0.5 mi
0   0.5 km

JEFFREY'S
STEAKHOUSE

W 200 N   E 200 N

BOWEN
MOTEL

LOVE
MUFFIN

N MAIN ST

N 100 E

RIM
CYCLERY

JAILHOUSE
CAFÉ

E 100 N

RED ROCK
LODGE
MOTEL

N 100 W

POST
OFFICE

MIGUEL'S
BAJA GRILL

SLICKROCK
CAFÉ

E CENTER ST

MUSEUM OF
MOAB

BEST WESTERN
CANYONLANDS
INN

RIO

DESERT
BISTRO

S 100 W

RED ROCK
BAKERY

ZAX

S MAIN ST

MOAB
INFORMATION
CENTER

EDDIE
MCSTIFF'S

KOKOPELLI
LODGE

S 100 E

PUBLIC
LIBRARY

W 100 S   E 100 S

BEST WESTERN
GREENWELL MOTEL

© AVALON TRAVEL

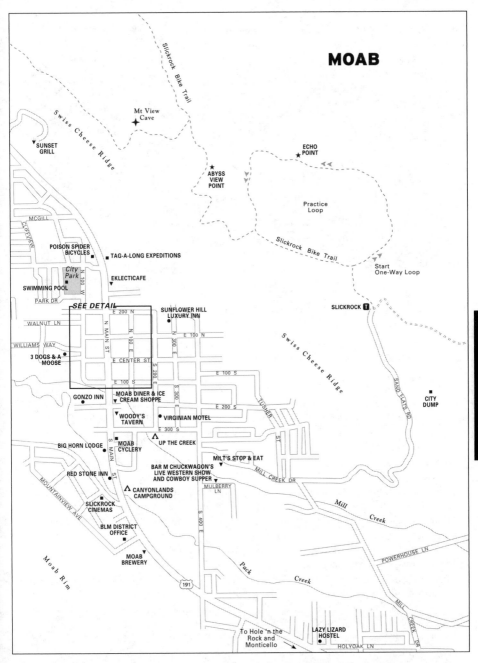

MOAB

Dead Horse Point State Park, just northwest of Moab, is full of outstanding views.

© PAUL LEVY

make a 40-acre corral. They chose the desirable animals from the herd and let the rest go. According to one tale, a group of horses left behind after such a roundup became confused by the geography of the point. They couldn't find their way off and circled repeatedly until they died of thirst within sight of the river below. You may also hear other stories of how the point got its name.

Besides the awe-inspiring views, the park also has a **visitors center** (8am-6pm daily mid-Mar.-mid-Oct., 9am-5pm daily mid-Oct.-mid-Mar.), a very popular campground, a picnic area, a group area, a nature trail, hiking trails, and great mountain biking on the **Intrepid Trail System.** Spectacularly scenic hiking trails run along the east and west rims of the peninsula-like park; hikers are also allowed to use the Intrepid trails. Rangers lead hikes during the busy spring season and on some evenings during the summer, including monthly full-moon hikes. Whether you're visiting for

the day or camping at Dead Horse Point, it's best to bring plenty of water. Although water is available here, it is trucked in.

Dead Horse Point is easily reached by paved road, either as a destination itself or as a side trip on the way to the Island in the Sky District of Canyonlands National Park. From Moab, head northwest 10 miles on U.S. 191, then turn left and travel 22 miles on Highway 313. The drive along Highway 313 climbs through a scenic canyon and tops out on a ridge with panoramas of distant mesas, buttes, mountains, and canyons. There are several rest areas along the road.

SCENIC DRIVES

Each of the following routes is at least partly accessible to standard low-clearance highway vehicles. If you have a 4WD vehicle, you have the option of additional off-road exploring.

You'll find detailed travel information on these and other places in Charles Wells's *Guide to Moab, UT Backroads & 4-Wheel Drive Trails,*

MOAB'S MINING BOOM AND BUST

Moab is within the Paradox Salt Basin, a geologic formation responsible for the area's famous arch formations and accumulations of valuable minerals relatively near the surface. In addition to significant mineral wealth, mining and oil exploration has provided the region with some of its liveliest history and most colorful characters. French scientist Marie Curie, who discovered the element radium in uranium ore in 1898, visited the Moab area in 1899 to inspect a uranium-processing operation near the Dolores River.

Oil exploration in the 1920s caused some excitement in Moab, but nothing like that of the uranium boom that began in 1952. A down-on-his-luck geologist from Texas named Charles Steen struck it rich at his Mi Vida claim southeast of Moab. Steen's timing was exquisite: Uranium was highly sought-after by the federal government, primarily for use in Cold War-era atomic weapons and in nuclear power plants. An instant multimillionaire, Steen built a large mansion overlooking Moab and hosted lavish parties attended by Hollywood celebrities (his home is now the Sunset Grill restaurant). The Mi Vida mine alone would ultimately be worth more than $100 million, and it put Moab on the map.

By the end of 1956, Moab was dubbed "The Richest Town in the USA" and "The Uranium Capital of the World." In the wake of Steen's discovery, thousands of prospectors, miners, laborers, and others descended on the area, hoping to cash in on the mother lode. Moab's population tripled in just three years as eager prospectors swarmed into the canyons.

By the mid-1960s, the boom had died out. As the uranium played out, however, mining operations began in 1965 in one of the largest potash deposits in the world, on the Colorado River between Moab and Dead Horse Point, and work continues there today. Other valuable materials mined in the Moab area over the years include vanadium (used in steel processing), lead, gold, copper, and silver, along with helium, natural gas, and oil.

Cleanup of 16 million tons of uranium tailings is now underway near the U.S. 191 Colorado River crossing. The toxic tailings are being hauled 30 miles north to a disposal site near I-70. It's expected that this project will be completed no sooner than 2019.

which, along with a good selection of maps, is available at the **Moab Information Center** (25 E. Center St., at Main St., 435/259-8825 or 800/635-6622, www.discovermoab.com). Staff at the info center usually know current road and trail conditions.

Utah Scenic Byway 279

Highway 279 goes downstream along the west side of the Colorado River Canyon on the other side of the river from Moab. Pavement extends 16 miles past fine views, prehistoric rock art, arches, and hiking trails. A potash plant marks the end of the highway; a rough dirt road continues to Canyonlands National Park. From Moab, head north 3.5 miles on U.S. 191, then turn left on Highway 279. The highway enters the canyon at the "portal," 2.7 miles from the turnoff. Towering sandstone cliffs rise on the right, and the Colorado River drifts along just below on the left.

Stop at a signed pullout on the left, 0.6 miles past the canyon entrance, to see **Indian Ruins Viewpoint,** a small prehistoric Native American ruin tucked under a ledge across the river. The stone structure was probably used for food storage.

Groups of **petroglyphs** cover cliffs along the highway 5.2 miles from U.S. 191, which is 0.7 miles beyond milepost 11. Look across the river to see the Fickle Finger of Fate among the sandstone fins of Behind the Rocks. A petroglyph of a bear is 0.2 miles farther down the highway. Archaeologists think that the Fremont people and the later Utes did most of the artwork in this area.

A signed pullout on the right, 6.2 miles from U.S. 191, points out **dinosaur tracks** and petroglyphs visible on rocks above. Sighting tubes help locate the features. It's possible to hike up the steep hillside for a closer look.

Ten miles west of the highway turnoff is the trailhead for the **Corona Arch Trail** (3 miles round-trip).

The aptly named **Jug Handle Arch,** with an opening 46 feet high and 3 feet wide, is close to the road on the right, 13.6 miles from U.S. 191. Ahead the canyon opens up where underground pressure from salt and potash has folded the rock layers into an anticline.

At the **Moab Salt Plant,** mining operations inject water underground to dissolve potash and other chemicals, then pump the solution to evaporation ponds. The ponds are dyed blue to hasten evaporation, which takes about a year. You can see these colorful ponds from Dead Horse Point and Anticline Overlook on the canyon rims.

High-clearance vehicles can continue on the unpaved road beyond the plant. The road passes through varied canyon country, with views overlooking the Colorado River. At a road junction in Canyonlands National Park's Island in the Sky District, you have a choice of turning left for the 100-mile White Rim Trail (4WD vehicles only past Musselman Arch), continuing up the steep switchbacks of the Shafer Trail Road (4WD recommended) to the paved park road, or returning the way you came.

Utah Scenic Byway 128

Highway 128 turns northeast from U.S. 191 just south of the Colorado River Bridge, two miles north of Moab. This exceptionally scenic canyon route follows the Colorado for 30 miles upstream before crossing at Dewey Bridge and turning north to I-70. The entire highway is paved. The Lions Park picnic area at the turnoff from U.S. 191 is a pleasant stopping place. Big Bend Recreation Site is another good spot 7.5 miles up Highway 128.

The rugged scenery along this stretch of the Colorado River has been featured in many films—mostly Westerns, but also *Thelma and*

Louise—and commercials. If you're intrigued, stop by the free **Film Museum** at Red Cliffs Ranch, a resort near mile marker 14.

The paved and scenic **La Sal Mountains Loop Road,** with viewpoints overlooking Castle Valley, Arches and Canyonlands National Parks, Moab Rim, and other scenic features, has its northern terminus at Castle Valley, climbs high into the La Sals, and then loops back to Moab. Vegetation along the drive runs the whole range from the cottonwoods, sage, and rabbitbrush of the desert to forests of aspen, fir, and spruce. The 62-mile loop road can easily take a full day with stops for scenic overlooks, a picnic, and a bit of hiking or fishing. Because of the high elevations, the loop's season usually lasts May-October. Before venturing off the Loop Road, it's a good idea to check current back-road conditions with the Moab Information Center (25 E. Center St., at Main St., 435/259-8825 or 800/635-6622, www.discovermoab.com). You can also ask for a road log of sights and side roads. The turnoff from Highway 128 is 15.5 miles up from U.S. 191.

A graded county road, **Onion Creek Road** turns southeast off Highway 128 about 20 miles from U.S. 191 and heads up Onion Creek, crossing it many times. Avoid this route if storms threaten. The unpleasant-smelling creek contains poisonous arsenic and selenium. Colorful rock formations of dark red sandstone line the creek. After about eight miles, the road climbs steeply out of Onion Creek to upper Fisher Valley and a junction with Kokopelli's Trail, which follows a jeep road over this part of its route.

One of the area's most striking sights are the gothic spires of **Fisher Towers,** which soar as high as 900 feet above Professor Valley. Supposedly, the name Fisher is not that of a pioneer but a corruption of the geologic term *fissure* (a narrow crack). In 1962, three climbers from Colorado made the first ascent of Titan Tower, the tallest of the three towers. The almost vertical rock faces, overhanging bulges, and sections of rotten rock made for

ROCK ART AROUND MOAB

The fertile valley around Moab has been home to humans for thousands of years. Prehistoric Fremont and Anasazi people once lived and farmed in the bottoms of the canyons around Moab. Their rock art, granaries, and dwellings can still be seen here. Nomadic Utes had replaced the earlier groups by the time the first white settlers arrived. They left fewer signs of settlement but added their artistry to the area's rock-art panels. You don't need to travel far to see excellent examples of native pictographs and petroglyphs.

Sego Canyon: If you approach Moab along I-70, consider a side trip to one of the premier rock-art galleries in Utah. Sego Canyon is about five miles north of I-70; take exit 185, the Thompson Springs exit. Drive through the slumbering little town and continue up the canyon behind it (BLM signs also point the way). A side road leads to a parking area where the canyon walls close in. Sego Canyon is a showcase of prehistoric rock art—it preserves rock drawings and images that are thousands of years old. The Barrier Canyon Style drawings may be 8,000 years old; the more recent Fremont Style images were created in the last 1,000 years. Compared to these ancient pictures, the Ute etchings are relatively recent: Experts speculate that they may have been drawn in the 1800s, when Ute villages still lined Sego Canyon. The newer petroglyphs and pictographs are more representational than the older ones. The ancient Barrier Canyon figures are typically horned ghostlike beings that look like aliens from early Hollywood sci-fi thrillers. The Fremont Style images depict stylized human figures made from geometric shapes; the crudest figures are the most recent. The Ute images are of bison and hunters on horseback.

Potash Road (Hwy. 279): From U.S. 191 just north of the Colorado River bridge, take Highway 279 west along the river 5.2 miles to these easily accessed petroglyphs. There's even a sign ("Indian Writing") to guide you to them.

Golf Course Rock Art: Take U.S. 191 south to the Moab Golf Course, which is about four miles from the corner of Main and Center Streets in downtown Moab. Turn left and proceed to Spanish Trail Road. Approximately one mile past the fire station, turn right onto Westwater Drive. Proceed 0.5 miles to a small pullout on the left side of the road. An area approximately 30 by 90 feet is covered with human and animal figures, including "Moab Man" and what is popularly referred to as the "reindeer and sled."

Kane Creek Boulevard: Kane Creek Boulevard (south of downtown Moab; watch for the McDonald's) follows the Colorado River and leads to a number of excellent rock-art sites. From the junction with U.S. 191, turn west and proceed 0.8 miles to the intersection of Kane Creek Drive and 500 West. Keep left and continue along Kane Creek Drive approximately 2.3 miles to the mouth of Moon Flower Canyon. Along the rock cliff just beyond the canyon, you will see a rock-art panel behind a chain-link fence (vandalism has been a problem). Continue another 1.2 miles to another rock-art panel, where a huge rock surface streaked with desert varnish is covered with images of bighorn sheep, snakes, and human forms. For a unique rock-art image, continue on Kane Creek Boulevard past the cattle guard, where the road turns from pavement to graded gravel road. After traveling 1.7 miles from the previous site, a total of 5.3 miles from the intersection of Kane Creek Drive and 500 West, watch for two pullouts. Down the slope from the road is a large boulder with rock art on all four sides. The most amazing image is of a woman giving birth.

Courthouse Wash: Although this site is located within Arches National Park, it is accessed from a parking lot off U.S. 191 just north of the Colorado River bridge, one mile north of Moab. A 0.5-mile hike leads to the panel, which is almost 19 feet high and 52 feet long. It has both pictographs and petroglyphs, with figures resembling ghostly humans, bighorn sheep, scorpions, and a large beaked bird.

A *Rock Art Auto Tour* brochure is available at the Moab Information Center (25 E. Center St., at Main St., Moab, 435/259-8825 or 800/635-6622, www.discovermoab.com, 8am-8pm Mon.-Sat. and 9am-7pm Apr.-Sept., reduced hours Mon.-Sat. Oct.-Mar.).

MOAB

© PAUL LEVY

The Fisher Towers are nearly 1,000 feet tall.

an exhausting 3.5 days of climbing; the party descended to the base for two of the nights. Their final descent from the summit took only six hours. In 2008 a slackliner walked a rope strung between the two tallest towers, and visitors to the towers can frequently see climbers and occasionally slackline walkers. The Bureau of Land Management (BLM) has a small campground and picnic area nearby, and a hiking trail skirts the base of the three main towers. An unpaved road turns southeast off Highway 128 near milepost 21, which is 21 miles from U.S. 191, and continues two miles to the picnic area.

The existing **Dewey Bridge,** 30 miles up the highway, replaced a picturesque wood-and-steel suspension bridge built in 1916, which burned in 2008. Here, the BLM has built the Dewey Bridge Recreation Site, with a picnic area, a trailhead, a boat launch, and a small campground.

Upstream from Dewey Bridge are the wild rapids of **Westwater Canyon.** The Colorado River cut this narrow gorge into dark metamorphic rock. You can raft or kayak down the river in one day or a more leisurely two days; many local outfitters offer trips. Camping is limited to a single night. Unlike most desert rivers, this section of the Colorado River also offers good river-running at low water levels in late summer and autumn. Westwater Canyon's inner gorge, where boaters face their greatest challenge, is only about 3.5 miles long; however, you can enjoy scenic sandstone canyons both upstream and downstream.

The rough 4WD **Top-of-the-World Road** climbs to an overlook with outstanding views of Fisher Towers, Fisher Valley, Onion Creek, and beyond. Pick up a map at the Moab Information Center (25 E. Center St., at Main St., 435/259-8825 or 800/635-6622, www.discovermoab.com) to guide you to the rim. The elevation here is 6,800 feet, nearly 3,000 feet higher than the Colorado River.

Kane Creek Scenic Drive

Kane Creek Road heads downstream along the Colorado River on the same side as Moab. The four miles through the Colorado River Canyon are paved, followed by six miles of good dirt road through Kane Springs Canyon. This route also leads to several hiking trails and camp-grounds. People with high-clearance vehicles or mountain bikes can continue across Kane Springs Creek to Hurrah Pass and an extensive network of 4WD trails. From Moab, drive south on Main Street (U.S. 191) for one mile, then turn right onto Kane Creek Boulevard, which becomes Kane Creek Road.

Recreation

Moab is at the center of some of the most picturesque landscapes in North America. Even the least outdoorsy visitor will want to explore the river canyons, natural arches, and mesas. Mountain biking and river tours are the recreational activities that get the most attention in the Moab area, although hikers, climbers, and horseback riders also find plenty to do. If you're less physically adventurous, you can explore the landscape on scenic flights or follow old mining roads in a jeep to remote backcountry destinations.

It's easy to find outfitters and sporting goods rental operations in Moab; it's the largest business segment in town. And there's a remarkable cohesion to the town's operations: It seems that everyone markets everyone else's excursions and services, so just ask the closest outfitter for whatever service you need, and chances are excellent you'll get hooked up with what you want.

Make the **Moab Information Center** (25 E. Center St., at Main St., 435/259-8825 or 800/635-6622, www.discovermoab.com) your first stop in town. It's an excellent source for information about the area's recreational options. The center is staffed by representatives of the National Park Service, the BLM, the U.S. Forest Service, and the Canyonlands Field Institute; they can direct you to the adventure of your liking. The center also has literature, books, and maps for sale. BLM officials can point you to the developed and undeveloped designated campsites near the Moab Slickrock Bike Trail, Kane Creek, and along the Colorado River; you must use the designated sites in these areas.

To reach most of Moab's prime hiking trails requires a short drive to trailheads. For more options, head to nearby Arches and Canyonlands National Parks. **Canyonlands Field Institute** (435/259-7750 or 800/860-5262, www.canyonlandsfieldinst.org) leads day hikes from (Sat.-Sun. mid-Apr.-mid-Oct., $40-45, includes transportation and park admission) at various locations near Moab; join one to really learn about the area's natural history.

HIKING KANE CREEK SCENIC DRIVE AND U.S. 191 SOUTH

The high cliffs just southwest of town provide fine views of the Moab Valley, the highlands of Arches National Park, and the La Sal Mountains.

Moab Rim Trail

- Distance: 6 miles round-trip
- Duration: 4 hours
- Elevation change: 940 feet
- Effort: moderate
- Trailhead: Kane Creek Boulevard, 2.6 miles northwest of its intersection with U.S. 191 in Moab

If you're hiking, expect to share this route with mountain bikers and 4WD enthusiasts. The trail climbs northeast 1.5 miles along tilted rock strata of the Kayenta Formation to the top of the plateau west of Moab, with the first of several great views over town and the Spanish Valley. Once on top, hikers can follow jeep roads southeast to Hidden Valley Trail, which descends to U.S. 191 south of Moab—a 5.5-mile trip one-way. Experienced hikers can also

ODD FORMATIONS BEHIND THE ROCKS

A look at a topographic map will show that something strange is going on in the area called **Behind the Rocks.** Massive fins of Navajo sandstone, 100-500 feet high, 50-200 feet thick, and up to 0.5 miles long cover a large area. Narrow vertical cracks, sometimes only a few feet wide, separate the fins. The concentration of arches in the area is similar to that in Arches National Park, with more than 20 major named arches. Where canyon drainages penetrate the sandstone, pour-offs form into 400-1,000-foot-deep sheer-walled canyons, often exposing perennial springs at the bottom. Behind the Rocks was inhabited extensively by the Anasazi and Fremont peoples, the two cultures apparently overlapping here. Petroglyph panels, habitation caves, stone ruins, and middens abound throughout the area.

No maintained trails exist, and some routes require technical climbing skills. The maze offers endless routes for exploration. If you get lost, which is very easy to do, remember that the fins are oriented east-west; the rim of the Colorado River Canyon is reached by going west, and Spanish Valley is reached by going east. Bring plenty of water, a topographic map (Moab 7.5-minute), and a compass. Access routes are Moab Rim and Hidden Valley Trails (from the north and east) and Pritchett Canyon (from the west and south). Although it is only a couple of miles from Moab, Behind the Rocks seems a world away.

head south from the rim to Behind the Rocks, a fantastic maze of sandstone fins.

Hidden Valley Trail

- Distance: 2.3 miles round-trip to Behind the Rocks overlook
- Duration: 3 hours
- Elevation change: 680 feet
- Effort: moderate
- Trailhead: 3 miles south of Moab on U.S. 191 and right onto Angel Rock Road. After two blocks, turn right onto Rimrock Road and drive to the parking area.

You'll see not only a hidden valley from this trail, but also panoramas of the Moab area and the Behind the Rocks area. The trail ascends a series of switchbacks to a broad shelf below the Moab Rim, then follows the shelf (hidden valley) to the northwest. It then crosses a low pass and follows a second shelf in the same direction. Near the end of the second shelf, the trail turns left to a divide, where you can see a portion of the remarkable fins of Behind the Rocks. The trail continues 0.3 miles from the divide down to the end of the Moab Rim Trail, with

the possibility of hiking on loop trails. Instead of turning left to the divide, you can make a short side trip (no trail) to the right for views of Moab.

Hunters Canyon

- Distance: 4 miles round-trip
- Duration: 4 hours
- Elevation change: 240 feet
- Effort: moderate
- Trailhead: on Kane Creek Scenic Drive, 7.5 miles west of its intersection with U.S. 191. Hunters Canyon is on the left, 1 mile beyond the switchbacks.
- Directions: To reach the trailhead from Moab, drive eight miles on Kane Creek Boulevard along the Colorado River and up Kane Creek Canyon. The road is asphalted where it fords Hunters Creek, but the asphalt is usually covered with dirt washed over it by the creek.

A rock arch and other rock formations in the canyon walls and the lush vegetation along the creek are highlights of a Hunters Canyon hike. Off-road vehicles have made tracks a short way up; you'll be walking, mostly along the creek bed. Short sections of trail lead around thickets of tamarisk and other water-loving plants. Look for Hunters Arch on the right, about 0.5 miles up. Most of the water in Hunters Canyon comes from a deep pool surrounded by hanging gardens of maidenhair ferns. A dry fall and a small natural bridge are above the pool. This pretty spot marks the hike's three-mile point and an elevation gain of 240 feet. At this point, the hike becomes very brushy.

You can make a longer hike by going up Hunters Canyon and descending on Pritchett Canyon Road. The road crosses the normally dry creek bed just upstream from the deep pool. To bypass the dry fall above the pool, backtrack 300 feet down the canyon and rock-scramble up a short steep slope on the right heading upstream. At a junction just east of here, a jeep road along the north rim of Hunters Canyon meets Pritchett Canyon Road. Walk northeast 0.5 miles on Pritchett Canyon Road to a spur trail (on the left) leading to Pritchett Arch. Then continue 4.5 miles on Pritchett Canyon Road to Kane Creek Boulevard. This country is more open and desertlike than Hunters Canyon. A 3.2-mile car shuttle or hike is required for the return to Hunters Canyon trailhead.

HIKING HIGHWAY 279
Portal Overlook Trail

- Distance: 4 miles round-trip
- Duration: 3 hours
- Elevation change: 980 feet
- Effort: moderate
- Trailhead: JayCee Park Recreation Site, Highway 279, 4.2 miles west of the Highway 279-U.S. 191 junction

The Portal Overlook Trail switchbacks up a slope, then follows a sloping sandstone ledge of the Kayenta Formation for two miles to an overlook. A panorama (the "portal") takes in the Colorado River, Moab Valley, Arches National Park, and the La Sal Mountains. This trail is a twin of the Moab Rim Trail across the river. Expect to share it with mountain bikers.

◖ Corona Arch and Bowtie Arch Trail

- Distance: 3 miles round-trip
- Duration: 2 hours
- Elevation change: 200 feet
- Effort: moderate
- Trailhead: Highway 279, 10 miles west of the Highway 279-U.S. 191 junction

If you have time for only one hike in the Moab area, this one is especially recommended. The trail leads across slickrock country to two impressive arches. You can't see them from the road, although a third arch—Pinto—is visible. The trail climbs 1.5 miles up from the parking area, crosses railroad tracks, and follows a jeep road and a small wash to an ancient gravel bar. Pinto Arch, also called Gold Bar Arch, stands to the left, but there's no trail to it. Follow rock cairns to Corona and Bowtie Arches. Handrails and a ladder help in the few steep spots.

Despite being only a few hundred yards

© PAUL LEVY

Bowtie Arch was formed when a pothole in the cliffs above met a cave below.

© PAUL LEVY

The trail up Negro Bill Canyon is cooler and shadier than many trails around Moab.

apart, each arch has a completely different character and history. Bowtie formed when a pothole in the cliffs above met a cave underneath. It used to be called Paul Bunyan's Potty before that name was appropriated for an arch in Canyonlands National Park. The hole is about 30 feet in diameter. Corona Arch, reminiscent of the larger Rainbow Bridge, eroded out of a sandstone fin. The graceful span is 140 feet long and 105 feet high. Both arches are composed of Navajo sandstone.

HIKING HIGHWAY 128
Negro Bill Canyon

- Distance: 4 miles round-trip
- Duration: 3-4 hours
- Elevation change: 330 feet
- Effort: easy-moderate
- Trailhead: Highway 128, 3 miles east of the Highway 128-U.S. 191 junction

One of the most popular hiking destinations in the Moab area, the Negro Bill Canyon trail follows a lively stream dammed by beavers and surrounded by abundant greenery and sheer cliffs. The high point of the hike is Morning Glory Natural Bridge, the sixth-longest natural rock span in the country at 243 feet.

William Granstaff was the first non-Native American to live in the area, about 1877-1881; modern sensibilities have changed his nickname to "Negro Bill." The trailhead and a large parking area are on the right just after crossing a concrete bridge three miles from U.S. 191. The Granstaff campground, run by the BLM, is on the banks of the Colorado River just across the road from the trailhead.

The trail follows the creek up the canyon, with numerous stream crossings. Although the crossings are not difficult, hikers must be comfortable with stepping from rock to rock.

To see Morning Glory Natural Bridge, head two miles up the main canyon to the second side canyon on the right, then follow a good but fairly steep side trail for 0.5 miles up to the long slender bridge. The spring and small pool underneath keep the air cool even in summer; ferns, columbines, and abundant poison ivy grow here.

Experienced hikers can continue up the main canyon about eight miles and rock-scramble (there's no trail) up the right side, then drop into Rill Creek, which leads to the North Fork of Mill Creek and into Moab. The total distance is about 16 miles one-way; you'll have to find your own way between canyons. The upper Negro Bill and Rill Canyons can also be reached from Sand Flats Road. The Moab and Castle Valley 15-minute and Moab 1:100,000 topographic maps cover the route. This makes a good overnight trip, although fast hikers have done it in a day. Expect to do some wading and rock scrambling. Water from the creeks and springs is available in both canyon systems, but be sure to purify it first.

A car shuttle is necessary between the Negro Bill and Mill Creek trailheads. You can reach Mill Creek from the end of Powerhouse Lane on the east edge of Moab, but don't park here: Vehicle break-ins are a serious problem. Have someone meet you or drop you off here or park closer to town near houses. A hike up the North Fork offers very pretty scenery. A deep pool and waterfall are 0.75 miles upstream; follow Mill Creek upstream and take the left (north) fork. Negro Bill and Mill Creek Canyons are BLM wilderness study areas.

◖ Fisher Towers

- Distance: 4.4 miles round-trip
- Duration: 4 hours
- Elevation change: 670 feet
- Effort: moderate
- Trailhead: off Highway 128; 21 miles east of the Highway 128-U.S. 191 junction, turn right and go 2.2 miles on an improved dirt road to a parking lot

These spires of dark-red sandstone rise 900 feet above Professor Valley. You can hike around the base of these needle rocks on a trail accessed by a short flight of stairs from the BLM picnic area. The trail follows a small slickrock-covered ridge leading away from the main cliffs; when the ridge narrows, go left into the ravine

through a small cut in the ridge. From the bottom of the ravine, the trail heads steeply up and then begins to wind directly beneath the Fisher Towers. After skirting around the largest tower, the Titan, the trail ascends and ends after 2.2 miles on a ridge with a panoramic view. The Fisher Towers attract many very good rock climbers, and hikers may find that they linger along the trail to watch some spectacular climbing exploits. Carry water, as much of the trail is exposed and is frequently quite hot.

BIKING

The first mountain bikes came to Moab in 1982, when they were used to herd cattle. That didn't work out so well, but within a decade or so, Moab had become the West's most noted mountain bike destination. In addition to riding the famed and challenging slickrock trails (slickrock is the exposed sandstone that composes much of the land's surface here, and despite its name, bike tires grab it quite nicely) that wind through astonishing desert landscapes, cyclists can pedal through alpine meadows in the La Sal Mountains or take nearly abandoned 4WD tracks into the surrounding backcountry. Beware: The most famous trails—like the Slickrock Bike Trail—are not for beginners. Other trails are better matched to the skills of novices.

It's a good idea to read up on Moab-area trails before planning a trip; heaps of books and pamphlets are available. You can also hire an outfitter to teach you about the special skills needed to mountain-bike in slickrock country, or join a guided tour. The Moab Information Center's website (www.discovermoab.com) also has good information about bike trails.

Most people come to Moab to mountain bike mid-March-late May, and then again in the fall mid-September-end of October. Unless you are an early riser, summer is simply too hot for extended bike touring in these desert canyons. Be prepared for crowds, especially in

MOAB

MOUNTAIN BIKE ETIQUETTE

When mountain biking in the Moab area, don't expect an instant wilderness experience. Because of the popularity of the routes, the fragile desert environment is under quite a bit of stress, and you'll need to be considerate of the thousands of other people who share the trails. By keeping these rules in mind, you'll help keep Moab from being loved to death.

- **Ride only on open roads and trails.** Much of the desert consists of extremely fragile plant and animal ecosystems, and riding recklessly through cryptobiotic soils can destroy desert life and lead to erosion. If you pioneer a trail, chances are someone else will follow the tracks, leading to ever more destruction.

- **Protect and conserve scarce water sources.** Don't wash, swim, walk, or bike through potholes, and camp well away from isolated streams and water holes. The addition of your insect repellent, body oils, suntan lotion, or bike lubrication can destroy the thriving life of a pothole. Camping right next to a remote stream can deprive shy desert wildlife of life-giving water access.

- **Leave all Native American sites and artifacts as you find them.** First, it's against the law to disturb antiquities; second, it's stupid. Enjoy looking at rock art, but don't touch the images—body oils hasten their deterioration. Don't even think about taking potsherds, arrowheads, or artifacts from where you find them. Leave them for others to enjoy or for archaeologists to interpret.

- **Dispose of solid human waste thoughtfully.** The desert can't easily absorb human fecal matter. Desert soils have few microorganisms to break down organic material, and, simply put, mummified turds can last for years. Be sure to bury solid waste at least 6-12 inches deep in sand and at least 200 feet away from streams and water sources. Pack out toilet paper in plastic bags.

mid-March during spring break. The Slickrock Trail alone has been known to attract more than 150,000 riders per year.

If you've never biked on slickrock or in the desert, here are a few basic guidelines. Take care if venturing off a trail—it's a long way down some of the sheer cliff faces. A trail's steep slopes and sharp turns can be tricky, so a helmet is a must. Knee pads and riding gloves also protect from scrapes and bruises. Fat bald tires work best on the rock; partially deflated knobby tires do almost as well. Carry plenty of water—one gallon in summer, half a gallon in cooler months. Tiny plant associations, which live in fragile cryptobiotic soil, don't want you tearing through their homes; stay on the rock and avoid sandy areas.

Dozens of trails thread through the Moab area; one good place for beginners to start is on the

Intrepid trail system at Dead Horse Point State Park. Descriptions of several local trails follow.

MOAB Brand Trails

The interconnected loops and spur trails here form a trail system with several options that are especially good for beginners or riders who are new to slickrock.

The seven-mile **Bar-M** loop is easy and makes a good family ride, although you might share the packed-dirt trail with motor vehicles; try **Circle O** (no motor vehicles) for a good three-mile initiation to slickrock riding.

More experienced slickrock cyclists can find some challenges on the **Deadman's Ridge, Long Branch,** and **Killer-B** routes at the southern end of the trail system.

To reach the trailhead for all these rides, head about eight miles north of town on U.S.

191 to the Bar M Chuckwagon, and park at the south end of their private lot.

Slickrock Bike Trail

Undulating slickrock in the Sand Flats Recreation Area just east of Moab challenges even the best mountain bike riders; this is not an area in which to learn riding skills. Originally, motorcyclists laid out this route, although now most riders rely on leg and lung power. The 1.7-mile practice loop near the trail's beginning allows first-time visitors a chance to get a feel for the slickrock. The "trail" consists only of painted white lines. Riders following it have less chance of getting lost or finding themselves in hazardous areas. Plan on about five hours to do the 10.5-mile main loop, and expect to do some walking.

Side trails lead to viewpoints overlooking Moab, the Colorado River, and arms of Negro Bill Canyon. Panoramas of the surrounding canyon country and the La Sal Mountains add to the pleasure of biking.

To reach the trailhead from Main Street in Moab, turn east and go 0.4 miles on 300 South, turn right and go 0.1 miles on 400 East, turn left (east) and go 0.5 miles on Mill Creek Drive, then turn left and go 2.5 miles on Sand Flats Road. The Sand Flats Recreation Area, where the trail is located, charges $5 for an automobile day pass, $2 for a bicycle or motorcycle. Camping ($10) is available, but there is no water.

Farther up Sand Flats Road, the quite challenging, often rock-strewn **Porcupine Rim Trail** draws motorcyclists, jeeps, and mountain bikers; after about 11 miles, the trail becomes single-track, and four-wheelers drop out. The whole trail is about 15 miles long.

◖ Gemini Bridges Trail

This 14-mile one-way trail passes tremendous twin rock arches (the bridges) and the slickrock fins of the Wingate Formation, making this one of the most scenic of the trails in the Moab area; it's also one of the more moderate trails in terms of necessary skill and fitness. The trail begins 12.5 miles up Highway 313, just before the turnoff to Dead Horse Point State Park. It's a stiff 21-mile uphill ride from Moab to reach the trailhead, so you may want to consider a shuttle. Several companies, including **Coyote Shuttle** (435/260-2097, $20), provide this service, enabling cyclist to concentrate on the fun, mostly downhill ride back toward Moab. The Gemini Bridges Trail, which is shared with motorcycles and 4WD vehicles, ends on U.S. 191 just north of town.

Intrepid Trail System

Mountain bikers, including novices, should bring their rides to Dead Horse Point, where the Intrepid Trail System offers about 15 miles of slickrock and sand single-track trails in three loops that range from a one-mile beginner's loop to a more challenging nine-mile loop. All routes start at the visitors center and have great views into the canyon country. To reach Dead Horse Point State Park (435/259-2614, $10) from Moab, take U.S. 191 nine miles north, then turn west on Highway 313 and follow it 23 miles to the park entrance.

Monitor and Merrimac Trail

A good introduction to the varied terrains of the Moab area, the 13.2-mile Monitor and Merrimac Trail also includes a trip to a dinosaur fossil bed. The trail climbs through open desert and up Usher Canyon, then explores red sandstone towers and buttes across slickrock before dropping down Mill Canyon. At the base of the canyon, you can leave your bike and hike the Mill Canyon Dinosaur Trail before completing the loop to the parking area. Reach the trailhead by traveling 15 miles north of Moab on U.S. 191 and turning west (left) onto Mill Canyon Road, just past mile marker 141.

MOAB

MOAB

Sovereign Single Track

Not every bike trail here is over slickrock; the challenging single-track Sovereign trail is good to ride in hot weather. The trail, which contains rocky technical sections, a bit of slickrock, and more flowing single track, is shared with motorcycles. Several trailheads access this trail; a popular one is from Willow Springs Road. From Moab, travel 11 miles north on U.S. 191 and turn right onto Willow Springs Road, following this sandy road 2.5 miles to the trailhead. To best see the options, pick up a map at a local bike store.

Kokopelli's Trail

Mountain bikers have linked a 142-mile series of back roads, paved roads, and bike trails through the magical canyons of eastern Utah and western Colorado. The trail is usually ridden from east to west, starting in Loma, Colorado, and passing Rabbit Valley, Cisco Boat Landing, Dewey Bridge, Fisher Valley, and Castle Valley before landing on Sand Flats Road in Moab. Lots of optional routes, access points, and campsites allow for many possibilities. This multiday trip requires a significant amount of advance planning; **Bikerpelli Sports** (www.bikerpelli.com) is a good place to start this process.

Moab Canyon Pathway (Road Biking)

Although the Moab area is great for biking, riding along busy U.S. 191 is no fun. The recently completed Moab Canyon Pathway starts at the Colorado River bridge at the north end of town and closely parallels the highway north to Arches National Park. From the entrance to the park, the path, which is separated from the road, continues north, climbing to the junction of Highways 191 and 313, the road to Dead Horse Point State Park and Canyonlands' Island in the Sky district. From this intersection, the bike path is on a relatively wide shoulder; it's a 35-mile ride to Canyonlands' Grand View Point, or a mere 24-mile uphill chug to Dead Horse Point.

The paved route provides easy cycling access to the MOAB Brand mountain bike trails just off U.S. 191 and a more challenging ride to the Intrepid trails in Dead Horse Point State Park and the Gemini Bridges trail, which starts just outside the park.

Bike Tours

Most of the bicycle rental shops in Moab offer day-long mountain bike excursions, while outfitters offer multiday tours that vary in price depending on the difficulty of the trail and the degree of comfort involved. The charge for these trips is usually around $200-250 per day, including food and shuttles. Be sure to inquire whether rates include bike rental.

Rim Tours (1233 S. U.S. 191, 435/259-5223 or 800/626-7335, www.rimtours.com) is a well-established local company offering several half-day (around $85 pp for 2-3 cyclists), full-day (around $120 pp for 2-3 cyclists), and multi-day trips. **Magpie Cycling** (800/546-4245, magpieadventures.com) is a small local business that runs day trips that include instruction on mountain biking techniques and overnight rides, mostly in Canyonlands, including a four-day tour of the White Rim Trail ($875).

Western Spirit Cycling (478 Mill Creek Dr., 435/259-8732 or 800/845-2453, www.western-spirit.com) offers mountain and road bike tours in the western United States, with about one-third of them in Utah. Moab-area trips include the White Rim, the Maze, and the Kokopelli Trail (5 days, $1,200). Another Moab-based company with tours all over the West is **Escape Adventures** (Moab Cyclery, 391 S. Main St., 435/259-7423 or 800/596-2953, www.escapeadventures.com), which leads multiday mountain bike trips, including one into the remote Maze section of Canyonlands National Park (5 days, $1,270); some of the tours combine cycling with rafting, climbing, and hiking.

Rentals and Repairs

Rim Cyclery (94 W. 100 N., 435/259-5333 or 888/304-8219, www.rimcyclery.com, 9am-6pm daily) is Moab's oldest bike and outdoor gear store, offering both road and mountain bike sales, rentals, and service. Mountain bike rentals are also available at **Poison Spider Bicycles** (497 N. Main St., 435/259-7882 or 800/635-1792, www.poisonspiderbicycles.com, 8am-7pm daily spring and fall, 9am-6pm daily winter and summer) and **Chile Pepper** (702 S. Main St., 435/259-4688 or 888/677-4688, www.chilebikes.com, 8am-6pm daily Mar.-Nov., 9am-5pm daily Dec.-Feb.). **Moab Cyclery** (391 S. Main St., 435/259-7423 or 800/559-1978, www.moabcyclery.com, 8am-6pm daily) offers rentals, tours, shuttles, and gear. Expect to pay about $45-70 per day to rent a mountain bike, a little less for a road bike.

Shuttle Services

Several of the Moab area's best mountain bike trails are essentially one-way, and unless you want to cycle back the way you came, you'll need to arrange a shuttle service to pick you up and bring you back to Moab or your vehicle.

© BILL MCRAE

Colorado River Canyon, just outside Moab

Also, if you don't have a vehicle or a bike rack, you will need to use a shuttle service to get to more distant trailheads. **Coyote Shuttle** (435/260-2097, www.coyoteshuttle.com) and **Roadrunner Shuttle** (435/260-2724, www.roadrunnershuttle.com) both operate shuttle services; depending on distance, the usual fare is $15-25 pp. Both companies also shuttle hikers to trailheads and pick up rafters.

RAFTING AND BOATING

Even a visitor with a tight schedule can get out and enjoy the canyon country on rafts and other watercraft. Outfitters offer both laid-back and exhilarating day trips, which usually require little advance planning. Longer multi-day trips include gentle canoe paddles along the placid Green River and thrilling expeditions down the Colorado River.

You'll need to reserve well in advance for most of the longer trips because the BLM and the National Park Service limit trips through the backcountry, and space, especially in high season, is at a premium. Experienced rafters can also plan their own unguided trips, although you'll need a permit for all areas except for the day-long Fisher Towers float upstream from Moab.

The rafting season runs April-September, and jet-boat tours run February-November. Most do-it-yourself river-runners obtain their permits by applying in January-February for a March drawing; the Moab Information Center's BLM ranger can advise on this process and provide the latest information about available cancellations.

Rafting and Kayaking Trips

For most of the following trips, full-day rates include lunch and beverages, while part-day trips include just lemonade and soft drinks. On overnight trips you'll sleep in tents in backcountry campgrounds.

The **Colorado River** offers several exciting options. The most popular day run near Moab

MOAB

starts upstream near Fisher Towers and bounces through several moderate rapids on the way back to town. Full-day raft trips (about $65 pp adults) run from Fisher Towers to near Moab. Half-day trips ($45-50 pp adults) run over much the same stretch of river but don't include lunch.

For a more adventurous rafting trip, the Colorado's rugged **Westwater Canyon** offers lots of white water and several class III-IV rapids near the Utah-Colorado border. These long day trips are more expensive, typically around $160-170 per day. The Westwater Canyon is also often offered as part of multiday adventure packages. The **Dolores River** joins the Colorado about two miles upstream from Dewey Bridge, near the Colorado border. The Dolores River offers exciting white water in a narrow canyon during the spring runoff; the season is short, though, and the river is too low to run by mid-June. With plenty of class III-IV rapids, this 32-mile trip usually takes 2-5 days and costs around $325-975 pp.

The **Cataract Canyon** section of the Colorado River, which begins south of the river's confluence with the Green River and extends to the backwater of Lake Powell, usually requires four days of rafting to complete. However, if you're in a hurry, some outfitters offer time-saving trips that motor rather than float through placid water and slow down only to shoot rapids, enabling these trips to conclude in as little as two days. This is the wildest white water in the Moab area, with big boiling class III-IV rapids. Costs range $600-1,200, depending on what kind of craft, the number of days, and whether you fly, hike, or drive out at the end of the trip.

The **Green River** also offers class II-III rafting and canoeing opportunities, although they are milder than those on the Colorado. Trips on the Green make good family outings. Most trips require five days, leaving from the town of Green River and taking out at Mineral Bottom, just before Canyonlands National Park. Highlights of the Green River include Labyrinth Canyon and Bowknot Bend. Costs range $650-900 for a five-day rafting trip.

Rafting or Kayaking on Your Own

The class II-III **Fisher Towers** section of the Colorado River is gentle enough for amateur rafters to negotiate on their own. A popular one-day raft trip with mild rapids begins from the Hittle Bottom Recreation Site (Hwy. 128, 23.5 miles north of Moab, near Fisher Towers) and ends 14 river miles downstream at Take-out Beach (Hwy. 128, 10.3 miles north of U.S. 191). You can rent rafts and the mandatory life jackets in Moab, but you won't need a permit on this section of river.

Experienced white-water rafters can obtain permits from the BLM's Westwater Ranger Station (82 E. Dogwood Ave., 435/259-7012, www.blm.gov, 8am-noon Mon.-Fri.) up to two months prior to launch date. Don't show up at the office expecting to get a same-day or next-day permit; it's important to plan well in advance. The usual put-in is at the Westwater ranger station nine miles south of I-70's exit 227; another option is the Loma boat launch in Colorado. A start at Loma adds a day or two to the trip along with the sights of Horsethief and Ruby Canyons. Normal takeout is at Cisco, although it's possible to continue 16 miles on slow-moving water through open country to Dewey Bridge.

Canyon Voyages (211 N. Main St., 435/259-6007 or 800/733-6007, www.canyonvoyages.com) and **Navtec Expeditions** (321 N. Main St., 435/259-7983 or 800/833-1278, www.navtec.com) are two local rafting companies that rent rafts (from $60 per day) and kayaks (about $35 per day) for those who would rather organize their own river adventures.

Rafting Outfitters

Moab is full of river-trip companies, and most offer a variety of day and multiday trips; in addition, many will combine raft trips with biking, horseback riding, hiking, or 4WD excursions. Check out the many websites at www.discovermoab.com/tour.htm. The following list includes major outfitters offering a variety of rafting options. Most lead trips to the main river destinations on the Colorado and Green Rivers as well as other rivers in Utah and the West. Red River Adventures runs trips in smaller self-paddled rafts and inflatable kayaks. Inquire about natural history or petroglyph tours if these specialty trips interest you.

- **Adrift Adventures** (378 N. Main St., 435/259-8594 or 800/874-4483, www.adrift.net)
- **Canyon Voyages** (211 N. Main St., 435/259-6007 or 800/733-6007, www.canyonvoyages.com)
- **Navtec Expeditions** (321 N. Main St., 435/259-7983 or 800/833-1278, www.navtec.com)
- **Red River Adventures** (1140 S. Main St., 435/259-4046 or 877/259-4046, www.redriveradventures.com)
- **Sheri Griffith Expeditions** (503/259-8229 or 800/332-2439, www.griffithexp.com)
- **Tag-A-Long Expeditions** (452 N. Main St., 435/259-8946 or 800/453-3292, www.tagalong.com)
- **Western River Expeditions** (225 S. Main St., 435/259-7019 or 866/904-1163, www.westernriver.com)

Canoeing

Canoeists can also sample the calm waters of the Green River on multiday excursions with **Moab Rafting and Canoe Company** (805 N. Main St., 435/259-7722, www.moab-rafting.com), which runs scheduled guided trips (about $150 pp per day) to four sections of the Green and to calmer stretches of the Colorado River. They also rent canoes (around $35 per day), including the necessary equipment.

Another good source for DIY canoe and kayak trips on the Green is **Tex's Riverways** (435/259-5101 or 877/662-2839, www.texsriverways.com), which specializes in rentals, shuttles, and support for self-guided trips.

Jet Boats and Motorboats

Guided jet-boat excursions through Canyonlands National Park start at around $75 for a half-day trip. **Tag-A-Long Expeditions** (452 N. Main St., 435/259-8946 or 800/453-3292, www.tagalong.com) and **Adrift Adventures** (378 N. Main St., 435/259-8594 or 800/874-4483, www.adrift.net) both offer half-day trips and full-day combination jet boat-jeep excursions.

Canyonlands by Night & Day (435/259-5261 or 800/394-9978, www.canyonlandsbynight.com, Apr.-mid-Oct., $65 adults, $55 ages 4-12) tours leave at sunset in an open motorboat and go several miles upstream on the Colorado River; a guide points out canyon features. The sound and light show begins on the way back; music and historic narration accompany the play of lights on the canyon walls. Package tours with chuckwagon dinners are available. Reservations are a good idea because the boat fills up fast. Daytime jet-boat tours ($80 adults, $70 children) are longer—about four hours—and go a little farther. Trips depart from the Spanish mission-style office just north of Moab, across the Colorado River.

4WD EXPLORATION

Road tours offer visitors a special opportunity to view unique canyon-country arches and spires, indigenous rock art, and wildlife. An interpretive brochure at the Moab Information Center (25 E. Center St., at Main St., 435/259-8825 or 800/635-6622, www.discovermoab.com) outlines the Moab Area Rock Art Auto Tour, which routes motorists to petroglyphs tucked away behind golf courses and ranches. You might also pick up a map of Moab-area 4WD trails: four rugged 15-54-mile loop routes through the desert that take 2.5-4 hours to drive. Those who left their trusty four-by-fours and off-road-driving skills at home can take an off-road jeep tour with a private operator. Most Moab outfitters offer jeep or Hummer tours,

MOAB

Four-wheeling and outlandish art both find homes in Moab.

often in combination with rafting or hiking options. The **Moab Adventure Center** (452 N. Main St., 435/259-7019 or 888/622-4097, www.moabadventurecenter.com) runs two-hour ($81 adults, $49 youths) and half-day ($169 adults, $122 youths) guided Hummer safaris. The Adventure Center, which can book you on any number of trips, can also arrange jeep rentals (from $180 per day).

Jeep and other 4WD-vehicle rentals are available at a multitude of Moab outfits, including **Farabee Jeep Rentals** (35 Grand Ave., 435/259-74944 or 877/970-5337, www.moabjeeprentals.com), **Canyonlands Jeep Adventures** (225 S. Main St., 435/259-4412, www.canyonlandsjeep.com), and **Cliffhanger Jeep Rentals** (40 W. Center St., 435/259-0889, www.cliffhangerjeeprental.com). Expect to pay from $180 per day.

ATVS AND DIRT BIKES

As an alternative to four-by-four touring in the backcountry, there's all-terrain vehicle (ATV)

and motorcycle "dirt biking," typically but not exclusively geared toward youngsters and families. Although youths ages 8-15 may operate an ATV, provided they possess an Education Certificate issued by Utah State Parks and Recreation or an equivalent certificate from their home state, parents should research ATV safety before agreeing to such an outing. Much of the public land surrounding Moab is open to ATV exploration, with many miles of unpaved roads and existing trails on which ATVs can travel. However, ATV and dirt bike riding is not allowed within either Arches or Canyonlands National Park.

One particularly popular area for ATVs is **White Wash Sand Dunes,** with many miles of dirt roads in a strikingly scenic location. It is 48 miles northwest of Moab, reached by driving 13 miles south from I-70's exit 175, just east of Green River. The dunes are interspersed with large cottonwood trees and bordered by red sandstone cliffs. In addition to the dunes, White Wash is a popular route around three sides of the dunes.

ATVs and dirt bikes are available from a number of Moab-area outfitters, including **High Point Hummer** (281 N. Main St., 435/259-2972 or 877/486-6833, www.highpointhummer.com) and **Moab Tour Company** (543 N. Main St., 435/259-4080 or 877/725-7317, www.moabtourcompany.us). A half-day dirt bike or ATV rental starts at around $150.

◖ AIR TOURS

You'll have a bird's-eye view of southeastern Utah's incredible landscape from Moab's Canyonlands Field with **Redtail Aviation** (435/259-7421 or 800/842-9251, www.redtailaviation.com). Flights (minimum 2 people, $165 pp) include Canyonlands National Park's Needles, Island in the Sky, and Maze Districts. Longer tours are also available, and flights operate year-round. A 3.5-hour tour (minimum 4 people, $435 pp) over Canyonlands, Natural Bridges, Lake Powell, and the Capitol Reef area includes a stop for lunch (extra cost) at the Marble Canyon Lodge.

SKYDIVING

If you think the Arches and Canyonlands area looks dramatic from an airplane, imagine the excitement of parachuting into the desert landscape. **Skydive Moab** (Canyonlands Fields Airport, U.S. 191, 16 miles north of Moab, 435/259-5867, www.skydivemoab.com) offers jumps for both first-time and experienced skydivers. First-timers receive 30 minutes of ground schooling, followed by a half-hour flight before a tandem parachute jump with an instructor from 10,000 feet. A tandem skydive, including instruction and equipment, starts at $215. For experienced skydivers with their own equipment, jumps start at $18; equipment and parachutes are available for rent.

CLIMBING

Just outside town, the cliffs along Highway 279 and Fisher Towers attract rock climbers. For world-class crack climbing, head south to Indian Creek, near the Needles District of Canyonlands National Park.

Moab has a couple of stores with rock climbing gear and informative staff: **Gearheads** (471 S. Main St., 435/259-4327) and **Pagan Mountaineering** (59 S. Main St., 435/259-1117, www.paganclimber.com). The friendly folks at Pagan also offer a climbing guide service to the local rock. **Moab Desert Adventures** (415 N. Main St., 435/260-2404 or 877/765-6622, www.moabdesertadventures.com) offers rock climbing and canyoneering lessons, both for beginners and experienced climbers; families are welcome. A half day of climbing instruction is $165 pp; rates are lower for groups of 2-3 students.

HORSEBACK RIDING

Head up the Colorado River to **Red Cliffs Lodge** (milepost 14, Hwy. 128, 435/259-2002 or 866/812-2002, www.redcliffslodge.com) for guided trail rides amid the dramatic scenery of Castle Valley. Half-day rides are $80 pp; children must be at least eight years old, and an adult must accompany children. Riders must weigh less than 220 pounds. Several tour operators, including **Adrift Adventures** (378 N. Main St., 435/259-8594 or 800/874-4483, www.adrift.net) and the **Moab Adventure Center** (225 S. Main St., 435/259-7019 or 866/904-1163, www.moabadventurecenter.com), offer horseback rides in conjunction with rafting, hiking, and jeep exploration.

GOLF

The **Moab Golf Club** (2705 SE Bench Rd., 435/259-6488, www.moabcountryclub.com/golf, $47) is an 18-hole par-72 public course in a well-watered oasis amid stunning red-rock formations. To get here from Moab, go south five miles on U.S. 191, turn left on Spanish Trail Road, follow it two miles; then go right on Murphy Lane, and follow it to Bench Road and the golf course.

MOAB

LOCAL PARKS

The **city park** (181 W. 400 N.) has shaded picnic tables and a playground. It's also home to the **Moab Recreation and Aquatic Center** (374 Park Ave., 435/259-8226), a new community center with indoor and outdoor swimming pools, a weight room, and group exercise classes.

Two miles north of town, **Lions Park** (U.S. 191 and Hwy. 128) offers picnicking along the Colorado River, although ongoing bridge construction makes it less than peaceful. **Rotary Park** (Mill Creek Dr.) is family-oriented and has lots of activities for kids.

Entertainment and Events

For a town of its size, Moab puts on a pretty good nightlife show, with lots of young hikers, bikers, and rafters reliving their daily conquests in bars and brewpubs. There are also notable seasonal music events, ranging from folk to classical.

NIGHTLIFE

A lot of Moab's nightlife focuses on the rowdy and well-loved **Eddie McStiff's** (57 S. Main St., 435/259-2337, www.eddiemcstiffs.com, 11:30am-close daily), right downtown, with 12 handcrafted beers on draft, two outdoor seating areas, and live music several times a week. Although the **Moab Brewery** (686 S. Main St., 435/259-6333, www.themoabbrewery.com) brews on the premises and is a pleasant place to sample good beer, it is more a restaurant than a bar.

Woody's Tavern (221 S. Main St., 435/259-9323) has live bands on the weekend—you might hear bluegrass, roots rock, reggae, or jam bands.

Come for some barbecue and stay for the blues (or vice versa; both are good) at **Blu Pig** (811 S. Main St., 435/259-3333). Another restaurant with a lively bar scene is **Buck's Grill House** (1393 U.S. 191, 435/259-5201); they bring in bands a couple of times a week.

For a more family-friendly evening out, consider the **Bar M Chuckwagon's Live Western Show and Cowboy Supper** (7000 N. U.S. 191, 435/259-2276, http://barmchuckwagon.com, hours vary), a kind of Western-themed dinner theater that includes mock gunfights,

live country music, and other Old West entertainment in addition to a chuckwagon buffet dinner.

Another longtime tradition for evening entertainment is **Canyonlands by Night** (435/259-5261, www.canyonlandsbynight.com), a cruise on the Colorado River that ends with a sound-and-light presentation along the sandstone cliffs. Dinner packages are available; children under age four are not permitted, per Coast Guard regulations.

For a selection of movies, head for **Slickrock Cinemas** (580 Kane Creek Blvd., 435/259-4441).

EVENTS

To find out about local happenings, contact the Moab Information Center (25 E. Center St., at Main St., 435/259-8825 or 800/635-6622, www.discovermoab.com) or browse *Moab Happenings,* available free around town or online (www.moabhappenings.com). Unsurprisingly, Moab offers quite a few annual biking events. The **Moab Skinny Tire Festival,** held the first week of March, and the **Moab Century Tour,** held in September, are both supported road bike events that benefit the Lance Armstrong Foundation. For information on both, visit www.skinnytire-festival.com or call 435/259-3193. The mountain bike endurance race event **24 Hours of Moab** (www.grannygear.com/Races/Moab), held in early October, pits four-person relay teams against the rugged terrain of the Behind the Rocks area. This is one of North America's major events for mountain bikers, bringing more than 500 teams and 5,000 spectators to Moab.

Other major annual athletic events include the **Canyonlands Half Marathon and Five Mile Run** (www.moabhalfmarathon.org), held the third Saturday in March. A women's half marathon, the **Thelma and Louise Half Marathon,** run in May, is organized by the same group.

Moab's most popular annual event, more popular than anything celebrating two wheels, is the **Easter Jeep Safari** (www.rr4w.com), which is the Sturgis or Daytona Beach of recreational four-wheeling. Upward of 2,000 4WD vehicles (it's not exclusively for jeeps, although ATVs are not allowed) converge on Moab for a week's worth of organized backcountry trail rides. "Big Saturday" (the day before Easter) is the climax of the event, when all participating vehicles parade through Moab. Plan well ahead for lodging if you are planning to visit Moab during this event, as hotel rooms are often booked a year in advance.

Memorial Day weekend brings artists, musicians, and art cars to the city park for the **Moab Arts Festival** (435/259-2742, www.moabartsfestival.org).

The dust is kicked up at the Spanish Trail Arena (3641 S. U.S. 191, just south of Moab) with the professional **Canyonlands PRCA Rodeo,** held the first weekend in June, with a rodeo, a parade, a dance, horse racing, and a 4-H gymkhana.

The **Moab Music Festival** (435/259-7003, www.moabmusicfest.org) is first and foremost a classical chamber music festival, but every year a few jazz, bluegrass, or folk artists are included in the lineup. More than 30 artists are currently involved in the festival, held the first two weeks of September. Many of the concerts are held in dramatic outdoor settings. The **Moab Folk Festival** (www.moabfolkfestival.com) is the town's other big annual musical event, attracting top-notch acoustic performers to Moab the first weekend of November.

SHOPPING

Main Street, between 200 North and 200 South, has nearly a dozen galleries and gift

MOAB

© BILL MCRAE

Moab's old downtown

shops with T-shirts, outdoor apparel, Native American art, and other gifts. **Back of Beyond Books** (83 N. Main St., 435/259-5154) features an excellent selection of regional books and maps. Pick up those missing camping items at **Gearheads** (471 S. Main St., 435/259-4327, 8am-10pm daily spring-fall, shorter hours winter), an amazingly well-stocked outdoor store. If you're heading out to camp or hike in the desert, Gearheads is a good place to fill your water jugs with free filtered water.

Moab's largest grocery store, **City Market** (425 S. Main St., 435/259-5181, 6am-11pm daily), is a good place to pick up supplies; it has a pharmacy and a gas station.

Stop by the **Moonflower Market** (39 E. 100 N., 435/259-5712, 9am-8pm daily) for natural-food groceries; it's a well-stocked store.

Accommodations

Moab has been a tourism destination for generations and offers a wide variety of lodging choices, ranging from older motels to new upscale resorts. U.S. 191 is lined with all the usual chain motels, but we tend to go for the smaller local operations, and that's mostly what you'll find listed here.

Moab/Canyonlands Central Reservations (435/259-5125 or 800/505-5343, www.moabutahlodging.com) can make bookings at area vacation homes, which include some relatively inexpensive apartments. Another handy tool is www.moab-utah.com, which has a complete listing of lodging websites for the Moab area.

The only time Moab isn't busy is in the dead of winter, November-February. At all other times, be sure to make reservations well in advance. Summer room rates are listed here; in winter rates typically drop 40 percent.

UNDER $50

The **Lazy Lizard Hostel** (1213 S. U.S. 191, 435/259-6057, www.lazylizardhostel.com) costs just $10 for simple dorm-style accommodations. To stay at this casual classic Moab lodging, you won't need a hostel membership, and all guests share access to a hot tub, a kitchen, a barbecue, a coin-operated laundry, and a common room with cable TV. Showers for nonguests ($3) and private guest rooms ($26) are also offered. Log cabins can sleep two ($34) to six ($48) people.

The Lazy Lizard is one mile south of town, behind A-1 Storage; the turnoff is about 200 yards south of Moab Lanes.

$50-100

There's nothing fancy about the **Red Rock Lodge Motel** (51 N. 100 W., 435/259-5431 or 877/253-5431, www.red-rocklodge.com, from $60), but it has a great location, pet-friendly guest rooms with fridges and coffeemakers, a hot tub, and a locked bicycle storage facility.

A simple but quite adequate place is the **Bowen Motel** (169 N. Main St., 435/259-7132 or 800/874-5439, www.bowenmotel.com, from $74), a homey motel with an outdoor pool and included continental breakfast. The Bowen offers a variety of room types, including three-bedroom family suites and an 1,800-square-foot three-bedroom house with full kitchen. A couple of older but well-cared-for motels just north of downtown have guest rooms starting at about $75: the **Adventure Inn** (512 N. Main St., 435/662-2466 or 866/662-2466, www.adventureinnmoab.com) and the **Inca Inn** (570 N. Main St., 435/259-7261 or 866/462-2466, www.incainn.com).

A reasonably priced motel that's simple, friendly, and noncorporate is the **Kokopelli Lodge** (72 S. 100 E., 435/259-7615 or 888/530-3134, www.kokopelilodge.com, from $76), offering small but colorful pet-friendly guest

© JUDY JEWELL

Moab has a few modest but well-kept motels such as the Kokopelli Lodge.

rooms and a convenient location one block off the main drag. Kokopelli also offers a number of condos on its website if you're looking for a relatively inexpensive option with multiple beds and full kitchens.

A few blocks south of downtown, the **Red Stone Inn** (535 S. Main St., 435/259-3500 or 800/772-1972, www.moabredstone.com, from $90) is a one-story, knotty pine-sided motel; all guest rooms have efficiency kitchens. Other amenities include a bicycle maintenance area, a covered patio with a gas barbecue grill, a hot tub, and guest laundry. Motel guests have free access to the hotel pool next door. Pets are permitted only in smoking rooms.

$100-150

The Red Stone's sister property, the sprawling **Big Horn Lodge** (550 S. Main St., 435/259-6171 or 800/325-6171, www.moabbighorn.com, from $99) has similar knotty-pine guest rooms equipped with microwaves and fridges as well as a pool and a steak restaurant. Package deals for a guest room plus jeep tours, raft trips, and other activities are offered.

At the heart of downtown Moab, **Best Western Greenwell Motel** (105 S. Main St., 435/259-6151 or 800/528-1234, www.best-westernmoab.com, from $139) has a pool, fitness facilities, an on-premises restaurant, and some kitchenettes.

At the **Virginian Motel** (70 E. 200 S., 435/259-5951 or 800/261-2063, www.moab-utah.com/virginian, $109), more than half of the guest rooms have kitchenettes, and pets are permitted. During the winter, room rates are less than half the high-season rates.

Eight very long blocks from downtown, on a quiet property that backs on the Mill Creek and Nature Conservancy holdings, is **Adobe Abode** (778 Kane Creek Blvd., 435/259-7716, www.adobeabodemoab.com, from $139), a B&B-style inn with large guest rooms done up in handsome Southwestern style. The inn also offers a pool table and evening refreshments, a large and tasty breakfast, and a hot tub.

If you want seclusion in a quiet community 18 miles east of Moab, stay at the **Castle Valley Inn B&B** (424 Amber Lane, Castle Valley, 435/259-6012, www.castlevalleyinn.com, $105-220). The inn adjoins a wildlife refuge in a stunning landscape of red-rock mesas and needle-pointed buttes. You can stay in one of the main house's five guest rooms or in one of the three bungalows with kitchens. Facilities include a hot tub. To reach Castle Valley Inn, follow Highway 128 east from Moab for 16 miles, turn south, and continue 2.3 miles toward Castle Valley.

OVER $150

The **Best Western Canyonlands Inn** (16 S. Main St., 435/259-2300 or 800/649-5191, www.canyonlandsinn.com, from $170) is at the heart of Moab, with suites, a pool, a fitness room and spa, a restaurant, and a bike storage area.

One of the most interesting accommodations

Saddle horses await their riders at Sorrel River Ranch.

options in Moab is the **Gonzo Inn** (100 W. 200 S., 435/259-2515 or 800/791-4044, www.gonzoinn.com, from $169). With a look somewhere between an adobe inn and a postmodern warehouse, the Gonzo doesn't try to appear anything but hip. Expect large guest rooms with vibrant colors and modern decor, a pool, and a friendly welcome.

Located in a lovely and quiet residential area, the **Sunflower Hill Luxury Inn** (185 N. 300 E., 435/259-2974 or 800/662-2786, www.sunflowerhill.com, from $165) offers high-quality accommodations. Choose from a guest room in one of Moab's original farmhouses, a historic ranch house, or a garden cottage. All 12 guest rooms have private baths, air-conditioning, and queen beds; there are also two suites. Guests share access to an outdoor swimming pool and a hot tub, bike storage, patios, and large gardens. Children over age seven are welcome, and the place is open year-round.

Families or groups might want to rent a condo at **Moab Springs Ranch** (1266 N. U.S. 191, 435/259-7891 or 888/259-5759, www.moabspringsranch.com, from $274), located on the north end of town on the site of Moab's oldest ranch. The townhomes have a parklike setting with a swimming pool and a hot tub, and they sleep up to 10.

A cluster of four charming and pet-friendly cottages dubbed **3 Dogs & a Moose** (171 and 173 W. Center St., 435/260-1692, www.3dogsandamoosecottages.com) is just off the main drag. The two smaller cottages ($125-175) are perfect for couples, and the larger cottages ($275-285) sleep up to six.

GUEST RANCHES

A short drive from Moab along the Colorado River's red-rock canyon is the region's premium luxury guest ranch, the **Sorrel River Ranch** (Hwy. 128, 17 miles northeast of Moab, 435/259-4642 or 877/317-8244, www.sorrelriver.com, from $399). The ranch sits on 240 acres in one of the most dramatic landscapes in the Moab area—just across the river from Arches National Park and beneath the soaring mesas of Castle Valley. Accommodations are in a series of beautifully furnished wooden lodges, all tastefully fitted with Old West-style furniture. All units have kitchenettes and a patio with a porch swing or back deck overlooking the river; some guest rooms have both. Horseback rides are offered into the arroyos behind the ranch, and kayaks and bicycles are available for rent. The ranch's restaurant, the River Grill (435/259-4642, 7am-2pm and 6pm-9pm daily Apr.-Oct., 7am-10am and 6pm-9pm daily Nov.-Mar., $28-36), has some of the best views in Utah and an adventurous menu offering everything from blue corn-dusted halibut to grilled elk chops.

Sharing a similar view of the Colorado River and Castle Valley but three miles closer to Moab is the sprawling **Red Cliffs Lodge** (milepost 14, Hwy. 128, 435/259-2002 or 866/812-2002, www.redcliffslodge.com, from $239), which houses guests in "mini suites" in the main lodge building and in a number of riverside cabins that can sleep up to six ($339). The lodge offers the Cowboy Grill bar and restaurant, horseback rides, and mountain bike rentals and will arrange river raft trips. The lodge is also the headquarters for Castle Creek Winery and the site of the free Moab Museum of Film & Western Heritage, which displays a collection of movie memorabilia from westerns filmed in the area.

CAMPGROUNDS
Moab Campgrounds

It's really easy and comfy to camp at ◖ **Up the Creek** (210 E. 300 S., 435/260-1888, www. moabupthecreek.com, mid-Mar.-early Nov., $25 for 1 person, $30 for 2, $35 for 3, $5 dogs), a walk-in, tents-only campground tucked into

© JUDY JEWELL

Shade trees, an in-town location, and a nice bathhouse make Up the Creek campground a pleasant place to stay.

a residential neighborhood near downtown Moab. The shady campground, with a bathhouse and showers, picnic tables, and a few propane grills (campfires are prohibited), is right alongside a bike path.

RV parks cluster at the north and south ends of town. **Moab Valley RV Resort** (1773 N. U.S. 191, at Hwy. 128, 2 miles north of Moab, 435/259-4469, www.moabvalleyrv.com, $25 tents, from $40 RVs) is open year-round; it has showers, a pool, a playground, and free wireless Internet access. There's also a selection of cabins (bedding provided, $57-80) available—some are simple sleeping rooms, others have baths and fridges. Pets are allowed only in RVs. Although this place is convenient, it is pretty close to a large ongoing environmental cleanup project involving removal of radioactive mine tailings. **Moab KOA** (3225 S. U.S. 191, 435/259-6682 or 800/562-0372, http://moabkoa.com, Mar.-Nov., $25 tents, from $65 RVs with hookups, $65-170 cabins), just off the highway four miles south of town, has showers, a laundry room, a store, miniature golf, and a pool.

More convenient to downtown, **Canyonlands Campground** (555 S. Main St., 435/259-6848 or 800/522-6848, www.canyonlandsrv.com, $26-33 tents, $40-46 RVs, $60-65 cabins) is open year-round; it has showers, a laundry room, a store, a pool, and two-person air-conditioned cabins—bring your own bedding. One mile north of Moab, **Slickrock Campground** (1301½ N. U.S. 191, 435/259-7660 or 800/448-8873, http://slickrockcampground.com, $25 tents or RVs without hookups, $32-39 with hookups, $52 cabins with air-conditioning and heat but no bath or kitchen) remains open year-round; it has nice sites with some shade as well as showers, a store, an outdoor café, and a pool.

You'll also find campgrounds farther out at Arches and Canyonlands National Parks, Dead Horse Point State Park, Canyon Rims Recreation Area, and east of town in the cool La Sal Mountains.

BLM Campgrounds

There are 26 BLM campgrounds (most $8-12) in the Moab area. Although these spots can't be reserved, sites are abundant enough that campers are rarely unable to find a spot. The campgrounds are concentrated on the banks of the Colorado River—along Highway 128 toward Castle Valley, along Highway 279 toward the potash factory, and along Kane Creek Road—and at the Sand Flats Recreation Area near the Slickrock Trail. Only a few of these campgrounds can handle large RVs, none have hookups, and few have piped water. For a full list of BLM campground and facilities, visit www.discovermoab.com/campgrounds_blm.htm.

Dead Horse Point State Park Campground

Soak in Dead Horse Point's spectacular scenery at the park's **Kayenta Campground** (reservations 800/322-3770, www.reserveamerica.com, $20 camping, $9 reservations fee), just past the visitors center, which offers sites with water and electric hookups but no showers. The campground nearly always fills up during the main season, so it's almost essential to reserve well in advance. Winter visitors may camp on the point; no hookups are available, but the restrooms have water.

If you aren't able to secure a spot inside the park, try the BLM's **Horsethief Campground** (no drinking water, $12) on Highway 313 a few miles east of the state park entrance. It has nearly 60 sites, all first-come, first-served, so it's usually possible to find a site.

Food

Moab has the largest concentration of good restaurants in southern Utah; no matter what else the recreational craze has produced, it has certainly improved the food. Several Moab-area restaurants are closed for vacation in February, so call ahead if you're visiting in winter.

BREAKFAST AND LIGHT MEALS

Food isn't limited to muffins at **Love Muffin** (139 N. Main St., 435/259-6833, www.lovemuffincafe.com, 7am-1pm daily, $6-8), but if you decide to skip the breakfast burritos or insanely tasty red quinoa, the Burple Nurple muffin may be just what you need. While you're eating breakfast, order a Muffaletta or barbecued tofu sandwich to pack along for lunch.

Another good option for a tasty but healthy breakfast or lunch is **EklectiCafe** (352 N. Main St., 435/259-6896, 7am-2:30pm Mon.-Sat., 7am-1pm Sun., $6-9), a charming and busy little café serving delicious organic and vegetarian dishes. For a more traditional breakfast, try the **Jailhouse Café** (101 N. Main St., 435/259-3900, 7am-noon daily, $7-11), a Moab classic.

Dense, chewy bagels and good sandwiches make the **Red Rock Bakery** (74 S. Main St., 435/259-5941, 7am-2pm daily) worth a visit.

Two Moab diners have an old-fashioned ambience and really good food. At the **Moab Diner & Ice Cream Shoppe** (189 S. Main St., 435/259-4006, http://moabdiner.com, 6am-9pm Mon.-Sat., $5-12), the breakfasts are large, with a Southwestern green chili edge to much of the food. The ice cream is delicious. Another spot with great burgers and shakes is **Milt's Stop & Eat** (356 Millcreek Dr., 435/259-7424, www.miltsstopandeat.com, 11am-8pm, $3.50-7)—it's a local classic, and just the place to stop after a day of biking or hiking.

CASUAL DINING

Unless otherwise noted, each of the following establishments has a full liquor license.

Zax (96 S. Main St., 435/259-6555, www.zaxmoab.com, 6:30am-close daily, $7-13) is a high-volume all-things-to-all-people restaurant in the heart of downtown. If you're with kids, this might be the ticket for sandwiches, steaks, pasta, pizza, or salad.

The **Slickrock Café** (5 N. Main St., 435/259-8004, www.slickrockcafe.com, 11am-close daily, $10-27) is another versatile restaurant in a historic building downtown. The Slickrock is a casual place serving a wide range of American standards; large salads ($4-14) are a decent bet.

Check out **Miguel's Baja Grill** (51 N. Main St., 435/259-6546, www.miguelsbajagrill.com, 5pm-9pm daily, $10-20) for well-prepared Baja-style seafood, including good fish tacos. It's a busy place, so make a reservation or be prepared to wait.

Get away from high-volume assembly-line restaurants at **Sabaku Sushi** (90 E. Center St., 435/259-4455, 5pm-10pm daily, rolls $4-15), which offers surprisingly good sushi in a friendly atmosphere. Arrive at 5pm for the sushi happy hour.

For a Western night out, consider **Bar M Chuckwagon Supper** (541 S. Mulberry Lane, 435/259-2276, www.barmchuckwagon.com, show starts at 6:30pm Apr.-Oct., days vary by season, beer only, $28 over age 12, $14 ages 4-12, free under age 4), located on the banks of Mill Creek just southeast of town. Tasty cowboy-style cooking is served up from chuckwagons, followed by a variety of live Western entertainment including mock gunfights and live music.

BREWPUBS

After a hot day out on the trail, who can blame you for thinking about a cold brew and a hearty meal? Luckily, Moab has two excellent pubs to fill the bill. **Eddie McStiff's** (57 S. Main St., 435/259-2337, www.eddiemcstiffs.com, 11:30am-close daily, $9-19) is an extremely

MOAB

MOAB

MOAB-AREA WINERIES

Southern Utah is not exactly the first place you think of when you envision fine wine, but for a handful of wine pioneers, the Moab area is the *terroir* of choice. Actually, conditions around Moab are similar to parts of Spain and the eastern Mediterranean, where wine grapes have flourished for millennia. The area's first wine grapes were planted in the 1970s through the efforts of the University of Arizona and the Four Corners Regional Economic Development Commission. The results were positive, as the hot days, cool nights, and deep sandy soil produced grapes of exceptional quality and flavor. A fruit-growing cooperative was formed in Moab to grow wine grapes, and by the 1980s the co-op was producing wine under the Arches Winery label. As teetotal Utah's first winery, Arches Winery was more than a novelty—its wines were good enough to accumulate nearly 40 prizes at national wine exhibitions.

Arches Winery was a true pioneer, and now two wineries produce wine in the Moab area, both open for wine tasting. In addition, many of Moab's fine restaurants offer wine from these local wineries.

Castle Creek Winery (Red Cliffs Lodge, Hwy. 128, 14 miles east of Moab, 435/259-3332, http://redcliffslodge.com/winery, noon-5:30pm Mon.-Sat.), formerly Arches Winery, produces pinot noir, merlot, cabernet sauvignon, chenin blanc, chardonnay, and late-harvest gewürztraminer.

Spanish Valley Vineyards and Winery (4710 Zimmerman Lane, 6 miles south of Moab, 435/259-8134, www.moab-utah.com/spanishvalleywinery, noon-7pm Mon.-Sat. Mar.-Oct., noon-5pm Mon.-Sat. Feb. and Nov.) produces riesling, gewürztraminer, cabernet sauvignon, and syrah.

---

popular place to sip a cool beer or a mojito, eat standard pub food (the pizza is a good bet), and meet other travelers; in good weather there's seating in a nice courtyard. You'd have to try hard not to have fun here.

There's more good beer and perhaps better food at the **Moab Brewery** (686 S. Main St., 435/259-6333, www.themoabbrewery.com, 11:30am-10pm Sun.-Thurs., 11:30am-11pm Fri.-Sat., $8-21), although it doesn't attract the kind of scene you'll find at Eddie McStiff's. The atmosphere is light and airy, and the food is good—steaks, sandwiches, burgers, and a wide selection of salads. Try the spinach salad with smoked salmon ($9) or prime rib ($19). There's deck seating when weather permits.

FINE DINING

The **C Desert Bistro** (36 S. 100 W., 435/259-0756, www.desertbistro.com, reservations recommended, dinner from 5:30pm Tues.-Sun. Mar.-Nov., $22-50), a longtime favorite for regional fine dining, has moved to a new location in downtown Moab. Its seasonal, sophisticated Southwest-meets-continental cuisine features local meats and game plus fresh fish and seafood. The patio dining is some of the nicest in Moab, and the indoor dining rooms are pretty and peaceful.

Buck's Grill House (1393 N. U.S. 191, 435/259-5201, www.bucksgrillhouse.com, 5pm-close daily, $9-33) is a steak house with an easygoing Western atmosphere and imaginative refinements on standard steak house fare. Dishes like duck tamales, elk stew with root vegetables, and a vegetarian meatless loaf are excellent.

Jeffrey's Steakhouse (218 N. 100 W., 435/259-3588, www.jeffreyssteakhouse.com, 5pm-close daily, $22-40), tucked off the main drag in an elegantly renovated small house with an upstairs bar, is about as classy and upscale as you'll find in Moab, with a small menu of steaks, chicken, lamb, and salmon.

The **River Grill** (Sorrel River Ranch, Hwy. 128, 17 miles northeast of Moab, 435/259-4642, www.sorrelriver.com, 7am-2pm and 6pm-9pm daily Apr.-Oct., 7am-10am and 6pm-9pm daily Nov.-Mar., $28-36) has a lovely dining room that overlooks spires of red rock and the dramatic cliffs of the Colorado River. The scenery is hard to top, and the food is good, with a focus on prime beef and continental specialties. Dinner reservations are strongly recommended.

The **Sunset Grill** (900 N. U.S. 191, 435/259-7146, www.moab-utah.com/sunsetgrill, 5pm-close Mon.-Sat., $14-24) is located in uranium king Charlie Steen's mansion, situated high above Moab, with million-dollar sweeping views of the valley. Choose from steaks, fresh seafood, and a selection of pasta dishes—what you'll remember is the road up here and the view.

Information and Services

Moab is a small town, and people are generally friendly. Between the excellent Moab Information Center (25 E. Center St., at Main St., 435/259-8825 or 800/635-6622, www.discovermoab.com) and the county library—and the friendly advice of people in the street—you'll find it easy to assemble all the information you need to have a fine stay.

INFORMATION

The **Moab Information Center** (25 E. Center St., at Main St., 435/259-8825 or 800/635-6622, www.discovermoab.com, 8am-8pm Mon.-Sat. and 9am-7pm Apr.-Sept., reduced hours Mon.-Sat. Oct.-Mar.) is the place to start for nearly all local and area information. The National Park Service, the BLM, the U.S. Forest Service, the Grand County Travel Council, and the Canyonlands Natural History Association are all represented here. Visitors who need help from any of these agencies should start at the information center rather than at the agency offices. Free literature is available, the selection of books and maps for sale is large, and the staff is knowledgeable. The center's website is also well organized and packed with information.

The **BLM district office** (82 E. Dogwood Ave., 435/259-2100, 7:45am-4:30pm Mon.-Fri.) is on the south side of town behind Comfort Suites. Some land-use maps are sold here, and this is the place to pick up river-running permits.

SERVICES

The **Grand County Public Library** (257 E. Center St., 435/259-1111, 9am-8pm Mon.-Fri., 9am-5pm Sat.) is a good place for local history and general reading.

The **post office** (50 E. 100 N., 435/259-7427) is downtown. **Moab Regional Hospital** (450 W. Williams Way, 435/719-3500) provides medical care. For ambulance, sheriff, police, or fire emergencies, dial 911.

GETTING THERE

Great Lakes Airlines (800/554-5111, www.greatlakesav.com) provides daily scheduled air service between Canyonlands Field (CNY, U.S. 191, 16 miles north of Moab, 435/259-4849) and Denver. Grand Junction, Colorado, is 120 miles east of Moab via I-70 and has better air service; Salt Lake City is 240 miles northwest of Moab.

Moab Luxury Coach (435/940-4212, www.moabluxurycoach.com) runs SUVs and buses between Moab and Salt Lake City ($149 one-way); advance reservations are required. **Red Rock Express** (435/260-0595, www.redrockexpress.com) has SUV shuttles between Moab and the Grand Junction, Colorado, airport ($100).

Enterprise (711 S. Main St., 435/259-8505, www.enterprise.com) rents cars at the airport.

MOAB

THE SOUTHEASTERN CORNER

Although Arches and Canyonlands capture more attention, Utah's southeastern corner contains an incredible wealth of scenic and culturally significant sites. Consider rounding out your trip to this part of Utah with a tour of Anasazi ruins, remote desert washes, soaring natural bridges, snowy mountain peaks, and a vast reservoir.

Highway 191 runs south from Moab between Canyonlands National Park and the surprisingly tall Abajo Mountains to the west and the La Sal Mountains to the east. In the heat of the summer, these mountains are cool refuges. Also east of the highway, nearly to the Colorado border is Hovenweep National Monument, an Anasazi site with an astounding collection of masonry buildings. Here the Anasazi lived in more or less of a city until they suddenly departed about 900 years ago.

The San Juan River runs across the southern tier of the region, with Cedar Mesa to the north and Monument Valley and Navajo tribal land to the south. Bluff, a charming town that's now the put-in for most river trips on the San Juan, was settled in 1880 by Mormon pioneers who made the incredible wagon train trip from Escalante through steep canyons, including Hole-in-the-Rock.

Cedar Mesa is a place to explore on foot; canyons here often shelter Anasazi ruins. To the west of the mesa, Natural Bridges National Monument is often overlooked, probably because it's rather remote. But its soaring stone

© PAUL LEVY

HIGHLIGHTS

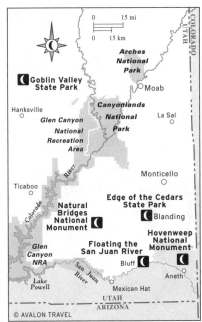

© AVALON TRAVEL

LOOK FOR C TO FIND RECOMMENDED SIGHTS, ACTIVITIES, DINING, AND LODGING.

C Edge of the Cedars State Park: Indoor and outdoor archeological exhibits make this Blanding museum a good introduction to the area and its Anasazi, Ute, Navajo, and Anglo history (page 248).

C Floating the San Juan River: Take a few days away from the rest of the world and paddle from Bluff to Lake Powell. You'll go through deep canyons, past rock art and ruins, and down a few Class III rapids (page 250).

C Hovenweep National Monument: It's worth taking the detour to this impressive collection of masonry dwellings. Six villages with varying architectural styles are among the ruins here (page 252).

C Natural Bridges National Monument: Hike an 8.6-mile loop to visit three spectacular natural bridges. If you're short on time or energy, a nine-mile drive with short hikes to each bridge will also do the trick (page 259).

C Goblin Valley State Park: Big mushroom-shaped rock formations, some with eroded "eyes," cluster around the valley floor of this state park. Tromp down into the valley and wander among these sandstone oddities (page 267).

bridges (carved by streams and spanning a streambed) are beautiful, even elegant, and a night in the campground will allow you to see stars in one of the nation's darkest places.

At Lake Powell the Colorado River is backed up by the Glen Canyon Dam. Lake Powell draws boaters—including visitors who rent houseboats to motor to the huge reservoir's remote inlets and canyons—but for a quick look, the car ferry across the lake is far less expensive. The surrounding Glen Canyon Recreation Area encompasses the rugged canyons that drop down toward Lake Powell; before the dam was built, Glen Canyon was considered the equal of the Grand Canyon for drama and

beauty, and in low-water years, a few peeks into the past are possible. A popular side trip—usually visited via tour boats from one of the lake's marinas—is to Rainbow Bridge National Monument, where the enormous stone bridge spans an arm of the lake.

On the western edge of the region, about 25 miles south of I-70, Goblin Valley State Park has rock formations that would be worthy of national park status if they weren't so close to Arches. Here you can hike among hoodoos, spires, and balancing rocks, many with wind-carved "eyes" that explain the area's supernatural moniker.

Remember that this is remote country and fill your gas tank when you have the

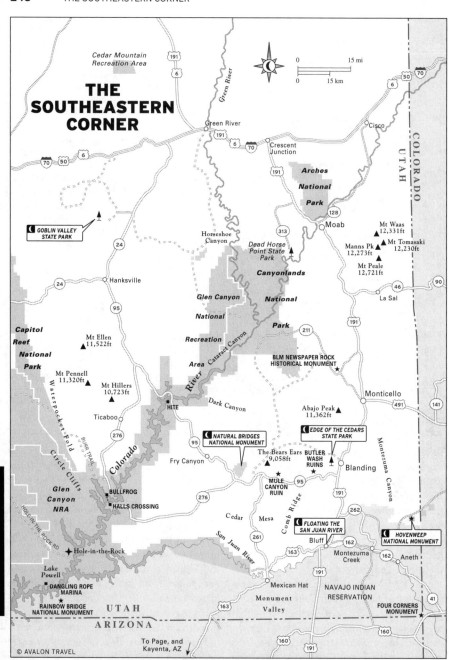

THE
SOUTHEASTERN
CORNER

Cedar Mountain
Recreation Area

0   15 mi

0   15 km

Green River

Green River

Crescent
Junction

Cisco

COLORADO
UTAH

Arches

National

Park

Moab

GOBLIN VALLEY
STATE PARK

Horseshoe
Canyon

Dead Horse
Point State
Park

Mt Waas
12,331ft

Mt Tomasaki
12,230ft

Manns Pk
12,273ft

Canyonlands

Mt Peale
12,721ft

Hanksville

La Sal

Glen Canyon

National

Capitol
Reef
National
Park

Mt Ellen
11,522ft

Recreation

Area

BLM NEWSPAPER ROCK
HISTORICAL MONUMENT

Mt Pennell
11,320ft

Mt Hillers
10,723ft

Dark Canyon

Monticello

Abajo Peak
11,362ft

Waterpocket Fold

HITE

Ticaboo

NATURAL BRIDGES
NATIONAL MONUMENT

EDGE OF THE CEDARS
STATE PARK

The Bears Ears
9,058ft

BUTLER
WASH
RUINS

Fry Canyon

Blanding

Circle Cliffs

BURR TRAIL

Colorado

MULE
CANYON
RUIN

Cedar   Mesa

Glen
Canyon
NRA

BULLFROG

HALLS CROSSING

Comb Ridge

FLOATING THE
SAN JUAN RIVER

HOVENWEEP
NATIONAL MONUMENT

HOLE-IN-THE-ROCK RD

Hole-in-the-Rock

San Juan River

Bluff

Montezuma
Creek

Aneth

Lake
Powell

DANGLING ROPE
MARINA

Mexican Hat

NAVAJO INDIAN
RESERVATION

RAINBOW BRIDGE
NATIONAL MONUMENT

UTAH

ARIZONA

Monument

Valley

FOUR CORNERS
MONUMENT

To Page, and
Kayenta, AZ

© AVALON TRAVEL

opportunity. Hanksville and Blanding are good places to check your gauge; if it's showing less than half a tank, definitely fill up. Likewise, pack a lunch and plenty of water when exploring remote areas such as Cedar Mesa, Hovenweep, or Glen Canyon.

PLANNING YOUR TIME

Although it's possible to spend many days exploring the backcountry of Cedar Mesa, floating the San Juan River, houseboating to remote reaches of Lake Powell, or really getting to understand the ancient dwellings at Hovenweep National Monument, most travelers will, at least initially, just pass through. Be sure to allow a day to visit Hovenweep and the Edge of the Cedars Museum in Blanding. From there, if you are short on time, head west across Cedar Mesa to Natural Bridges National Monument and north through Hanksville to Goblin Valley State Park.

Although there are motels in all of the towns included in this chapter, you'll have more flexibility if you are camping. There are many campgrounds and even more de facto primitive campsites, where you can make your own camp; however, be certain that you have the necessary permits before camping in the Cedar Mesa area.

South of Moab

U.S. 191 runs south out of Moab, with the La Sal Mountains to the east and Canyonlands National Park to the west. A string of small towns—Monticello, Blanding, and Bluff—offer places to stop for a meal or a motel room as well as opportunities to explore mountains, desert, rivers, and archeological sites.

MONTICELLO

This small Mormon town (population 2,000) is about 50 miles south of Moab and pretty much its polar opposite. Quiet and relatively untouristed, it's the best place to stay if you're visiting the Needles District and don't want to camp. Monticello ("mon-tuh-SELL-o") is at an elevation of 7,069 feet, just east of the Abajo Mountains. It is 46 miles east of the entrance to the Needles District of Canyonlands National Park.

The local golf course, **The Hideout** (549 S. Main St., 435/587-2200, $40 for 18 holes) is popular in the summer because, at over 7,000 feet in elevation, it's not too hot.

Accommodations

Monticello has a number of comfortable and affordable motels. The **Inn at the Canyons** (533 N. Main St., 435/587-2458, www.monticellocanyonlandsinn.com, from $75) is nicely renovated and has an indoor pool, a pretty basic continental breakfast, and microwaves and fridges in the guest rooms. The **Monticello Inn** (164 E. Central St., 435/587-2274, www.themonticelloinn.org, from $65) is a well-maintained older motel with a pleasant in-town setting and a few guest rooms that allow pets.

Eight miles north of town, the **Runnin' Iron Inn** (milepost 79.5, U.S. 191, 435/587-2351, http://canyonlandsbestkeptsecret.com, from $59) is a small motel with an Old West ambience, fitting for its middle-of-nowhere location, which happens to be pretty convenient to the Needles District. If you don't need a luxurious guest room or a microwave and fridge, this is a fun place to stay. It's part of a faux-Western town called Roughlock, which also houses an RV park ($20) with tent sites ($20), a few camping cabins ($39) that have no bath or cooking facilities, and a steak house.

The local B&B, the **Grist Mill Inn** (64 S. 300 E., 435/587-2597, www.oldgristmillinn.com, from $89) is indeed housed in an old flour mill.

But rest assured, you won't be sleeping under an old millstone; the seven guest rooms are all furnished in typical B&B fashion, and all have private baths and TVs.

Camping

Campgrounds in the nearby Manti-La Sal National Forest include Buckboard and Dalton Springs (435/587-2041, $10). **Buckboard,** seven miles west of town on Blue Mountain Road (Forest Rd. 105), is at 8,600 feet in elevation, so it's not your best bet early in the spring. But when the rest of southeastern Utah swelters in the summer, this shady campground is perfect. **Dalton Springs** is along the same road, a couple of miles closer to town, at 8,200 feet. An abandoned ski area nearby is a good place for mountain biking.

Food

Not only can you get a good cup of coffee and freshly made juice at **Peace Tree Juice Cafe** (516 N. Main St., 435/587-5063, 7am-5pm daily, $79), this is also the only place this side of Moab that you're likely to get a vegetarian Thai wrap sandwich (and it tastes really good).

It's just like a backyard cookout at **K&A Chuckwagon** (196 N. Main St., 435/587-3468, 5pm-9pm daily May-Sept., $15). Settle in at one of the long tent-covered picnic tables and wait for your steak or salmon to be cooked on the big kettle grill. Chuckwagon beans and potatoes accompany the meal, and dessert is included. It's all highly informal and friendly, much like all of Monticello.

Up the road at the Roughlock encampment, the **Line Camp** (milepost 79.5, U.S. 191, 435/587-2351, 5pm-8pm daily, $17-26) is another good steak house with sides of potatoes, beans, and salad as well as a big extra helping of Western atmosphere accompanying every meal. Beer is available at this restaurant, and you can bring your own wine (free corkage).

Information and Services

The expansive new **Southeastern Utah Welcome Center** (216 S. Main St., 435/587-3401, www.southeastutah.com, 9am-6pm Wed.-Mon. Mar.-Oct., 9am-6pm Fri.-Sun. Nov.-Feb.) is a great place to stop for information about southeastern Utah, including Canyonlands National Park.

The **public library** (80 N. Main St., 435/587-2281) is in the city park.

The **San Juan Hospital** (364 W. 100 N., 435/587-2116) is friendly and small, and it's a good place to have any camping-related injuries repaired.

BLANDING

The largest town in San Juan County, Blanding (population 3,290, elevation 6,105 feet) is also a handy stop for travelers, especially for visitors to Hovenweep National Monument. If you're heading east toward Hovenweep or west into the Cedar Mesa area, check your gas gauge; Blanding is a good place to gas up.

◖ Edge of the Cedars State Park

One mile north of present-day Blanding, prehistoric Anasazi people built at least six groups of pueblo structures between 700 and 1220. The **Edge of the Cedars State Park Museum** (660 W. 400 N., 435/678-2238, www.stateparks.utah. gov, 9am-5pm Mon.-Sat., $5 adults, $3 children) features an excellent array of pottery, baskets, sandals, jewelry, and stone tools. The pottery collection on the second floor stands out for its rich variety of styles and decorative designs. The museum also has exhibits and artifacts of the people who followed the Anasazi—the Utes and Navajo and the early Anglo pioneers.

A short trail behind the museum leads past six clusters of ruins, each of which contains both rectangular rooms on the surface and circular depressions of underground kivas and pit houses. Only Complex 4 has been excavated and partly restored to suggest the village's appearance when the Anasazi lived here. You may enter the kiva by descending a ladder through the restored roof; the walls and interior features are original.

The Dinosaur Museum

The Dinosaur Museum (754 S. 200 W., 435/678-3454, www.dinosaur-museum.org, 9am-5pm Mon.-Sat. Apr. 15-Oct. 15, $3 adults, $2 seniors, $1.50 children) showcases the prehistoric plant and animal life of this corner of Utah. Exhibits include life-size models of dinosaurs as well as fossils and skeletons. Don't miss the models of feathered dinosaurs.

Accommodations

With one exception, Blanding's motels are all pretty generic. That exception is **Stone Lizard Lodging** (88 W. Center St., 435/678-3323, www.stonelizardlodging.com, $59), an older motel with nicely remodeled guest rooms at very reasonable rates. The **Four Corners Inn** (131 E. Center St., 435/678-3257 or 800/574-3150, www.fourcornersinn.com, from $62), which has a restaurant next door and a simple continental breakfast, is a fine enough place to spend a night. Another good option is the **Gateway Inn** (88 E. Center St., 435/678-2278 or 888/921-2279, http://gatewayinnblanding.com, from $66), with an outdoor pool and pet-friendly guest rooms.

CAMPGROUNDS

At the south edge of town, **Blue Mountain RV Park** (1930 S. Main St., 435/678-7840, www.bluemountainrvpark.com, $32 RVs) is also home to a trading post with some high-quality Native American rugs, jewelry, and baskets. Although tent campers are welcome at the RV park, **Devil's Canyon Campground** (reservations 877/444-6777, www.recreation.gov, $10, $9 reservation fee), at an elevation of 7,100 feet in the Manti-La Sal National Forest, is a better bet for tents. It has sites with water early May-late October (no water or fees off-season). A 0.25-mile nature trail begins at the far end of the campground loop. From

Blanding, go north eight miles on U.S. 191, then turn west onto a paved road for 1.3 miles; the turn-off from U.S. 191 is between mileposts 60 and 61.

Food

Blanding is a somewhat unlikely spot to find an outpost of the **Peace Tree Juice Cafe** (164 N. Grayson Pkwy., 435/678-3969, 7am-5pm daily, $3-8), with its vaguely hippie vibe, tasty wraps, and fresh juices. Although **Fattboyz Grillin'** (733 S. Main St., 435/678-3777, 7am-9pm daily, $5-19) is open for all meals, it's best at dinner, when the ribs are well marinated and the locals are shoulder-to-shoulder. In addition to ribs, there are chicken, burgers, and Navajo tacos on the menu. Since Blanding is a dry town, no alcohol is served.

BLUFF

Bluff, a sleepy community of about 300 inhabitants, is nestled in a striking physical location. In the past few years, Bluff has become a rather unlikely mecca for recreationists and escapees from urban congestion. The quality of lodging is better than that of almost any other town of this size in the state, and local outfitters make it easy to get out and enjoy the remarkable scenery hereabouts.

Bluff is the oldest non-Native American community in southeastern Utah; it was settled in 1880 by Mormon pioneers who had traveled the excruciatingly difficult Hole-in-the-Rock Trail from the town of Escalante down into what's now Lake Powell.

Spend an afternoon poking around local washes or examining a large pictograph panel, found along the cliff about 0.3 miles downstream from the Sand Island campground. **Fort Bluff** is being reconstructed; it is located near the north end of town. The visitors center, located in the small museum, is worth a stop; the staff can give you detailed directions for good informal hikes in the nearby washes.

If you want a guided trip into the backcountry

© JUDY JEWELL

The San Juan River runs by the town of Bluff.

of southeastern Utah, **Far Out Expeditions** (425/672-2294, www.faroutexpeditions.com) is a local company with lots of experience leading day trips and overnights in the area.

◖ Floating the San Juan River

From the high San Juan Mountains in southern Colorado, the San Juan River winds its way into New Mexico, enters Utah near Four Corners, and twists through spectacular canyons before ending at Lake Powell. Most boaters put in at Sand Island Campground near Bluff and take out at the town of Mexican Hat, 30 river miles downstream. This trip combines ancient Native American ruins, rock art, and a trip through Monument Upwarp and the Upper Canyon, with fast water for thrills (Class III rapids) and weirdly buckled geology to ponder. Longer trips continue on through the famous Goosenecks, the "entrenched meanders" carved thousands of feet below the desert surface, and through more Class III rapids on the way to

Clay Hills Crossing or Paiute Farms (not always accessible) on Lake Powell. Allow at least four days for the full trip, though more time will allow for exploration of side canyons and visits to Anasazi sites. Rafts, kayaks, and canoes can be used. The season usually lasts year-round because of adequate water flow from Navajo Reservoir upstream.

Many commercial river-running companies offer San Juan trips. If you go on your own, you should have river-running experience or be with someone who does. Private groups need to obtain permits ($6-18 pp) from the Bureau of Land Management's San Juan Resource Area office (435/587-1544, www.blm.gov); permits are issued through a preseason lottery, although boaters with flexible schedules can usually get permits close to their time of travel. Permit fees vary depending on how far you're floating.

Some people also like to run the river between Montezuma Creek and Sand Island, a leisurely trip of 20 river miles. The solitude often makes up for the lack of scenery. It's easy to get a river permit for this section because no use limits or fees apply.

If you're looking for a multiday trip on the San Juan River, contact local **Wild Rivers Expeditions** (101 Main St., 435/672-2244 or 800/422-7654, www.riversandruins.com), which offers both day and multiday trips out of Bluff; trips run daily in summer, and only a day's notice is usually needed to join a float. Eight-hour, 26-mile day excursions to Mexican Hat cost $165 adults, $123 under age 13; motors may be used if the water level is low. Some of the larger Moab-based outfitters offer San Juan River trips when interest allows.

Accommodations

Attractive ◖ **Desert Rose Inn** (701 W. Main St., 735/672-2303 or 888/475-7673, www.desertroseinn.com, from $119) is one of the nicest lodgings in this corner of the state. The large lodge-like log structure has two-story wraparound porches and guest rooms furnished with pine furniture, quilts, and Southwestern art. At the edge of the property are a number of handsome one-bedroom log cabins. This is definitely a class act.

The other great place to stay is **Recapture Lodge** (220 E. Main St., 435/672-2281, www.recapturelodge.com, $75). For many years the heart and soul of Bluff, the lodge is operated by longtime outfitters and has an easy nonchalance that is immediately welcoming. Besides guest rooms and kitchenettes, Recapture Lodge has trails out the back door, a swimming pool, a hot tub, a coin laundry, tours, and llama pack trips. The Recapture also rents a couple of fully equipped homes in Bluff for families and groups.

Kokopelli Inn Motel (160 E. Main St., 435/672-2322, www.kokoinn.com, from $82), just next door to the Recapture, is a fine place to stay, though it pales in comparison to Bluff's unique lodges.

CAMPGROUNDS

Sand Island Recreation Area (435/587-1500, www.blm.gov, $10) is a Bureau of Land Management (BLM) camping area along the San Juan River, three miles south of town, with piped water. Large cottonwood trees shade this pretty spot, but tenters need to watch for thorns in the grass. River-runners often put in at the campground, so it can be a busy place. Two RV parks are right in town: **Cadillac Ranch RV Park** (U.S. 191, 435/672-2262, www.cadillacranchrv.com, year-round, $28) is in the center of town and **Cottonwood R.V. Park** (U.S. 191, 435/672-2287, http://cottonwoodrvpark.blogspot.com, Mar. 15-Nov. 15, $30) is at the west end of Bluff.

Food

It's worth spending the night in Bluff just to eat at the ◖ **San Juan River Kitchen** (435/672-9956, www.sanjuanriverkitchen.com, 5:30-about 9pm Tues.-Sat., $10-18), where as much food as possible comes from the restaurant's organic garden. The food is not just local; it's also delicious. Smoked chicken enchiladas feature homemade green chili, and a steak-and-egg sandwich turns into a real treat when braised chard and grilled mushrooms share the space between slices of *ciabatta*. The kitchen serves good beer and wine, which is not so easy to come by in these parts. Lastly, the space is quite lovely—modern and simple yet warm.

A longtime local hangout and a good place for a meal and a friendly vibe is the **Twin Rocks Cafe** (435/672-2341, www.twinrockscafe.com, 7am-8pm daily, $5-20), next to the trading post just below the impossible-to-miss Twin Rocks. Here you can dine on Navajo tacos (fry bread with chili) or Navajo pizza (fry bread with pizza toppings) as well as more standard fare. Be sure to visit the trading post for high-quality Native American crafts, many of them produced locally by Navajo artisans.

Settle in under the big cottonwood tree for a

© PAUL LEVY

Hovenweep was the site of six Anasazi villages.

flame-grilled steak dinner at the **Cottonwood Steakhouse** (Main St. and 4th St. E., 435/672-2282, 5:30pm-9:30pm daily spring-fall, $17-25). Dinners come with salad, beans, and potatoes; for $9, you can split an entrée with someone else and get full servings of side dishes. Indoor dining is also an option.

Stop by the **Comb Ridge Coffee House** (680 S. U.S. 191, 435/672-9931, 7am-5pm Tues.-Sun., sandwiches $5-6.25) for a breakfast muffin or slice of quiche, a cup of coffee, and a dose of friendly community spirit. Premade sandwiches and ice cream round out the menu at this sweet spot.

◖ HOVENWEEP NATIONAL MONUMENT

Delve into the region's cultural history and architecture at remote Hovenweep National Monument (970/562-4283, www.nps.gov/hove, $6 per vehicle, $3 cyclists and pedestrians, $25 annual Local Passport also includes entrance to Canyonlands and Arches National Parks and Natural Bridges National Monument), where the Anasazi built many impressive masonry buildings during the early-mid-1200s, near the end of their 1,300-year stay in the area. A drought that began in 1274 and lasted 25 years probably hastened their migration from this area. Several centuries of intensive farming, hunting, and woodcutting had already taken a toll on the land. Archaeologists believe the inhabitants retreated south in the late 1200s to sites in northwestern New Mexico and northeastern Arizona. The Ute word *hovenweep* means "deserted valley," an appropriate name for the lonely high-desert country they left behind. The Anasazi at Hovenweep had much in common with the Mesa Verde culture, although the Dakota sandstone here doesn't form large alcoves suitable for cliff-dweller villages. Ruins at Hovenweep remain essentially unexcavated, awaiting the attention of future archaeologists.

The Anasazi farmers had a keen interest in the seasons because of their need to know the best time for planting crops. Astronomical stations (alignments of walls, doorways, and tiny openings) allowed the sun priests to determine the equinoxes and solstices with an accuracy of 1-2 days. This precision also may have been necessary for a complex ceremonial calendar. Astronomical stations at Hovenweep have been discovered at Hovenweep Castle, House of Square Tower Ruins, and Cajon Ruins.

Planning Your Time

Hovenweep National Monument protects six groups of villages left behind by the Anasazi. The sites are near the Colorado border, southeast of Blanding. **Square Tower Ruins Unit,** where the visitors center is located, has the most ruins and the most varied architecture. In fact, you can find all of the Hovenweep architectural styles here. There are other ruins that are good to visit if you'd like to spend more time in the area; you'll need a map and directions from a ranger to find them because they aren't signed. One group, the Goodman Point, near Cortez, Colorado, offers relatively little to see except unexcavated mounds.

Visitors Center

The visitors center (970/562-4282, 8am-6pm daily May-Sept., 8am-5pm daily Apr. and Oct., 8am-4:30pm daily Nov.-Mar.) has a few exhibits on the Anasazi, photos of local wildlife, and a small bookstore. A ranger can answer your questions, provide brochures and handouts about various aspects of the monument, and give directions for visiting the other groups of ruins. Mesa Verde National Park (970/529-4465, www.nps.gov/meve) administers Hovenweep.

Square Tower Ruins

This extensive group of Anasazi towers and dwellings lines the rim and slopes of Little Ruin Canyon, located a short walk from the visitors center. Obtain a trail-guide booklet from the ranger station. You can take easy walks of less than 0.5 miles on the rim; combine all the trails for a loop of about two miles with only one up-and-down section in the canyon. The booklet has good descriptions of Anasazi life and architecture and of the plants growing along the trail. You'll see towers (D-shaped, square, oval, and round), cliff dwellings, surface dwellings, storehouses, kivas, and rock art. Keep an eye out for the prairie rattlesnake, a subspecies of the Western rattlesnake, which is active at night in summer and during the day in spring and fall. And stay on the trail: Don't climb the fragile walls of the ruins or walk on rubble mounds.

Holly Ruins

Holly Ruins group is noted for its Great House, Holly Tower, and Tilted Tower. Most of Tilted Tower fell away after the boulder on which it sat shifted. Great piles of rubble mark the sites of structures built on loose ground. Look for remnants of farming terraces in the canyon below the Great House. A hiking trail connects the campground at Square Tower Ruins with Holly Ruins; the route follows canyon bottoms and is about eight miles round-trip. Ask a ranger for a map and directions. Hikers can also continue to Horseshoe Ruins (one mile farther) and Hackberry Ruins (just beyond Horseshoe). All of these are just across the Colorado border and about six miles one-way by road from the visitors center.

Horseshoe and Hackberry Ruins

Horseshoe Ruins and Hackberry Ruins are best reached by an easy trail (one mile round-trip) off the road to Holly Ruins. Horseshoe House, built in a horseshoe shape similar to Sun Temple at Mesa Verde, has exceptionally good masonry work. Archaeologists haven't determined the purpose of the structure. An alcove in the canyon below contains a spring and a small shelter. A round tower nearby on the rim has a strategic view. Hackberry House has only one room still intact. Rubble piles and wall remnants abound in the area. The spring under an alcove here still has a good flow and supports lush growths of hackberry and cottonwood trees along with smaller plants.

Cutthroat Castle Ruins

Cutthroat Castle Ruins were remote even in Anasazi times. The ruins lie along an intermittent stream rather than at the head of a canyon like most other Hovenweep sites. Cutthroat Castle is a large multistory structure with both straight and curved walls. Three round towers stand nearby. Look for wall fragments and the circular depressions of kivas. High-clearance vehicles can get close to the ruins, about 11.5 miles one-way from the visitors center. Visitors with cars can drive to a trailhead and then walk to the ruins, 1.5 miles round-trip on foot.

Cajon Ruins

Cajon Ruins are at the head of a little canyon on Cajon Mesa on the Navajo Reservation in Utah, about nine miles southwest of the visitors center. The site has a commanding view across the San Juan Valley as far as Monument Valley. Buildings include a large multiroom structure, a round tower, and a tall square tower. An alcove just below has a spring and some rooms. Look for pictographs, petroglyphs, and grooves in the rock used for tool grinding. Farming terraces were located on the canyon's south side.

Camping

A small **campground** near the visitors center (no reservations, $10) has 31 sites geared toward tent campers, although a few sites will accommodate RVs up to 36 feet long. Running water is available only during summer, when five gallons are allotted to each camper. Like Hovenweep's ancient inhabitants, campers are often treated to excellent stargazing; the monument is far from light pollution, and the dark night skies are frequently clear.

Getting There

One approach is from U.S. 191 between Blanding and Bluff; head east nine miles on Highway 262, continue straight six miles on a small paved road to Hatch Trading Post, and then follow the signs for 16 miles. A good way in from Bluff is to go east 21 miles on the paved road to Montezuma Creek and Aneth, then follow the signs north for 20 miles. A scenic 58-mile route through Montezuma Canyon begins five miles south of Monticello and follows unpaved roads to Hatch and on to Hovenweep; you can stop at the BLM's Three Turkey Ruin on the way. From Colorado, take a partly paved road west and north 41 miles from U.S. 491 (the turnoff is four miles south of Cortez).

Don't expect your cell phone to work in this remote area.

Cedar Mesa and Vicinity

Head way off the beaten track to explore ancient ruins and stunning geography in the area west of U.S. 191 and east of Glen Canyon and Lake Powell. Experienced hikers can wander deep into this rugged area; those with less experience or fortitude may want to focus on the trails at Natural Bridges National Monument.

CEDAR MESA

Just south of Blanding, Highway 95—here labeled Trail of the Ancients National Scenic Byway—heads west across a high plateau toward the Colorado River, traversing Comb Ridge, Cedar Mesa, and many canyons. This is remote country, so fill up with gas before leaving Blanding; you can't depend on finding gasoline until Hanksville, 122 miles away. Hite and the other Lake Powell marinas do have gas and supplies, but their hours are limited.

Cedar Mesa and its canyons have an exceptionally large number of prehistoric Anasazi sites. Several ruins are just off the highway, and hikers will discover many more. If you would like to explore the Cedar Mesa area, be sure to drop in at the **Kane Gulch Ranger Station** (435/587-1532, www.blm.gov, 8am-noon daily spring and fall), at the west end of Cedar Mesa, four miles south of Highway 95 on Highway 261. BLM staff issue the permits required to explore the Cedar Mesa backcountry for day-use ($2) and for overnight stays ($8 pp) in Grand Gulch, Fish Creek Canyon, and Owl Creek Canyon. The number of people permitted to camp at a given time is limited, so call ahead. BLM staff will also tell you about archaeological sites and their historic value, current hiking conditions, and where to find water. Cedar Mesa is managed for more primitive recreation, so hikers in the area should have good route-finding skills and come prepared with food and water. The ranger station sells maps but has no water.

Butler Wash Ruins

Well-preserved pueblo ruins left by the Anasazi are tucked under an overhang across the wash. Find the trailhead on the north side of Highway 95, 11 miles west of U.S. 191, between mileposts 111 and 112. Follow cairns for 0.5 miles through juniper and piñon pine woodlands and across slickrock to the overlook, where you can see four kivas and several other structures. Parts have been reconstructed, but most of the site is about 900 years old.

Comb Ridge

Geologic forces have squeezed up the earth's crust in a long ridge running 80 miles south from the Abajo Peaks into Arizona. Sheer cliffs plunge 800 feet into Comb Wash on the west side. Engineering the highway down these cliffs took considerable effort. A parking area near the top of the grade offers expansive panoramas across Comb Wash.

Arch Canyon

This tributary canyon of Comb Wash has spectacular scenery and many Native American ruins. Much of the canyon can be seen on a day hike, but 2-3 days are required to explore the upper reaches. The main streambeds usually have water, but purify it before drinking it. To reach the trailhead, turn north onto Comb Wash Road (between mileposts 107 and 108 on Hwy. 95) and go 2.5 miles on the dirt road, past a house and a water tank, then park in a grove of cottonwood trees before a stream. The mouth of pretty Arch Canyon is just to the northwest (it's easy to miss). Look for a Native American ruin just up Arch Canyon on the right. More ruins are tucked under alcoves farther up-canyon.

Arch Canyon Overlook

A road and a short trail to the rim of Arch Canyon provide a beautiful view into the depths. Turn north on Texas Flat Road (County Rd. 263) from Highway 95, between mileposts 102 and 103, continue four miles, park just before the road begins a steep climb, and walk east on an old jeep road to the rim. This is a fine place for a picnic, although there are no facilities or guardrails. Texas Flat Road is dirt but passable when dry for cars with good clearance. Trucks can continue up the steep hill to other viewpoints of Arch and Texas Canyons.

Mule Canyon Ruin

Archaeologists have excavated and stabilized this Anasazi village on the gentle slope of Mule Canyon's South Fork. A stone kiva, circular tower, and 12-room structure are all visible, and all were originally connected by tunnels. Cave Towers, two miles southeast, would have been visible from the top of the tower here. Signs describe the ruins and periods of Anasazi development. Turn north from Highway 95 between mileposts 101 and 102 and continue 0.3 miles on a paved road. Hikers can explore other ruins in the North and South Forks of Mule Canyon; check with the Kane Gulch Ranger Station for advice and directions. You might see pieces of pottery and other artifacts in this area. Federal laws prohibit the removal of artifacts: Please leave every piece in place so that future visitors can enjoy the discovery too. Be sure to have a BLM day hiking permit when exploring this area.

GRAND GULCH PRIMITIVE AREA

Within this twisting canyon system are some of the most captivating scenery and largest concentrations of Anasazi ruins in southeastern Utah. The main canyon begins only about six miles southeast of Natural Bridges National Monument. From an elevation of 6,400 feet, Grand Gulch cuts deeply into Cedar Mesa on a tortuous path southwest to the San Juan River, dropping 2,700 feet in about 53 miles. Sheer cliffs, alcoves, pinnacles, Anasazi cliff dwellings, rock-art sites, arches, and a few natural bridges line Grand Gulch and its many tributaries.

From the Kane Gulch Ranger Station, a trail leads four miles down Kane Gulch to the upper end of Grand Gulch, where a camping area is shaded by cottonwood trees. Junction Ruin, a cave dwelling, is visible from here, and less than one mile farther into Grand Gulch are more ruins and an arch.

Kane Gulch and Bullet Canyon provide access to the upper end of Grand Gulch from the east side. A popular loop hike using these canyons is 23 miles long (3-4 days); arrange a 7.5-mile car shuttle or hitch. Ask at the ranger station if a shuttle service is available. Collins Canyon, reached from Collins Spring Trailhead, leads into lower Grand Gulch from the west side. Hiking distance between Kane Gulch and Collins Spring Trailheads is 38 miles one-way (5-7 days). A car

shuttle of about 29 miles (including eight miles of dirt road) is required. Be sure to visit the BLM's Kane Gulch Ranger Station or Monticello office for a permit and information. You must have a day-use ($2) or overnight camping permit ($8) to enter the area.

MEXICAN HAT

South of the Kane Gulch Ranger Station, Highway 261 loses its pavement and becomes contorted into a series of steeply banked switchbacks known as the Moki Dugway. Slow down and take this stretch of road (with 1,100 feet of elevation change and 5-10 percent grades) at 5-10 mph. About 10 miles south of the Dugway is the town of Mexican Hat, a modest trade and tourism center.

Spectacular geology surrounds this tiny community perched on the north bank of the San Juan River. Folded layers of red and gray rock stand out dramatically. Alhambra Rock, a jagged remnant of a volcano, marks the

© BILL MCRAE

Mexican Hat is about 10 miles south of the Moki Dugway, a series of steep switchbacks.

© JUDY JEWELL

The tightly wound San Juan River flows 1,000 feet below this viewpoint at Goosenecks State Park.

southern approach to Mexican Hat. Another rock, which looks just like an upside-down sombrero, gave Mexican Hat its name; you'll see this formation from U.S. 163, two miles north of town. Monument Valley, Valley of the Gods Scenic Drive, Goosenecks State Park, and Grand Gulch Primitive Area are only short drives away. The riverbanks near town can be a busy place in summer as river-runners on the San Juan put in, take out, or just stop for ice and beer.

Goosenecks State Park

The San Juan River winds through a series of incredibly tight bends 1,000 feet below. So closely spaced are the bends that the river takes six miles to cover an air distance of only 1.5 miles. The bends and exposed rock layers form exquisitely graceful curves. Geologists know the site as a classic example of entrenched mean-ders, caused by gradual uplift of a formerly level plain. Signs at the overlook explain the geo-logic history and identify the rock formations.

Goosenecks State Park (435/678-2238, http://stateparks.utah.gov) is an undeveloped area with a few picnic tables and vault toilets. A **campground** (free) is available but has no water. From the junction of U.S. 163 and Highway 261, four miles north of Mexican Hat, go one mile northwest on Highway 261, then turn left and go three miles on Highway 316 to its end.

Muley Point Overlook

One of the great views in the Southwest is just a short drive from Goosenecks State Park and more than 1,000 feet higher in elevation. Although the view of the Goosenecks below is less dramatic than at the state park, the 6,200-foot elevation provides a magnificent panorama across the Navajo Reservation to Monument Valley and countless canyons and moun-tains. To get here, travel northwest nine miles on Highway 261 from the Goosenecks turn-off. At the top of the Moki Dugway switch-backs, turn left (southwest) and go 5.3 miles on gravel County Road 241 (the turnoff may

SOUTHEASTERN CORNER

not be signed), and follow it toward the point. This road is not suitable for wet-weather travel.

Accommodations and Food

The **San Juan Inn and Trading Post** (435/683-2220 or 800/447-2022, www.sanjuaninn.net, from $84), at a dramatic location above the river, just west of town, offers clean guest rooms without extras, a few yurts, Native American trade goods, and a restaurant, the **Olde Bridge Bar and Grill** (435/683-2220, 7am-9pm daily, $8-15), serving American, Mexican, and Navajo food. **Hat Rock Inn** (435/683-2221, www.hatrockinn.com, $145) offers the nicest guest rooms in town and a swimming pool. **Mexican Hat Lodge** (435/683-2222, www.mexicanhat.net, from $84) offers guest rooms, a pool, and a fun but somewhat expensive restaurant (lunch and dinner daily) with grilled steaks and burgers.

Valle's Trading Post and RV Park (435/683-2226, year-round, $20), has tent and RV sites with hookups. The camping area is pretty basic, but great scenery surrounds it. The trading post offers crafts, groceries, showers, vehicle storage, and car shuttles. **Goosenecks State Park** has free camping with great views but no amenities.

Valley of the Gods

Great sandstone monoliths, delicate spires, and long rock fins rise from the broad valley. This strange red-rock landscape resembles better-known Monument Valley but on a smaller scale. A 17-mile dirt road winds through the spectacular scenery. Cars can usually travel the road at low speeds if the weather is dry (the road crosses washes). Allow 1-1.5 hours for the drive; it's studded with viewpoints, and you'll want to stop at all of them. The east end of the road connects with U.S. 163 at milepost 29 (7.5 miles northeast of Mexican Hat, 15 miles southwest of Bluff); the west end connects with Highway 261 just below the Moki Dugway switchbacks

(four miles north of Mexican Hat on U.S. 163, then 6.6 miles northwest on Hwy. 261).

MONUMENT VALLEY

Towering buttes, jagged pinnacles, and rippled sand dunes make this area along the Utah-Arizona border an otherworldly landscape. Changing colors and shifting shadows during the day add to the enchantment. Most of the natural monuments are remnants of sandstone eroded by wind and water. Agathla Peak and some lesser summits are the roots of ancient volcanoes, whose dark rock contrasts with the pale yellow sandstone of the other formations. The valley is at an elevation of 5,564 feet in the Upper Sonoran Life Zone; annual rainfall averages about 8.5 inches.

In 1863-1864, when Kit Carson was ravaging Canyon de Chelly in Arizona to round up the Navajo, Chief Hoskinini led his people to the safety and freedom of Monument Valley.

Hollywood movies made the splendor of Monument Valley widely known to the outside world. *Stagecoach,* filmed here in 1938 and directed by John Ford, became the first in a series of Westerns that has continued to the present. John Wayne and many other movie greats rode across these sands.

The Navajo have preserved the valley as a park with a scenic drive, visitors center, and campground. From Mexican Hat, drive 22 miles southwest on U.S. 163, and turn left and go 3.5 miles to the visitors center. At the turnoff on U.S. 163 is a village's worth of outdoor market stalls and a modern complex of enclosed shops where you can stop to buy Navajo art and crafts.

Visitors Center

At the entrance to the **Monument Valley Navajo Tribal Park** is a visitors center (435/727-5874, 6am-8pm daily May-Sept., 8am-5pm daily Oct.-Apr., $5 pp age 10 and up, free under age 10) with exhibits and crafts. This is a good place to get a list of Navajo tour guides to lead you on driving or hiking trips into the monument. Lots of folks along the road will also offer these services.

Tours

Take one of several guided tours leaving daily year-round from the visitors center to visit sites such as a hogan, a cliff dwelling, and petroglyphs in areas beyond the self-guided drive. The trips last 1.5-4 hours and cost $45-90 pp. Guided horseback rides from near the visitors center cost around $75 for two hours; longer day and overnight trips can be arranged too. If you'd like to hike in Monument Valley, you must hire a guide. Hiking tours of two hours to a full day or more can be arranged at the visitors center.

Monument Valley Drive

A 17-mile self-guided scenic drive (6am-8:30pm daily May-Sept., 8am-4:30pm daily Oct.-Apr.) begins at the visitors center and loops through the heart of the valley. Overlooks provide sweeping views from different vantage points. The dirt road is normally OK for cautiously driven cars. Avoid stopping or you may get stuck in the loose sand that sometimes blows across the road. Allow 90 minutes for the drive. No hiking or driving is allowed off the signed route. Water and restrooms are available only at the visitors center.

Accommodations

Don't be surprised to find that lodgings at Monument Valley are expensive; they're also extremely popular, so be sure to book well ahead.

The Navajo-owned **◖ View Hotel** (435/727-5555, www.monumentvalleyview.com, from $199) provides the only lodging in Monument Valley Tribal Park. Views are terrific from this stylish newer hotel; reserve a room well in advance.

◖ Goulding's Lodge and Trading Post (435/727-3231, www.gouldings.com, from $140) is another great place to stay in the

Monument Valley area. Harry Goulding and his wife, Mike, opened this dramatically located trading post in 1924. It's a large complex tucked under the rimrocks two miles west of the U.S. 163 Monument Valley turn-off, just north of the Arizona-Utah border. Modern motel rooms offer incredible views of Monument Valley. Guests can use a small indoor pool; meals are available in the dining room. A gift shop sells a wide range of souvenirs, books, and Native American crafts. The nearby store has groceries and gas pumps, a restaurant is open daily for all meals, and tours and horseback rides are available. The lodge stays open year-round, and rates drop in winter and early spring. Goulding's Museum, in the old trading post building, displays prehistoric and modern artifacts, movie photos, and memorabilia of the Goulding family. The Gouldings **campground** ($25 without hookups, $42 with hookups) is pleasant and well managed.

About 30 minutes south in Kayenta, Arizona, the adobe-style **Hampton Inn** (U.S. 160, 520/697-3170 or 800/426-7866, from $189) is the nicest place in town, and it's only a little more expensive than its Kayenta neighbors.

◖ NATURAL BRIDGES NATIONAL MONUMENT

Streams in White Canyon and its tributaries cut deep canyons, then formed three impressive bridges, now protected as Natural Bridges National Monument (435/692-1234, www.nps.gov/nabr, $6 per vehicle, $3 cyclists and pedestrians, $25 annual Local Passport also includes entrance to Natural Bridges and Hovenweep National Monuments and Arches and Canyonlands National Parks). Silt-laden floodwaters sculpted the bridges by gouging tunnels between closely spaced loops in the meandering canyons. You can distinguish a natural bridge from an arch because the bridge spans a streambed and was initially carved out of the rock by flowing water. In the

© PAUL LEVY

the fragile and elegant Owachomo Bridge, in Natural Bridges National Monument

monument, these bridges illustrate three different stages of development, from the massive, newly formed Kachina Bridge to the middle-aged Sipapu Bridge to the delicate and fragile span of Owachomo. All three natural bridges will continue to widen and eventually collapse under their own weight. A nine-mile scenic drive has overlooks of the picturesque bridges, Anasazi ruins, and twisting canyons. You can follow short trails down from the rim to the base of each bridge or hike through all three bridges on an 8.6-mile loop.

Ruins, artifacts, and rock art indicate a long occupation by Native Americans ranging from archaic groups to the Anasazi. Many fine cliff dwellings built by the Anasazi still stand. In 1883, prospector Cass Hite passed on tales of the huge stone bridges that he had discovered on a trip up White Canyon. Adventurous travelers, including those on a 1904 *National Geographic* magazine expedition, visited this isolated region to marvel at the bridges. The

public's desire for protection of the bridges led President Theodore Roosevelt to proclaim the area a national monument in 1908. Federal administrators then changed the original bridge names from Edwin, Augusta, and Caroline to the Hopi names used today. Although the Hopi never lived here, the Anasazi of White Canyon very likely have descendants in the modern Hopi villages in Arizona.

Visitors Center

From the signed junction on Highway 95, it is 4.5 miles on Highway 275 to the visitors center (435/692-1234, 8am-6pm daily May-Sept., 8am-5pm daily Apr. and Oct., 8am-4:30pm daily Nov.-Mar.), at an elevation of 6,505 feet. Monument Valley Overlook, two miles in, offers views south across a vast expanse of piñon pine and juniper to Monument Valley and distant mountains. A slide show in the visitors center illustrates how geologic forces and erosion created the canyons and natural bridges. Exhibits introduce the people who once lived here, as well as the area's geology, wildlife, and plants. Outside, labels identify common plants of the monument.

Rangers can answer your questions about the monument and the surrounding area. If asked, staff will provide details on locations of ruins and rock art sites. You can purchase regional books, topographic and geologic maps, postcards, and slides. Checklists of birds, other wildlife, and plants are available too.

The Bridge View Drive is always open during daylight hours, except after heavy snowstorms. A winter visit can be very enjoyable; ice or mud often close the steep Sipapu and Kachina Trails, but the short trail to Owachomo Bridge usually stays open. Pets aren't allowed on the trails or in the backcountry at any time.

Other than the small but popular campground at the national monument, the nearest accommodations are 40 miles east near Blanding or 50 miles west at Hite.

Bright Sun, Dark Nights

A large **solar electric-power station** is across the road from the visitors center. This demonstration system, the largest in the world when it was constructed in 1980, has 250,000 solar cells spread over nearly an acre and produces up to 100 kilowatts. Batteries, located elsewhere, store a two-day supply of power. The monument is far from the nearest power lines, so the solar cells provide an alternative to continuously running diesel-powered generators.

When the sun sets, Natural Bridges becomes one of the darkest places in the United States. In fact, the International Dark Sky Association has named this the world's first dark-sky park. Come here for some serious stargazing!

Bridge View Drive

This nine-mile drive begins its one-way loop just past the campground. You can stop for lunch at a picnic area. Allow about 1.5 hours

for a quick trip around. To make all the stops and do a bit of leisurely hiking takes most of a day. The cross-bedded sandstone of the bridges and canyons is part of the 265-million-year-old Cedar Mesa Formation.

Sipapu Bridge viewpoint is two miles from the visitors center. The Hopi name refers to the gateway from which their ancestors entered this world from another world below. Sipapu Bridge has reached its mature or middle-age stage of development. The bridge is the largest in the monument and has a span of 268 feet and a height of 220 feet. Many people think Sipapu is the most magnificent of the bridges. Another view and a trail to the base of Sipapu are 0.8 miles farther. The viewpoint is about halfway down on an easy trail; allow half an hour. A steeper and rougher trail branches off the viewpoint trail and winds down to the bottom of White Canyon, which is probably the best place to fully appreciate the bridge's size. The total round-trip distance is 1.2 miles, with an elevation change of 600 feet.

Horse Collar Ruin, built by the Anasazi, looks as though it has been abandoned for just a few decades, not 800 years. A short trail leads to an overlook 3.1 miles from the visitors center. The name comes from the shape of the doorway openings in two storage rooms. Hikers walking in the canyon between Sipapu and Kachina Bridges can scramble up a steep rock slope to the site. Like all ancient ruins, these are fragile and must not be touched or entered. Only with such care will future generations of visitors be able to admire the well-preserved structures. Other groups of Anasazi dwellings can also be seen in or near the monument; ask a ranger for directions.

The **Kachina Bridge** viewpoint and trailhead are 5.1 miles from the visitors center. The massive bridge has a span of 204 feet and a height of 210 feet. A trail, 1.5 miles round-trip, leads to the canyon bottom next to the bridge; the elevation change is 650 feet. Look for pictographs near the base of the trail. Some of the figures resemble Hopi kachinas (spirits) and inspired the bridge's name. Armstrong Canyon joins White Canyon just downstream from the bridge; floods in each canyon abraded opposite sides of the rock fin that later became Kachina Bridge.

The **Owachomo Bridge** viewpoint and trailhead are 7.1 miles from the visitors center. An easy walk leads to Owachomo's base—0.5 miles round-trip with an elevation change of 180 feet. Graceful Owachomo spans 180 feet and is 106 feet high. Erosive forces have worn the venerable bridge to a thickness of only nine feet. Unlike the other two bridges, Owachomo spans a smaller tributary stream instead of a major canyon. Two streams played a role in the bridge's formation. Floods coming down the larger Armstrong Canyon surged against a sandstone fin on one side while floods in a small side canyon wore away the rock on the other side. Eventually a hole formed, and waters flowing down the side canyon took the shorter route through the bridge. The word *owachomo* means "flat-rock mound" in the Hopi language; a large rock outcrop nearby inspired the name. Before construction of the present road, a trail winding down the opposite side of Armstrong Canyon provided the only access for monument visitors. The trail, little used now, connects with Highway 95.

Natural Bridges Loop Trail

- Distance: 8.6 miles round-trip
- Duration: 5-6 hours
- Elevation change: 500 feet
- Effort: moderate-strenuous
- Trailhead: Sipapu Bridge

A canyon hike through all three bridges can be the highlight of a visit to the monument. Unmaintained trails make a loop in White and Armstrong Canyons and cross a wooded plateau.

The trip is easier if you start from Sipapu and come out on the relatively gentle grades at Owachomo. You can save 2.5 miles by arranging a car shuttle between the Sipapu and Owachomo trailheads. Another option is to go in or out on the Kachina Bridge Trail midway to cut the hiking distance in half. As you near Owachomo Bridge from below, a small sign points out the trail, which bypasses a deep pool. The canyons remain in their wild state; you'll need some hiking experience, water, proper footwear, a compass, and a map (the handout available at the visitors center is adequate). The USGS 7.5-minute topographic maps also cover this area.

When hiking in the canyons, keep an eye out for natural arches and Native American writing. Try not to step on midget faded rattlesnakes or other living entities (including the fragile cryptobiotic soil). And beware of flash floods, especially if you see big clouds billowing in the sky in an upstream direction. You don't need a hiking permit, although it's a good idea to talk beforehand with a ranger to find out current conditions. Overnight camping within the monument is permitted only in the campground. Backpackers, however, can go up or down the canyons and camp outside the monument boundaries. Note that vehicles can't be parked overnight on the loop drive.

Campgrounds

The **Natural Bridges Campground** (first-come, first-served, year-round, $10) is in a forest of piñon pine and juniper. Obtain water from a faucet in front of the visitors center. Rangers give talks several evenings each week during the summer season. The campground is often full, but there is a rather grim designated overflow area near the intersection of Highways 95 and 261. RVs and trailers longer than 26 feet must use this parking area. To reach the campground, drive 0.3 miles past the visitors center and turn right.

Lake Powell and Glen Canyon

Lake Powell is at the center of the Glen Canyon National Recreation Area (520/608-6404, 7 days $15 per vehicle or $7 cyclists and pedestrians, no charge for passing through Page on U.S. 89), a vast land covering 1.25 million acres in Arizona and Utah. When the Glen Canyon Dam was completed in 1964, conservationists deplored the loss of the remote and beautiful Glen Canyon of the Colorado River beneath the lake's waters. In terms of beauty and sheer drama, Glen Canyon was considered the equal of the Grand Canyon. Today, we have only words, pictures, and memories to remind us of its wonders. On the other hand, the 186-mile-long lake now provides easy access to an area most had not even known existed. Lake Powell is the second-largest artificial lake in the United States. Only Lake Mead,

farther downstream, has a greater water-storage capacity. Lake Powell, however, has three times more shoreline—1,960 miles—and when full, it holds enough water to cover the state of Pennsylvania one foot deep. Just a handful of roads approach the lake, so access is basically limited to boats—bays and coves offer nearly limitless opportunities for exploration by boaters—as well as long-distance hiking trails.

NATURAL BRIDGES TO BULLFROG MARINA BY FERRY

Eight miles west of the entrance to Natural Bridges National Monument, travelers must make a decision: whether to continue on Highway 95 to cross the Colorado by bridge at Hite or to follow Highway 276 to the Halls Crossing Marina and cross the river, at this point tamed by the Glen Canyon Dam and known as Lake Powell, by car ferry.

Obviously, the ferry is the more exotic choice, and both Halls Crossing and Bullfrog Marinas offer lodging and food, a relative scarcity in this remote area. Crossing the Colorado on the ferry also makes it easy to access Bullfrog-Notom Road, which climbs for 60 miles through dramatic landscapes on its way to Capitol Reef National Park's otherwise remote Waterfold Pocket. The road ends at Notom, just four miles from the eastern entrance to Capitol Reef Park on Highway 24. Drivers can also turn west on the Burr Trail and follow back roads to Boulder, near the Escalante River Canyon.

Halls Crossing and Bullfrog Ferry

At the junction of Highways 95 and 276, a large sign lists the departure times for the ferry; note that these may be different than the times listed in the widely circulated flyer or on the website. Confirm the departure times (435/684-3088,

© JUDY JEWELL

A ferry crosses Lake Powell from Halls Crossing to Bullfrog.

www.udot.utah.gov) before making the 42-mile journey to Halls Crossing.

The crossing time for the three-mile trip from Halls Crossing to Bullfrog is 27 minutes. Fares are $25 for cars, which includes the driver and all passengers, $10 bicycles and foot passengers, and $15 motorcycles. Vehicles longer than 20 feet pay $1.50 per foot.

Ferry service runs late April-early October, and there's a trip every other hour daily beginning with the 9am boat from Halls Landing, which then leaves Bullfrog at 10am The final ferry from Halls Crossing departs at 3pm, and the final ferry from Bullfrog departs at 4pm The ferry does not run early October-late April.

If drought or downstream demand lowers the level of Lake Powell beyond a certain point, there may not be enough water for the ferry to operate. If this is the case, there will be notices about the ferry's status at just about every park visitors center in southern Utah.

For reservations and information regarding lodging, camping, tours, boating, and recreation at both Halls Crossing and Bullfrog Marina, contact **Lake Powell Resorts & Marinas** (888/896-3829, www.lakepowell.com).

Arriving at Halls Crossing by road, you'll first reach a small store offering three-bedroom units in trailer houses and an RV park. Continue for 0.5 miles on the main road to the boat ramp and **Halls Crossing Marina** (435/684-2261). The marina has a larger store (groceries and fishing and boating supplies), tours to Rainbow Bridge, a boat-rental office (fishing, waterskiing, and houseboats), a gas dock, slips, and storage. The **ranger station** is nearby, although rangers are usually out on patrol; look for their vehicle in the area if the office is closed.

On the western side of the lake, **Bullfrog Marina** is more like a small town (albeit one run by Aramark), with a **visitors center** (435/684-7420), a clinic, stores, a service station, and a handsome hotel and restaurant. The marina rents boats ranging from kayaks ($45 per day) to 12-person party boats ($600 per day) to houseboats ($4,320-15,000 per week), but for guided boat tours of Lake Powell, you'll have to go to the Wahweap Marina near Page, Arizona.

Defiance House Lodge (888/896-3829, www.lakepowell.com, from $146) offers comfortable lake-view accommodations and the **Anasazi Restaurant** (breakfast, lunch, and dinner daily summer, $9-32). The front desk at the lodge also handles family units (well-equipped trailers, about $300 per night), an RV park ($46), and houseboat rentals (from $750 per day, 3-day minimum). Showers, a laundry room, a convenience store, and a post office are at **Trailer Village.** Ask the visitors center staff or rangers for directions to primitive camping areas with vehicle access elsewhere along Bullfrog Bay.

Bullfrog Marina can be reached from the north via paved Highway 276. It is 40 miles between Bullfrog and the junction with Highway 95. Ticaboo, 20 miles north of Bullfrog, has another good lodging option. The **Ticaboo Lodge** (435/788-2110 or 800/842-2267, from $122) is a hotel with a swimming pool, a restaurant, and a service-station complex that pretty much constitutes all of Ticaboo.

NATURAL BRIDGES TO LAKE POWELL VIA HIGHWAY 95

If the Lake Powell ferry schedule doesn't match your travel plans, Highway 95 will quickly get you across the Colorado River to the junction with Highway 24 at Hanksville.

Hite

In 1883 Cass Hite came to Glen Canyon in search of gold. He found some at a place later named Hite City, which set off a small gold rush. Cass and a few of his relatives operated a small store and post office, which were the only services for many miles. Travelers who wanted to cross the Colorado River here had the difficult task of swimming their animals across. Arthur Chaffin, a later resident, put through the first road and opened a ferry service in 1946. The Chaffin Ferry served uranium prospectors and adventurous motorists until the lake backed up to the spot in 1964. A steel bridge now spans the Colorado River upstream from Hite Marina. Cass Hite's store and the ferry site are underwater about five miles down the lake from Hite Marina.

Beyond Hite, on the tiny neck of land between the Colorado River bridge and the Dirty Devil bridge, an unmarked dirt road turns north. Called Hite Road, or Orange Cliffs Road, this long and rugged road eventually links up with backcountry routes—including the Flint Trail—in the Maze District of Canyonlands National Park.

The uppermost marina on Lake Powell, Hite is 141 lake miles from Glen Canyon Dam. It is hit hard when water levels drop in Lake Powell, which has been most of the time in recent years. When water is available, boats can continue up the lake to the mouth of Dark Canyon in Cataract Canyon at low water or into Canyonlands National Park at high water. During times of low water, the boat ramp is often high above the lake. Hite tends to be quieter than the other marinas and is favored by some anglers and families. Facilities include a small **store** with gas, three-bedroom housekeeping units in trailer houses (about $300), and a primitive **campground** (free) with no drinking water. Primitive camping is also available nearby, off Highway 95 at Dirty Devil, Farley Canyon, White Canyon, Blue Notch, and other locations. A **ranger station** (435/684-2457) is occasionally open; look for the rangers' vehicle at other times. Contact **Lake Powell Resorts & Marinas** (888/896-3829, www.lakepowell.com) for accommodations reservations.

PAGE, ARIZONA

Although the town of Page is hot, busy, and not particularly appealing, it is the largest community anywhere near Lake Powell, and it offers travelers a number of places to stay and eat. The town overlooks Lake Powell and Glen Canyon Dam; the large Wahweap Resort and Marina is just six miles away.

Accommodations

Nearly all Page motels are on or near Lake Powell Boulevard (U.S. 89L), a 3.25-mile loop that branches off the main highway. Page is a busy place in summer, however, and a call ahead is a good idea if you don't want to chase around town looking for vacancies. Expect to pay top dollar for views of the lake. The summer rates listed here drop in winter (Nov.-Mar.).

In a way, the most appealing lodgings are in the small apartments-turned-motels on and around 8th Avenue, a quiet residential area two blocks off Lake Powell Boulevard. These apartments date back to 1958-1959, when they housed supervisors for the dam construction project. One such place is **Bashful Bob's Motel** (750 S. Navajo Dr., 928/645-3919, www.bashfulbobsmotel.com, from $39), a great little budget place with simple two-bedroom apartments, all with kitchenettes. **Debbie's Hide A Way** (117 8th Ave., 928/645-1224, www.debbieshideaway.com, from $99) is another place with a personal touch and a quiet garden in back; all guest rooms are suites with kitchens. Debbie's also has a two-bedroom apartment ($75) a couple of blocks from the motel. **Lulu's Sleep Ezze** (105 8th Ave., 928/608-0273 or 800/553-6211, www.lulussleepezzemotel.com, from $95, cash discount) is especially sweet.

Courtyard Page (600 Clubhouse Dr., 928/645-5000 or 877/905-4495, www.marriott.com, from $159) is a good chain hotel with a great setting, with views, a restaurant, a pool, a spa, an exercise room, and an adjacent 18-hole golf course.

Food

Dam Bar and Grill (644 N. Navajo Dr., 928/645-2161, 5pm-11pm daily, $8-25), in the

Dam Plaza, serves up steaks, barbecue, seafood, pasta, and sandwiches; it also has a sports bar. **Fiesta Mexicana** (201 S. Lake Powell Blvd., 928/645-3999, 11am-9pm daily, $8-15) is a busy but friendly little Mexican place (and here in Arizona, it's easy to get a margarita).

West of Canyonlands

It's a lonely road that leads north from the Glen Canyon Recreational Area and Lake Powell to I-70, just west of the town of Green River. The crossroads town of Hanksville is a good place to gas up (don't expect any bargains on gas) and grab a burger, and Goblin Valley State Park is worth the detour. Highway 24 north of Hanksville also provides access to Canyonlands National Park's Maze District and the incredible rock art in the park's Horseshoe Canyon Unit.

HANKSVILLE

Even by Utah standards, tiny Hanksville (population just over 200) is pretty remote. Ebenezer Hanks and other Mormon settlers founded this out-of-the-way community in 1882 along the Fremont River, then known as the Dirty Devil River. The isolation attracted polygamists like Hanks and other fugitives from the law. Butch Cassidy and his gang found refuge in the rugged canyon country of "Robbers' Roost," east of town. Several houses and the old stone church on Center Street, one block south of the highway, survive from the 19th century.

Travelers exploring this scenic region find Hanksville a handy if lackluster stopover; Capitol Reef National Park is to the west, Lake Powell and the Henry Mountains are

© JUDY JEWELL

This waterwheel is the most scenic thing in the crossroads town of Hanksville.

to the south, the remote Maze District of Canyonlands National Park is to the east, and Goblin Valley State Park is to the north.

Wolverton Mill

E. T. Wolverton built this ingenious mill during the 1920s at his gold-mining claims in the Henry Mountains. A 20-foot waterwheel, still perfectly balanced, powered ore-crushing machinery and a sawmill. Owners of claims at the mill's original site didn't like a steady stream of tourists coming through to see the mill, so it was moved to the BLM office at Hanksville. Drive south 0.5 miles on 100 West to see the mill and some of its original interior mechanism.

Accommodations

Whispering Sands Motel (68 E. 100 N., 435/542-3238, from $89) has spacious guest rooms with cable TV and phones. In the center of town, the **Red Rock Campground** (435/542-3235 or 800/894-3242, mid-Mar.-Oct., $28 RVs) has showers, laundry, and a restaurant.

Food

Hanksville's restaurants cluster at the south end of town; don't expect anything fancy. The **Red Rock** (26 E. 100 N., 435/542-3235, 8am-8pm or later daily Apr.-Oct., $9-23) is at the campground, with home cooking, beer, and wine. **Blondie's Eatery** (3 N. Hwy. 95, 435/542-3255, 7am-9pm daily, $5-13) is a casual sit-down place with chicken and burgers across from Whispering Sands motel. **Stan's Burger Shack** (140 S. Hwy. 95, 435/542-3441, 7am-10pm daily, $5-8), at the Chevron station, is more a fast-food burger joint that's a step up from the chains.

Information and Services

The **Bureau of Land Management** (435/542-3461) has a field station 0.5 miles south of Highway 24 on 100 West, with information on road conditions, hiking, camping, and the buffalo herd in the Henry Mountains.

GOBLIN VALLEY STATE PARK

Thousands of rock formations, many with goblin-like "faces," inhabit Goblin Valley State Park (435/564-8110, reservations 800/322-3770, www.reserveamerica.com, year-round, $7 per vehicle day-use, $16 camping). All of these so-called goblins have weathered out of the Entrada Formation, here a soft red sandstone and even softer siltstone. **Carmel Canyon Trail** (1.5-mile loop) begins at the northeast side of the parking lot at road's end, then drops down to the desert floor and a strange landscape of goblins, spires, and balanced rocks. Just wander around at your whim; this is a great place for the imagination. A 1.3-mile trail connects the campground and the goblin-studded Carmel Canyon Trail.

Curtis Bench Trail begins on the road between the parking lot and the campground and goes south to a viewpoint of the Henry Mountains; cairns mark the 1.5-mile (one-way) route.

The turnoff from Highway 24 is at milepost 137, which is 21 miles north of Hanksville and 24 miles south of I-70; follow signs west five miles on a paved road, then south seven miles on a gravel road.

Although there are off-road vehicle and motorcycle riding areas just west of the park, bicycling is limited to the park's roads. However, 12 miles north, the **Temple Mountain Bike Trail** traverses old mining roads, ridges, and wash bottoms. Popular hikes near the state park include the Little Wild Horse and Bell Canyons Loop, Chute and Crack Canyons Loop, and Wild Horse Canyon. The park is also a good base for exploring the **San Rafael Swell** area to the northwest.

Camping at Goblin Valley is a real treat; the late-evening and early-morning sun makes the sandstone spires glow. If you're not much of

Goblin Valley State Park

a camper, consider booking one of the park's two yurts ($60). They're tucked back among the rock formations, and each is equipped with bunk beds and a futon, a swamp cooler, and a propane stove. There are only 26 camping sites, so it's best to reserve well in advance.

GREEN RIVER

Green River (population about 950) is, except for a handful of motels and a lively tavern, pretty run-down, but it's the only real settlement on the stretch of I-70 between Salina and the Colorado border. Travelers can stop for a night or a meal, set off on a trip down the Green River, or use the town as a base for exploring the scenic San Rafael Swell country nearby.

Green River is known for its melons. In summer, stop at roadside stands and partake of wondrous cantaloupes and watermelons. The blazing summer heat and ample irrigation water make such delicacies

possible. **Melon Days** celebrates the harvest on the third weekend of September with a parade, a city fair, music, a canoe race, games, and lots of melons.

John Wesley Powell River History Museum

Stop by this fine museum (1765 E. Main St., 435/564-3427, www.johnwesleypowell.com, 8am-7pm daily summer, call for hours fall-spring, $6 adults, $2 ages 3-12) to learn about Powell's daring expeditions down the Green and Colorado Rivers in 1869 and 1871-1872. An excellent multimedia presentation about both rivers uses narratives from Powell's trips. Historic riverboats on display include a replica of Powell's *Emma Dean*.

Labyrinth and Stillwater Canyons

The Green River's Labyrinth and Stillwater Canyons are downstream, between the town of Green River and the river's confluence with

© PAUL LEVY

the Colorado River in Canyonlands National Park. Primarily a canoeing or kayaking river, the Green River at this point is calm and wide as it passes into increasingly deep, rust-colored canyons. This isn't a wilderness river; regular powerboats can also follow the river below town to the confluence with the Colorado River and head up the Colorado to Moab, 2-3 days and 186 river miles away.

The most common trip on this portion of the Green River begins just south of town and runs south through the Labyrinth Canyon, ending at Mineral Bottom, a distance of 68 river miles. **Moab Rafting and Canoe Company** (805 N. Main St., Moab, 435/259-7722, http://moab-rafting.com, $625 for a 5-day trip) offers this trip in canoes and has rentals available. **Sherry Griffith Expeditions** (435/259-8229 or 800/332-2439, www.griffithexp.com, $900 for a 5-day trip), also based in Moab, offers the same trip in kayaks. For longer excursions, inquire about special 10-day guided trips that go all the way down the Green to its confluence with the Colorado River. Alternatively, you can plan your own self-guided trip down the Green River. **Tex's Riverways** (435/259-5101, www.texsriverways.com) offers canoe and touring kayak rentals and all the other equipment you need to outfit a multiday trip, plus shuttle services to and from the river. Permits are required to paddle in Labyrinth Canyon; they're free and available to download from the BLM website (www.blm.gov) or can be picked up in town at the John Wesley Powell Museum (1765 E. Main St.) or Green River State Park (150 S. Green River Blvd.).

Crystal Geyser

With some luck, you'll catch the spectacle of this cold-water geyser on the bank of the Green River. The gusher shoots as high as 60 feet, but only 3-4 times daily, so you may have to spend half a day here in order to see it. The eruption, typically lasting seven minutes, is powered by carbon dioxide and other gases. A 2,267-foot-deep petroleum test well drilled in 1935-1936 concentrated the geyser flow, but thick layers of old travertine deposits attest that mineral-laden springs have long been active at this site. Colorful newer travertine forms delicate terraces around the opening and down to the river. The orange and dark red of the minerals and algae make this a pretty spot, even if the geyser is only quietly gurgling.

Crystal Geyser is 10 miles south of Green River by road; boaters should look for the geyser deposits on the left, about 4.5 river miles downstream from Green River. From downtown, drive east one mile on Main Street, turn left, and go three miles on signed Frontage Road (near milepost 4), then turn right and go six miles on a narrow paved road just after going under a railroad overpass. The road goes under I-70, then is unpaved for the last 4.5 miles; keep right at a fork near some power lines. Some washes have to be crossed, so the drive isn't recommended after rains. When the weather is fair, cars shouldn't have a problem. Buildings and antennas passed on the way belong to the Utah Launch Complex of White Sands Missile Range. From 1963 to 1979 several hundred Pershing and Athena rockets blasted off here for targets at White Sands, New Mexico, 400 miles away.

Accommodations

Green River has a few rather shabby older motels as well as newer chain motels to choose from; unless noted, each of the following has a swimming pool—a major consideration in this often sweltering desert valley.

One of the older places, the **Robber's Roost Motel** (325 W. Main St., 435/564-3452, www.rrmotel.com, from $39) is cheap and basic and right in the center of town; it does not have a pool. Green River's newer motels are on the east end of town. The **Super 8** (1248 E. Main St., 435/564-8888 or 800/888-8888, $75), out by I-70's exit 162, is a good value, with spacious, comfortable guest rooms. The **Holiday Inn Express** (1845 E. Main St., 435/564-4439, $124) is predictably comfortable—not a bad thing if you're coming out of the desert or off the river.

The nicest place to stay in town is (**The River Terrace** (1740 E. Main St., 435/564-3401 or 877/564-3401, www.river-terrace.com, from $106), with somewhat older but large guest rooms, some of which overlook the Green River and some with balconies. Breakfast is included, plus there's a restaurant adjacent to the hotel. The very pleasant outdoor pool area is flanked by patios and shaded tables.

CAMPGROUNDS

Several campgrounds, all with showers, offer sites for tents and RVs year-round. **Green River State Park** (150 S. Green River Blvd., 435/564-3633 or 800/322-3770, www.reserveamerica.com, year-round, $5 day-use, $16 camping) has a great setting near the river; it's shaded by large cottonwoods and has a boat ramp. **Shady Acres RV Park** (350 E. Main St., 435/564-8290 or 800/537-8674, www.shadyacresrv.com, year-round, $20 tents, $27-35 hookups, $42 cabins) is not all that shady and may be a bit too close to the noisy road for tent campers; it has a store, showers, and a laundry. **Green River KOA** (235 S. 1780 E., 435/564-3651, $29 tents, $46 hookups, from $64 cabins) has campsites and cabins (bring sleeping bags) across from the John Wesley Powell Museum and next to the Tamarisk Restaurant.

Food

Other than motel restaurants and fast food, the one really notable place to eat in Green River is (**Ray's Tavern** (25 S. Broadway, 435/564-3511, 11am-10pm daily, $8-26). Ray's doesn't look like much from the outside, but inside you'll find a friendly welcome, tables made from tree trunks, and some of the best steaks, chops, and burgers in this part of the state. Don't expect haute cuisine, but the food is good, and the atmosphere is truly Western; beer drinkers will be glad for the selection of regional microbrews after a long day navigating the river or driving desert roads.

Directly adjacent to the River Terrace hotel is a decent American-style restaurant, **The Tamarisk** (880 E. Main St., 435/564-8109, 7am-10pm daily, $6-27), with riverfront views.

BACKGROUND

The Colorado Plateau

Utah's five national parks and the Grand Staircase-Escalante National Monument are all part of the Colorado Plateau, a high, broad physiographic province that includes southern Utah, northern Arizona, southwest Colorado, and northwestern New Mexico. This roughly circular plateau, nearly the size of Montana, also contains the Grand Canyon, the Navajo Nation, and the Hopi Reservation.

Created by a slow but tremendous uplift and carved by magnificent rivers, the plateau is mostly between 3,000 and 6,000 feet elevation, with some peaks reaching nearly 13,000 feet. Although much of the terrain is gently rolling, the Green and Colorado Rivers have sculpted remarkable canyons, buttes, mesas, arches, and badlands. Isolated uplifts and foldings have formed such features as the San Rafael Swell, Waterpocket Fold, and Circle Cliffs. The rounded Abajo, Henry, La Sal, and Navajo Mountains are examples of intrusive rock—an igneous layer that is formed below the earth's surface and later exposed by erosion.

The Colorado Plateau province is broken down into six physiographic sections: the Grand Canyon, Datil, Navajo, Uinta Basin,

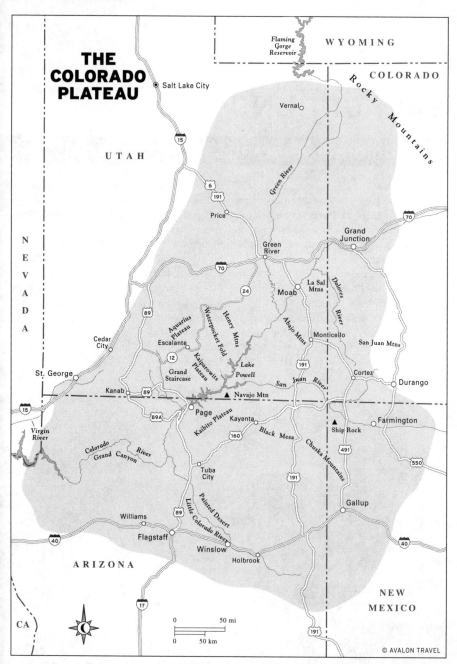

THE COLORADO PLATEAU

WYOMING

Flaming Gorge Reservoir

COLORADO

Salt Lake City

Vernal

Rocky Mountains

UTAH

15

6
191

Price

Green River

70

Grand Junction

70

N E V A D A

24

Moab

La Sal Mtns

Dolores River

89

Aquarius Plateau

Waterpocket Fold

Henry Mtns

Abajo Mtns

Monticello

San Juan Mtns

Cedar City

Escalante

12

Kaiparowits Plateau

Lake Powell

191

Cortez

Durango

Grand Staircase

Grand Staircase

San Juan River

Kanab

89

▲ Navajo Mtn

15

Virgin River

89A

Page

Kaibito Plateau

Kayenta

160

Black Mesa

▲ Ship Rock

Chuska Mountains

491

Farmington

550

Colorado River

Grand Canyon

Tuba City

191

Painted Desert

Little Colorado River

Gallup

Williams

89

40

Flagstaff

Winslow

Holbrook

40

ARIZONA

17

NEW MEXICO

CA

0   50 mi
0   50 km

191

© AVALON TRAVEL

Canyon Lands, and High Plateaus. Utah's national parks are spread across the High Plateaus and Canyon Lands sections. The westernmost parks, Zion and Bryce, are in the High Plateaus; Capitol Reef, Arches, and Canyonlands are, not surprisingly, in the Canyon Lands section; and the Escalante River forms the dividing line between the two sections.

The High Plateaus (the Paunsaugunt, Markagunt, and Aquarius Plateaus) are lava-topped uplands reaching above the main height of the Colorado Plateau, then dropping off to the south in a series of steps known as the Grand Staircase. Exposed layers range from the relatively young rocks of the Black Cliffs (lava flows) in the north to the increasingly older Pink Cliffs (visible at Bryce), Gray Cliffs (which include the Straight Cliffs of Grand Staircase-Escalante), White Cliffs (Zion's Navajo sandstone), and Vermilion Cliffs (surrounding Kanab, Utah) toward the south.

The Canyon Lands section is noted for its synclines, anticlines, and folds—nongeologists can picture the rock layers as blankets on a bed, and then imagine how they look before the bed is made in the morning. This warping, which goes on deep beneath the earth's surface, has affected the overlying rocks, permitting the development of deeply incised canyons.

GEOLOGY

When you visit any one of Utah's national parks, the first things you're likely to notice are rocks. Vegetation is sparse and the soil is thin, so there's not much to hide the geology here. Particularly stunning views are found where rivers have carved deep canyons through the rock layers.

By the standards of the American West, the rocks forming the Colorado Plateau have had it pretty easy. Although faults have cracked and uplifted rocks, and volcanoes have spewed lava across the plateau, it's nothing like the surrounding Rocky Mountains or Basin and Range provinces, both of which are the result of eons of violent geology. Mostly, sediments piled up, younger layers on top of older, then eroded, lifted up, and eroded some more.

The clean, orderly stair steps from the young rocks in Bryce Canyon to the much older Grand Canyon show off the clearly defined layers of rock. Weird crenellations, hoodoos, and arches occur as a result of the way erosion acted on the various rocks that make up this big Colorado Plateau layer cake.

Sedimentation

Water made this desert what it is today. Back before the continents broke apart and began drifting to their present-day locations, Utah was near the equator, just east of a warm ocean. Ancient seas washed over the land, depositing sand, silt, and mud. Layer upon layer, the soils piled up and were—over time—compressed into sandstones, limestones, and shales.

The ancestral Rocky Mountains rose to the east of the ocean, and, just to their west, a trough-like basin formed and was intermittently flushed with sea water. Evaporation caused salts and other minerals to collect on the basin floor; when the climate became wetter, more water rushed in.

As the ancestral Rockies eroded, their bulk washed down into the basin. The sea level rose, washing in more mud and sand. When the seas receded, dry winds blew sand across the region, creating enormous dunes.

Over time, the North American continent drifted north, away from the equator, but this region remained near the sea and was regularly washed by tides, leaving more sand and silt. Just inland, freshwater lakes filled, then dried, and the lakebeds consolidated into shales. During wet periods, streams coursed across the area, carrying then dropping their loads of mud, silt, and sand.

As the ancestral Rockies wore down to mere hills, other mountains rose, then eroded, contributing their sediments. A turn toward dry weather meant more dry winds, kicking up the sand and building it into massive dunes.

NATURE'S PALETTE

In Utah, you'll get used to seeing a lot of colorful rock formations. The color gives you clues to the composition and geologic history of the rock. In general:

- **Red rocks** are stained by rusty iron-rich sediments washed down from mountains, and they are a clue that erosion has occurred.

- **Gray or brown rocks** were deposited by ancient seas.

- **White rocks** are colored by their "glue," the limey remains of dissolved seashells that leach down and harden sandstones.

- **Black rocks** are volcanic in origin, though not all volcanic, or igneous, rocks are black. Igneous are present in the La Sal, Abajo, and Henry Mountains near Canyonlands. These mountains are "laccoliths," formed by molten magma that pushed through the sedimentary layers, leaking deeper into some layers than others and eventually forming broad dome-shaped protuberances, which were eroded into soft peaks, then carved by glaciers into the sharp peaks we see today.

A layer of lava also caps the Paunsaugunt, Markagunt, and Aquarius Plateaus, which have lifted above the main level of the Colorado Plateau. This mostly basalt layer was laid down about 37 million years ago, before the Colorado Plateau began to uplift.

Uplift

About 15 million years ago, the sea-level plateau began to lift slowly, steadily, and by geologic standards, incredibly gently. Some areas were hoisted as high as 10,000 feet above sea level.

Along the western edge of the plateau, underlying faults—like those common in the Basin and Range area—shot through the sedimentary layers. Along these faults, the High Plateaus—the Paunsaugunt, Markagunt, and Aquarius—rose above the height of the main Colorado Plateau.

Uplift is still occurring. A 1992 earthquake just outside Zion National Park was one strong reminder that the plateau continues to move.

Erosion

As the Colorado Plateau rose, its big rivers carved deep gorges through the uplifting rocks. Today, these rivers—the Green, Colorado, Escalante, Paria, and Virgin—are responsible for much of the dramatic scenery in Utah's national parks.

More subtle forms of erosion have also contributed to the plateau's present-day form. Water percolating down through the rock layers is one of the main erosive forces, washing away loose material and dissolving ancient salts, often leaving odd formations, such as thin fins of resistant rock.

The many layers of sedimentary rocks forming the Colorado Plateau are all composed of different minerals and have varying densities, so it's not surprising that erosion affects each layer a bit differently. For instance, sandstones and limestones erode more readily than the harder mudstones or shales.

Erosion isn't limited to the force of water against rock. Rocks may be worn down or eaten away by a variety of forces, including wind, freezing and thawing, exfoliation (when sheets of rock peel off), oxidation, hydration and carbonation (chemical weathering), plant roots or animal burrows, and dissolving of soft rocks. Rockfalls in Zion, the ever-deepening channel of the Colorado River through Canyonlands, and the slow thinning of pedestals supporting Arches' balanced rocks are all clues that erosion continues unabated.

CLIMATE

The main thing for southern Utah travelers to remember is that they're in the desert.

The high-desert country of the Colorado

© PAUL LEVY

Arches occur when erosion dissolves salt formations surrounded by more resistant rock.

Plateau lies mostly between 3,000 and 6,000 feet in elevation. Annual precipitation ranges from an extremely dry 3 inches in some areas to about 10 inches in others. Mountainous regions between 10,000 and 13,000 feet receive abundant rainfall in summer and heavy snows in winter.

Sunny skies prevail through all four seasons. Spring comes early to the canyon country, with weather that's often windy and rapidly changing. Summer can make its presence known in April, although the real desert heat doesn't set in until late May-early June. Temperatures then soar into the 90s and 100s at midday, although the dry air makes the heat more bearable. Early morning is the choice time for travel in summer. A canyon seep surrounded by hanging gardens or a mountain meadow filled with wildflowers provides a refreshing contrast to the parched desert; other ways to beat the heat include hiking in the mountains and river rafting.

Summer thunderstorm season begins anywhere from mid-June until August; huge billowing thunderstorm clouds bring refreshing rains and coolness. During this season, canyon hikers should be alert for flash flooding.

Fall begins after the rains cease, usually in October, and lasts into November or even December; days are bright and sunny with ideal temperatures, but nights become cold. In all of the parks, evenings will be cool even in midsummer. Although the day may be baking hot, you'll need a jacket and a warm sleeping bag for the night.

Elevation matters: Bryce Canyon National Park is at 8,000 feet and is significantly cooler than nearby Zion, at about 4,000 feet. Bryce is the only park regularly covered with enough snow for cross-country skiing or snowshoeing. It's also where, during early spring, a motel room will seem like a good idea to all but the most hardy tent campers. Winter lasts only about two months at the lower elevations. Light snows on the canyon walls add new beauty to the rock layers. Nighttime temperatures commonly dip into the teens, which is too cold for most campers.

Yuccas have long tap roots that dig deep to find moisture.

Otherwise, winter can be a fine time for travel. Heavy snows rarely occur below 8,000 feet.

Flash Floods

Rainwater runs quickly off the rocky desert surfaces and into gullies and canyons. A summer thunderstorm or a rapid late-winter snowmelt can send torrents of mud and boulders rumbling down dry washes and canyons. Backcountry drivers, horseback riders, and hikers need to avoid hazardous locations when storms threaten or unseasonably warm winds blow on the winter snowpack.

Flash floods can sweep away anything in their path, including boulders, cars, and campsites. Do not camp or park in potential flash flood areas. If you come to a section of flooded roadway—a common occurrence on desert roads after storms—wait until the water goes down before crossing (it shouldn't take long). Summer lightning causes forest and brush fires, posing a danger to hikers who are foolish enough to climb mountains when storms threaten.

The bare rock and loose soils so common in the canyon country do little to hold back the flow of rain or meltwater. In fact, slickrock is effective at shedding water as fast as it comes in contact. Logs and other debris wedged high on canyon walls give proof enough of past floods.

FLORA

Within the physiographic province of the Colorado Plateau, several different life zones are represented.

In the low desert, shrubs eke out a meager existence. Climbing higher, you'll pass through grassy steppe, sage, and piñon-juniper woodlands to ponderosa pine. Of all these zones, the piñon-juniper is most common.

But it's not a lockstep progression of plant A at elevation X and plant B at elevation Z. Soils are an important consideration, with sandstones being more hospitable than shales. Plants will

© JUDY JEWELL

Find biscuitroot on the Devils Garden or Fiery Furnace Trails in Arches National Park.

grow wherever the conditions will support them, and Utah's parks have many microenvironments that can lead to surprising plant discoveries. Look for different plants in these different habitats: slickrock (where cracks can gather enough soil to host a few plants), riparian (moist areas with the greatest diversity of life), and terraces and open space (the area between riverbank and slickrock, where shrubs dominate). With more than 800 native species, Zion has the greatest plant diversity of any of Utah's parks.

How Plants Survive in the Desert

Most of the plants you'll see in Utah's national parks are well adapted to desert life. Many are succulents, which have their own water storage systems in their fleshy stems or leaves. Cacti are the most obvious succulents; they swell with stored moisture during the spring, then slowly shrink and wrinkle as the stored moisture is used. Other plants have different strategies for making the most of scarce water. Some, such as yucca, have deep roots, taking advantage of what moisture exists in the soil. The leaves of desert plants are often vertical, exposing less surface area to the sun. Leaves may also have very small pores, slowing transpiration, or stems coated with a resinous substance, which also slows water loss. Hairy or light-colored leaves help reflect sunlight.

Desert wildflowers are annuals; they bloom in the spring, when water is available, then form seeds, which can survive the dry hot summer, and die. A particularly wet spring means a bumper crop of wildflowers.

Even though mosses aren't usually thought of as desert plants, they are found growing in seeps along canyon walls and in cryptobiotic soils. When water is unavailable, mosses dry up; when the water returns, the moss quickly plumps up again.

Junipers have a fairly drastic way of dealing with water shortage: self-pruning. During a prolonged dry spell, a juniper tree can shut off the flow of water to one or more of its branches, sacrificing these branches to keep the tree alive.

Hanging Gardens

Look along Zion's Virgin River canyon for clumps of ferns and mosses lit with maidenhair ferns, shooting stars, monkey flowers, columbine, orchids, and bluebells. These unexpectedly lush pockets are called "hanging gardens," gemlike islands of plantlife nestled into canyon walls.

Hanging gardens take advantage of a unique microclimate created by the meeting of two rock layers: Navajo sandstone and Kayenta shale. Water percolates down through porous sandstone and, when it hits the denser shale layer, travels laterally along the top of the harder rock and emerges at cliff's edge. These little springs support lush plantlife.

Tamarisk

One of the Colorado Plateau's most common

© BILL MCRAE

Squirrels are common visitors to picnics.

trees, the nonnative tamarisk is also one of the peskiest. Imported from the Mediterranean and widely planted along the Colorado River to control erosion, the tamarisk has spread wildly, and its dense stands have crowded out native trees such as cottonwoods. Tamarisks are notoriously thirsty trees, sucking up vast amounts of water, but they give back little in the way of food or habitat for local wildlife. Their thick growth also increases the risk of fire. State and federal agencies are taking steps to control tamarisk; tamarisk beetles, imported from Kazakhstan and China, have been released in sites in southern Utah as a biocontrol agent.

Cryptobiotic Soil

Over much of the Colorado Plateau, the soil is alive. What looks like a grayish-brown crust is actually a dense network of filament-forming blue-green algae intertwined with soil particles, lichens, moss, green algae, and microfungi. This slightly sticky, crusty mass holds the soil together, slowing erosion. Its sponge-like consistency allows it to soak up water and hold it. Plants growing in cryptobiotic soil have a great advantage over plants rooted in dry sandy soil.

Cryptobiotic soils take a long time to develop and are extremely fragile. Make every effort to avoid stepping on them—stick to trails, slickrock, or rocks instead.

FAUNA

Although they're not thought of as great "wildlife parks" like Yellowstone or Denali, Utah's national parks are home to plenty of animals. Desert animals are often nocturnal and unseen by park visitors.

Rodents

Rodents include squirrels, packrats, kangaroo rats, chipmunks, and porcupines, most of which spend their days in burrows.

One of the few desert rodents out foraging during the day is the white-tailed antelope squirrel, which looks much like a chipmunk. Its white tail reflects the sunlight, and when it needs to cool down a bit, an antelope squirrel smears its face with saliva (yes, that probably would work for you too, but that's why you have sweat glands). The antelope squirrel lives at lower elevations; higher up you'll see golden-mantled ground squirrels.

Look for rabbits—desert cottontails and jackrabbits—at dawn and dusk. If you're rafting the Green or Colorado River, keep an eye out for beavers.

Kangaroo rats are particularly well adapted to desert life. They spend their days in cool burrows, eat only plants, and never drink water. Instead, a kangaroo rat metabolizes dry food in a way that produces water.

Utah prairie dogs have been given a new lease on life in Bryce National Park. In 1973 the animals were listed as an endangered species and reintroduced to Bryce. Today nearly 200 animals live in the park—the largest protected

MOUNTAIN LION ENCOUNTERS

Imagine hiking down a trail and suddenly noticing fresh large paw prints. Mountain lion or Labrador retriever? Here's the way to tell the difference: Mountain lions usually retract their claws when they walk. Dogs, of course, can't do this. So if close inspection of the print reveals toenails, it's most likely from a canine's paw.

But about those mountain lions: In recent years incidents of mountain lion-human confrontations have increased markedly and received much publicity. These ambush hunters usually prey on sick or weak animals but will occasionally attack people, especially children and small adults. When hiking or camping with children in mountain lion territory—potentially all of Utah's national parks—it is important to keep them close to the rest of the family.

If you are stalked by a mountain lion, make yourself look big by raising your arms, waving a big stick, or spreading your coat. Maintain direct eye contact with the animal, and do not turn your back to it. If the mountain lion begins to approach, throw rocks and sticks, and continue to look large and menacing as you slowly back away. In the case of an attack, fight back; do not "play dead."

To put things in perspective, it's important to remember that mountain lions are famously elusive. If you do see one, it will probably be a quick glimpse of the cat running away from you.

population of Utah prairie dogs. Prairie dogs live together in social groups called colonies or towns, which are laced with burrows, featuring a network of entrances for quick pops in and out of the ground. Prairie dogs are preyed on by badgers, coyotes, hawks, and snakes, so a colony will post lookouts, who are constantly searching for danger. When threatened, the lookouts "bark" to warn the colony. Utah prairie dogs hibernate during the winter and emerge from their burrows to mate furiously in early April.

Porcupines are common in Capitol Reef and Zion; although they prefer to live in forested areas, especially the piñon-juniper zone, they sometimes forage in streamside brush. These nocturnal creatures have also been known to visit campsites, where they like to gnaw on sweaty boots or backpack straps.

Bats

As night falls in canyon country, bats emerge from the nooks and crannies that protect them from the day's heat and begin to feed on mosquitoes and other insects. The tiny gray western pipistrelle is common. It flies early in the evening, feeding near streams, and can be spotted by its somewhat erratic flight. The pallid bat spends a lot of its time creeping across the ground in search of food and is a late-night bat; look for it after 10pm in the summer at Capitol Reef. Another common bat here and across the United States is the prosaically named big brown bat.

Large Mammals

Mule deer are common in all of the parks, as are coyotes. Other large mammals include the predators: mountain lions and coyotes. If you're lucky, you'll get a glimpse of a bobcat or a fox.

If you're hiking the trails of Bryce Canyon early in the morning and see something that looks like a small dog in a tree, it's probably a gray fox. These small (5-10 pounds) foxes live in forested areas and have the catlike ability to climb trees. They're most commonly seen on the connecting trail between the Queen's Garden and Navajo Loop trails. Kit foxes, which are even tinier than gray foxes, with prominent ears and a big bushy tail, are common in Arches and Canyonlands. Red foxes also live across the plateau.

Desert bighorn sheep live in Arches, Canyonlands, and Capitol Reef; look for them trotting across steep, rocky ledges. In Arches, they're frequently sighted along U.S. 191 south of the visitors center. They also roam the talus slopes and side canyons near the Colorado River. Desert bighorns have been reintroduced in Zion and can occasionally be spotted in steep, rocky areas on the park's east side.

Reptiles

Reptiles are well-suited to desert life. As cold-blooded, or ectothermic, animals, their body temperature depends on the environment, rather than on internal metabolism, and it's easy for them to keep warm in the desert heat. When it's cold, reptiles hibernate or drastically slow their metabolism.

The western whiptail lizard is common in Arches. You'll recognize it because its tail is twice as long as its body. Also notable is the western collared lizard, with a bright green body set off by a black collar.

Less flashy but particularly fascinating are the several species of parthenogenetic lizards. All of these lizards are female, and they reproduce by laying eggs that are clones of themselves. Best known is the plateau striped whiptail, but 6 of the 12 species of whiptail present in the area are all-female.

The northern plateau lizard is common at altitudes of about 3,000-6,000 feet. It's not choosy about its habitat—juniper-piñon woodlands, prairies, riparian woodlands, and rocky hillsides are all perfectly acceptable. This is the lizard you'll most often see scurrying across your campsite in Zion or Capitol Reef.

Rattlesnakes are present across the area, but given a chance, they'll get out of your way rather than strike. (Still, they're another good reason to wear sturdy boots.) The midget faded rattlesnake, a small subspecies of the western rattlesnake, lives in burrows and rock crevices and is mostly active at night. Although this snake has especially toxic venom, full venom injections occur in only one-third of all bites.

© EMILY ROTH

rattlesnake warming against a rock

Amphibians

Although they're not usually thought of as desert animals, a variety of frogs and toads live on the Colorado Plateau. Tadpoles live in wet springtime potholes as well as in streams and seeps. If you're camping in a canyon, you may be lucky enough to be serenaded by a toad chorus.

Bullfrogs are not native to the western United States, but since they were introduced in the early 1900s, they have flourished at the expense of native frogs and toads, whose eggs and tadpoles they eat.

The big round toes of the small spotted canyon tree frog make it easy to identify—that is, if you can see this well-camouflaged frog in the first place. These frogs are most active at night, spending their days on streamside rocks or trees.

Toads present in Utah's parks include the Great Basin spadefoot, red spotted toad, and western woodhouse toad.

Birds

Have you ever seen a bird pant? Believe it or not,

© PAUL LEVY

chukar at Kodachrome Basin State Park

wren is—as its name implies—a rock collector: It paves a trail to its nest with pebbles, and the nest itself is lined with rocks. Another canyon bird, the white-throated swift, swoops and calls as it chases insects and mates, rather dramatically, in flight. Swifts are often seen near violet-green swallows, which are equally gymnastic fliers, in Canyonlands, Arches, and Grand Staircase-Escalante.

The chukar—a chunky game bird introduced for the benefit of hunters in the 1930s—is common at Capitol Reef, where it is often seen on or near the ground, foraging in low-lying shrubs and grasses.

Several species of hummingbird (mostly black-chinned, but also broad-tailed and rufous) are often seen in the summer. Woodpeckers are also common, including the northern flicker and red-naped sapsucker, and flycatchers like Say's phoebe, western kingbird, and western wood pewee can be spotted too. Two warblers—the yellow and the yellow-rumped—are common in the summer, and Wilson's warbler stops in during spring and fall migrations. Horned larks are present year-round.

Mountain bluebirds are colorful, easy for a novice to identify, and common in Canyonlands and Arches. Look for the American dipper along the Virgin River in Zion. This small gray bird distinguishes itself from other similar birds by its habit of plunging headfirst into the water in search of insects.

Both the well-known scrub jay and its local cousin, the piñon jay, are noisy visitors to almost every picnic. Other icons of western avian life—the turkey vulture, the raven, and the magpie—are widespread and easily spotted.

that's how desert birds expel heat from their bodies. They allow heat to escape by drooping their wings away from their bodies, exposing thinly feathered areas (sort of like pulling up your shirt and using it to fan your torso).

The various habitats across the Colorado Plateau, such as piñon-juniper, perennial streams, dry washes, and rock cliffs, allow many species of bird to find homes. Birders will find the greatest variety of birds near rivers and streams. Other birds, such as golden eagles, kestrels (small falcons), and peregrine falcons nest high on cliffs and patrol open areas for prey. Common hawks include the red-tailed hawk and northern harrier; late-evening strollers may see great horned owls. California condors were reintroduced in 1996 to Zion, and can now be seen in the Lava Point, Canyon Overlook, and Angels Landing areas.

People usually detect the canyon wren by its lovely song; this small long-beaked bird nests in cavities along cliff faces. The related rock

Fish

Obviously, deserts aren't particularly known for their aquatic life, and the big rivers of the Colorado Plateau are now dominated by non-native species such as channel catfish and carp. Many of these fish were introduced as game fish. Native fish, like the six-foot, 100-pound Colorado pikeminnow, are now uncommon.

Spiders and Scorpions

Tarantulas, black widow spiders, and scorpions all live across the Colorado Plateau, and all are objects of many a visitor's phobias. Although the black widow spider's venom is toxic, tarantulas deliver only a mildly toxic bite (and they rarely bite humans), and a scorpion's sting is about like that of a bee.

ENVIRONMENTAL ISSUES

Utah's national parks have generally been shielded from the environmental issues that play out in the rest of the state, which has always been business-oriented, with a heavy emphasis on extractive industries such as mining and logging.

The main environmental threats to the parks are the consequences of becoming too popular. During the summer, auto and RV traffic can clog park roads, with particularly bad snarls at viewpoint parking areas. Both Zion and Bryce have made attempts to control park traffic by running shuttle buses along scenic drives. At Zion, it's mandatory to ride the bus (or your bike) during the summer high season, and that has made a significant difference.

Hikers also have an impact, especially when they tread on fragile cryptobiotic soil. Killing this living soil crust drastically increases erosion in an already easily eroded environment.

ATV Overkill

Off-road vehicles, or ATVs (all-terrain vehicles), have gone from being the hobby of a small group of off-road enthusiasts to being one of the fastest-growing recreational markets in the country. Although use of ATVs is prohibited in the national parks, these dune buggies on steroids are having a huge impact on public lands adjacent to the parks and on Bureau of Land Management (BLM) lands that are currently under study for designation as wilderness. The scope of the issue is easy to measure. In 1979 there were 9,000 ATVs registered in Utah. In 2010 there were over 120,000. In addition, the power and dexterity of the machines has greatly increased. Now essentially military-style assault machines that can climb near-vertical cliffs and clamber over any kind of terrain, ATVs are the new "extreme sports" toy of choice, and towns like Moab are now seeing more visitors coming to tear up the backcountry on ATVs than to mountain bike. The problem is that ATVs are extremely destructive to the delicate natural environment of the Colorado Plateau deserts and canyon lands, and the more powerful, roaring, exhaust-belching machines put even the most remote and isolated areas within reach of large numbers of potentially destructive revelers.

Between the two camps—one that would preserve the public land and protect the ancient human artifacts found in remote canyons, the other that sees public land as a playground to be zipped over at high speed—is the BLM. The Moab BLM office has seemed to favor the ATV set, abdicating its role to protect the land and environment for all. Groups like Southern Utah Wilderness Alliance (SUWA, www.suwa. org) are constantly strategizing to force the BLM to comply with its responsibility for environmental stewardship of public land.

Nonnative Species

Nonnative species don't respect park boundaries, and several nonnative animals and plants have established strongholds in Utah's national parks, altering the local ecology by outcompeting native plants and animals.

Particularly invasive plants include tamarisk (salt cedar), cheatgrass, Russian knapweed, and Russian olive. Tamarisk is often seen as the most troublesome invader. This thirsty Mediterranean plant was imported in the 1800s as an ornamental shrub and was later planted by the Department of Agriculture to slow erosion along the banks of the Colorado River in

Arizona. It rapidly took hold, spreading upriver at roughly 12 miles per year, and is now firmly established on all of the Colorado's tributaries, where it grows in dense stands. Tamarisk consumes a great deal of water and rarely provides the food and shelter necessary for the survival of wildlife. It also outcompetes cottonwoods because tamarisk shade inhibits the growth of cottonwood seedlings.

Courthouse Wash in Arches is one of several sites where the National Park Service has made an effort to control tamarisk. Similar control experiments have been established in nearby areas, mostly in small tributary canyons of the Colorado River.

History

The landscape isn't the only vivid aspect of southern Utah. The area's human history is also noteworthy. This part of the West has been inhabited for over 10,000 years, and there are remnants of ancient villages and panels of mysterious rock art in now remote canyons. More recently, colonization by Mormon settlers and the establishment of the national parks have brought human history back to this dramatic corner of the Colorado Plateau.

PREHISTORY

Beginning about 15,000 years ago, nomadic groups of Paleo-Indians traveled across the Colorado Plateau in search of game animals and wild plants, but they left few traces.

Nomadic bands of hunter-gatherers roamed the Colorado Plateau for at least 5,000 years. The climate was probably cooler and wetter when these first people arrived, with both food plants and game animals more abundant than today.

© PAUL LEVY

Ancient Native Americans left behind astonishing arrays of rock art throughout Utah.

ANASAZI OR ANCESTRAL PUEBLOAN?

As you travel through the Southwest, you may hear reference to the "Ancestral Puebloans." In this book, we've chosen to use the more familiar name for these people—the Anasazi. The word *anasazi* is actually a Navajo term that archaeologists chose, thinking it meant "old people." A more literal translation is "enemy ancestors." For this reason, some consider the name inaccurate. The terminology is in flux, and which name you hear depends on whom you're talking to or where you are. The National Park Service now uses the more descriptive term Ancestral Puebloan. These prehistoric people built masonry villages and eventually moved south to Arizona and New Mexico, where their descendants, such as the Acoma, Cochiti, Santa Clara, Taos, and Hopi Mesas, live in modern-day pueblos.

Agriculture was introduced from the south about 2,000 years ago and brought about a slow transition to a settled village life. The Fremont culture emerged in the northern part of the region, including present-day Capitol Reef and Arches National Parks and Grand Staircase-Escalante National Monument, and the Anasazi in the southern part (there was a settlement in present-day Zion National Park). In some areas, including Escalante and Arches, both groups lived contemporaneously. Although both groups made pots, baskets, bowls, and jewelry, only the Anasazi constructed masonry villages. Thousands of stone dwellings, ceremonial kivas, and towers built by the Anasazi still stand. Both groups left behind intriguing rock art, either pecked in (petroglyphs) or painted (pictographs).

The Anasazi and Fremont departed from this region about 800 years ago, perhaps because of drought, warfare, or disease. Some of the Anasazi moved south and joined the Pueblo people of present-day Arizona and New Mexico. The fate of the Fremont people remains a mystery.

After the mid-1200s and until white settlers arrived in the late 1800s, small bands of nomadic Ute and Paiute moved through southern Utah. The Navajo began to enter Utah in the early 1800s. None of the three groups established firm control of the region north of the San Juan River, where the present-day national parks are located.

AGE OF EXPLORATION

In 1776, Spanish explorers of the Dominguez-Escalante Expedition were the first Europeans to visit and describe the region. They had given up partway through a proposed journey from Santa Fe to California and returned to Santa Fe along a route passing through the sites of present-day Cedar City and Hurricane, crossing the Colorado River in a place that is now covered by Lake Powell.

The Old Spanish Trail, used 1829-1848, ran through Utah to connect New Mexico with California, crossing the Colorado River near present-day Moab. Fur trappers and mountain men, including Jedediah Smith, also traveled southern Utah's canyons in search of beaver and other animals during the early 1800s; inscriptions carved into the sandstone record their passage. In 1859 the U.S. Army's Macomb Expedition made the first documented description of what is now Canyonlands National Park. Major John Wesley Powell's pioneering river expeditions down the Green and Colorado Rivers in 1869 and 1871-1872 filled in many blank areas on the maps.

MORMON SETTLEMENT

In 1849-1850, Mormon leaders in Salt Lake City took the first steps toward colonizing southern Utah. Parowan, now a sleepy community along I-15, became the first Mormon settlement in southern Utah, and Cedar City the second—both were established in 1851. In 1855 a successful experiment in growing cotton along Santa Clara Creek near present-day St. George aroused considerable interest among the Mormons. New settlements soon arose in the Virgin River Valley. Poor roads hindered development, and floods, droughts, disease, and hostile Native Americans discouraged some Mormon pioneers, but many of those who stayed prospered by raising food crops and livestock.

Also in 1855, the Elk Ridge Mission was founded near present-day Moab. It lasted only a few months before skirmishes with the Utes led to the deaths of three Mormon settlers and sent the rest fleeing for their lives. Church members had better success later in the Escalante area (1876) and Moab (1877).

For sheer effort and endurance, the efforts of the Hole-in-the-Rock Expedition of 1879-1880 are remarkable. Sixty families with 83 wagons and more than 1,000 head of livestock crossed some of the West's most rugged canyon country in an attempt to settle at Montezuma Creek on the San Juan River. They almost didn't make it: A journey expected to take six weeks turned into a six-month ordeal. The exhausted company arrived on the banks of the San Juan River on April 5, 1880. Too tired to continue just 20 easy miles to Montezuma Creek, they stayed and founded the town of Bluff. The Mormons also established other towns in southeastern Utah, relying on ranching, farming, and mining for their livelihoods. None of the communities in the region ever reached a large size; Moab is the biggest, with a current population of 5,500.

NATIONAL PARK MOVEMENT IN UTAH

In the early 1900s, people other than Native Americans, Mormon settlers, and government explorers began to notice that southern Utah was a remarkably scenic place and that it might be developed for tourism.

In 1909 a presidential Executive Order designated Mukuntuweap (now Zion) National Monument in Zion Canyon. Roads were built to improve access, and by 1917 a tent camping resort was operating in the canyon. Two years later, Congress passed a bill forming Zion National Park. In the 1920s the Union Pacific Railroad completed a rail line to Cedar City and Zion; Zion Lodge was built; and the technically challenging construction of the Zion-Mt. Carmel Highway, including its impressive 5,613-foot tunnel, began.

Early homesteaders around Bryce took visiting friends and relatives to see the incredible rock formations, and pretty soon they found themselves in the tourism business. In 1923, when Bryce Canyon National Monument was dedicated, the Union Pacific Railroad took over the fledgling tourist camp and began building Bryce Lodge. Tours of the hoodoos proved to be spectacularly popular, and Bryce became a national park in 1928.

Like Bryce and Zion, Arches was also helped along by railroad executives looking to develop their own businesses. In 1929 President Herbert Hoover signed the legislation creating Arches National Monument.

Capitol Reef became a national monument in 1937, thanks largely to one vigorous and enthusiastic local, and for years it was loved passionately by a handful of Utah archaeology buffs but largely ignored by the federal government, who put it under the administrative control of Zion National Park.

During the 1960s the National Park Service responded to a huge increase in park visitation nationwide by expanding facilities, spurring Congress to change the status of several national monuments to national parks. Canyonlands became a national park in the 1960s; after a spate of uranium prospecting in the nuclear-giddy 1950s, Capitol Reef and Arches gained national park status in 1971.

As visitors continued to flood the parks during the 1980s and 1990s, park managers realized they needed to develop strategies to deal with the crowds and especially the traffic. New trails, campgrounds, and visitors centers were built, and Zion and Bryce have both made attempts to control traffic on their scenic roads.

In 1996, President Bill Clinton used provisions of the National Antiquities Act to establish the Grand Staircase-Escalante National Monument, a sudden announcement that angered many locals. This vast tract of land, which totals more than 1.8 million acres, is the largest national monument land grouping in the Lower 48, bringing under federal Department of the Interior management tracts of land previously administered by the Bureau of Land Management, the National Forest Service, and the state of Utah. Designation as a national monument means that the land is off-limits to specific kinds of development and that the land is managed to preserve its wilderness characteristics as much as possible. The timing of the designation was apparently motivated by plans to develop a large strip coal mine in the slickrock Escalante River canyons, a well-loved destination for long-distance hikers and adventurers.

The People

One of the oddest statistics about Utah is that it's the most urban of the country's western states. Eighty-five percent of the state's population of 2.8 million live in urban areas, and a full 80 percent reside in the Wasatch Front area. That means that there aren't many people in remote southern Utah. With the exception of St. George, Cedar City, Kanab, and Moab, there are no sizable communities in this part of the state. Even the undaunted Mormon settlers found this a forbidding place to settle during their 19th-century agrarian colonization of Utah.

Moab is known as a youthful and dynamic town, and its mountain bikers set the civic tone more than the Mormon Church. However, outside Moab, most small ranching communities in southeastern Utah are still deeply Mormon. It's a good idea to develop an understanding of Utah's predominant religion if you plan on spending any time here outside the parks.

LATTER-DAY SAINTS

One of the first things to know is that the term *Mormon* is rarely used by church members themselves. The church's proper title is the Church of Jesus Christ of Latter-day Saints, and members prefer to be called Latter-day Saints, Saints (usually this term is just used among church members), or LDS. While calling someone a Mormon isn't wrong, it's not quite as respectful.

The religion is based in part on the Book of Mormon, the name given to a text derived from a set of golden plates found by Joseph Smith in 1827 in western New York State. Smith claimed to have been led by an angel to the plates, which were covered with a text written in "reformed Egyptian." A farmer by upbringing, Smith translated the plates and published an English-language version of the Book of Mormon in 1830.

The Book of Mormon tells the story of the lost tribes of Israel, which, according to Mormon teachings, migrated to North America and became the ancestors of today's Native Americans. According to the Book of Mormon, Jesus also journeyed to North America, and the book includes teachings and prophecies that Christ supposedly gave to the ancient Native Americans.

The most stirring and unifying aspect of Mormon history is the incredible westward migration made by the small, fiercely dedicated band of Mormon pioneers in the 1840s. Smith and his followers were persecuted in New York and then in their newly founded utopian communities in Ohio, Missouri, and Illinois. After Smith was murdered near Carthage, Illinois, in 1844, the group decided to press even farther westward toward the frontier, led by church president Brigham Young. The journey across the then very Wild West to the Great Salt Lake basin was made by horse, wagon, or handcart—hundreds of Mormon pioneers pulled their belongings across the Great Plains in small carts. The first group of Mormon pioneers reached what is now the Salt Lake City area in 1847. The bravery and tenacity of the group's two-year migration forms the basis of many Utah residents' fierce pride in their state and their religion.

Most people know that LDS members are clean-living, family-focused people who eschew alcohol, tobacco, and stimulants, including caffeine. This can make it a little tough for visitors to feed their own vices, and indeed, it may make what formerly seemed like a normal habit feel a little more sinister. But Utah has loosened up a lot in the last decade or so, largely thanks to having hosted the 2002 Winter Olympics, and it's really not too hard to find a place to have a beer with dinner, although you may have to make a special request. Towns near the national parks are particularly used to hosting non-Mormons, and residents attach virtually no stigma to waking up with a cup of coffee or winding down with a glass of wine.

SOUTHERN UTAH'S NATIVE AMERICANS

It's an oddity of history that most visitors to Utah's national parks will see much more evidence of the state's ancient native residents—in the form of eerie rock art, stone pueblos, and storehouses—than they will of today's remaining Native Americans. The prehistoric residents of the canyons of southeastern Utah left their mark on the land but largely moved on. The fate of the ancient Fremont people has been lost to history, and the abandonment of Anasazi, or Ancestral Puebloan, villages is a mystery still being unearthed by archaeologists. When the Mormons arrived in the 1840s, isolated bands of Native Americans lived in the river canyons. Federal reservations were granted to several of these groups.

Ute

Several bands of Utes, or Núuci, ranged over large areas of central and eastern Utah and adjacent Colorado. Originally hunter-gatherers, they acquired horses around 1800 and became skilled raiders. Customs adopted from Plains people included the use of rawhide, tepees, and the travois, a sled used to carry goods. The discovery of gold in southern Colorado and the pressures of farmers there and in Utah forced the Utes to move and renegotiate treaties many times. They now have the large Uintah and Ouray Indian Reservation in northeast Utah, the small White Mesa Indian Reservation in southeast Utah, and the Ute Mountain Indian Reservation in southwest Colorado and northwest New Mexico.

Southern Paiute

Six of the 19 major bands of Southern Paiutes, or Nuwuvi, lived along the Santa Clara, Beaver, and Virgin Rivers and in other parts of southwest Utah. Historically, extended families hunted and gathered food together. Fishing and the cultivation of corn, beans, squash, and sunflowers supplemented the diet of most of the communities. Today, Utah's Paiutes have their headquarters in Cedar City and scattered small parcels of reservation land. Southern Paiutes also live in southern Nevada and northern Arizona.

Navajo

Calling themselves Diné, the Navajo moved into the San Juan River area around 1600. The Navajo have proved exceptionally adaptable in learning new skills from other cultures: Many

Navajo crafts, clothing, and religious practices have come from Native American, Spanish, and Anglo neighbors. The Navajo were the first in the area to move away from hunting and gathering lifestyles, relying instead on the farming and shepherding techniques they had learned from the Spanish. The Navajo are one of the largest Native American groups in the country, with 16 million acres of exceptionally scenic land in southeast Utah and adjacent Arizona and New Mexico. The Navajo Nation's headquarters is at Window Rock, Arizona.

ESSENTIALS

Getting There

If you're driving from other points in North America, Utah is easy to reach. The parks are east of I-15, which runs parallel to the Rocky Mountains from Montana to Southern California. And they're south of I-70, which links Denver to I-15.

International travelers flying into the region have numerous options. Salt Lake City is convenient as a terminus for travelers who want to make a road-trip loop tour through all of Utah's parks. For other travelers, Utah's national parks may be best seen as part of a longer U.S. road trip. Many European travelers fly into Denver, rent vehicles or RVs, cross the Rocky Mountains, and explore the parks of southern Utah and perhaps the Grand Canyon on the way to Las Vegas, whence they return.

Public transportation, like regularly scheduled flights, is almost nonexistent in southern Utah and the parks; you'll need your own vehicle to explore the area.

FROM SALT LAKE CITY

Many tours of Utah's national parks begin in Salt Lake City. Its busy airport and plethora of hotels make it an easy place to begin and end a trip.

© PAUL LEVY

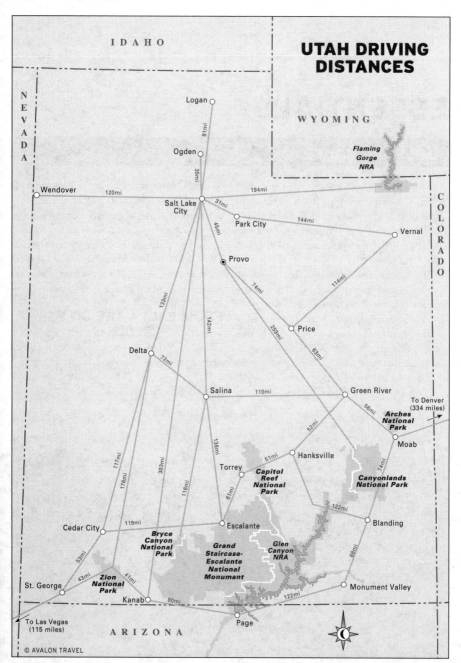

UTAH DRIVING DISTANCES

IDAHO

NEVADA

WYOMING

Flaming Gorge NRA

Logan

118mi

Ogden

35mi

Wendover — 120mi — Salt Lake City — 194mi

COLORADO

31mi — Park City — 144mi — Vernal

45mi

Provo

133mi

74mi

114mi

142mi

Price

255mi

Delta

72mi

63mi

Salina — 110mi — Green River

To Denver (334 miles)

56mi

Arches National Park

52mi

136mi

Moab

117mi

303mi

51mi — Hanksville

Torrey

Capitol Reef National Park

Canyonlands National Park

74mi

176mi

118mi

61mi

122mi

Cedar City — 119mi — Escalante

Blanding

Bryce Canyon National Park

Grand Staircase-Escalante National Monumant

Glen Canyon NRA

88mi

53mi

St. George

43mi

Zion National Park

41mi

Kanab — 80mi

122mi

Monument Valley

To Las Vegas (115 miles)

Page

ARIZONA

© AVALON TRAVEL

Airport

Salt Lake City is a hub for Delta Airlines, and all other major airlines have regular flights into **Salt Lake City International Airport** (SLC, 776 N. Terminal Dr., 801/575-2400, www.slcairport.com). The airport is an easy seven miles west of downtown; reach it via I-80 or North Temple Boulevard.

SkyWest Airlines (800/453-9417, www.skywest.com), Delta's and United's commuter partner, flies to Cedar City and St. George in Utah and to towns in adjacent states. Great Lakes Airlines (800/554-5111, www.flygreatlakes.com) provides daily scheduled air service between Canyonlands Field (CNY), just north of Moab, and Denver.

The Salt Lake City airport has three terminals; in each you'll find a ground transportation information desk, restaurants, motel and hotel courtesy phones, and car rentals (all the major companies are either on-site or a short shuttle ride away). Terminal 2 houses Zion's First National Bank for currency exchange. Terminal 3 is dedicated to international arrivals and departures.

Train

The only passenger train through Salt Lake City is Amtrak's *California Zephyr,* which heads west to Reno and Oakland and east to Denver and Chicago four times a week. **Amtrak** (station 340 S. 600 W., 800/872-7245, www.amtrak.com) prices tickets as airlines do, with discounts for advance booking, special seasonal fares, and other discounts available. Amtrak office hours are irregular and timed to meet the trains, so call first.

Long-Distance Bus

Salt Lake City is at a crossroads of several major highways and has good bus service from **Greyhound** (160 W. South Temple, 801/355-9579 or 800/231-2222, www.greyhound.com). Generally speaking, buses run north and south along I-15 and east and west along I-80; you won't be able to take the bus to any of Utah's national parks.

Car

From Salt Lake City, it's a long 238-mile drive to Moab, the center for exploring Arches and Canyonlands National Parks. The fastest route takes you south from Salt Lake City on I-15, cutting east at Spanish Fork on U.S. 6/89 to Price, south to Green River and I-70, and then to Moab on U.S. 191. Dramatic scenery highlights the entire length of this four-hour drive. To get to Zion and Bryce, simply take I-15 south from Salt Lake City; driving time is about four hours.

You'll find all of the major car rental companies at the Salt Lake City airport (www.slcairport.com).

RV and Motorcycle Rentals

Access RV Rental (2240 S. State St., Salt Lake City, 801/936-1200 or 800/327-6910, http://rentmotorhome.com) is a local company with relatively good rates on RV rentals. **Cruise America** (4125 S. State St., Salt Lake City, 801/288-0930, www.cruiseamerica.com) is a larger company with RV rentals available. **El Monte RV** (250 U.S. 89, North Salt Lake City, 888/337-2214, www.elmonterv.com) also provides rentals. Expect to pay $1,000-1,800 per week to rent an RV, depending on the season and the size of the vehicle; small travel trailers are less expensive but frequently unavailable.

Rent a motorcycle from **Street Eagle/ BMW Motorcycles of Utah** (339 W. 9000 S., Sandy, 801/658-7368, www.streeteagle.com, about $150 per day).

Accommodations

Salt Lake City has many hotel rooms across all price categories. We've included a few of our favorites here. Although most aren't airport hotels, the airport is pretty easy to get to from all of them.

If you're driving into town and just want to

find a hotel room fast, head south and west of downtown, where chain hotels proliferate. The area around 600 South and 200 West is especially fertile ground for mid-priced hotels.

UNDER $50

The Avenues Hostel (107 F St., 801/363-3855, www.saltlakehostel.com, $18 dorm, $40 d, only half have private baths), one mile east of Temple Square, offers lodging with the use of a kitchen, a TV room, and laundry. Information-packed bulletin boards list city sights and goings-on, and you'll meet travelers from all over the world. Reservations (with first night's deposit) are advised in the busy summer travel and winter ski seasons. From downtown, head east on South Temple Street to F Street, then turn north and go two blocks.

$50-100

The **Howard Johnson Express Inn** (121 N. 300 W., 801/521-3450 or 800/541-7639, www.hojo.com, from $64) is an older but well-maintained motor-court motel near Temple Square with a pool, complimentary continental breakfast, and free HBO.

Just east of Temple Square is the pleasant, well-maintained **Carlton Hotel** (140 E. South Temple, 801/355-3418 or 800/633-3500, www.carltonhotel-slc.com, from $74). The Carlton is an older hotel in a great location and offers guest laundry, an exercise room, a sauna, a hot tub, and in-room VCRs with free movies; there are also five suites.

$100-150

On the campus of the University of Utah, the **University Guest House and Conference Center** (110 S. Ft. Douglas Blvd., 801/587-1000 or 888/416-4075, www.universityguesthouse.com, from $95) is a good choice if you want a comfortable room, free parking, and nice walks nearby (check out the Red Butte Garden). Good restaurants are nearby,

and downtown is a short drive or light-rail trip away.

Comfortable guest rooms, an outdoor pool, and a better-than-average included continental breakfast make the **Comfort Inn Airport** (200 N. Admiral Byrd Rd., 801/537-7444 or 800/535-8742, www.comfortinn.com, $129 and up) an appealing place to spend a night.

The **Radisson Hotel Salt Lake City Airport** (2177 W. North Temple, 801/364-5800 or 800/967-9033, www.radisson.com, $112 and up) is an attractive lodge-like building with nicely furnished guest rooms. Guests receive a complimentary continental breakfast and newspaper, and in the evenings there's a manager's reception with free beverages. Facilities include a pool, a spa, and a fitness room. Suites come with a loft bedroom area. There's quite a range in room rates, and package rates and promotions can bring the rates down dramatically. At the **Airport Hilton** (5151 Wiley Post Way, 801/539-1515 or 800/999-3736, www1.hilton.com, from $135), guest rooms are spacious and nicely furnished, and facilities include two pools, a putting green, a sports court, and an exercise room and whirlpool. The hotel even has its own lake.

OVER $150

If you really want to do Salt Lake City in style, two downtown hotels are good places to splurge. **Hotel Monaco** (15 W. 200 S., 801/595-0000 or 877/294-9710, www.monaco-saltlakecity.com, from $219) occupies a grandly renovated historic office building in a convenient spot in the middle of downtown; on the main floor is Bambara, one of the most sophisticated restaurants in Utah. Guest rooms are sumptuously furnished with real élan: This is no anonymous upscale hotel in beige and mauve. Expect wild colors and contrasting fabrics, lots of flowers, and excellent service. Facilities include an on-site fitness center, meeting rooms, and concierge and valet services.

Pets are welcome, and if you forgot your own pet, the hotel will deliver a companion goldfish to your room. Room rates vary greatly; check the website to discover unexpected bargains.

The gigantic **Grand America Hotel and Suites** (75 E. 600 S., 800/533-3525, www.grandamerica.com, $309 and up), is Salt Lake City's take on the Vegas fantasy hotel. A block square (that's 10 acres in this land of long blocks), its 24 stories contain 775 guest rooms, more than half of them suites. Guest rooms have luxury-level amenities; expect all the perks and niceties that modern hotels can offer.

Camping

Of the several commercial campgrounds around the periphery of Salt Lake City, **Camp VIP/Salt Lake City KOA** (1350 W. North Temple, 801/328-0224, www.koa.com) is the most convenient, located between downtown and the airport. It offers tent sites (from $27) and RV sites (from $47) year-round with showers, a swimming pool, a game room, a playground, a store, and laundry. From I-15 northbound, take exit 308 onto I-80; go west 1.3 miles on I-80, exit north on Redwood Road (Hwy. 68) and go 0.5 miles, then turn right and continue another 0.5 miles on North Temple. From I-15 southbound, take exit 310 and go south 1.5 miles on 900 West, then turn right and drive less than one mile on North Temple. From I-80 take either the North Temple exit or Redwood Road (Hwy. 68), and go 0.5 miles, then turn right and continue another 0.5 miles on North Temple.

There are two good Forest Service campgrounds in Big Cottonwood Canyon, about 15 miles southeast of downtown Salt Lake City, and another two up Little Cottonwood Canyon, about 19 miles southeast of town. All have drinking water, and all prohibit pets because of local watershed regulations; sites range $19-22, and some can be reserved (877/444-6777, www.recreation.gov, $10 reservation fee).

Spruces Campground (elevation 7,400 feet, early June-mid-Oct.) is 9.1 miles up Big Cottonwood Canyon. **Redman Campground** (elevation 8,300 feet, no reservations, mid-June-early Oct.) is between Solitude and Brighton, 14 miles up Big Cottonwood Canyon.

Tanners Flat Campground (elevation 7,200 feet, no reservations, mid-May-mid-Oct.) is 4.3 miles up Little Cottonwood Canyon. **Albion Basin Campground** (elevation 9,500 feet, no reservations, early July-late Sept.) is high in the mountains a few miles past Alta Ski Area; go 11 miles up the canyon, the last 2.5 miles on gravel.

Food

If you're going to be camping on your trip through southeastern Utah's national parks, you may want to pick up some provisions in Salt Lake City before hitting the road south. Just east of I-15, off I-80 in the Sugar House district, **Whole Foods Market** (1131 E. Wilmington Ave., 801/359-7913) has a good deli, lots of organic produce, bulk foods, and good bread (likely the last you'll see for a while). It's in a complex that also contains some good restaurants, a camping supply store, and the brightest, shiniest tattoo parlor you'll ever lay eyes on.

Downtown, stop at **Tony Caputo Market & Deli** (308 W. Broadway, 801/531-8669, www.caputosdeli.com, 9am-7pm Mon., 9am-9pm Tues.-Sat., 10am-5pm Sun.), an old-style Italian deli brimming with delicious sausages, cheeses, and olives. Don't forget to get a sandwich to go.

For Salt Lake City's best restaurants, you have to head downtown. **Lamb's** (169 S. Main St., 801/364-7166, www.lambsgrill.com, 7am-9pm Mon.-Fri., 8am-9pm Sat., $13-15) claims to be Utah's oldest restaurant. You can still enjoy the classic 1930s diner atmosphere as well as the tasty food. Lamb's is an especially good place for breakfast.

Red Iguana (736 W. North Temple, 801/322-1489, www.rediguana.com, 11am-10pm Mon.-Thurs., 11am-11pm Fri., 10am-11pm Sat.,

10am-9pm Sun., $8-22), on the way in from the airport, is one of the city's favorite Mexican restaurants and offers excellent south-of-the-border cooking with a specialty in Mayan and regional foods. Best of all, the flavors are crisp, fresh, and earthy. The Red Iguana is very popular, so arrive early—especially at lunch—to avoid the lines.

For fine dining, the **Metropolitan** (173 W. Broadway, 801/362-3472, www.themetropolitan.com, 11:30am-2pm and 6pm-9pm Mon.-Thurs., 11:30am-2pm and 6pm-9:30pm Fri., 6pm-9:30pm Sat., 6pm-9pm Sun., $25-35) is easily Salt Lake City's most ambitious restaurant, taking "fusion cuisine" to new lengths. In this high-design dining room (reserve tables near the fireplace and water sculpture), the foods of the world meet and mingle on your plate in preparations that are sometimes unexpected but always stylish.

In the Hotel Monaco, **Bambara** (202 S. Main St., 801/363-5454, www.bambara-slc.com, 7am-10am, 11am-2pm, and 5:30pm-10pm Mon.-Thurs., 7am-10am, 11am-2pm, and 5:30pm-10:30pm Fri., 8am-11am and 5:30pm-10:30pm Sat., 8am-noon and 5:30pm-9pm Sun., $20-25) has a menu that emphasizes the freshest and most flavorful local meats and produce, with preparations in a wide-awake New American style that is equal parts tradition and innovation.

Utah's oldest brewpub is **Squatters Pub Brewery** (147 W. Broadway, 801/363-2739, www.squatters.com, 11am-midnight Mon.-Thurs., 11am-1am Fri., 10:30am-1am Sat., 10:30am-midnight Sun., $8-18). In addition to fine beers and ales, the pub serves sandwiches, burgers, and other light entrées in a handsome old warehouse. In summer there's seating on the back deck. Another popular brewpub is the **Red Rock Brewing Company** (254 S. 200 W., 801/521-7446, www.redrockbrewing.com, 11am-midnight Sun.-Thurs., 11am-1am Fri.-Sat., $10-20), offering pasta, salads, and sandwiches, including an excellent variation on the hamburger, baked in a wood-fired oven inside a bread pocket. There's often a wait to get in the door, but the food and brews are worth it.

FROM LAS VEGAS

Just because you're going to Utah, don't assume it's best to fly into Salt Lake City. If you're traveling to Zion, Bryce, or Grand Staircase-Escalante, consider flying into Las Vegas rather than Salt Lake City. Not only is it closer to these parks, but car rentals are usually about $100 a week cheaper. Even if you have absolutely no interest in gambling, many casino hotels have very good midweek rates.

Airport

McCarran International Airport (LAS, 5757 Wayne Newton Blvd., 702/261-5743, www.mccarran.com) is just a few minutes south of the Strip (a.k.a. Las Vegas Blvd. S.), the six-mile stretch of casinos and hotels.

Las Vegas is well served by major domestic airlines, and also by smaller or "no-frills" carriers such as Frontier Airlines (800/432-1359, www.frontierairlines.com), Spirit Airlines (800/772-7117, www.spiritair.com) and Southwest Airlines (800/435-9792, www.southwest.com), whose bargain prices keep the other airlines competitive.

The airport has two terminals—Terminal 1 has most of the domestic traffic, while the massive new high-tech Terminal 3 serves international and charter flights (Terminal 2 was closed when 3 opened in 2012). Exchange foreign currency in Terminal 3; find full-service banking and check-in for some of the larger casino hotels in Terminal 1. Slot machines, of course, are everywhere.

Long-Distance Bus

Greyhound (220 S. Main St., 702/383-9792, www.greyhound.com) serves communities along the I-15 corridor, including St. George.

Car

From Las Vegas, it's just 120 miles northeast on I-15 to St. George, with Zion just 43 miles farther.

It's relatively inexpensive to rent a car in Las Vegas; an economy car will run about $120 per week, before taxes. At the airport, find **Avis** (702/261-5591 or 800/331-1212), **Budget** (800/922-2899), **Dollar** (702/739-8403 or 800/800-4000), **Hertz** (702/736-4900 or 800/654-3131), **National** (702/261-5391 or 800/227-7368), **Payless** (702/736-6147 or 800/729-5377), **Alamo** (800/462-5266), and **Thrifty** (702/896-7600 or 800/367-2277).

RV Rentals

Rent an RV from **Cruise America** (551 N. Gibson Rd., Henderson, 888/980-8282, www.cruiseamerica.com). **El Monte RV** (13001 Las Vegas Blvd., 702/269-8000 or 888/337-2214, www.elmonterv.com) is another good bet. Rates typically start at about $1,000 a week.

Accommodations

For its sheer number of hotel rooms, Las Vegas can't be beat. Even if you have no desire to visit Vegas, it may make sense to spend the first or final night of your trip here. During the week, it's relatively easy to find a good rate at a casino hotel. However, beware of weekends if you're watching your pennies: on Saturday night rooms often cost triple what they cost during the week. Reservation services, such as **Las Vegas Hotels Reservation Service** (877/477-8005, www.lasvegasnevadahotels.org) or the **Las Vegas Convention and Visitor Authority** (702/892-0711, www.visitlasvegas.com), may be able to help you find a good deal on a room. Most of the major casino hotels (Caesar's Palace, New York New York, the Venetian, and others) have guest rooms for over $100, but specials in the $60-80 range are easy to find. You'll find them listed on reservation services, which makes it easy to locate a room that suits your taste and budget.

About one mile from the airport, and not too far off the south end of the Strip, find the **Ambassador Strip Travelodge** (5075 Koval Lane, 702/736-3600 or 888/844-3131, $49 weekdays, $99 weekends). This motel, with an outdoor pool and continental breakfast included, is a good alternative to a casino hotel. Just a little more expensive and also off the Strip near the airport is the **Best Western McCarran Inn** (4970 Paradise Rd., 702/798-5530 or 800/626-7575, www.bestwestern.com, $70-80 weekdays, $90-110 weekends).

Food

As celebrity chefs from around the country have established outposts in various upscale casinos, Las Vegas has become a destination for fine dining. Nearly every casino hotel has multiple restaurants, sometimes multiple fine dining restaurants. For instance, at the MGM Grand (3799 Las Vegas Blvd. S., 702/891-7374, www.mgmgrand.com) there's both **Craftsteak** for the high-end steak house experience, courtesy of Tom Colicchio, and **Joel Robuchon,** the eponymous restaurant of the renowned French chef. And talk about an embarrassment of riches—at the Venetian Hotel (3355 Las Vegas Blvd. S., 702/414-3737, www.venetian.com), Emeril Lagasse owns the **Delmonico,** a steak house that goes well above and beyond your basic rib eye; Thomas Keller has **Bouchon,** promising high-end Napa Valley dining; Mario Batali has an Italian outpost called **B&B Ristorante;** and Wolfgang Puck operates **Postrio Bar and Grill.**

Expect main courses at all of these restaurants to be $30-40 and up. Dine less expensively on a selection of appetizers. Cheaper dining can be found at casino buffets, or try **Pink Taco** (Hard Rock Hotel, 4455 Paradise Rd., 702/693-5525, www.hardrockhotel.com, $15-25) for Mexican food in a hip, freewheeling atmosphere.

Finally, if you want a taste of old Vegas, head up to the 24th floor of Binion's Horseshoe to **Binion's Ranch Steakhouse** (128 E. Fremont

St., 702/382-1600, www.binions.com, $31-50), a Las Vegas institution with huge steaks and reasonable prices.

FROM DENVER

Although it may not seem intuitive to start your tour of Utah's national parks in Denver, that's exactly what works best for many folks, especially those who fly from European capital cities to Denver International Airport. From there, it's easy to rent a car or RV and begin a tour that typically includes Rocky Mountain National Park, Utah's five national parks, and the Grand Canyon before terminating at Las Vegas.

Airport

Locals joke that **Denver International Airport** (DEN, 8500 Peña Blvd., 303/342-2000, www.flydenver.com), often referred to as DIA, is in Kansas; it's actually 23 miles northeast of downtown Denver on Highway 470, north of I-70. Major airlines using DIA include American, British Airways, Continental, Delta, and United.

DIA's Jeppesen Terminal has a giant atrium and three concourses connected by a light-rail train. Car-rental counters are in the central terminal atrium between security screening areas.

Car

To drive from Denver to the parks, follow I-70 west, up over the Continental Divide along the Rocky Mountains, and down to the Colorado River. Cross into Utah and take I-70 exit 212 at Cisco. From Denver to Cisco is 297 miles, all on the freeway. From Cisco, follow Highway 128 for 37 highly scenic miles through red-rock canyons to Moab. Allow 5.5 hours of driving time between Moab and Denver.

All major car rental agencies have facilities near DIA.

RV Rentals

B&B RV (6960 Smith Rd., Denver, 303/322-6013, www.bb-rv.com) is a local company that rents RVs. **Moturis Inc./Camping World** (4100 Youngfield St., Denver, 800/222-6795, www.moturis.com) is west of downtown Denver. Regional corporations with offices in Denver include **Cruise America** (8950 N. Federal Blvd., Denver, 303/650-2865, www.cruiseamerica.com) and **El Monte RV** (5989 Main St., Louviers, 303/426-7998 or 888/337-2214, www.elmonterv.com).

Accommodations

Chain hotels have set up shop in the area surrounding DIA. Almost all offer shuttles to and from the airport.

For budget travelers, the **11th Avenue Hotel and Hostel** (1112 N. Broadway, 303/861-7777, http://innkeeperrockies.com, $21 dorm, $29 pp private rooms) is a 1903 hotel on the edge of downtown that's now a blend of hotel and hostel. Facilities include laundry, Internet access, and cable TV. There's no kitchen, but guests have access to a barbecue grill, a microwave, and a toaster oven.

The closest lodgings to DIA are about six miles from the airport. The **DIA Microtel Inn** (18600 E. 63rd Ave., 303/371-8300 or 800/771-7171, www.microtelinn.com, from $79) offers free breakfast. The **Quality Inn** (6890 Tower Rd., 303/371-5300 or 877/424-6423, www.qualityinn.com, from $89) is easy to find north of I-70 exit 286. About 12 miles south of the airport, near the intersection of I-70 and Peña Boulevard, is a cluster of chain motels, including **Comfort Inn** (16921 E. 32nd Ave., 303/367-5000, www.comfortinn.com, from $89).

The **Hilton Garden Inn Denver Airport** (16475 E. 40th Circle, 303/371-9393, www1.hilton.com, from $149) is near the intersection of I-70 and Peña Boulevard, south of the airport. Other comfortable DIA-area hotels include **Comfort Suites** (6210 Tower Rd., 303/371-9300, www.comfortsuites.com, from $109), where all guest rooms are suites, and the **Fairfield Inn Denver Airport** (6851

Tower Rd., 303/576-9640, www.marriott.com, $139). If you're looking for the classic swanky downtown-Denver hotel, try the **Brown Palace** (321 17th St., 303/297-3111 or 800/321-2599, www.brownpalace.com, from $233), a historic and ornate hotel from Denver's 1890s heyday.

Food

If you're just passing through DIA on your way to Utah, you'll find that there's not a lot of fine dining near the airport; inside the terminals there is a **Wolfgang Puck Express** (Concourse B, 303/342-7611), which is worth knowing about. You'll have to travel into Denver if you want to explore the dining scene.

There's a large Hispanic population, so it's no surprise that Denver has lots of Latin American restaurants, and these are often good and reliable places for inexpensive meals. However, some of Denver's most exciting restaurants are Nuevo Latin American restaurants—where familiar tacos, tortillas, and enchiladas are updated into zippy fine dining. One of the best is **Lola** (1575 Boulder St., 720/570-8686, www.loladenver.com, 4pm-10pm Mon.-Fri., 10am-10pm Sat.-Sun., entrées under $25), a hip and happening restaurant with over 150 tequilas to choose from and main courses like grilled pork with habañero sauce. Guacamole is prepared table-side, like Caesar salad in traditional American steak houses. More upscale is **Tamayo** (1400 Larimer St., 720/946-1433, www.richardsandoval.com, 11:30am-2pm and 5pm-10pm Mon.-Thurs., 11:30am-2pm and 5pm-11pm Fri., 5pm-11pm Sat., 5pm-10pm Sun., entrées $20-28), a hybrid of French refinement and zesty Mexican flavors. Views from this rooftop dining room overlook Larimer Square and the Rockies, making it a top spot for margaritas and appetizers, particularly the excellent shrimp tacos.

At **Deluxe** (30 S. Broadway, 303/722-1550, http://deluxedenver.com, 5pm-10pm Tues.-Sat., $10-28), the emphasis is on seasonal ingredients and perfect execution of international comfort foods such as spring vegetable risotto and lamb *ragù* with fresh pasta ribbons, along with delicious cocktails. The **Barolo Grill** (3030 E. 6th Ave., 303/393-1040, www.barologrilldenver.com, 5:30pm-10:30pm Tues.-Sat., $15-30) is a comfortable northern Italian restaurant with good salads and pasta as well as grilled fish, game, and chicken main courses. The wine list is outstanding. Denver is known for its steak houses, and one of the best is the locally owned **Capital Grille** (1450 Larimer St., 303/539-2500, www.thecapitalgrille.com, 11:30am-2:30pm and 5pm-10pm Mon.-Thurs., 11:30am-2:30pm and 5pm-11pm Fri., 5pm-11pm Sat., 4pm-9pm Sun., $19-40), with swank surroundings, an attentive staff, and excellent steaks, prime rib, and chops. For a lighter meal, go to **Falling Rock Tap House** (1919 Blake St., 303/293-8338, www.fallingrocktaphouse.com, 11am-2am daily, $8-20), one of Denver's top regional beer pubs, with over 75 brews on tap and tasty pub grub.

Getting Around

For most travelers, getting around southern Utah will require using some form of automobile. Public transport is nonexistent in and between the parks, and distances are great—although the parks cover a relatively compact area, the geography of the land is so contorted that there are few roads that connect the dots. For instance, from Moab to the Arizona border, a distance of nearly 130 miles, only one bridge crosses the Colorado River once it drops into its canyon. Cars are easily rented in gateway cities, and in towns like Moab there is a plethora of jeep and Humvee rentals as well.

Bicycle touring is certainly an excellent option, but cyclists need to be in good shape and be prepared for intense heat during summer trips. For detailed information on cycling Utah, read the classic *Bicycle Touring in Utah* by Dennis Coello, now out of print but available from libraries and used from online sources.

STREET NUMBERING AND GRID ADDRESSES

Many towns founded by Mormon settlers share a street-numbering scheme that can be confusing to first-time visitors but quickly becomes intuitive. A city's address grid will generally have its temple at the center, with blocks numbered by hundreds out in every direction. For instance, 100 West is one block west of the center of town, then comes 200 West, and so on. In conversation, you may hear the shorthand "4th South," "3rd West," and so on to indicate 400 South or 300 West.

While this street-numbering system is a picture of precision, it's also confusing at first. All addresses have four parts: When you see the address 436 North 100 West, for instance, the system tells you that the address will be found four blocks north of the center of town, on 100 West. One rule of thumb is to remember that the last two segments of an address (300 South, 500 East, 2300 West) are the street's actual name—the equivalent of a single street signifier such as Oak Street or Front Street.

TRAVELING BY RV

Traveling the Southwest's national parks in an RV is a time-honored tradition, and travelers will have no problem finding RV rentals in major cities like Denver, Salt Lake City, and Las Vegas, which serve as gateways to the parks of southern Utah. The parks have good campgrounds, and towns like Moab and Springdale have some very spiff campground options with extras like swimming pools and wireless Internet. Note that some parks attempt to limit vehicle access—to visit Bryce and Zion, you have need to leave the RV behind and tour the narrow park roads by free shuttle bus.

DRIVING THE PARKS

During the summer, patience is the key to driving in Utah's national parks. Roads are often crowded with slow-moving RVs, and traffic jams are not uncommon. At Zion, shuttle buses have replaced private vehicles along the scenic Zion Canyon Road, and a voluntary shuttle runs through the main Bryce Canyon amphitheater.

If you're traveling on back roads, especially in the Grand Staircase-Escalante National Monument, make sure you have plenty of gas, even if it means paying top dollar at a small-town gas pump.

Summer heat in the desert puts an extra strain on both cars and drivers. It's worth double-checking your vehicle's cooling system, engine oil, transmission fluid, fan belts, and tires to make sure they are in top condition. Carry several gallons of water in case of a breakdown or radiator trouble. Never leave children or pets in a parked car during warm weather; temperatures inside can cause fatal heatstroke in minutes.

At times the desert has too much water, when late-summer storms frequently flood low spots in the road. Wait for the water level to subside before crossing. Dust storms can completely block visibility but tend to be short-lived. During such storms, pull completely off the road, stop, and turn off your lights so as not to confuse other drivers. Radio stations carry frequent weather updates when weather hazards exist.

If stranded, stay with your vehicle unless you're positive of where to go for help, then leave a note explaining your route and departure time. Airplanes can easily spot a stranded car (tie a piece of cloth to your antenna), but a person walking is more difficult to see. It's best to carry emergency supplies: blankets or sleeping bags, a first-aid kit, tools, jumper cables, a shovel, traction mats or chains, a flashlight, rain gear, water, food, and a can opener.

Obey road signs and check in locally to make sure roads are open and passable.

Maps

The Utah Department of Transportation prints and distributes a free, regularly updated map of Utah. Ask for it when you call for information or when you stop at a visitor information office. Benchmark Maps' *Utah Road and Recreation Atlas* is loaded with beautiful maps, recreation information, and global positioning system (GPS) grids. If you're planning on extensive backcountry exploration, be sure to ask locally about conditions.

Off-Road Driving

Here are some tips for safely traversing the backcountry in a vehicle (preferably one with four-wheel drive):

- Drive slowly enough to choose a safe path and avoid obstacles such as rocks or giant potholes, but keep up enough speed to propel yourself through sand or mud.
- Keep an eye on the route ahead of you. If there are obstacles, stop, get out of your vehicle, and survey the situation.
- Reduce the tire pressure if you're driving across sand.
- Drive directly up or down the fall line of a slope. Cutting across diagonally may seem less frightening, but it puts you in a position to slide or roll over.

If you really want to learn to drive your 4WD rig, consider signing up for a class.

SHUTTLES

Both Zion and Bryce National Parks offer shuttle bus service during peak summer season along their primary entrance roads to reduce traffic and vehicular impact on the parks. In Zion, shuttles pick up visitors at various points around Springdale and take them to the park gate, where another shuttle runs park visitors up Zion Canyon Road, stopping at trailheads, scenic overlooks, and Zion Lodge. Essentially, private cars are no longer allowed on Zion

Canyon Road during peak season. (Registered overnight guests at Zion Lodge can drive their own vehicles to the hotel.)

In Bryce, the shuttle bus picks up visitors at the park gate and drives the length of the main parkway, making stops at all the major trailheads and vista points in addition to campgrounds, Ruby's Inn, and the Bryce Canyon Lodge. Using the shuttle bus is not required in Bryce, although it is highly recommended.

In both parks, the shuttle ticket cost is covered by park entrance fees.

TOURS

Bus tours of the southern Utah national parks, often in conjunction with Grand Canyon National Park, are available from several regional tour companies. **Southern Utah Scenic Tours** (435/656-1504 or 888/404-8687, www.utahscenictours.com) offers multiday scenic and thematic tours of the Southwest, including the Utah national parks.

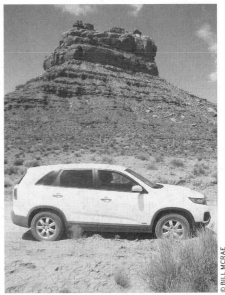
A high-clearance vehicle is a good idea on Utah back roads.

© BILL MCRAE

Road Scholar (800/454-5768, www.roadscholar.org) operates programs out of St. George, including a bus tour of southern Utah and northern Arizona's national parks and monuments. These trips are geared toward older adults (this is the organization formerly known as Elderhostel) and involve a bit of easy hiking.

For a truly unusual bus tour, consider the

Adventure Bus (375 S. Main St., Moab, 909/633-7225 or 888/737-5263, www.adventurebus.com), a bus that's had most of its seats removed to make lounge and sleeping areas. Guests live on the bus (some meals are provided) as it makes tours of Utah and other Southwest hot spots.

Recreation

Utah's national parks are home to epic landscapes—red-rock canyons, towering arches, and needles of sandstone that are best explored by foot, by bike, or on the water. Hikers will find a variety of trails, ranging from paved all-abilities paths to remote backcountry tracks. Rafts and jet boats out of Moab provide another means to explore rugged canyons otherwise inaccessible to all but the hardiest trekkers. The sheer rock cliff faces and promontories in

the parks provide abundant challenges to experienced rock climbers; be certain to check park regulations before climbing, however, as restrictions may apply.

HIKING

Utah's national parks offer lots of opportunities for hikers and backcountry enthusiasts interested in exploring the scenery on foot. Each of the parks has a variety of well-maintained

HOW TO CHOOSE AN OUTFITTER

Utah has many outfitters, guides, trail-drive operators, and guest ranches, all of which promise to get you outdoors and into an Old West adventure. But all outfitting and recreational services are not created equal. The most important consideration in choosing an outfitter is safety; the second is comfort. Make sure you feel confident on both counts before signing on.

Here are some points to ponder while you plan your adventure vacation.

All outfitters should be licensed or accredited by the state and be happy to provide you with proof. This means that they are bonded, carry the necessary insurance, and have money and organizational wherewithal to register with the state. This rules out fly-by-night operations and college students who've decided to set up business for the summer. If you're just starting to plan an excursion, contact the Utah Travel Council (Capitol Hill, Salt Lake City, 801/538-1030 or 800/200-1160, www.utah.com). The council's website contains an extensive network of outfitters and guides.

Many outfitters offer similar trips. When you've narrowed down your choices, call and talk to the outfitters on your short list. Ask lots of questions, and try to get a sense of who the people are; you'll be spending a lot of time with them, so make sure you feel comfortable. If you have special interests, like bird- or wildlife-watching, be sure to mention them to your potential outfitter. A good outfitter will take your interests into account when planning a trip.

If there's a wide disparity in prices among outfitters for the same trip, find out what makes up the difference. The cheapest trip may not be the best choice for you. Food is one of the most common areas to economize in. If you don't mind having cold cuts each meal for your five-day pack trip, then maybe the cheapest outfitter is OK. If you prefer a cooked meal, or alcoholic beverages, or a choice of entrées, then be prepared to pay more. On a long trip, it might be worth it. Also be sure you know what kinds of accommodations are included in multiday trips. You may pay more to have a tent or cabin to yourself, but again, it may be worth it.

Ask how many years an outfitter has been in business and how long your particular escort has guided this trip. Although a start-up outfitting service can be perfectly fine, you should know what level of experience you are buying. If you have questions, especially for longer or more dangerous trips, ask for referrals.

Most outfitters will demand that you pay a portion (usually half) of your fee well in advance to secure your place, so be sure to ask about cancellation policies. Some lengthy float trips can cost thousands of dollars; if cancellation means the forfeiture of the deposit, you need to know that. Also, find out what the tipping or gratuity policy is for your outfitter. Sometimes 15 or 20 percent extra is added to your bill as a tip for the "hands." Although this is undoubtedly nice for the help, you should be aware that your gratuities for a week's stay can run into the hundreds of dollars.

---

hiking trails, ranging from easy strolls to multiday backcountry treks. In fact, much of the Needles and Maze districts in Canyonlands and the most compelling parts of Capitol Reef and Zion are accessible only by foot; visits to remote Anasazi ruins and petroglyphs are among the rewards for the long-distance hiker.

One increasingly popular activity is canyoneering—exploring mazelike slot canyons. Hundreds of feet deep but sometimes only wide enough for a hiker to squeeze through, these canyons are located across southern Utah, with some great ones near Escalante and in the Paria River area. You'll need to be fit to explore these regions—and watch the weather carefully for flash floods.

CAMPING

All of Utah's national parks have campgrounds, with each park keeping at least one campground open year-round. Most campgrounds are first-come, first-served; reservations (www.recreation.gov, $9 reservation fee) are accepted

© PAUL LEVY

hiking ridges above the Escalante River

seasonally at Zion's Watchman Campground, Bryce's Sunset Campground, and Arches' Devils Garden Campground. During the summer and on holiday weekends during the spring and fall, it's best to arrive at the park early in the day and select a campsite immediately. Don't expect to find hookups or showers at National Park Service campgrounds. For these comforts, look just outside the park entrance, where you'll generally find at least one full-service commercial campground.

Backcountry Camping

Backcountry campers in national parks must stop by the park visitors center for a backcountry permit. Backcountry camping may be limited to specific sites in order to spread people out a bit; if so, a park ranger will consult with you and assign you a campground.

Before heading into the backcountry, check with a ranger about weather, water sources, fire danger, trail conditions, and regulations. Backpacking stores are also good sources of information. Here are some tips for traveling safely and respectfully in the backcountry:

- Tell rangers or other reliable people where you are going and when you expect to return; they'll alert rescuers if you go missing.
- Travel in small groups for the best experience (group size may also be regulated).
- Avoid stepping on—or camping on—fragile cryptobiotic soils.
- Use a portable stove to avoid leaving fire scars.
- Resist the temptation to shortcut switchbacks; this causes erosion and can be dangerous.
- Avoid digging tent trenches or cutting vegetation.
- Help preserve old Native American and other historic ruins.
- Camp at least 300 feet away from springs, creeks, and trails. Camp at least 0.25 miles from a lone water source to avoid scaring away wildlife and livestock.
- Avoid camping in washes at any time; be alert to thunderstorms.
- Take care not to throw or kick rocks off trails—someone might be below you.
- Don't drink water directly from streams or lakes, no matter how clean the water

AMERICA THE BEAUTIFUL INTERAGENCY PASSES

The U.S. government revamped its year-long park pass system in 2007, doing away with the old Golden Eagle, Golden Age, and Golden Access passes. The new passes are the result of a cooperative effort between the National Park Service, the Forest Service, the U.S. Fish and Wildlife Service, the Bureau of Land Management, and the Bureau of Reclamation.

The basic pass is called the **America the Beautiful–National Parks and Federal Recreational Lands Pass** (valid for 1 year from date of purchase, $80), which is available to the general public and provides access to, and use of, federal recreation sites that charge an entrance or standard amenity fee. Passes can be obtained in person at a park; by calling 888-ASK-USGS–888/275-8747, ext. 1; or at http://store.usgs.gov/pass.

U.S. citizens or permanent residents age 62 or older can purchase a lifetime version of the America the Beautiful pass for $10. This pass can only be obtained in person at a park. The Senior Pass provides free access to federal parks and recreational areas, plus a 50 percent discount on some fees, such as camp-ing, swimming, boat launch, and specialized interpretive services. The pass is good for the cardholder plus three adults (children 16 and under are free). The pass is nontransferable and generally does not cover or reduce special recreation permit fees or fees charged by park concessionaires.

U.S. citizens or permanent residents with permanent disabilities are eligible for a free lifetime America the Beautiful Access Pass. Documentation such as a statement from a licensed physician, the Veterans Administration, or Social Security is required to obtain this pass, which can only be obtained in person at a park. Like the Senior Pass, the Access Pass provides free access to federal parks and recreational areas, plus a 50 percent discount on some fees, such as camping, swimming, boat launch, and specialized interpretive services. Free annual passes are also available to members of the U.S. military and their families.

Volunteers who have amassed 250 service hours with one of the participating federal agencies are eligible for a free one-year pass, which is available through their supervisor.

appears; it may contain the parasitic proto-zoan *Giardia lamblia,* which causes giardia-sis. Boiling water for several minutes will kill giardia as well as most other bacterial or viral pathogens. Chemical treatments and water filters usually work too, although they're not as reliable as boiling (giardia spends part of its life in a hard shell that protects it from most chemicals).

- Bathe and wash dishes away from lakes, streams, and springs. Use biodegradable soap, and scatter your wash water.
- Bring a trowel for personal sanitation. Dig 6-8 inches deep and cover your waste; in some areas, you'll be required to carry portable human waste disposal systems.
- Pack out all your trash, including toilet paper and feminine hygiene items.
- Bring plenty of feed for your horses and mules.

- Leave dogs at home; they're not permitted on national park trails.
- If you realize you're lost, find shelter. If you're sure of a way to civilization and plan to walk out, leave a note with your departure time and planned route.
- Visit the Leave No Trace website (www.lnt.org) for more details on responsible back-country travel.

CLIMBING

Most visitors to Utah's national parks enjoy spotting rock climbers scaling canyon walls and sandstone pillars, but for a few, the whole reason to visit southern Utah is to climb. These folks need a climbing guide, either the classic *Desert Rock* by Eric Bjørnstad or *Rock Climbing Utah,* by Stewart M. Green.

Prospective climbers should take note: Just

© PAUL LEVY

Camping at Utah's national parks gets you closer to the spirit of the land.

because you're the star of the local rock gym, don't think that climbing Zion's high exposed big walls or Canyonlands' remote sandstone towers is going to be simple. Sandstone poses its own set of challenges; it weakens when wet, so it's wise to avoid climbing in damp areas or after rain. The Entrada sandstone in Arches is particularly tough to climb.

Climbers in the national parks should take care to use clean climbing techniques. Approach climbs via established trails to prevent further erosion of slopes. Camp in park campgrounds, or on multiday climbs, get a backcountry permit. Because white chalk leaves unsightly marks on canyon walls, add red pigment to your chalk. Do not disturb vegetation growing in cracks along your route. Tube or bag human waste and carry it out. Remove all old worn rope and equipment, but do not remove fixed pins. Make sure your climb is adequately protected by visually inspecting any preexisting bolts or fixed pins. It is illegal to use a power drill to place bolts. Never climb

directly above trails, where hikers may be hit by dislodged rocks.

In Canyonlands, even stricter regulations are in place. Here, no new climbing hardware may be left in a fixed location; protection may not be placed with the use of a hammer except to replace existing belay and rappel anchors and bolts on existing routes (or for emergency self-rescue); and unsafe slings must be replaced with earth-colored slings.

Plan to climb in the spring or fall. During the summer, the walls become extremely hot. Some climbing areas may be closed during the spring to protect nesting raptors. Check at the visitors centers for current closures.

4WD EXPLORATION

Utah's national parks are all blessed with fine paved roads—but if you have a high-clearance vehicle, you should explore some of the back roads of southern Utah. The following roads are either graded dirt or gravel, often with a bit of paved road to begin with, and in dry conditions they are passable by most passenger

VISITOR INFORMATION

General tourism literature and maps are available from the **Utah Travel Council** (Council Hall/Capitol Hill, Salt Lake City, UT 84114-7420, 801/538-1030, fax 801/538-1399, www.utah.com). Call or write in advance of your visit to obtain maps and brochures from the parks.

Arches National Park
P.O. Box 907
Moab, UT 84532-0907
435/719-2299
www.nps.gov/arch

Bryce Canyon National Park
P.O. Box 640201
Bryce Canyon, UT 84764-0201
435/834-5322
www.nps.gov/brca

Canyonlands National Park
2282 SW Resource Blvd.
Moab, UT 84532-3298
435/719-2100
www.nps.gov/cany

Capitol Reef National Park
HC 70 Box 15
Torrey, UT 84775-9602
435/425-3791
www.nps.gov/care

Grand Staircase-Escalante National Monument
669 S. U.S. 89A
Kanab, UT 84741
435/644-1200
www.ut.blm.gov/monument

Zion National Park
Springdale, UT 84767-1099
435/772-3256
www.nps.gov/zion

vehicles, including cars. You'll travel with less concern if you have a higher clearance vehicle (if you're renting, get an SUV); always check in locally to make sure that roads are open and passable. By getting off the highway, you'll leave behind 99 percent of the crowds and have some of Utah's most amazing scenery to yourself.

From Escalante or Boulder, **Hell's Backbone Road** climbs up through alpine forests to 9,200 feet before dropping down onto a one-lane bridge that vaults across a chasm between two precipitous canyons. Bring a camera—and some Xanax.

Handy **Notom-Bullfrog Road** links the northern reaches of Capitol Reef National Reef with Lake Powell and other sites in remote southeastern Utah. Best of all, you'll get a feel for the Waterpocket Fold, the formation that makes up most of Capitol Reef park, but that travelers who stick to paved Highway 24 don't really experience. Time your trip right, and you can cross Lake Powell on Utah's only public car ferry.

Burr Trail, a former cattle route, departs from Boulder to skirt the northern canyons of the Escalante River system, ending near the Waterpocket Fold in Capitol Reef National Park, which it descends in an amazing series of switchbacks—dropping 800 feet in less than one mile. Good brakes are a plus.

Wet weather frequently closes **Cottonwood Canyon Road,** but it's one of the most scenic in the Grand Staircase-Escalante National Monument if for no other reason than it's the access road for wonderful Kodachrome Basin and Grosvenor Arch. Continue south to U.S. 89 for excellent canyon hiking and visits to vintage movie sets.

Follow **Hole in the Rock Road** to its end to parallel the route of intrepid Mormon pioneers and to catch a peek of Lake Powell, or simply use this well-maintained gravel road as access to the amazing slot canyons of the Escalante River system (at least check out the Devils Garden).

Tips for Travelers

Southern Utah may seem a remote, uninhabited, and even hostile destination, but it sees hundreds of thousands of travelers each year and has sufficient facilities to ensure that visitors have a pleasant vacation. Before you visit, here are a few tips to ensure that your Utah vacation goes well.

FOREIGN VISITORS
Entering the United States
Citizens of Canada must provide a passport to enter the United States, but a visa is not required for Canadian citizens.

Citizens of 28 other countries can enter the United States under a reciprocal visa-waiver program. These citizens can enter for up to 90 days for tourism or business with a valid passport, and no visa is required. These countries include most of Western Europe plus Japan, Australia, New Zealand, and Singapore. For a full list of reciprocal visa-waiver countries (along with other late-breaking news for travelers to the United States), check out www.travel.state.gov. Visitors on this program who arrive by sea or air must show round-trip tickets out of the United States dated within 90 days, and they must present proof of financial solvency (credit cards are usually sufficient). If citizens of these countries are staying longer than 90 days, they must apply for and present a visa.

Citizens of countries not covered by the reciprocal visa-waiver program are required to present both a valid passport and a visa to enter the United States. These are obtained from U.S. embassies and consulates. These travelers are also required to offer proof of financial solvency and show a round-trip ticket out of the United States dated within the timeline of the visa.

Once in the United States, foreign visitors can travel freely among states without restrictions.

Customs
U.S. Customs allows each person over the age of 21 to bring one liter of liquor and 200 cigarettes into the country duty-free. Non-U.S. citizens can bring in $100 worth of gifts without paying duty. If you are carrying more than $10,000 in cash or traveler's checks, you are required to declare it.

Money and Currency Exchange
Except in Salt Lake City, there are few opportunities to exchange foreign currency or traveler's checks in non-U.S. funds at Utah banks or exchanges. Traveler's checks in U.S. dollars are accepted at face value in most businesses without additional transaction fees.

By far the best way to keep yourself in cash is by using bank, debit, or cash cards at ATMs (automated teller machines). Not only does withdrawing funds from your own home account save on fees, but you also often get a better rate of exchange. Nearly every town in Utah has an ATM. Most ATMs at banks require a small fee to dispense cash. Most grocery stores allow you to use a debit or cash card to purchase food, with the option of a cash withdrawal. These transactions are free to the withdrawer.

Credit cards are accepted nearly everywhere in Utah. The most common are Visa and MasterCard. American Express, Diners Club, and Discover are also used, although these aren't as ubiquitous.

Electricity
As in all of the United States, electricity is 110 volts, 60 hertz. Plugs have either two flat prongs or two flat prongs plus one round prong. Older homes and hotels may have outlets that only have two-prong outlets. If you're traveling with computers or appliances that have three-prong plugs, ask your hotel or motel manager for an adapter. You may need to buy a three-prong adapter, but the cost is small.

SAY IT RIGHT!

The following place names are easy to mispronounce. Say it like a local!

- Duchesne: du-SHANE
- Ephraim: EE-from
- Hurricane: HUR-ken
- Kanab: kuh-NAB
- Lehi: LEE-high
- Manti: MAN-tie
- Monticello: mon-ta-SELL-o
- Nephi: NEE-fi
- Panguitch: PAN-gwich
- Tooele: too-WILL-uh
- Uinta: you-IN-tuh
- Weber: WEE-ber

Escalante poses an unusual problem. Utahans from northern parts of the state pronounce the name of the town and the famous river canyons as es-ka-LAN-tay; citizens of the town, however, pronounce it without the final long e, as es-ka-LANT.

ACCESS FOR TRAVELERS WITH DISABILITIES

Travelers with disabilities will find Utah progressive when it comes to accessibility. All of the parks, except Grand Staircase-Escalante National Monument, have all-abilities trails and services. All five national parks have reasonably good facilities for visitors with limited mobility. Visitors centers are all accessible, and at least a couple of trails in each park are paved or smooth enough for wheelchair users to navigate with some assistance. Each park has a few accessible campsites.

Most hotels also offer some form of barrier-free lodging. It's best to call ahead and inquire what these accommodations are, however, because these services can vary quite a bit from one establishment to another.

Because the Grand Staircase-Escalante National Monument is almost entirely undeveloped, trails are generally inaccessible to wheelchair users.

TRAVELING WITH CHILDREN

The parks of southern Utah are filled with dramatic vistas and exciting recreation. The parks provide lots of opportunities for adventures, whether it's rafting the Colorado River or hiking to ancient Anasazi ruins, and most children will have the time of their young lives in Utah.

Utah is a family-vacation type of place, and no special planning is required to make a national park holiday exciting for children. Children do receive discounts on a number of things, ranging from motel rooms (where they often stay for free, but inquire about age restrictions, which vary) to museum admissions. One exception to this family-friendly rule is B&Bs, which frequently don't allow children at all.

Utah law requires all children age four or younger to be restrained in a child safety seat. Child seats can be rented from car-rental agencies—ask when making a car reservation.

SENIOR TRAVELERS

The parks and Utah in general are hospitable for senior travelers. The long-standing National Park Service-issued Golden Age Passport has been replaced by the America the Beautiful—National Parks and Federal Recreational Lands Senior Pass. This is a lifetime pass for U.S. citizens or permanent residents age 62 or over. The pass provides access to, and use of, federal parks and recreation sites that charge an entrance fee or standard amenity. The pass admits the pass holder and passengers in a noncommercial vehicle at per-vehicle fee areas, not to exceed four adults. The pass costs $10 and can only be obtained in person at the park. There is a similar discount program at Utah state parks.

UTAH'S DRINKING LAWS

The state's liquor laws can seem rather confusing and peculiar to outsiders. Changes to Utah's once prohibitive rules have made it easier to buy and consume alcohol. Note that it's no longer necessary to be a member of a private club in order to consume alcohol in a bar–no more buying a temporary membership or signing in on someone else's membership just to enjoy a drink.

Several different kinds of establishments are licensed to sell alcoholic beverages:

Taverns, which include brewpubs, can sell only 3.2 percent beer (beer that is 3.2 percent alcohol by volume). Taverns can't sell wine, which is classed as hard liquor in Utah. Stronger beer is available in Utah, but only in bottles, and this beer is also regulated as hard liquor. You don't need to purchase food to have a beer in a tavern. With the exception of brewpubs, taverns are usually fairly derelict and not especially cheery places to hang out.

Licensed restaurants are able to sell beer, wine, and hard liquor, but only with food orders. In many parts of Utah, you'll need to specifically ask for a drink or the drink menu to begin the process. In Salt Lake City, Moab, and Park City, most restaurants have liquor licenses. In small towns, few eating establishments offer alcohol.

Cocktail bars, lounges, live music venues, and nightclubs, which once operated on the private-club system, can now serve alcohol without asking for membership. However, some continue the income flow by demanding a cover charge for entry. Depending on which county you are in, you may still be required to order some food to have a drink.

Nearly all towns will have a state-owned **liquor store,** though they can be difficult to find, and 3.2 percent beer is available in most grocery stores and gas station minimarts. Many travelers find that carrying a bottle of your favorite beverage to your room is the easiest way to enjoy an evening drink. The state drinking age is 21.

GAY AND LESBIAN TRAVELERS

Utah is not the most enlightened place in the world when it comes to equality issues, but that shouldn't be an issue for travelers to the national parks. Needless to say, a little discretion is a good idea in most public situations, and don't expect to find much of a gay scene anywhere in southeastern Utah. Moab is notably more progressive than anywhere else in this part of the state, but there are no gay bars or gathering places.

PETS

Unless you really have no other option, it's best not to bring your dog (or cat, or bird, or ferret) along on a national park vacation. Although pets are allowed in national parks, they aren't permitted on the trails. This limits you and your dog to leashed walks along the roads, around campground loops, and in parking areas. During much of the year, it's far too hot to leave an animal in a parked car. In Zion, private cars are prohibited on the scenic canyon drive, and no pets are allowed on the shuttle buses that drive this route.

Several pet boarding services are available in Moab:

- **Karen's Canine Campground** (2781 S. Roberts Rd., 435/259-7922)
- **Desert Doggie Daycare** (4890 Sunny Acres Lane, 435/259-4841, http://moabdesertdoggiedaycare.com)
- **Moab Veterinary Clinic** (4575 Spanish Valley Dr., 435/259-8710, http://moabvetclinic.com)

When in Moab, visit the **Moab Bark Park** (300 S. 100 E.), a fenced off-leash dog park.

CONDUCT AND CUSTOMS
Alcohol and Nightlife

Observant Mormons don't drink alcoholic beverages, and state laws make purchasing alcohol relatively awkward. If going out for drinks and nightclubbing is part of your idea of

GOURMET DELIGHTS

Small-town Utah is not known for its cuisine. However, there are a few outposts of good food scattered around the parklands of southern Utah, where good chefs have unpacked their knives and whisks, and where the best local produce and meats are featured. Be sure to stop by and support these fine locally owned restaurants.

BLUFF

Tiny Bluff was already appealing before the **San Juan River Kitchen** opened—now, it's a must-visit destination. From the cooling modern architecture to the locally grown salad greens and chocolate cayenne cake, eating here is a real treat.

BOULDER

The restaurant at the inviting Boulder Mountain Lodge, **Hell's Backbone Grill,** offers incongruously fine dining. The regularly changing menu features regionally based cuisine: a blend of Western Range, Pueblo, and Southwestern flavors, with local organically grown vegetables and herbs and locally raised natural meats.

ESCALANTE

The specialty of the **Circle D Eatery** is beef that comes straight from a local ranch; the Circle D chefs also smoke all their own meats (brisket, ribs, even cheese). If you're around for breakfast, chow down on some good Mexican-style eggs.

KANAB

It's a special treat to dine at the **Rocking V Café,** in a storefront on Kanab's main drag. As at most of southern Utah's best restaurants, chef-owners Victor and Vicky use local ingredients whenever possible to make Southwestern-style food, and they cater to everybody from vegans to steak lovers.

MOAB

Moab has several fine dinner restaurants, but for good food and a taste of laid-back local culture, stop for breakfast at the **Love Muffin Cafe.** While eating your breakfast burrito, order a sandwich to take along for lunch on the trail.

Just off Main Street, find the **Desert Bistro,** housed in a lovely renovated building that was, when it was built in 1892, Moab's first dance hall. Fresh seafood and meats, including a deluxe antelope and mushroom burger, have subtle Southwestern touches, making this one of the top restaurants in southern Utah.

SPRINGDALE

Some of the best food in town, including an amazing spaghetti squash enchilada, comes out of the tiny kitchen at the **Whiptail Grill,** set in an old gas station. And in a town with a relative abundance of good restaurants, that's worth a bit.

TORREY

Inventive Southwestern cuisine is the specialty at **Cafe Diablo.** Chef-owner Gary Pankow, a graduate of the Culinary Institute of America, adds zest and finesse to locally grown organic meats and produce. In addition to freshly baked bread, the desserts and ice cream are all homemade.

---

entertainment, you'll find that only Moab offers much in the way of nightspots. Most towns have a liquor store; outside Moab, many restaurants don't serve alcohol.

Smoking

Smoking is taboo for observant Mormons, and smoking is prohibited in almost all public places. You're also not allowed to smoke on church grounds. Obviously, take care when smoking in national parks and pick up your own butts. Besides the risk of fire, there's nothing that ruins a natural experience more than windblown piles of cigarette filters.

Small-Town Utah

If you've never traveled in Utah before, you may find that Utahans don't initially seem as welcoming and outgoing as people in other Western states. In many smaller towns, visitors from outside the community are a relatively new phenomenon, and not everyone in the state is anxious to have their towns turned into tourism or recreational meccas. The Mormons are very family- and community-oriented, and if certain individuals initially seem insular and uninterested in travelers, don't take it as unfriendliness.

Mormons are also orderly and socially conservative people. Brash displays of rudeness or use of foul language in public will not make you popular.

Health and Safety

There's nothing inherently dangerous about Utah's national parks, though a few precautions can help minimize what risks do exist. For the most part, using common sense about the dangers of extreme temperatures, remote backcountry exploration, and encounters with wildlife will assure a safe and healthy trip.

HEAT AND WATER

Southern Utah in summer is a very hot place. Be sure to use sunscreen, or else you risk having an uncomfortable vacation. Wearing a wide-brimmed hat and good sunglasses, with full UV protection, can shield you from the sun's harmful effects. Heat exhaustion can also be a problem if you're hiking in the hot sun. In midsummer, try to get an early start if you're hiking in full sun. If you're out during the heat of the afternoon, look for a shady spot and rest until the sun begins to drop.

Drink steadily throughout the day, whether you are thirsty or not, rather than gulping huge amounts of water once you feel thirsty. For hikers, one of the best ways to drink enough is to carry water in a hydration pack (the two top brands are Camelbak and Platypus). These collapsible plastic bladders come with a hose and a mouthpiece, so you can carry your water in your pack, threading the hose out the top of the pack and over your shoulder, which keeps the mouthpiece handy for frequent sips of water. One easy way to tell if you're getting enough to drink is to monitor your urine output. If you're only urinating a couple of times a day, and the color and odor of your urine are both strong, it's time to start drinking more water.

HYPOTHERMIA

Don't think that just because you're in the Utah desert that you're immune to hypothermia. This lowering of the body's temperature below 95°F causes disorientation, uncontrollable shivering, slurred speech, and drowsiness. The victim may not even realize what's wrong. Unless corrective action is taken immediately, hypothermia can lead to death. Hikers should therefore travel with companions and always carry wind and rain protection. Space blankets are lightweight and cheap and offer protection against the cold in emergencies. Remember that temperatures can plummet rapidly in Utah's dry climate—a drop of 40 degrees between day and night is common. Be especially careful at high elevations, where sunshine can quickly change into freezing rain or a blizzard. Simply falling into a mountain stream can also lead to hypothermia and death unless proper action is taken. If you're cold and tired, don't waste time: Seek shelter and build a fire, change into dry clothes, and drink warm liquids. If a victim isn't fully conscious, warm him or her by skin-to-skin contact in a sleeping bag. Try to keep the victim awake and offer plenty of warm liquids.

GIARDIA

Giardia lamblia is a protozoan that has become common in even the most remote mountain streams. It is carried in animal or human waste that is deposited or washed into the water. When ingested, it begins reproducing, causing intense cramping and diarrhea in the host; this can become serious and may require medical attention.

No matter how clear a stream looks, it's best to assume that it is contaminated and to take precautions against giardia by filtering, boiling, or treating water with chemicals before drinking it. A high-quality filter will remove giardia and a host of other things you don't want to be drinking. (Spend a bit extra for one that removes particles down to one micrometer in size.) It's also effective to simply boil your water; 2-5 minutes at a rolling boil will kill giardia even in the cyst stage. Because water boils at a lower temperature as elevation increases, increase the boiling time to 15 minutes if you're at 9,000 feet. Two drops of bleach left in a quart of water for 30 minutes will remove most giardia, although some microorganisms are resistant to chemicals.

HANTAVIRUS

Hantavirus is an infectious disease agent that was first isolated during the Korean War and then discovered in the Americas in 1993 by a task force of scientists in New Mexico. This disease agent occurs naturally throughout most of North and South America, especially in dry desert conditions. The infectious agent is airborne, and in the absence of prompt medical attention, its infections are usually fatal. This disease is called hantavirus pulmonary syndrome (HPS). It can affect anyone, but given some fundamental knowledge, it can also be easily prevented.

The natural host of the hantavirus appears to be rodents, especially mice and rats. The virus is not usually transmitted directly from rodents to humans; rather, the rodents shed hantavirus particles in their saliva, urine, and droppings. Humans usually contract HPS by inhaling particles that are infected with the hantavirus. The virus becomes airborne when the particles dry out and get stirred into the air (especially from

sweeping a floor or shaking a rug). Humans then inhale these particles, which leads to the infection.

HPS is not considered a highly infectious disease, so people usually contract HPS from long-term exposure. Because transmission usually occurs through inhalation, it is easiest for a human being to contract hantavirus within a contained environment, where the virus-infected particles are not thoroughly dispersed. Being in a cabin or barn where rodents can be found poses elevated risks for contracting the infection.

Simply traveling to a place where the hantavirus is known to occur is not considered a risk factor. Camping, hiking, and other outdoor activities also pose low risks, especially if steps are taken to reduce rodent contact. If you happen to stay in a rodent-infested cabin, thoroughly wet any droppings and dead rodents with a chlorine bleach solution (one cup of bleach per gallon of water) and let them stand for a few minutes before cleaning them up. Be sure to wear rubber gloves for this task, and double-bag your garbage.

The first symptoms of HPS can occur anywhere between five days and three weeks after infection. They almost always include fever, fatigue, aching muscles (usually in the back, shoulders, or thighs), and other flu-like symptoms. Other early symptoms may include headaches, dizziness, chills, and abdominal discomfort such as vomiting, nausea, or diarrhea. These symptoms are shortly followed by intense coughing and shortness of breath. If you have these symptoms, seek medical help immediately. Untreated infections of hantavirus are almost always fatal.

THINGS THAT BITE OR STING

Although travelers in Utah's national parks are not going to get attacked by a grizzly bear, and encounters with mountain lions are rare, there are a few animals to watch out for. Snakes, scorpions, and spiders are all present in considerable numbers, and there are a few key things to know about dealing with this phobia-inducing trio.

Snakes

Rattlesnakes, including the particularly venomous midget faded rattlesnake, are present throughout southern Utah. The midget faded snakes live in Arches and Canyonlands, where they frequent burrows and rock crevices and are mostly active at night. Even though their venom is toxic, full venom injections are relatively uncommon, and, like all rattlesnakes, they pose little threat unless they're provoked.

If you see a rattlesnake, observe it at a safe distance. Be careful where you put your hands when canyoneering or scrambling—it's not a good idea to reach above your head and blindly plant your hands on a sunny rock ledge. Hikers should wear sturdy boots to minimize the chance that a snake's fangs will reach the skin if a bite occurs. Do not walk barefoot outside after dark, as this is when snakes hunt for prey.

First aid for rattlesnake bites is full of conflicting ideas: to suck or not to suck; to apply a constricting bandage or not; to take time treating in the field versus rushing to the hospital. Most people who receive medical treatment after being bitten by a rattlesnake live to tell the story. Prompt administration of antivenin is the most important treatment, and the most important aspect of first aid is to arrange transportation of the victim to a hospital as quickly as possible.

Scorpions

A scorpion's sting isn't as painful as you'd expect (it's about like a bee sting), and the venom is insufficient to cause any real harm. Still, it's not what you'd call pleasant, and experienced desert campers know to shake out their boots every morning, as scorpions and spiders are attracted to warm, moist, dark places.

Spiders

Tarantulas and black widow spiders are present across much of the Colorado Plateau. Believe it or not, a tarantula's bite does not poison humans; the enzymes secreted when they bite do turn the insides of frogs, lizards, and insects to a soft mush, allowing the tarantula to suck the guts from its prey. Another interesting tarantula fact: While males live about as long as you'd expect a spider to live, female tarantulas can live for up to 25 years. Females do sometimes eat the males, which may account for some of this disparity in longevity.

Black widow spiders, on the other hand, have a toxic bite. Although the bite is usually painless, it delivers a potent neurotoxin, which quickly causes pain, nausea, and vomiting. It is important to seek immediate treatment for a black widow bite; although few people actually die from these bites, recovery is helped along considerably by antivenin.

RESOURCES

Suggested Reading

ARCHAEOLOGY

Childs, Craig. *House of Rain: Tracking a Vanished Civilization across the American Southwest.* New York: Back Bay Books, 2006. Only part of this book deals with Utah, but it's a great read about the Anasazi.

Lister, Robert, and Florence Lister. *Those Who Came Before.* Southwest Parks and Monuments, 1983. A well-illustrated guide to the history, artifacts, and ruins of prehistoric Southwestern people. The author also describes parks and monuments containing archaeological sites.

Simms, Steven R. *Traces of Fremont: Society and Rock Art in Ancient Utah.* Salt Lake City: University of Utah Press and Price, UT: College of Eastern Utah Prehistoric Museum, 2010. Great photos accompany the text in this look into Fremont culture.

Slifer, Dennis. *Guide to Rock Art of the Utah Region: Sites with Public Access.* Albuquerque: University of New Mexico Press, 2000. The most complete guide to rock-art sites, with descriptions of more than 50 sites in the Four Corners region. Complete with maps and directions, and with an overview of rock art styles and traditions.

GUIDEBOOKS AND TRAVELOGUES

Benchmark Maps. *Utah Road & Recreation Atlas.* Medford, OR: Benchmark Maps, 2008. Shaded relief maps emphasize landforms, and recreational information is abundant. Use the atlas to locate campgrounds, back roads, and major trailheads, although there's not enough detail to rely on it for hiking.

Huegel, Tony. *Utah Byways: 65 of Utah's Best Backcountry Drives.* Berkeley, CA: Wilderness Press, 2006. If you're looking for off-highway adventure, this is your guide. The spiral-bound book includes detailed directions, human and natural history, outstanding photography, full-page maps for each of the 65 routes, and an extensive how-to chapter for beginners.

Zwinger, Ann. *Wind in the Rock: The Canyonlands of Southeastern Utah.* Tucson: University of Arizona Press, 1986. Well-written accounts of hiking in the Grand Gulch and nearby canyons. The author tells of the area's history, archaeology, wildlife, and plants.

HISTORY AND CURRENT EVENTS

Dellenbaugh, Frederick S. *A Canyon Voyage: The Narrative of the Second Powell Expedition.* Tucson: University of Arizona Press, 1984. A well-written account of John Wesley Powell's second expedition down the Green and Colorado Rivers, 1871-1872. The members took the first Grand Canyon photographs and obtained much valuable scientific knowledge.

Powell, John Wesley. *The Exploration of the Colorado River and Its Canyons.* Mineola, NY: Dover Publications, reprinted 1997 (first published in 1895). Describes Powell's 1869 and 1871-1872 expeditions down the Green and Colorado Rivers. His was the first group to navigate through the Grand Canyon. A description of the 1879 Uinta Expedition is also included.

Stegner, Wallace. *Beyond the Hundredth Meridian: John Wesley Powell and the Second Opening of the West.* New York: Penguin Books, 1992 (first published in 1954). Stegner's book tells the story of Powell's wild rides down the Colorado River, then goes on to point out why the United States should have listened to what Powell had to say about the U.S. Southwest.

MEMOIRS

Abbey, Edward. *Desert Solitaire.* New York: Ballantine Books, 1991. A meditation on the Red Rock Canyon country of Utah. Abbey brings his fiery prose to the service of the American outback, while excoriating the commercialization of the West.

Childs, Craig. *The Secret Knowledge of Water.* Boston: Back Bay Books, 2001. Childs looks for water in the desert, and finds plenty of it.

Meloy, Ellen. *Raven's Exile.* New York: Henry Holt & Company, 1994. Throughout a summer of Green River raft trips, Meloy reflects on natural and human history of the area.

Zwinger, Ann. *Run, River, Run: A Naturalist's Journey down One of the Great Rivers of the American West.* Tucson: University of Arizona

Press, 1984. An excellent description of the author's experiences along the Green River, from its source in the Wind River Range of Wyoming to the Colorado River in southeastern Utah. The author weaves geology, Native American ruins, plants, wildlife, and her personal feelings into the text and drawings.

NATURAL SCIENCES

Chronic, Halka. *Roadside Geology of Utah.* Missoula, MT: Mountain Press Publishing, 1990. This layperson's guide tells the story of the state's fascinating geology as seen by following major roadways.

Fagan, Damian. *Canyon Country Wildflowers.* Helena, MT: Falcon Publishing, 1998. A comprehensive field guide to the diverse flora of the Four Corners area.

Fagan, Damian, and David Williams. *A Naturalist's Guide to the White Rim Trail.* Seattle: Wingate Ink, 2007. Take your time to explore nature on the White Rim Trail.

Williams, David. *A Naturalist's Guide to Canyon Country.* Helena, MT: Falcon Publishing, 2000. If you want to buy just one field guide, this is the one to get. It's well written, beautifully illustrated, and a delight to use.

OUTDOOR ACTIVITIES

Adkison, Ron. *Best Easy Day Hikes Grand Staircase-Escalante and the Glen Canyon Region.* Helena, MT: Falcon Publishing, 2010. Features 19 hikes in south-central Utah's canyon country, including Paria Canyon.

Allen, Steve. *Canyoneering 3.* Salt Lake City: University of Utah Press, 1997. Provides excellent, detailed descriptions of a variety of hikes in the Grand Staircase-Escalante National Monument, ranging from day hikes to multiday treks.

Belnap, Bill, and Buzz Belnap. *Canyonlands River Guide.* Evergreen, CO: Westwater Books, 2008. River map guide to the Colorado and Green Rivers, printed on waterproof paper.

Bickers, Jack. *Canyon Country Off-road Vehicle Trails: Maze Area.* Moab, UT: Canyon Country Publications, 1988. Descriptions of backcountry roads and off-road vehicle trails in the Maze area; out of print, but relatively easy to track down.

Bjørnstad, Eric. *Desert Rock: Rock Climbs in the National Parks.* Helena, MT: Falcon Publishing, 1996. A classic climbing guide by one of Utah's most respected climbers.

Crowell, David. *Mountain Biking Moab,* 2nd edition. Guilford, CT: Globe Pequot, 2004. A guide to the many trails around Moab, from the most popular to the little explored, in a handy size—small enough to take on the bike with you.

Day, David. *Utah's Favorite Hiking Trails.* Provo, UT: Rincon Publishing, 2002. Good simple maps and detailed descriptions of trails all over the state, including many in southern Utah's national parks and monuments.

Green, Stewart M. *Rock Climbing Utah.* Helena, MT: Falcon Publishing, 1998. Good detail on climbs in all of Utah's national parks, including many line drawings and photos with climbing routes highlighted.

Kelsey, Michael R. *Canyon Hiking Guide to the Colorado Plateau.* Provo, UT: Kelsey Publishing, 2006. One of the best guides to hiking in southeastern Utah's canyon country. Geologic cross sections show the formations you'll be walking through.

Lambrechtse, Rudi. *Hiking the Escalante.* Salt Lake City: Wasatch Publishers, 1999. "A wilderness guide to an exciting land of buttes, arches, alcoves, amphitheaters, and deep canyons," this introduction to history, geology, and natural history of the Escalante region in southern Utah contains descriptions and trailhead information for 42 hiking destinations.

Schneider, Bill. *Best Easy Day Hikes Canyonlands and Arches.* Helena, MT: Falcon Publishing, 2005. Twenty hikes in this popular vacation area, geared to travelers who are short on time or aren't able to explore the canyons on more difficult trails.

Wells, Charles A. *Guide To Moab, UT Backroads & 4-Wheel Drive Trails.* Monument, CO: Funtreks, 2008. Good descriptions and GPS waypoints for Moab-area four-wheelers.

Internet Resources

Although a virtual visit to Utah cannot replace the real thing, you'll find an enormous amount of helpful information online. Thousands of websites cover everything from ghost towns to the latest community news.

The American Southwest
www.americansouthwest.net/utah
Utah Guide provides an overview of national parks, national recreation areas, and some state parks.

Canyonlands Utah
www.canyonlands-utah.com
Good source for information on Moab and the surrounding areas, including Canyonlands and Arches National Parks.

Desert USA
www.desertusa.com
Desert USA's Utah section discusses places to visit and what plants and animals you might meet there. Here's the best part of this site: you can find out what's in bloom at www.desertusa.com/wildflo/wildupdates.

Moab Area Travel Council
www.discovermoab.com
Upcoming events, mountain bike trails, local restaurants and lodging, and outfitters are all easy to find at this comprehensive site.

National Park Service
www.nps.gov
The National Park Service offers pages for all its areas at this site. You can also enter this address followed by a slash and the first two letters of the first two words of the place (first four letters if there's just a one-word name); for example, www.nps.gov/brca takes you to Bryce

Canyon National Park and www.nps.gov/zion leads to Zion National Park.

Recreation.gov
www.recreation.gov
If a campground is operated by the federal government, this is the place to make a reservation. You can expect to pay close to $10 for this convenience.

Reserve America
www.reserveamerica.com
Use this website to reserve campsites in state campgrounds. It costs a few extra bucks to reserve a campsite, but compare that with the cost of being skunked out of a site and having to resort to a motel room.

State of Utah
www.utah.gov
The official State of Utah website has travel information, agencies, programs, and what the legislature is up to.

U.S. Forest Service
www.fs.fed.us/r4
Utah falls within U.S. Forest Service Region 4. The Manti-La Sal National Forest (www.fs.fed.us/r4/mantilasal) is in southeast Utah around Moab and Monticello.

Utah Mountain Biking
www.utahmountainbiking.com
Details mountain biking routes listed in this book as well as other local trails.

Utah's Dixie
www.utahsdixie.com
The southwestern Utah city of St. George is the

focus of this site, which also covers some of the smaller communities outside Zion National Park.

Utah State Parks
www.stateparks.utah.gov
The Utah State Parks site offers details on the large park system, including links to reserve campsites.

Utah Travel Council
www.utah.com
The Utah Travel Council is a one-stop shop for all sorts of information on Utah. It takes you around the state to sights, activities, events, and maps, and offers links to local tourism offices. The accommodations listings are the most up-to-date source for current room rates and options.

Zion Park
www.zionpark.com
This site will point you to information on Springdale and the area surrounding Zion National Park, with links to lodging and restaurant sites.

Index

List of Maps

www.moon.com

DESTINATIONS | ACTIVITIES | BLOGS | MAPS | BOOKS

MOON.COM is ready to help plan your next trip! Filled with fresh trip ideas and strategies, author interviews, informative travel blogs, a detailed map library, and descriptions of all the Moon guidebooks, Moon.com is all you need to get out and explore the world—or even places in your own backyard. While at Moon.com, sign up for our monthly e-newsletter for updates on new releases, travel tips, and expert advice from our on-the-go Moon authors. As always, when you travel with Moon, expect an experience that is uncommon and truly unique.

KEEP UP WITH MOON ON FACEBOOK AND TWITTER
JOIN THE MOON PHOTO GROUP ON FLICKR

MAP SYMBOLS

▭▭▭	Expressway	【	Highlight	✗	Airfield	⚑	Golf Course
▭▭	Primary Road	○	City/Town	✈	Airport	🅿	Parking Area
▭▭	Secondary Road	◉	State Capital	▲	Mountain	◢◣	Archaeological Site
======	Unpaved Road	⊛	National Capital	✦	Unique Natural Feature	♠	Church
-------	Trail	★	Point of Interest			⛽	Gas Station
....	Ferry	•	Accommodation	⌇	Waterfall	◌	Glacier
▪▬▪▬▪	Railroad	▾	Restaurant/Bar	▴	Park	▨	Mangrove
▭▭▭	Pedestrian Walkway	▪	Other Location	🚩	Trailhead	▨	Reef
▥▥▥	Stairs	∧	Campground	⛷	Skiing Area	⬕	Swamp

CONVERSION TABLES

°C = (°F – 32) / 1.8
°F = (°C x 1.8) + 32
1 inch = 2.54 centimeters (cm)
1 foot = 0.304 meters (m)
1 yard = 0.914 meters
1 mile = 1.6093 kilometers (km)
1 km = 0.6214 miles
1 fathom = 1.8288 m
1 chain = 20.1168 m
1 furlong = 201.168 m
1 acre = 0.4047 hectares
1 sq km = 100 hectares
1 sq mile = 2.59 square km
1 ounce = 28.35 grams
1 pound = 0.4536 kilograms
1 short ton = 0.90718 metric ton
1 short ton = 2,000 pounds
1 long ton = 1.016 metric tons
1 long ton = 2,240 pounds
1 metric ton = 1,000 kilograms
1 quart = 0.94635 liters
1 US gallon = 3.7854 liters
1 Imperial gallon = 4.5459 liters
1 nautical mile = 1.852 km

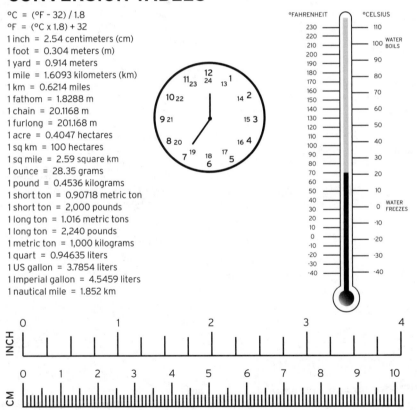

MOON ZION & BRYCE

Avalon Travel
a member of the Perseus Books Group
1700 Fourth Street
Berkeley, CA 94710, USA
www.moon.com

Editor: Kathryn Ettinger
Series Manager: Sabrina Young
Copy Editor: Christopher Church
Graphics Coordinator: Lucie Ericksen
Production Coordinator: Lucie Ericksen
Cover Designer: Lucie Ericksen
Map Editor: Mike Morgenfeld
Cartographers: Chris Henrick, Kat Bennett
Indexer: Greg Jewett

ISBN-13: 978-1-61238-289-0
ISSN: 1540-3823

Printing History
1st Edition – 2003
5th Edition – April 2013
5 4 3 2 1

Text © 2013 by W. C. McRae & Judy Jewell.
Maps © 2013 by Avalon Travel.
All rights reserved.

Front cover photo: view at sunrise from Sunset Point, Bryce Canyon National Park © Alan Palmer / Alamy
Title page photo: campground in Arches National Park © Paul Levy
Interior color photos: pages 8-9, 11 bottom-left, 18 left, 20, 21 left: © Bill McRae; pages 10, 11 top-right 12, 14, 15 left, 17, 18 right, 21 right, 24: © Paul Levy; pages 11 top-left and bottom-right, 15 right, 19, 22: © Judy Jewell

Printed in Canada by Friesens

KEEPING CURRENT

If you have a favorite gem you'd like to see included in the next edition, or see anything that needs updating, clarification, or correction, please drop us a line. Send your comments via email to feedback@moon.com, or use the address above.